Class Struggle and the Industrial Revolution

Class Struggle and the Industrial Revolution

Early industrial capitalism in three English towns

John Foster
with a Foreword by Professor E. J. Hobsbawm

Weidenfeld and Nicolson · London

Weidenfeld and Nicolson,
11 St John's Hill, London SW11

ISBN 0 297 76681 3

Printed in Great Britain by
REDWOOD BURN LIMITED
Trowbridge and Esher

Contents

Figures

Abbreviations

Tables

A*

Foreword

The history of the working class in industrial Britain has only just begun to be written. Traditionally it has most commonly been approached through the study of labour movements, justifiably enough, since the existence of the working class is inseparable from its struggles. However, this approach usually suffered from three defects. It tended to identify class and movement, movement and organization or the leadership of organizations, thus by-passing actual social realities. It followed the tracks of the pioneers of labour history, who were primarily concerned with national de-velopments, and thus neglected not only the substantial regional, sectional and local differences, but also important developments of wider interest, which happened not to be readily accessible through national documentation. Finally, it tended to accept with insufficient criticism a framework of chronological narrative and a pattern of interpretation which was itself the product of the movement's history as much as of research into it.

Considerable progress has been made since the 1950s, but to some extent at the cost of neglecting the fundamental problem which traditional labour history quite correctly, though not always consciously, sought to illuminate: the relationship between the emergence and development of the working class and its movement. We now possess a number of local and regional studies of labour movements, which have largely transformed our knowledge of – to take one example – Chartism, though unfortunately there are still too few studies of local working classes or occupational/indus-trial groups of workers. There has been a substantial advance in our knowledge of the attitudes of political rulers, governments and parties to the working class and its movements, though not so much advance in our knowledge of working-class attitudes to government and parties, and very little in our knowledge of the attitude of employers to industrial relations, at any rate before the twentieth century. From a different angle, sociological concepts and quantitative methods, especially those of historic demography, have been used to illuminate, or actually to discover, much of the social structure of working-class life. We know a great deal more about both the working classes and labour movements than most people thought likely twenty years ago. However, with very rare exceptions (which admittedly include the monumental one of E. P. Thompson's *The Making of the Working Class*) historians have shied away from directly confronting the relations between class, struggle and movement.

Hence the significance of John Foster's strikingly original and lucid study. Though it concentrates on Oldham, with side-glances at two other towns, it is not a piece of local history, or even a collection of 'case studies', a term which is usually a euphemism for a piece of very specialized history which wishes to pretend that it is of more general interest. It is an enquiry into certain central features of British industrial development, and into the nature of both the Victorian bourgeoisie and the working class. More generally, it is an attempt both to clarify and to provide analytical and preferably quantitative methods for investigating the concept of 'class consciousness'. Foster concentrates on his three towns not because they are themselves his major concern – though in studying Oldham he has incidentally and necessarily made important additions to our knowledge of the Industrial Revolution – but because the problems which concern him can be most conveniently explored in this way.

It is safe to say that this book has long been awaited by the numerous historians and students of urbanization who have already had a foretaste of the author's findings and some of his argument in a brief but already widely known and widely quoted article (J. O. Foster, 'Nineteenth century towns – a class dimension' in H. J. Dyos (ed.) *The Study of Urban History*, London 1968). The author may be safely left to speak for himself, for though his argument is complex and tight, it is set out with great clarity, and may be read independently of the impressive apparatus of references and special appendices which justify its factual basis.

Class Struggle and the Industrial Revolution will be widely discussed and intensively read, both by historians and sociologists. It deals both with important conceptual questions (such as the nature of 'class consciousness' and 'false consciousness'), with very fundamental problems of the structure of society (such as the nature of the relationship between antagonistic classes and of social control), and with crucial questions of nineteenth-century history, arising out of the author's major theme, 'the development and decline of a revolutionary class consciousness in the second quarter of the century', or in more general terms 'the nature of the change which British capitalism underwent in the middle years of the century.' This implies an enquiry into the composition, changes and variations of local class structure, which is based on important and pioneering research into a variety of problems ranging from poverty and the religious views of entrepreneurs to patterns of intermarriage, residential segregation and wealth. Whether or not Foster's views are accepted on all points his book will be essential reading for students of nineteenth-century Britain. Moreover it will greatly stimulate and advance the study of social history in general.

The interest of the subject will be evident even to general readers and obvious to students, who will certainly have to make themselves familiar with Foster's work. However, only specialists will appreciate the enormous labours of technically sophisticated research on which his arguments rest, and the vast amount of quite new information which they have produced. In fact this is a remarkable book. I think it will be recognized as such.

E. J. Hobsbawm

September 1973
London

never much more than an arbitary geographical bite out of a larger political system. And there is that of the system itself – seen statically at a particular moment in time. If adequate questions are to be directed at the material (and its full social significance grasped) both these levels of incompleteness have to be overcome.

The problem of 'liberalization' is an attempt to tackle the first (to relate community to political system) and is itself a typical example of how a process cutting across a number of areas – central government, economy, the local community – tends to escape systematic investigation. Obviously no study, local or otherwise, can provide any agreed summary of what happened at the 'national' level as a basis for research elsewhere. But it can at least project into it the main areas of controversy and this is what the following chapters will attempt to do.

As far as liberalization is concerned, the great question is whether it can be seen as a process at all. Many would claim that the developments assembled under this heading are quite unconnected. What we will be trying to establish here is the reverse: that liberalization was in fact a collective *ruling-class* response to a social system in crisis and integrally related to a preceding period of working-class consciousness. And while much of this cannot be tested at local level, there are other parts (like the existence of class consciousness itself and the deliberateness of subsequent attempts to develop an adequate reply) that can be tested there and nowhere else.

However, even this only takes us a certain distance. The second level of incompleteness – that of the system itself seen statically – is still unaccounted for, and though this level is undoubtedly more contentious it is also perhaps the most crucial. If basic social change did occur, what really needs to be settled is its precise significance in the overall development of capitalist society; the *place* of the forms of social structure it produced in relation to those that came before and after. In many ways it is this – rather than the mere establishment of liberalization – that would seem to be the most important task confronting a study of this kind, and dealing with it demands some discussion of capitalism as a system seen in its historical completion.

Most of those who have concerned themselves with this (and they start with Marx) would see capitalism's social development as being determined by people's response to it as a *class* system. It is the struggle against its class nature that helps drive the system forward and (on occasion) overthrows it. It is the response to the alienation it embodies that also (on occasion) helps sustain it. And it is finally the interplay of *both* with the underlying dimension of economic change which produces the system's characteristic pattern of development. The way in which this takes place provides – in its detailed working – much of the perspective we are looking for.

To start with the response to alienation. Alienation occurs in any system of society which denies part of its population equal control over social development – a denial which 'alienates' their full humanity as social beings. Under capitalism this alienation takes place in the process of production. By having to *sell* their labour, the bulk of the population loses control over the use to which it is put, a loss most immediately expressed in the unequal wage they get in return. It is the usual (passive) response to this 'alienation' which produces capitalism's typically fragmented social structure. In order to recreate the conditions for a meaningful 'social' existence – to establish *apparent* control over what society produces – people tend to limit their social contacts to those possessing roughly the same purchasing power as themselves. The result is a series of sectional groupings which – by possessing an approximate equality of consumption – serve to cancel out the most immediate expression of people's larger social irrelevance and, within these limits, allow them to find some measure of social fulfilment.

That is the explanation put forward for the usual *form* of capitalism's social structure: a method of restricting contact and comparison which provides a context for maintaining the *appearance* of real social participation. What is more difficult to explain is the *content* of the cultures that result: the great variety of sectional 'false consciousnesses' which – by insulating one section of the labour force from another – effectively block the development of any collective class consciousness.

On this level there is a good deal of disagreement. Some people would explain such false consciousness as *purely and simply* the result of bourgeois manipulation. Others would make the process considerably more complicated (and it is this line that is followed here). Obviously there can be no pretence that false consciousness does not work in favour of the ruling class. Clearly the particular cultural patterns – or codes of social recognition and rejection – developed by each grouping play a key part in filtering out disruptive contacts from society at large. And as their basic purpose is to obscure the reality of exploitation, they must also stand in fairly explicit opposition to any group that attempts to do the reverse. Indeed, more than this: because the whole process is based upon an unequal valuation of people's worth (as well as upon the more open definition of one group against the other) it also offers a ready channel for the penetration of ruling-class attitudes and controls.

In most situations, therefore, false consciousness undoubtedly does serve as a major prop to capitalist stability. Yet it is also more than this, and certainly cannot be seen as solely the product of bourgeois manipulation. Such an interpretation would fail even at the elementary level of explaining the great variety of sectional cultures. Worse still, it would also make nonsense of the whole process of capitalist social change. Were the bourgeoisie able to determine exactly what labour ought to believe, it would also be free to turn the clock back historically – free to ignore the 'legitimate' rights and standards already won. And this it is manifestly unable to do (at least without upsetting the whole structure).

It is here that we come to the most immediately relevant aspect of the whole argument: the fact that false consciousness is essentially *historical*. The patterns of culture that define any group's identity are not arbitrary but *concrete*, based upon particular historically determined levels of consumption. And the job of maintaining and defending this identity is clearly integral to the structure of any particular grouping. It cannot be imposed from outside. To maintain itself in a technologically changing society, a subgroup has to be able to both accept *and* reject. And within most it is possible to identify two distinct groupings (or 'poles') of leaders: one trying to open it up to developments in society at large (and especially to the rapidly changing occupational and cultural demands put upon it); the other – mediating at a more intense level – defending its traditional identity and particularly the objective rights and standards used to define it against others.

As a result each subgroup's identity is fairly irrevocably geared into the larger sequence of historical change. And it is the same internal tension that also makes it so dangerous for the bourgeoisie to put the clock back. Any such attack disrupts the vital network by which group leaderships both maintain their own authority and act (as they usually do in some institutional way) as go-betweens and message boys for the establishment. If, therefore, the system's *economic* contradictions force the ruling class to ask too much of these men – to countenance attacks on existing expectations and identities – then it runs the risk of forcing at least part of them into opposition. In these circumstances opponents of the *system itself* get the chance to take up their defence and, if the struggle goes on long enough, may even be able to merge sectional identities into a collective *class* identity developed around slogans incompatible with the existing order.

Hence false consciousness – while the antithesis of class consciousness – does contain within it (as a kind of historical ratchet stop) the crucial trigger capable of upsetting the whole system. And once this deeper organic crisis has occurred, once irreconcilably anti-capitalist ideas have been injected into it, there can be only two possible outcomes. Either the system is successfully overthrown or, if the old order is to survive, its whole political economy must be fundamentally modified – modified so that it can meet enough of the new demands to win back at least certain sections of the labour force. If this can be done, political stability may be restored (and new sectional identities developed), but at a higher level and around still more demanding expectations.

It is, therefore, this complex interplay between capitalism's underlying economic contradictions and these two forms of social response that determines the system's characteristically uneven, but usually progressive, pattern of development. In addition, however (and more immediately to the point), the essentially *historical* nature of the perspective that emerges ought also to have put a much sharper focus on the basic objects of this study. Above all, it should have underlined the importance of the specific. If the content of mass culture (and the effective form of any answering class ideology) necessarily *change* from one period to another, it is correspondingly futile to concentrate exclusively on establishing neat, all-embracing generalizations about the nature of 'class consciousness' or 'restabilization'. Not that there will not be very important basic continuities. But the really vital task is rather the other way about: to chart the concrete, developing human potential – the actual process of humanity's social self-creation – to which both changes and continuities relate.

It is from this angle that the potential richness of the material from the three towns finally becomes apparent.

As well as the overall process of liberalization itself, there were in the years between 1790 and 1860 three major (and unique) changes in English social structure. At the beginning of the century there was the development of what one might call 'labour consciousness'. As a result of the economic crises of the war years, one gets – for the very first time it seems – a major rupturing of capitalist authority systems and the continuing involvement of a large part of the labour force in economic struggle. Then, following renewed economic crises in the 1830s and 1840s, this 'labour consciousness' seems to have been converted (at least in certain areas) into a form of class consciousness sufficiently convincing for Marx and Engels to use it as a basis for their own political analysis. Finally, in the late 1840s and 1850s – and as part of the fundamental modification of the socio-economic system here called liberalization – one can trace the crystallization of an altogether new pattern of social subdivision within the labour force, a pattern which is of importance not just because it survived so long (in many cases until the First World War) but also because it provides a uniquely clear example of authority systems being rebuilt more or less from scratch around new sectional cultures.

It will be the precise content of these changes that will form our principal concern in what follows. Of the three towns, most attention will be focused on Oldham, the only one to go through all the stages mentioned. But comparison with the other two is also essential. Only by comparison – by a preliminary attempt to establish causes and connections – can one distinguish what is accidental and what essential, and while the scale on which this can be done is quite inadequate, the results will at least contribute to the growing body of work on which others can build.

The study will begin with an attempt to place Oldham within an overall perspective of capitalist development in England, so helping to break down the arbitrary incompleteness mentioned earlier. In particular, this opening chapter will examine the origin of those two key periods of crisis in which the ruling class was forced to attack labour's existing rights and standards. This will be followed by a description of how the *first* of these attacks helped produce a labour consciousness. The two central chapters will be concerned with the *class* consciousness. These will use material from all three towns to develop an explanation of Oldham's exceptional militancy and define its specific characteristics *as* class consciousness. Finally, the two concluding chapters will focus on the process of liberalization itself.

2 Industrialization and society

The operative weavers ... might truly be said to be placed in a higher state of 'wealth, peace and godliness' than they had ever before experienced ... the men each had a watch in their pocket and the women dressed to their fancy. . . . When they [the weavers] brought their work in a sort of familiarity continued to exist between us which in those days was the case between all masters and men (Radcliffe, an ex-handloom weaver employer, writing in 1826 about the early 1790s).

The relentless cruelty exercised by the fustian masters upon the poor weavers is such that it is unparalleled in the annals of cruelty, tyranny and oppression for it is a near impossibility for weavers to earn the common necessaries for life . . . (an Oldham handloom weaver writing in his diary for 11 August 1793).[1]

This chapter has two main tasks. One is to supply an outline perspective of capitalist development which can serve as a background for the rest of the study, and especially for understanding the economic origins of the two critical periods of conflict that occurred first in the 1790s and 1800s and then again in the 1830s. The other is to examine the detailed impact of the first of these periods in Oldham. This should help both to identify the structure of the labour community at the beginning of our period and pave the way for an analysis of the second, far more crucial, onslaught in the years after 1830.

The industrial revolution

In tackling capitalism's larger development it might be useful to start with the focus very close, namely on Oldham during the first years of factory-building in the 1780s and 1790s. We begin here not because this period marked any decisive change in social organization, but to dispose of claims that it *did*, claims which dangerously telescope England's very long road to fully fledged industrial capitalism and consequently obscure precisely those changes we are looking for.

Oldham stood in the classic heartland of England's cotton-based industrial revolution. It was situated, like the other early cotton towns, in the coal-bearing Pennine foothills and lay across one of the main routes between Lancashire and the ports and towns of Yorkshire. While its experience was undoubtedly different from that of the great mercantile centres of Liverpool and Manchester (or of the industry's outlying areas in Derby, Nottingham and Yorkshire), it seems to have been fairly typical of the general south Lancashire hinterland where the bulk of England's cotton was manufactured.[2] What, then, does it tell us? Did factory-building in Oldham involve some decisive break with 'traditional society' – the arrival of the self-made innovator, a new openness or mobility – which can be taken to mark the coming of a new industrial society?

On the quite full evidence we have for this particular area the answer is clear. Whatever the economic effects of factory-building (and these certainly were revolutionary), the immediate implications were small. Factory-building itself produced little mobility, no break with tradition, and a significant increase in economic concentration.

Of the first forty-two cotton mills built in Oldham between 1776 and 1811, the overwhelming majority were built by men who started out with capital. And most by men with a good deal: coal-owners, bankers, merchant hatters, wholesale tradesmen, yeoman manufacturers. Only two are known to have been built by men originating from worker families. One, James Lees, a Quaker mechanic, seems only to have lasted a dozen years. The other, James Gledhill, originally a shoemaker, made a moderate fortune and then sold out. The same story is repeated for the firms listed by name in the 1811 Crompton census of cotton spindlage. And looking at the origins of the big firms of the middle of the century, it seems that none were founded by men who came from labour families.

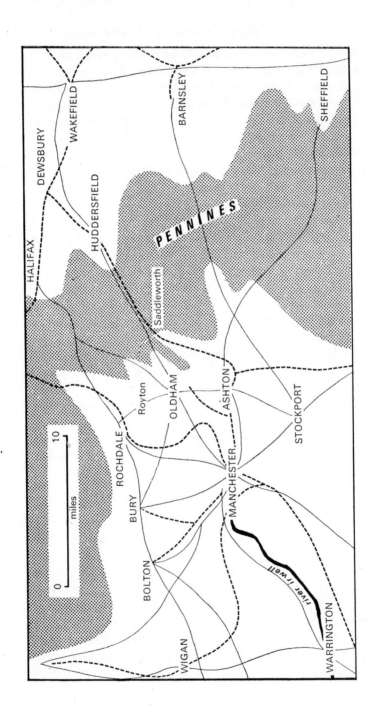

Figure 1 Principal canals and turnpikes, 1820: South-east Lancashire

land over 1000'   turnpikes   canal

PENNINES

WAKEFIELD
DEWSBURY
BARNSLEY
SHEFFIELD
HUDDERSFIELD
HALIFAX
Saddleworth
Royton
ROCHDALE
OLDHAM
ASHTON
STOCKPORT
BURY
MANCHESTER
BOLTON
WIGAN
WARRINGTON
river Irwell

miles
0   10

Table 1 Origins of early Oldham millowners[3]

	builders 1776–1811	spinners 1811	survivors 1825–51	founders big firms 1846
coal, hatting banking	13	9	9	6
outwork manufacturer wholesaler	21	10	21	5
immigrant	2	3	3	3
labour	2	1	0	0
not known	4	4	3	0
total	**42**	**27**	**36**	**14**

In the circumstances anything else would have been unlikely. The amount of capital required to purchase a couple of spinning mules, a water-twist frame or even a steam engine was not very much compared with what was wanted for a coal mine, a canal or a country house. But machinery was only a small part of what was needed. Far more important was competitive control over power, raw materials, labour and credit – and the men who built the *first* of the forty-two mills were not just men already in business but men coming from families in hatting and coal (industries demanding far larger capital than outwork manufacturing in either cotton or wool).[4] A worker *might* be able to get credit for the machinery but the rest would be altogether beyond him.

Even the general run of machine spinners seems to have come from the wealthier yeoman manufacturer families, and machine spinning to have formed only a part (though a critical part) of their business operations. At least nineteen of the twenty-seven spinning firms listed in the Crompton census of 1811 were engaged in out-work manufacturing. The smallest of them (with one thousand spindles) had two partners Wroe, a flour wholesaler, and Duncuft, a proprietor of the Werneth colliery whose family had been fairly substantial landholders in 1776. The firm employed hand-weavers to process its yarn and in 1810 had set up an abortive powerloom factory near Bolton.[5]

Hence the intending factory-builder needed not just capital but the right kind in the right place. In particular he needed land and the resources that went with it. At the end of the eighteenth century

the sixteen square miles of Oldham chapelry held a population of
sixteen thousand. The great bulk of it was employed by no more
than fifty families. Almost all had some kind of inherited landholding – and within the fifty just four were dominant: the Lees's
of Clarkfield and Werneth, the Cleggs and the Jones's. Each of
them had holdings going back to the seventeenth century. Together
they probably employed a near-majority of the textile workers and
certainly a majority of the miners. It was these families that
directed the building of the local turnpike system (and turnpikes
were always a matter of acute economic interest), who gave local
backing to the construction of canals and jointly enclosed the
town's commons in 1802.[6]

So if there was mobility in this situation (and in a sense the
Lees's, Cleggs and Jones's could all be described as upwardly
mobile), it was a mobility which led to a concentration of capital
and the narrowing – not widening – of opportunity. Moreover, it
was phased in terms of the family, not the individual It took place
over generations and its perspectives were essentially those of the
peasant proprietor: careful marriage, sharp bargaining, tenancy in
common. The Cleggs and the Jones's had been building up their
holdings since the 1680s, the Lees's for considerably longer. By the
end of the eighteenth century each of these families was made up
of a cluster of individual families bound together by a whole network of joint business ventures. The same pattern is repeated on a
smaller scale for Oldham's lesser families. John Wareing, for
instance, born in 1727, was an innkeeper and small landowner in
the neighbouring district of Saddleworth. His son set up as a flour
wholesaler in Oldham and bought more land in the 1780s. John
Wareing, the grandson, acquired further land and built (with his
brother) a mill on it in 1802. And finally his son, John, built a
new and much bigger mill in 1824.[7] 'Mobility' of this kind looked
to the past as much as the future and cannot easily be seen as
marking a decisive break with tradition.

Religion and way of life reveal the same pattern. Though (as
will be seen later) there is a fragment of truth in the Puritan-
capitalist story, the version that makes new types of belief cause
business activity is certainly not borne out in Oldham. Of the first
forty-two factory builders, the religion of fourteen is unknown
(though it seems unlikely that they were dissenters). Twenty-one
were Anglicans for certain. Only seven were definitely Nonconformists: six Presbyterian-Independents and one a Quaker.[8] Nor,

judging by the way they lived, do many of these early industrialists seem to have been particularly abstinent or in rebellion against old-style society. A local gazeteer describes their houses in 1817. James Clegg of Lower Bent owned a 'stone mansion plain but neat with an extensive garden and pleasure walks'. Pit Bank, the property of Daniel Lees, is described as 'the most elegant building in the township with a graceful parterre and shrubbery laid out with an artificial tumulus. If taste, if elegance of design . . . have charms to attract . . . here is a luxury'. John Lees of Fairfield lived in a 'plain stone building in modern taste consisting of centre and wings'. Orleans House, the 'newly erected mansion' of Joseph Rowland, 'promises to be as elegant as any other in the town'. New Clarksfield, belonging to a branch of the Clarksfield Lees, was a 'handsome edifice . . . ornamented with numerous plantations, handsome gardens and pleasure grounds'. The gazeteer spends more than a hundred pages describing the houses of fifty Oldham families.[9] From these houses came the twenty-one scarlet-uniformed officers of the 1798 Oldham Volunteers.[10]

So much, then, for factory building in Oldham. And while the situation there may not have been exactly typical, what happened elsewhere is unlikely to have been sufficiently different to justify claims that this very short period represented the coming of an altogether new industrial *society*. This is not to say that the industrial revolution had no social effects – it is precisely these we are ultimately concerned with – but it is clear that they can only be assessed as part of a very much longer process. It is this we must now try to define, and to do so we must reverse the level of analysis to one of pretty blunt generalization.

England's industrialization

The starting point for any useful treatment of England's industrialization must be the fact that it was *first*. This determined everything else. England's pioneering position meant that the path taken was uniquely complicated, and certainly cannot be seen as just the usual-style industrialization in slow motion. In essence, what we are dealing with is the process by which a new capitalist form of social organization emerged from an earlier, essentially antagonistic, feudal one. This involved an extremely devious roundabout route and probably the best way of getting at the basic logic behind it is by trying to identify the main incompatibilities between the two systems; working out, in effect, the preconditions of pioneer capitalist industrialization and then seeing why they could not be immediately fulfilled within the preceeding feudal type of society.

In themselves the preconditions for capitalist industrialization may not seem particularly difficult. Like any other form of industrialization its main requirement is the diversion of a relatively small amount of resources from immediate consumption (like building churches or country houses) to the sustained improvement of production methods. Consequently, the prime requirement in capitalist conditions is a rate of profit high enough to attract capital from other uses. On the *demand* side, this means having an unemployed reserve to prevent labour demanding a bigger share in the new wealth than it had in the old. And equally, to prevent primary producers doing the same, there has to be a readily expandable supply of raw material. On the *market* side, things are slightly more difficult. As 'labour reserve' industrialization is (as such) unlikely to add very much to mass purchasing power, outlets for the new goods have to be found within existing markets. And while over a short period this would present no problem – given the fact that industrial capital would find itself in highly profitable coexistence with craft producers – this could last only a limited time. Pre-industrial economies are usually small-scale and underdeveloped and so the amount of capital that could be invested in any given field without destroying the necessary super-profit margin is likely to be small.

For *sustained* investment much larger markets would be necessary, and ones where invested capital could somehow be guaranteed a monopoly position. In terms of a *single* pre-industrial economy this would be an almost impossible condition. If, however, there were a number of coexisting economies, all at different stages of development, then the matter is easily solved. The industrial goods of one country would simply invade the markets of the others, whose relative backwardness (and it need only be a matter of a few years) would prevent effective retaliation.

And this, of course, is eventually how England's industrial revolution did develop: a labour reserve, a quickly expandable supply of raw cotton, and a technological lead just sufficient to sustain a super-profit incursion into the world market for craft-produced textiles. Indeed, from this point of view, the preconditions for *pioneer* industrialization were easy compared with what was required from some subsequent attempts.

To understand why in fact they took so long to fulfil, one has to complete the equation and look at them *historically* from the angle of the preceding *type* of society. Here the picture is much less hopeful. At each level feudal society seems to have presented a series of almost impassable obstacles – obstacles which were all the more formidable because they were an essential part of feudal social organization and not just the result of general 'backwardness'. Feudal society existed as a precarious balance between the advanced and the primitive. Its luxuriant aristocracy, intercontinental trade, towns and universities all depended on the knife-edge economics of peasant farming. With near-stagnant productivity, the central equation in this balance – that determining the size of the feudal surplus – was the ratio between population and land. If peasant families got too big for the land available, either the surplus would be eaten up or the peasants starve. In either event the system's survival would be threatened. The basic function of feudal social organization was, therefore, to maintain just that balance between population and land which (in given technological conditions) would produce the biggest possible feudal surplus. It was the methods used to do this that formed the great barrier to capitalist growth.

For the majority of the peasant population the controls were fairly simple. It was enough to ensure that marriage and child-rearing were strictly tied (by customary practice and religion) to the inheritance of land, and rely on peasant self-interest to do the rest. For the small non-agricultural population – whose unrestricted expansion could easily upset the balance of the surrounding community – formal legal control had to be considerably tighter. Generally the whole sector was segregated into towns and the intake of labour governed by enforced apprenticeship. And, as with the peasant community, this solution generated a self-perpetuating momentum of its own. Restricted labour-intake gave workers a closed-shop bargaining position which enabled them to achieve a large measure of control over the process of production and, correspondingly, the merchants who provided the credit had to be guaranteed a monopoly of investment which they themselves enforced.

So at each level both the legal framework and group self-interest stood right against the development of the necessary conditions. The whole structure acted to prevent the emergence of a labour reserve. Overall landlord dominance made any rapid 'profitable' expansion of raw material cultivation unlikely. And craft control of production served to block the development of the critical super-profit trigger of labour-saving innovation.

The structure of feudal society does, therefore, provide a fairly convincing explanation of why the apparently simple conditions of pioneer industrialization took so long to fulfil. To discover how they eventually *were* fulfilled – and to plot the very devious route taken – one has in addition to see feudal society as a developing system; but developing in spite of itself and in response to certain inherent contradictions in its make-up.

The most important of these contradictions was that between its social organization and the small amount of technological advance it did succeed in generating. When – every other century or so – agricultural productivity did significantly move forward, the whole system (just because it was specifically geared to a stable level of productivity) got thrown off balance. The typical peasant reaction – bigger families and a mass demand for craft products – both threatened the old system at key points and created conditions for embryonic forms of capitalist production. And while these periods may not go far to explain the very different phenomenon of pioneer industrialization, they do help to explain why its achievement had to be so roundabout and devious. A number of cycles of agrarian advance and population rise can be distinguished within the development of European feudalism. Each produced short-lived forms of cheap labour, capitalist craft production, and while each cycle started at a higher technological level each also ended disastrously in demographic crisis and population decline. Each time the class logic of feudal society reasserted itself. Landowners had no interest in providing consumer goods for an agricultural labour force they did not need. To maintain the feudal surplus at the maximum level, the balance between population and land had to be restored.

Seen against this background, the great question posed by England's eventual breakthrough does not refer so much to what happened in the late eighteenth century as to what happened during the *preceding* cycle of advance during the sixteenth and early seventeenth centuries. By itself the late-eighteenth-century escape from the closed logic of a 'single economy' is easily explained: England used her lead in industrial technology to capture the markets of her neighbours. The real question is how England managed to achieve this lead, how during the previous century the apparently general feudal reaction was held off long enough to bridge the gap to the next agrarian upswing and in the meantime permit the development of a relatively advanced technology (which for the pioneer was bound to be a very lengthy and difficult process).

Taken on its own, an explanation in terms of bourgeois revolution – a capitalist seizure of state power – hardly seems enough. A bourgeois revolution certainly occurred in the 1640s, and what remained of the elaborate system of feudal controls was pretty thoroughly destroyed. Yet what really has to be explained is the economic situation which sustained the new set-up at a time when there could be no question of massive technological mastery over foreign competitors. No government, whatever its composition, could make continued industrial investment a viable, profitable proposition within the limits of one country – especially during the crisis-prone tail of a demographic cycle. And without such a prospect one would have expected the country's ruling class (whether originally landlord or merchant) to have reacted by restabilizing population and reviving feudal restrictions.

To understand what did, in fact, make possible this unparalleled suspension of feudal reaction, it is necessary to look once more at the development of late feudal society – this time more specifically.

During the final phase of the generally sixteenth- and seventeenth-century upswing-and-relapse, England's capitalists got two successive lucky breaks. The first resulted from the uneven growth of English and continental populations. While England's reacted far more quickly to the original impulse (and then suffered a hiccup of feudal reaction in the mid-sixteenth century), it eventually – and perhaps consequently – went on developing for a good generation after continental populations started to decline at the beginning of the seventeenth century. This meant that for over three decades England's textile producers could get plentiful supplies of labour no longer available to their continental (and especially Mediterranean) counterparts. Obviously the competitive advantages this offered were only small compared with those of the following century and seem to have been largely exhausted by the 1650s. But they were certainly enough to produce a massive expansion of the capitalist cheap-labour sector and push through a bourgeois revolution of unprecedented thoroughness.

The second lucky break followed directly on from this. Just when the textile expansion seemed to be reaching its limits, there came empire. England suddenly found herself in a position to seize an increasingly preponderant share of the massive *colonial* surplus that Europe had been exacting from neighbouring continents since the beginning of the sixteenth century. The old colonial master races, the Spanish, Portuguese and Dutch, were short of manpower. England was not. And it seems to have been this which finally did the trick. For obvious reasons this colonial surplus – in contrast to a feudal one – demanded a buoyant home population and also turned out to be most efficiently secured by precisely those capitalist, plantation-type techniques that England was in a position to pioneer. For the first time, it made the *continuing* relaxation of feudal restrictions also in the interest of the men who controlled the country's wealth.

England's pioneer industrialization seems, then, to have involved the following elements. Underlying the whole process, but not explaining it, were the general factors common to all Europe: the slow, spasmodic advance of agricultural productivity; the recurrent but abortive bursts of merchant capitalist production; and the new type of colonial surplus. Then, providing the necessarily devious escape route, came the factors that put England ahead. First, there was the out-of-step pattern of population growth that brought a boom in cheap labour, capitalist producion and bourgeois revolution. Next, there were the conditions that enabled the capture of Europe's colonial surplus, the long-term maintenance of capitalist forms of organization and continuing industrial and agrarian innovation. Then, finally (after the over-investment in colonial primary production had brought a collapse in colonial profits) one gets the massive switch of investment back to the home industrial sectors in the 1770s and 1780s: back in order to exploit the crucial super-profit techniques developed in the previous two generations. At this point, with all three basic preconditions fulfilled (labour, raw material and market) industrial revolution could begin.

That, then seems to have been the overall perspective, and on the social front it should at least have made clear what the late-eighteenth-century industrial revolution did *not* bring about. To start with, it obviously did not involve any basic change in the social system. In terms of the larger process of industrialization, it was essentially a revolution of scale, the expansion of an existing capitalist economy to an altogether new size. Just to create the situation that made it possible – to generate the vital technical lead over other countries – a secure, continuing framework for capitalist development had had to exist for over a century. By the time of the industrial revolution all essential capitalist institutions were already old.

Nor does there seem to have been any overwhelming impact on the social environment. Despite the critical cost-cutting advances made in certain sectors, the *bulk* of industrial technology would remain primitive – scarcely mechanized at all – for a long time to come. True, there was a massive increase in the size of the industrial labour force – almost doubling between 1780 and 1820. But even before 1780 it had been relatively large, and the proportion of industrial occupations (within a rapidly expanding total population) only rose from a minimum of perhaps 30 per cent in 1780 to around 40 per cent in 1820. Most of these workers would, moreover, still in 1820 be working in outwork occupations and in largely rural surroundings.

To say anything more positive means going back to theory, to the characteristic boom-slump pattern by which industrial capitalism developed. It seems to be this – rather than any impact on social institutions or environment – that holds the key to the industrial revolution's really fundamental effects on English society. What it meant was the appearance of a completely new *type* of situation in which the ruling class was (on occasion) forced to attack existing standards.

In the period under review this new situation had three distinct aspects. The first was the actual starting up of the boom-slump cycle itself. While economic fluctuations were, of course, nothing new, they had previously been largely the result of harvest failure and war. The new form of crisis was very different. It marked the arrival of the *industrial* stage of capitalist development, one demanding an increasing body of fixed investment which would only be sustained by the fundamentally contradictory private profit incentive. As in any system where goods are produced for profit (and so exchange at labour value), the ultimate, collective result of any burst of cost-cutting investment could only be to lower prices (and profits). And from the mid-1780s this is the pattern one begins to find in England – bursts of investment followed by falling prices and suspended investment: 1785, 1788, 1793, 1797, 1800.

Now obviously these crises themselves did not mean imminent disaster. (Indeed, from a Marxist standpoint they represented the process by which the capitalist economy evaded disaster; by which unrealistic prices were forced back to their new labour values and a rupture of exchange relations avoided.) But they did nonetheless introduce a fundamentally new element into class relations. Previously, labour's main experience of crisis had been through a rapid increase in food prices. Now – in a period which saw bursts of unpredecently fast growth in the size of the labour force (and at times wages) – crisis was expressed in unemployment and, even more, wage-cutting. And so while in pre-industrial capitalism it had usually been the food wholesaler who had been held responsible for the hunger and disease which crisis inflicted, it was now – to repeat a phrase from our opening quotation – the 'relentless cruelty of the masters'. This was a fundamental change which, as will be seen, cut right across the whole previous structure of social control.

For our period, however, there were two further elements in the situation which served to intensify its impact still further. For two quite lengthy spells there was not just repeated crisis but *deepening* crisis – with living standards for large sections of the industrial population ending each cycle at an absolutely lower level. The first lasted from about the mid-1790s to the second decade of the new century; the second from 1830 to the late 1840s. More than anything else it seems to have been these two periods which served to undermine the existing structure of English society, and for this reason it would be useful to say something more about their economic origin.

Both stemmed directly from the pioneer character of England's industrial revolution, and in particular from its extremely limited technological base. Indeed, it is remarkable just how little mechanization there was. The breakthrough of the 1780s and 1790s was based on scarcely more than the mechanization of *one* branch of *one* industry. And though the labour-saving achieved in that one branch (cotton spinning) was massive – and involved the coming together of a whole range of subsidiary innovations – the other branch of the industry (weaving) remained largely unmechanized for a period whose very length needs constantly restating – forty years. Throughout this period England was completely dependent on a vast army of handloom weavers to convert its yarn into exportable cloth. Moreover, outside the cotton industry England lacked almost all the technical equipment which today would be seen as essential pre-requisites for industrialization. There was no mechanized transport system for fifty years, no mass-produced machinery for sixty and no large-scale steel production for seventy.

It was the economic tensions set up by this situation that were largely responsible for both phases of 'deepening crisis'.

The first – 1790s to 1800s – principally resulted from the incomplete mechanization of the cotton industry itself. The failure to mechanize weaving brought the largest sector of England's industrial labour force into direct competition with the more cheaply fed workers of the continent, where industries had been surprisingly quick to reorganize in face of England's industrial offensive. Already by the mid-1790s they were making substantial imports of England's cheap machine-spun yarn and using it to edge England out of continental and later even some colonial markets for woven cloth. And although some respite was gained during the height of the continental blockade, the situation did not get much better till the mechanization of weaving finally got under way in the 1820s. So for over two decades the biggest section of the industry's labour force was exposed to an incessant downward pressure on its real wages.

The origins of the second phase of ruling-class attack – the 1830s and 1840s – correspond more closely to the classic formula for destabilizing crisis. Though the cotton industry was now well ahead of its continental rivals, the technological incompleteness of England's industry as a whole produced just the situation which Marx prescribed for a declining rate of profit. The extremely narrow base of the initial breakthrough meant that while there was a continual and dramatic decrease in the (labour) exchange value of cotton textiles – still in the 1830s producing half the country's exports – there was no corresponding fall in the price of food or machinery. So inevitably the value of industrial output relative to the costs of labour and the increasing mass of fixed capital would tend to fall from crisis to crisis. And this indeed is what the evidence from the cotton industry itself suggests: a fairly marked decline in the rate of profit from the early 1830s until well into the following decade.[11] Obviously this situation was only likely to last for a limited period. As soon as the development of heavy industry got under way – bringing both cheaper machinery and (with a mechanized world transport system) cheaper food – the trend was likely to be reversed. But while it lasted employers could only remain in business (and even then by no means all of them) by cutting wages.

So finally (to sum up) it seems to be this which was the essence of the new situation: the development of the industrial crisis cycle itself and the two phases of *deepening* crisis. And in assessing the industrial revolution's social effects, it should also have become clear that whatever happened in terms of environment and institutions, the most profound impact was not 'direct' but through this changed rhythm of the economy. What the rest of this chapter will be trying to do, therefore, is to analyze the social effects of the *first* phase of 'deepening crisis', and will start by attempting to make a local (Oldham) reconstruction of the pre-industrial social structure on which it acted.

Social structure before the industrial revolution

In the mid-sixteenth century the sixteen square miles that later made up the parliamentary borough probably supported less than seven hundred households – 5 per cent of Oldham's mid-nineteenth-century population. Even in terms of the country as a whole the area was backward. The land was held in knight's fee of the crown by seven families (Ashton, Byron, Chadderton, Cudworth, Radclyffe, Taylor and Tetlow) who seem to have lived off what fines and services they could exact from the peasants.[12] Acid, hillside soil limited cultivation to oats and a few sheep. Within a hundred years all this was changed. The feudal landlords had vanished. Two families were fined heavily for Catholicism.[13] Six of the seven fought on the losing side in the Civil War (the Cudworths kept out). And by the end of the seventeenth century all except the Radclyffes had sold off their lands – and the Radclyffes would lose most of theirs in the following century.[14]

Locally at least the catalyst seems to have been the early seventeenth-century burst of cheap-labour production. The development of European demand for the low quality 'new draperies' gave merchants the incentive to take production into hitherto untouched areas of the countryside. In Oldham the infiltration seems to have been managed from Manchester (though close commercial contact was kept with London). In response the population of the late sixteenth- and early seventeenth-century chapelry (approximately the parliamentary borough) underwent rapid expansion. And the resulting disruption of the peasant economy created a large number of landless cottagers and a small group of comparatively rich peasant-yeomanry. These richer peasants organized production for the Manchester merchants. However, before long the demand for 'new draperies' faltered and in the middle of the century declined substantially, leaving Oldham (not well placed to profit by the subsequent colonial expansion) to face a bad period of near-famine, plague and half a century of stagnant, if not declining, population.[15]

Yet, though short-lived, this period did not leave things altogether as they were. Before its end the peasant-employers had begun to grapple with the new problems of social control; they took over the church, placed the parish within the Manchester *classis* and laid the foundation of a useful system of charity patronage. Not all of this was destroyed. More important, the feudal landlords were gone for good. Their land went to two types of buyer: the larger peasants themselves (like the Lees); and more usually to wealthy merchants from outside looking for investment securities (Wood and Horton of London, Wrigley and later Perceval of Manchester).[16] Nationally, of course, the same period saw the end of any attempt by the state to regulate production either through the enforcement of apprenticeship or by monopoly company.

Eighteenth-century Oldham was not, then, in a position to offer much resistance to renewed activity by merchant capitalists. And the state was now squarely on their side (from the reign of Anne a whole series of penal statutes were passed weakening the bargaining position of outwork labour).[17] With the slow re-expansion of the European economy in the early years of the eighteenth century, all the old symptoms reappear. There was a burst of population growth in the first three decades, then a slight lull, and finally from the 1760s an uninterrupted period of expansion.[18] Already in the first decades the area's population had outstripped its food production and cottagers (whether they liked it or not) were forced to take manufacturer's outwork to supplement their cabbage patch diet; a situation which meant that manufacturing costs could, in fact, be kept well below what was normally required for subsistence.[19] In 1758 Perceval, a local magistrate, described the population as composed of 'a few rich traders amongst the numerous, half-starved, half-clothed poor weavers'.[20] The cottagers were in no position to argue. To survive they had to get every member of the family earning out-work wages as soon as possible. In the country, complained the Manchester craft weavers, there was no apprenticeship, no attempt to limit labour intake; it was a pattern of growth which put the country weavers still more in pawn to the manufacturers and the town weavers out of business.[21] It also made Oldham a very profitable place in which to process first Yorkshire wool and later American cotton (via Liverpool) and Canadian beaver (via London).[22]

That, then, seems to have been the economic impact of capitalism's *pre*-industrial development in one small area of Lancashire. The real task, however, is to reconstruct the type (or types) of social structure that sustained it and which ultimately had to bear the strains of industrial revolution.

This is something far more difficult and even its local aspect can only be tackled extremely inadequately. We are faced with a phase of development not just almost as long as the whole post-industrial revolution period (and which could well have contained within it quite as many distinct phases of social structure change) but also one which included a transition from one social *system* to another. So in addition to the problem of evidence – and there is very little – there is also a strong possibility that assumptions about capitalist social structure which seem to hold good for later centuries operated (if at all) in a quite different way. We know, for instance, that there was a vigorous local survival of certain peasant customs (like the annual wakes and rush carts) and it could well be that other more fundamental (but less visible) social routines associated with the pre-capitalist system could also have lingered on: the 'superstitions' which expressed the old peasant community's self-imposed discipline; the exclusive (almost caste-like) 'mystery' of the inherited craft.[23] And, if so, it is equally likely (especially in an area where proletarianized and non-proletarianized sectors – small peasants, cottagers and landless labourers – did coexist for a long period) that there was little development of specifically capitalist forms of social structure in the early period; that as yet there was no *generalized* response to the loss of control over what was produced in the way outlined in the previous chapter. All this is quite possible. And unfortunately the evidence that might allow us to test whether working people were in fact more divided up by occupational castes than income and consumption has not yet become available.

Where things do become a bit clearer is in the more directly political field of social control. Here some evidence has survived. And by looking at its social logic it should be possible to get at least some guide to the social tensions to which early capitalist society was exposed.

Probably the most typical *social* form of early capitalist production was what might be called the 'employer-dominated household'.

Two main problems of social control seem to have brought it into existence. The first was the actual coexistence of capitalist and pre-capitalist forms. At a time when the craft worker and small farmer maintained at least formal control over the use to which their labour was put, the capitalist worker – whether hired by the hour or on piecework – visibly did not. Moreover, in the new conditions he had little hope of becoming a master. The class division now ran through (and not round) the production unit. So on top of the problem of imposing a work discipline there was the constant danger of subversive 'levelling' comparisons. This seems to have been the *source* of the tension. The other constituent was the social context within which it had to be met. Early capitalist production involved immediate face-to-face contact between employer and employed. Even out-work manufacturing was intensely local, with the working cottagers living round the employer family and known to them over the years. Somehow a working relationship had to be maintained.

Historically, the solution evolved generally goes under the name 'Puritanism'. In this sense there is a fragment of truth behind the Protestant-capitalist story. But only a fragment. It was, of course, the wage-earner, not the capitalist, who was intended to be 'abstinent' and work hard. And it was not 'ideas' but the nature of production itself which provided the basic stimulus.

The essence of the solution seems to have been an attempt to gloss over the class split by binding the worker into the larger household of the employer and then asserting the moral priority of the overall group. On one side this involved emphasizing the similarities between employer and employed – the master, like the workman, was to live simply and hard. On the other side responsibility for 'moral' discipline was decentralized from the parish priest to the head of household: the patriarch armed with Geneva slogans about sloth and damnation.[24]

This, therefore, was a solution which involved direct conflict with pre-existing forms of social organization and in Oldham it was precisely the issue of Church control that brought the most dramatic confrontation of the Civil War period. The landlord-backed parish priest insisted on administering communion (and its dispensations) to his parishioners at large – a practice that openly undercut the authority of the larger peasant-employers.[25] As a result, these men eventually forced his resignation in favour of a minister-lecturer of their own choosing, and in 1646 established a presbytery of elders (a 'morals' court) which sent regular delegates to the Manchester *classis*.[26] From then on, members of the congregation were no longer equally sinful until redeemed by the church. Some were saved by God's grace (a state revealed by their assiduous attendance to their duties) and the rest, the damned, condemned to perpetual discipline by the community's elders. This local presbytery disappeared with the political changes of 1660 and the decline of the 'new draperies'. But in the hills along the Yorkshire border behind Oldham some woollen manufacturing continued, and the manufacturers built themselves a Presbyterian chapel on Greenacres Moor. During the political instability of 1715 this chapel was attacked and burnt by a mob – largely craft workers it seems – from Manchester.[27]

With the revival of trade in the eighteenth century roughly the same pattern was repeated, but in a way that gives the lie to the crude idealist determinism of the Protestant-capitalist argument. There was clearly no tradition – no initiating 'idea'. The Puritan pattern (now called 'Evangelicalism') was generated by force of circumstance; and generated *inside* the established Church.[28] This time there was no serious conflict with the state and, instead of any takeover of the parish church itself, an additional Anglican chapel was established, one in which authority was clearly delegated to the yeoman-employers. When the chancellor of the diocese consecrated St Peter's chapel in 1768 (some earlier building seems to have been used by the congregation from at least the 1750s), effective control was vested in the subscribers who put up the money and paid the minister's salary. These men were largely the grandfathers of the big industrialists of the early nineteenth century: Lees, Clegg, Duncuft, Worthington, Rowland, Taylor, Winterbottom.[29] The doctrine and ritual of the new church were predictable: the first minister was Hugh Grimshaw, the hymnal 'new version', and additional 'Thursday lectures' given by Wrigley, minister to the wool manufacturing congregation at Saddleworth.[30]

There can be little doubt, therefore, that as an instrument of social control the 'Puritan household' was closely associated with early capitalist production. And its appearance both underlines the fact that the period *was* transitional (did contain substantial survivals from the previous social system) and – if the foregoing diagnosis is correct – also gives very useful support to the argument that the new system's most basic social tension was that produced by the worker's immediate loss of control over his labour. However, the way in which this was handled differed significantly from what was to happen in later centuries. Instead of allowing labour to develop its own 'solution' – its own subcultures – the Puritan household attempted to eliminate the tension at source: to bind the worker so tightly into the cultural group of the employer that any consciousness of a loss of control was minimized.

The same could be said of the second main type of social control: the various religious sects that made their appearance in the last decades of the eighteenth century. These were also run fairly directly by the employers. The Methodists, who appeared in the early 1770s, first operated from St Peter's itself and were financially backed by several employer members of its congregation.[31] The Moravians came a bit later and set up a community in Lees more or less completely controlled by one of the area's biggest employers, John Lees of Fairfield.[32].

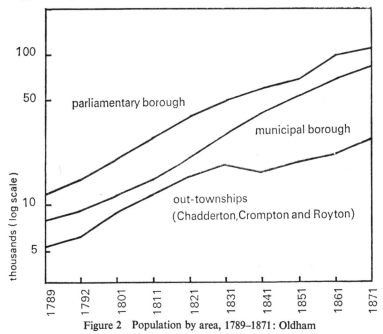

Figure 2 Population by area, 1789–1871: Oldham

What distinguished these later sects is the way they actively proselytized the general population instead of simply relying on the discipline of the employer household. In this they seem to reflect the increasing scale of local production. The population had risen from three to fifteen thousand in the course of the century and now included a much larger (as well as more remote and inscrutable) labour force of outwork cottagers.[33] If these were to be won for employer values, 'salvation' would have to be offered on very much more favourable terms than the harsh Calvinism of the previous century. And for the Methodists everyone could be saved – if they repented in time. Another reaction to the same problem was to work through the children. In the last few years of the century there seems to have been active use of Sunday schools to discipline the new child labour force in the factories. The curate of the *parish* church (always somewhat jealous of his rivals at St Peter's) wrote a rueful note to his bishop:

> They [the manufacturers] have the merit, it must be owned, of setting up Sunday schools for the instruction of the children who work in their factories, but their manner of conducting them is not altogether such as is consistent with our establishment, but if they are interrupted in their plans they generally withdraw their support and seem unwilling to have any clergyman connected with them but such as will be instruments in promoting their designs.[34]

This brings us to the third (and principal) area of social control: the *state establishment*. Though the state system was not (unlike that of the early seventeenth century) in actual conflict with that of the employers, it certainly did derive from a quite different area of social tension, namely that produced by the overall development of the country's economy. Post-Civil War England was following a path of development that was not just new but in terms of the preceding social system uniquely irresponsible. In the bid to maintain control over the world's colonial surplus, trade, industry, and population had all been allowed to run free. And while this gamble did eventually pay off, its success was by no means always certain. At times – when armies were defeated or the harvest failed – it often looked as though the new system might be smothered at birth by the country's mutinous, overgrown population. It was this type of crisis – like that in 1757 when Manchester had to be protected by regular troops – that the state system was designed to meet.

Partly it did so by maintaining state controls for the key areas of food pricing and supply. But more characteristic was an extremely elaborate (and predictably army-style) system of formal control over the labour population itself, a jealously guarded chain of command matched by a far-reaching system of local intelligence. The magistracy and Church served as its focal points. Above them were the county (and military) authorities. Below them an expanding network of what amounted to non-commissioned officers positioned within each main area of labour activity.

To this extent the state system also reflects the growth of the labour population in the course of the century. Originally, the Church alone handled almost everything: marriage, education, poor relief, ill health. By the middle of the century population growth had brought many manufacturing districts (including Oldham) near to the type of situation already found in the great port cities. Labour's social life now took place far more around the alehouse than the institutions specifically provided for it by the employers and Church authorities. This may not indicate the development of subculture itself, but it certainly meant a far more autonomous labour community, and its coming in Oldham is firmly documented by the visitation reports of the local clergymen, who mention the falling off of communion, the absence of the lower orders, the excessive drinking. Indeed, the thing to note from the figures in table 2 is not so much the massive relative decline in regular communicants between 1778 and 1821 as the low level of even the 1778 figure.

Table 2   Regular communicants in Oldham area churches[35]

	1778	1789	1804	1811	1821
St Mary's	110	300	–	–	45
St Peter's	–	–	250	350	250
Royton	50	50	–	20	70
Shaw	60	60	–	–	–
Hollinwood	40	60	15	–	–
Lees	–	80	100	–	35
total population in thousands	9	14	25	29	38

It was this development that created the need for a network of establishment henchmen *inside* the labour community, men who could be relied upon to hold it steady in times of crisis. The way this was achieved was to make as many key figures as possible legally dependent on the good graces of the authorities. The most important man of all, the alehouse-keeper, had to get his licence renewed annually.[36] In December 1792, when the magistrates cracked their whip, fifty-eight of the sixty Oldham area licencees signed a loyalty declaration.[37] A few months earlier a similar proportion had agreed to ban all 'seditious' persons from their houses.[38] Similarly with the friendly society, labour's principal mass organization. Even before the Act of 1793 the Oldham sick clubs seem to have been fairly subservient (financial difficulties made it easy for local magnates to step in as patrons), and their annual feast started off with a church service.[39] The Act of 1793 gave legal status only to those clubs which registered themselves and their rules with the Quarter sessions, a procedure which involved their treasurers entering into bond with the clerk of the peace.[40] The schoolmaster was equally tied. To teach (or preach) a man had to have a licence. Before the Act of 1779 this meant swearing a no-popery oath – which, as the authorities eventually realized, left a great deal unsaid. After 1779 there was the additional requirement that a man declares his belief in the scriptures as the 'revealed will' of God.[41]

By the late eighteenth century, therefore, the state system relied quite as much on this network of tied loyalists within the labour community as it did on its own traditional institutions, and it is interesting to note the parallel development of social groupings, which seem almost specifically designed to reinforce the loyalist activities of these men – above all, the freemasons. The first local lodge was founded in 1776 (by 1800 the number of lodges had risen to six) and from the incomplete returns made in 1799 it seems clear that the membership included many (if not most) of the sixty local innkeepers.[42] Later the Volunteers and Orangemen recruited from much the same base.

So although Oldham's later eighteenth-century labour force seems to have been socially fairly well-knit (and occupationally perhaps surprisingly fluid), there were also good reasons why it usually remained politically passive. Those dissatisfied with the existing system could not easily work through the existing labour institutions and were liable to get thrown out of the alehouses in which working people spent most of their spare time. Nonetheless, the mere description of all these tightening precautions should have indicated that some social tensions did exist, and it is at the nature of this opposition that we must look next.

Perhaps the first thing to emphasize is its *continuing* presence within the community. Recently much attention has been focused on food and excise riots. Undoubtedly these riots – accompanying the crisis years of the century (1757-8, 1766, 1773, 1782) – did mark the only occasions on which really large sections of the population were brought out against the authorities. These were the times when rapidly rising food prices (or taxes) seemed to mark an outright attack on living standards. On the other hand, locally it is also possible to identify more permanent cells of opposition, isolated groupings of families which provided at least some of the long-term continuity of language and direction. In the Oldham area two such groupings can be found: Lord Street in Oldham itself and Dob Lane two miles to the south. Both, like similar groupings in other parts of Lancashire, were in legal form *religious*.[43]

If, however, this means putting them alongside the parish church, the Evangelical employers or even the Methodists, such 'chapels' were altogether irreligious. In doctrine, they tended to free-thought and rejected all the usual weapons of social control – original sin, grace and after-life. Membership was entirely wage-earner or craft. There was no manipulation from outside. Above all, they were active. The emphasis was on seeing the world as it was – on using 'reason' against 'superstition' and 'oppression' – and consequently doing something about it. Several times during the century south Lancashire spawned crops of these congregations, often hiving themselves off from moribund Presbyterian chapels and taking over their buildings and endowments. Usually there was explicit reference to the Socinian-Anabaptist tradition of the previous century and links with a wider free-thought movement.[44] In 1753 Wesley noted in his journal finding 'a whole clan of infidel peasants' at Deryhulme (a few miles from Oldham) where an untypical 'alehouse-keeper drinks and laughs and argues into Deism all the ploughmen and dairymen he can light on.'[45] This religious underworld – attacked even more fiercely by dissent than the establishment (Bogue and Bennet, the official dissenter historians of 1808, talk of 'depravity', 'perversion of property' and 'evil disposition') – has not yet received the attention it deserves.[46]

Luckily, the public activity of the two Oldham area congregations is at least partially on record, and (significantly) it is reported for the years of military defeat and crisis. Dob Lane had its part to play in the mass actions of the late 1750s. In 1757, at the time of the food riots, there were two sermons (later published) 'on the great sin and danger of oppression: two sermons preached during the late high prices of corn'. And the manifesto issued by the striking check-weavers the following year has been attributed to the Dob Lane minister, Robinson. The language of this 'Apology' is noteworthy. It contrasts the wealth of the manufacturers with the 'misery of the mechanic from whose industry and hard work such immense riches have been acquired'.[47] During the late 1770s and early 1780s the Lord Street congregation, too, seems to have found the climate favourable for political activity. The titles of some of its public debates for 1784-5 have survived: 'Whether has done more towards the reformation of mankind, preaching or the law of all nations?'; 'Whether is more unworthy of his situation, the partial magistrate or the neglective clergyman?'; 'Do observation, reason and the holy writ confirm the doctrine of original sin?'[48]

Naturally the authorities were quite alive to the dangers. During the American crisis they put through the 'revealed will' oath, and the 1781 Act making unlawful Sunday debates 'held under the pretence of inquiring into religious doctrines by persons incompetent to explain the same'.[49] In 1786-7 the Manchester magistrates took a leading part in the nationwide 'suppression of vice' campaign, prosecuting seditious libels and illegal meetings, and closing down a good number of alehouses.[50]

How far this religion *was* merely a cover is difficult to tell. Sunday was the only day working people had free, and non-religious meetings were subject to restrictions which amounted to total ban by 1795.[51] But up till the last decade of the century it would seem that the religion of these groupings did represent something more than just camouflage and, if so, this itself would serve to underline the difficulty of maintaining an open, political challenge for all but very short periods, and even then the need to argue in terms dictated by the largely religious channels of social control. Amidst an overwhelmingly loyalist population, any opposition group that was to survive did very much need the kind of protection given by a separate, religiously defined identity (and especially perhaps the presence of a minister or teacher not tied to the establishment).

To end with, to place this 'working-class' opposition in perspective, it would be useful to quote from the diary of the local handloom weaver, Rowbottom, begun at the end of the period in 1787. Rowbottom probably provides a fairly typical picture of attitudes within the working population. Though articulate and obviously well integrated into the working community, he gives little indication of labour consciousness. When a fellow-weaver was imprisoned under the Piecework Acts (one of the employers' main weapons for increasing labour input) he merely wrote: 'At the sessions Jonathan Mellor was committed to prison for three months for keeping a warp and cotton above the statute time'.[52] He attended church and copied down the texts. He watched the gentry – a duel between Mr John Clegg and Dr Brennand, the departure for London of 'Sir Watts Horton, Lady Horton and Miss Horton accompanied by a large retinue' and transcribed the mottoes of the Derbys and the Greys.[53] There is a detailed description of the 'martial display' made by the shrill, fife-playing redcoats as they went on their rounds collecting replacement manpower.[54] It was on people like this that the men from Lord Street had to work and not surprisingly their influence was limited to periods of major crisis.

To sum up, therefore. On the basic lines of Oldham's social structure before the industrial revolution there can be no doubt. From the beginning of the century the area's working population was mainly composed of propertyless wage-labourers: miners, hatters and (always over 50 per cent of the total) weavers. The majority were employed by no more than a couple of dozen yeoman-manufacturer families. Mass activity of any kind was extremely spasmodic and continuing opposition limited to a handful of families operating half undercover. Most of the time the general population remained effectively cowed by the massive apparatus of intimidation.

For the immediate argument, however, the important thing is not so much the shape of social structure itself as that of the authority systems that sustained it. All had one thing in common. Either in terms of 'religion' or 'loyalty' they demanded a more or less direct identity with ruling-class values and ruled out any legitimate expression of separate labour interests. For the first phase of capitalist development this is, of course, just what one would expect. The overriding priority was to bind the emergent mass labour force to the new employer class – and to do so during a period when the old self-imposed disciplines of peasant-craft society were (at one and the same time) both disintegrating and still dangerously potent. What had to be killed right from the start was any idea of basic conflict between master and servant. If legitimate conflict existed, it was rather with monopolists and speculators who rigged food prices.

For most of the century this system was only too effective. For the period we are about to consider it could hardly have been worse. Within only a decade of building their first factories Oldham's employers had been forced to put on army uniforms and use their sabres,[55] and it will be argued here that the suddenness of this breakdown, far from being coincidental, stemmed directly from the inability of the old-style social structure to sustain the new pressures of *industrial* capitalism. As soon as the basic area of conflict started to shift from prices to wages, the very tightness of the old systems of control (above all their outlawry of a separate labour identity) proved their greatest liability. In the new conditions it was precisely the men who were themselves beyond the law, the previously isolated radicals, who were now (uniquely) in a position to express the interests of the great majority.

The politics of industrial revolution

In arguing this case, the sequence of events is important. Two distinct sets of potentially disruptive influences, ideological and economic, can be seen acting on Oldham in this period. Conveniently they are separated in time. First, ideologically, there were the ideas of the French revolution, already strongly felt in 1789, and which, while basically petty bourgeois, were still profoundly anti-establishment when translated into English terms. Then, bunched together between 1793 and 1795, there were three more material disruptions. In 1793 there was a trade depression (ending a boom which had lasted since 1789) that can be taken to mark, for the textile industry at least, the beginnings of the *industrial* capitalist economic cycle. Also in 1793 there was the start of a continental war, itself partly the result of Britain's economic breakthrough, which was to last for the next two decades and bring about an unprecedented level of price inflation. Finally in 1795 (a year of new economic downturn after a slight steadying in 1794) one gets the first direct pressure on English handloom weaving wages from continental competition. It is significant, therefore, that political breakdown did not come at all till 1793 and only became really serious in 1795. As one would expect from what has just been argued, it would seem to have been the change in politico-economic circumstances rather than the arrival of any new crop of anti-establishment ideas that provided the trigger for mass action. Indeed, the immediate consequences of the French revolution (especially its anti-monarchist phase) seem to have been quite the reverse. The level of activity appears to have declined from that of the previous decade. The events in France both strengthened the battered military credibility of the British ruling class and provided an ideal excuse for local witch-hunting. The loyalists enjoyed a brief golden age. From the summer of 1792 semi-authorized mobs roamed the Manchester area wrecking houses and 'working-class' meeting places. Among the places attacked was Dobb Lane chapel, and the experience was remembered long after. 'Persons stood before my father's house', recalled one subsequent radical, 'and shouted "Down with the Rump" . . . and others calling out "You are Jacobins, Painites and Presbyterians, you are enemies of your King and Country and deserve to be killed".'[56] In September and again in December 1792 local alehouse-keepers put out loyalty declarations.[57] In January 1793 there were meetings in liaison with the government-promoted London movement and locally directed by the Manchester Constitutional Association, at which the principal inhabitants showed their 'abhorrence of the inflammatory doctrines of levellers and republicans'.[58] And at a more popular level there was a Tom Paine bonfire. 'On New Year's Day', writes Rowbottom, 'the effigy was with the greatest solemnity brought out of the dungeon [the magistrate-controlled town lock-up] and attended by a band of music playing "God save the King" taken to the gallows.'[59]

By itself, therefore, the example of what happened in France does not seem to have been particularly disruptive, especially during the prosperity of 1792. The old controls were still quite effective. The real cracks did not start to appear till the second quarter of the following year. Then, within a few months, one had the beginning of war, a sharp rise in food prices and a similarly sharp cut in wages. The first big crisis of industrial capitalism had arrived. Overall, the weaver's purchasing power (and weavers, as has been noted, made up over half Oldham's working population) probably dropped by at least a quarter.[60] The diarist Rowbottom felt the pinch as much as anyone: *June 1793:* 'Most torturing misery'. *August:* 'Relentless cruelty of the fustian masters'. *December:* 'Inconceivable miseries . . . a great deal of heads of families enlist'.[61]

The radicals could now take the initiative. Already in May 1793 there had been some kind of street fighting in Oldham involving the Yorkshire militia.[62] Early summer saw the radical clubs in Manchester recruiting members fast, and in July the authorities struck at the ringleaders.[63] By the winter the radicals of Royton (the northernmost township of the Oldham area) were advertising a reform meeting.[64] And on the same day in April 1794 there was an open clash between radical and Church-and-King supporters in Royton, and an illegal strike meeting held by south Lancashire weavers on Newton Heath (a few miles to the west).[65]

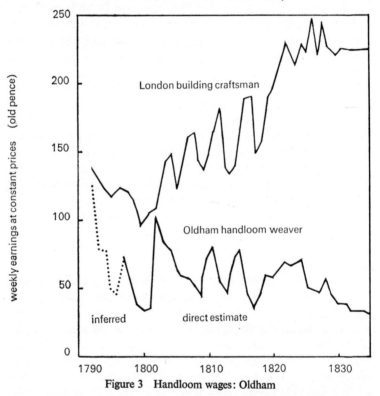

Figure 3   Handloom wages: Oldham

Up to this point the scale of radical activity had probably not gone much beyond that seen during the earlier crises of the 1780s. An altogether new level was reached in the summer of 1795. At one and the same time weaving wages suffered another collapse (with purchasing power down perhaps one-third on the 1792 level), and the war, after a short peace, was resumed. Letters began to reach Oldham from local men in the retreating English armies:

panic, disease, corruption.[66] 'The recent victories of the French',
wrote Rowbottom, 'have humbled the mind of the enthusiast so
that the poor cottager may be without oak at his door and the
traveller without a branch of it in his hat'.[67] In June came news
of the Oxford militia mutiny and the disorders in Birmingham,
followed quickly by trouble nearer home.[68] On three separate days
in late June and early August there was concerted action to force
a reduction in flour prices, culminating in an attack on a military
escort. Stocks were requisitioned and sold off at lower rates and
ultimately the local magistrate, Horton, intervened to fix prices.
Similar riots occurred in neighbouring towns.[69] That December two
Public Order Acts were passed more stringent than any seen so far.
One banned absolutely all meetings of more than fifty persons. The
other made verbal attack on the constitution a capital offence.[70]

War and the pressure on living standards was to continue, with
a few short breaks, for the next twenty years. Each successive
crisis – 1797, 1799, 1801, 1803, 1808 – further ruptured the authority of the establishment and its henchmen. Each strengthened the
hold of the radicals. Already in 1794 Rowbottom was beginning to
change his tune: 'The ministers set the war-hoop . . . harbinger of
future miseries'.[71] In the conditions of the time, war and the ruling
class were easily identified, and the Oldham radicals had little to
learn about propaganda techniques. Wall slogans ('Peace or no
King' – 'Cheap bread or no King'); armistice celebrations; food
boycotts and 'fair price' lists; political strikes; petitions (peace,
minimum wages, stricter apprenticeship); and a stream of seditious
broadsheets.[72] The issues at stake were well understood on both
sides. During a lull in 1805 the Bolton magistrate Fletcher (then
in charge of intelligence in south Lancashire) explained the dangers
to the home secretary:

> Whilst His Majesty's allies on the continent shall be able to
> make headway against the Common Enemy so long will Jacob-
> inism be obliged to hide its head, but the danger of its principles
> does not lie in open resistance but in being ever ready and in
> the presence of any disastrous event on the Public Mind (which
> in a war so extended can scarcely fail to happen some time or
> other) to raise a cry against the war. . . .[73]

And while Fletcher may have overestimated the universality of
the opposition, there can be no doubt that Oldham's radicals were

organized and active. In what was still a relatively small and close community they were known and marked. Rowbottom certainly knew their names; Knight, the 'noted Jacobin' from Saddleworth, John Jackson, John Stansfield,[74] Nor, in national terms, were they isolated. Links existed with a succession of larger groupings: Friends of Freedom (1796-8), United Englishmen (1799-1800), Patriots (1801). And significantly the outside contacts themselves remained roughly the same throughout – with the 'mechanics' group inside the Manchester movement and the Cartwright wing in London.[75] Locally, membership developed round the two 'working-class' congregations (Dob Lane and Lord Street) and the deist-atheist group which seems to have been their counterpart in Royton. These groups formed the inner core, bound together by loyalties of family and intermarriage.[76] By 1801 membership had expanded well beyond this (running to over a hundred twopence-a-month paying members in each of the four townships) held together by an elaborate underground organization.[77] Regular delegates went to Manchester, and in 1801 to national meetings in Yorkshire and London.[78]

It seems to have been this 1799-1801 period that saw the final turning point. Up till then conflict had remained at least partly focused around prices and to this extent the old controls retained their force. In 1795, for instance, the magistrate Horton was able to do at least something to maintain establishment credibility by intervening in the food riots. By the end of the decade the sheer persistence (and apparent inevitability) of rising prices had shifted attention decisively to the wages front – particularly in an industry like weaving where even money wages had fallen badly. By 1799 the weaver's purchasing power was well below half what it had been in 1792.[79] And in this situation the government itself dealt the final blow. Frightened by the degree to which political opposition seemed to be spreading into industry, it passed the Combination Acts. These Acts, conceived in the old spirit of total outlawry of labour activity, were designed to enable its more immediate prosecution at local petty sessions level. The result was merely to clinch the industrial control of those who were themselves outlaws, the working-class radicals. In south-west Lancashire almost every labour organization seems to have passed into their hands. 'The republicans', reported one agent, 'are drinking Mr. Pitt's health'.[80] At the height of the crisis in 1801 the Oldham leaders were able to assemble meetings several thousand strong on Tandle Hill (between Oldham and Royton) and on Buckland Castle Moor (some miles to the south). The Buckland Castle meeting only broke up after the military opened fire.[81]

It was also this particular period which saw the first really serious loss of nerve amongst employers. In mid-March 1801 Sir Robert Peel received two letters from business associates in Bury (six miles north of Oldham):

> Every link that bound subject to government seems broken – no confidence – no interest felt in the welfare of the country – feeling pinching hunger – seeing rising markets and no prospects – but the hand of oppression (as they think) continually upon them – any kind of change they say must be for the better. . . . I am, I admit, in low spirits . . . but I am and hope always shall be one that believes in a providence that overrules all things – believing that, I am of the opinion that the cries and distress of the poor in the midst of plenty will not be overlooked (I see a deal of their faces I assure you) and if the government does not interfere in respect to the price of provisions every day will grow worse and in the end it will not have it in its power to quell the rising spirit of the people.

And from the other (a magistrate) writing two days later to report an attack on the Bury garrison:

> I am sorry to say that what I have seen and heard today convinces me that the country is ripe for rebellion . . . and I firmly believe if provisions continue at the present high price a revolution will be the consequence – I shall be ready on every occasion to assist in the prevention of rioting, but my heart bled today to see so many children not half fed, and what rendered it more distressing I see no prospect of their situations being soon better. . . . [82]

Such crises occurred not just once but regularly through the war. Each time the radicals underlined the lesson: the war was fought on behalf of merchants and employers; the costs were passed to labour. One of their meetings in 1807 (demanding an immediate ceasefire) was described by a local coalowner as 'originating solely with these people and is neither more nor less than an attempt to disturb the peace of the country and to keep alive the spirit of discontent which they think so favourable to the ultimate achievement of their revolutionary designs. No opportunity of this kind will they ever let slip.'[83] Within the next few months the Oldham radicals had organized another minimum wage petition, a political strike by the weavers and a full-scale attack on the yeomanry.[84] In 1811-12 a guerilla campaign covering most of the north and midlands tied down twelve thousand regular troops for the best part of a year. At Middleton, just west of Oldham, there was a ragged two-day clash. A newspaper correspondent describes reinforcements coming in from Oldham on the second day: 'A body of men consisting of from one to two hundred, some armed with muskets with fixed bayonets, and others with colliers picks, marched into the village in procession [headed by a man who] waved a sort of red flag.'[85] Later in the day the same men stood their ground against a cavalry charge, firing two vollies and reloading for a third before being scattered.[86] By now Rowbottom's sympathies were more fully committed and he lists the local men among the dead: Daniel Knott (a glazier aged twenty and 'universally lamented'), Joseph Jackson (a sixteen year old hatter), John Siddall (twenty-two), George Albinson (a young man), John Johnson (a fifty-three year old joiner).[87]

'The spirit of turbulence', wrote a local coalowner immediately after the fight, '. . . peculiar to all manufacturing counties which used to exhaust itself with the gutting of a meal warehouse or two and the demolition of windows has assumed a new character since Jacobinism was infused into the lower orders and is now become perfectly infernal.'[88] Or as Major Cartwright put it to a Manchester correspondent in February 1813:

> You will recollect the information given us by Nicholson of Lees [Lees formed the southern portion of Oldham chapelry]. There can be no doubt but that the extraordinary success he reported was the effect of what he had told me in his letter of 7 December namely that the great population of their district had *induced them to form local unions*' in the several parishes of it. From that moment the active friends of reform were no longer a rope of sand but an organized body. . . .[89]

By 1812, therefore, the local establishment can be confidently said to have lost any sort of direct control over the labour community. Labour's loyalties now went in a quite different direction

– creating a dualism of authority that was to continue for a generation. And for the employers and magistrates the result was the development of a siege mentality that found concrete expression at a meeting of Lancashire deputy lieutenants in May 1812:

> We earnestly recommend . . . that a systematic arrangement among the different houses of business may be made to assist each other upon every necessary occasion. We are convinced that the most useful and effective mode of defence . . . will be by forming regular associations within the several subdivisions and districts of the county for mutual defence, and that without such active cooperation all other means by the government . . . will be very defective.[90]

Which takes us on to Peterloo and the culmination of the first classic period of English radicalism in the years immediately after the war.

Conclusion: what kind of radicalism?

Finally, therefore, to take stock of the arguments so far. Although the industrial revolution did have some massive social effects, one thing not included in these effects was the coming of some altogether new and 'open' industrial society. Instead, what we are faced with is more the breakdown of an old type of *social structure*, a transformation in the cultural organization of the labour community. The reasons for this seem quite clear. On the one side, there was the old system of establishment control inherited from the *pre*-industrial stage of capitalism's development – outlawing any separate labour identity and elaborating a whole series of very rigid cultural ties. On the other, there were the new pressures associated with the specific development of industrial capitalism in England: the recurrent crises, wage conflict superseding price conflict, and in weaving itself a steady downward pressure on real earnings. In this situation the infusion of 'Jacobinism' into the lower orders was almost inevitable. The only group capable of defending labour's existing standards were the previously outlawed radicals, with the very rigidity of existing controls (and the savagery of the establishment response) helping to build up a new structure of allegiance around them.

This explanation is also borne out by the sequence of events immediately after the war. Though the end of the war saw the final destruction of the last remnants of the revolutionary order in France, the scale of radical influence still increased in step with the intensity of economic crisis. In the winter of 1816-17 real earnings dipped again to the levels of 1800-1 and 1812-13 (see figure). And this time, in a deflationary price situation, and as manufacturers were forced to cut costs in face of continental competition, the pressures came solely on the wages front. Conversely, with the temporary stabilization of weaving wages after 1819, the ability of the radicals to bring large masses of workers into political action declined sharply. A similar conclusion comes from looking at the geographical spread of radical activity. It is precisely the areas with a similar economic experience to Oldham, the ring of south Lancashire and Cheshire cotton towns – Stockport, Ashton, Rochdale, Bury, Bolton and even more the entirely weaving-based communities in the Pennine foothills behind them – that stand out from the Home Office papers as the strongholds of anti-government organization.

Yet if the reasons for radical influence are obvious, its actual nature is not. Granted that the principal *social* effect of industrial revolution was to destroy an old type of social structure, what took its place? Was it a working class? On the positive side, one can see that it was this period that clinched the relationship between the radicals and industrial action – that for the first time wage-earners were seen as *the* potentially revolutionary class – and the historical significance of this cannot be overestimated. In each of the main crises, 1800, 1812, 1816-19, the whole energy of the southeast Lancashire leadership was devoted to harnessing labour's industrial claims to a wider mobilization.[91] But the real question is not so much this as another one. Did this 'harnessing' (and the breaking of cultural control from above) bring about any *mass* perspective that was specifically anti-capitalist?

Here the answer must be much less hopeful. Against the descriptions of 'popular ferment' for 1816 or 1819 (examined in chapter 5) one has to balance the fact that even then the radicals had to fight to get organized labour involved – and sometimes lost. And ideologically one must have doubts even about the leadership. True, there was always the leveller tradition, and a fairly full assimilation of Spence by 1816-19. But still more powerful was the influence of Paine and Cobbett, whose appeal was essentially to the independence of the small producer. Among local leaders even men like the redoubtable John Knight (already a leader in 1794, on the United Englishmen's county executive in 1801, arrested for his part in the crisis of 1812, and editor of the *Manchester Register* in 1817) seem at this stage to have been basically Jacobin in inspiration. So although the movement was mainly proletarian in composition and provided the soil in which socialist theory could grow (and would grow in the following decade) it seems too early to talk about 'working-class consciousness'.

More probably what one is dealing with on a mass scale is a very special form of *trade union* consciousness. If it was the defence of living standards that gave the radicals their position of leadership, its effective *practice* involved much more. It demanded the development of a coercive occupational solidarity extending to all sections of the labour community; a solidarity that was radically new, specifically illegal and in its practical application a direct challenge to state power. Though it may have stopped short of class consciousness, its importance should not be underestimated. Indeed, to a degree, it could be seen as more apposite, more useful – in its time – than class consciousness. The very fact that it was limited, did have an immediate and *continuing* pay-off within the system, enabled it to play the vital role of bridge between the first series of destabilizing crises and the *second* after 1830. In the 1820s it was this that seems to have successfully insulated labour from attempts to re-establish outside cultural controls (of which there were many). And by incorporating the effective gains of the previous period, it significantly raised labour's sensitivity to any new attack. (In the 1830s it would not take – as it had in the 1790s – a one-half cut in living standards to bring people on to the streets.) It is therefore this very specific experience that must be examined in the next chapter.

Note on handloom wages

So far, little overall material on handloom wages has come to light and certainly none that can provide an unbroken series from the 1790s to the 1830s. Moreover, even if it had, any single series would not be much general use for an industry that contained many varieties of cloth (continually changing in relative importance) and a range of production techniques that altered radically over the forty-year period. Nonetheless, for particular cloths and areas reasoned estimates are possible, and this is what has been attempted for Oldham in figure 3 (page 36).

This figure refers solely to weavers of velveteen fustian (the staple cloth of the Oldham area) and is mainly derived from three sources. The estimates for 1792 to 1800 are based on a series of gross prices paid to weavers taken from the evidence of the Oldham velveteen weaver Daniel Hurst to the 1800 committee on weavers' petitions (including Hurst's own estimate of his 'clear wage' for 1797 to 1800). For 1802 to 1808 the basis is a series of prices paid per score of velveteen fustian (a score represented ten and a half hours work) supplied by Daniel Hurst to the 1808 committee (including estimates for 'clear wages' in 1802 and 1808). For 1814 to 1833 the source is a direct average of earnings taken from the books of James Cheetham (a fustian manufacturer of Clough, near Oldham) by Joshua Milne for his evidence to the 1833 select committee on manufactures. The figures for 1801 and 1809 have been interpolated from Wood's series of Bolton prices (G. Wood, *Cotton Wages*, p. 107), and those for 1810 to 1813 from Edward Baines figures (*Cotton Manufacture*, p. 439) for Manchester velveteen.

For the period from 1797 the resulting estimates can be taken as fairly direct and reliable (those for 1802-8 have been calculated on the basis of the seventy-eight hour week that Hurst claimed to work). For the 1792-6 period the results can only be treated as inferences. They have been estimated from the gross velveteen prices by using the same ratio between prices and earnings that obtained for the four years 1797 to 1800 for which Hurst gives both gross prices and 'clear wage' (nine shillings in 1797, seven in 1798 and five in 1799 and 1800). This procedure could be open to a number of biases. One is changes in productivity. It has been suggested, on the basis of modern industrial experience, that one could expect a weaver's output per hour to increase from year to year, and unless this was taken into account the fall in wages during the 1790s could easily be exaggerated. Yet since one of the specific complaints to the 1800 committee was the increasing lengths of the pieces that weavers were expected to work (and this complaint was not challenged by an otherwise critical and expert committee), it seems unlikely that this could have made much difference for the comparatively short period under review. A more important bias, perhaps, might be the rising proportion of sub-contract costs, like that for spinning, which the weaver (at least in

Hurst's case) had to meet out of the gross price paid by the manufacturer. For a decade in which velveteen prices fell considerably faster than spinning costs, this could result in an underestimation of wage levels at the beginning of the period.

All in all, however, the ultimate figures seem to fit fairly well with the descriptive evidence found in Rowbottom's diary as well as the general trend of political events. For the early 1790s they also coincide in actual level with the figures Unwin calculated for Oldknow's Stockport muslin weavers (G. Unwin, *Oldknow*, p. 112), a series that shows an upward trend from the 1770s rising to a peak not far short of craft wages during the crests of expansion in 1784, 1788 and 1792 and then falling sharply.

Gross velveteen prices, 1792-1800
(PRO 30/8/301 f 300)

1792	24·0 pence per yard	1795	12·0 pence	1798	9·9 pence
1793	15·7 ,, ,, ,,	1796	10·4 ,,	1799	9·4 ,,
1794	13·6 ,, ,, ,,	1797	15·0 ,,	1800	9·5 ,,

Velveteen prices per score, 1802-8
PP 1808 II, Cotton weavers petitions, 29. These are given gross of deduction for working costs that fell from 51 to 45 pence a week between 1802 and 1808.

1802	32 pence	1805	23½ pence	1808	19 pence
1803	26½ ,,	1806	21½ ,,		
1804	25 ,,	1807	19 ,,		

Velveteen fustian weekly earnings, 1814-33
PP 1833 VI, evidence of Joshua Milne. One-sixth is deducted for winding costs but nothing for rent, light or loom repairs.

1814	137 pence	1820	90 pence	1826	64 pence
1815	118 ,,	1821	85 ,,	1827	69 ,,
1816	90 ,,	1822	90 ,,	1828	59 ,,
1817	63 ,,	1823	95 ,,	1830	49 ,,
1818	88 ,,	1824	95 ,,	1831	49 ,,
1819	100 ,,	1825	87 ,,	1832	44 ,,
				1833	44 ,,

Estimated weekly earnings at current prices

1792	159 pence	1795	72 pence	1798	84 pence
1793	104 ,,	1796	69 ,,	1799	60 ,,
1794	107 ,,	1797	108 ,,	1800	60 ,,

1801	65 pence	1807	94 pence	1813	101 pence
1802	183 ,,	1808	89 ,,	1814	137 ,,
1803	143 ,,	1809	95 ,,		and continuing
1804	136 ,,	1810	90 ,,		as in Milne's
1805	126 ,,	1811	144 ,,		evidence.
1806	103 ,,	1812	130 ,,		

Constant prices (1865-85)

To give a rough indication of purchasing power the above wages (expressed in current prices) have been weighted in figure 3 by Rousseaux's index of vegetable products linked (by a five-year average) to Schumpeter's consumer goods index for the pre-1800 years. The series of building wages comes from Bowley, *JRSS*, 1900.

3 Labour and state power

Whilst we have found great readiness to communicate information on the subject of the illegal proceedings, we have found few willing to give evidence. We have experienced that difficulty even on the part of persons engaged in the administration of the law. . . . In Oldham and also in other places it was stated to us that the owners of manufacturing property had introduced arms for self-defence, and were considering the formation of armed associations or self-protection. If the principle of self-protection were thus generally adopted which appears inevitable where due protection is not publicly provided, we need scarcely specify the serious inconveniences which are to be apprehended from each manufacturing town being rendered a fortress held by undisciplined troops' (first report RC county constabulary 1839).[1]

If the ruling power in any community allows other authorities to frame rules affecting, in their daily habits, their employments and properties, large bodies of men; to affix to the breach of these penalties rising . . . from simple insult to death, and proceed in the light of day to inflict these penalties; that ruling power has abdicated its functions. . . . It is obvious . . . as far as the manufacturing population is concerned the ruling power is not the state; the prevalent law is not the law of the land; and the punishments most to be feared are not those inflicted by the legal executive' (report RC handloom weavers 1841).[2]

Until recently there has been little systematic local research on the links between the earlier nineteenth-century breakdown in industrial law and order and the development of labour's political consciousness. It is, therefore, difficult to assess the general relevance of the findings presented here.[3] But even though Oldham's experience was probably somewhat exceptional, it seems likely that something of the same kind (in greater or less degree) happened elsewhere. Clearly, state power was dangerously eroded in a whole number of areas. Clearly, too, labour took advantage of it. The value of the Oldham evidence is to reveal the depth of cultural reorganization that could, in certain circumstances, result. The effective practice of illegal unionism demanded more than just the elaboration of a mass of institutional supports. It compelled the formation of a labour *community*. It is this process with which the present chapter will be concerned. It will begin by looking at the extent (and logic) of illegal unionism itself, then examine the capture of power in the local community, and finally describe the methods by which the state won back control.

Wage-bargaining by force

First we must look at the logic of illegal unionism. Up to 1824 union organization was itself illegal, and even after the repeal of the Combination Acts in 1825 attempts to enforce the *long-term* determinants of higher wages (the closed shop, apprenticeship, higher ratios of skilled to unskilled, more men per job, shorter hours) all remained common law offences. By this alone, organized labour was forced to place itself outside the law. But obviously to be effective (to *enforce* apprenticeship, the closed shop and the rest) unions had to go much further. They had to be able to establish a power of their own in the community at large, act, in Engel's phrase, as 'schools of war'; that is, frame rules, affix penalties and inflict punishments. This is why the social effects were so important, and is what the opening quotations are really about.

Naturally, from the point of view of contract enforcement and the bourgeois state, all this was quite intolerable. But on a national scale it was not easy to do much about it. We have already seen what happened in the early years of the century. As the authorities lost civil control of the population, existing forms of law enforcement had to be increasingly backed up with regular troops. The troubles of 1812 tied down twelve thousand soldiers. By the late 1830s the number on permanent garrison duty in England and Wales had risen to over thirty thousand. Even these were (not unnaturally) quite powerless against an opposition built so securely into the structure of the surrounding community. All the government could do was to maintain concentrations of troops in the key administrative areas – ready to strike out whenever trouble developed on a large scale. Small concentrations (anything smaller than two hundred) were seen as dangerous and for this reason Oldham lost its temporary garrison in 1820, 1827 and again in 1834. The same story is repeated for a good many other medium-sized industrial towns. Reassertion of government control depended on a whole variety of economic and military contingencies, and on the slow and costly establishment of local barracks and a state-controlled system of para-military and police forces. This process did not begin to make much solid headway until the 1840s.[4]

In the meantime labour could (in places) make real gains. Within the Lancashire cotton industry there were variations in wages of up to 15 per cent for the same job, highest in the places where the breakdown in law and order is known to have been most serious (Stockport, Ashton, Oldham).[5] In Oldham the rate was generally between 5 and 10 per cent above that in well garrisoned Manchester.[6] Three brief episodes will show what was involved.

Combination Act enforcement, 1818-22: The enforcement of this Act provides a very useful initial test. If there was a real failure of state power, it would presumably show up in the enforcement of an Act specifically designed to enable prosecution at local level.[7] Enforcement would be confined to those areas which were properly garrisoned. Was this so?

For Lancashire, luckily, material survives which permits at least a partial answer. Under the 1800 Act a parchment copy of every summary conviction had to be filed with the Quarter sessions.[8] For the years up to 1822 these parchments are still preserved (for 1823 and 1824 they seem to have been lost)[9] and for the five years 1818 to 1822 they have been analyzed.[10] There seems every reason to believe that registration was complete. Every petty sessions regularly sent parchment recognizances and copies of its summary convictions under other Acts to the sessions. So there would be no adminstrative difficulty. And as Quarter sessions appeal was more the rule than the exception, defaulting magistrates would soon have been found out.

The five years were marked by fairly intense union activity, and the area of the Quarter sessions jurisdiction covered all Lancashire except Wigan and Liverpool. Yet only seven convictions were filed. Three were from the well garrisoned administrative centres of Manchester, Preston and Rochdale; four from the less industrialized north (Burnley, Chorley, Blackburn and Colne).[11] From

Bolton, Bury, Oldham and Ashton (the real trouble areas) there was nothing – and not because there was no combination. For Oldham at least, there is firm evidence of active unionism (fund raising, strikes, assaults) among cotton spinners,[12] weavers,[13] colliers,[14] hatters,[15] and tailors.[16]

An explanation comes from Bolton's coalowner magistrate, Fletcher, in a letter of September 1818:

> About Oldham the colliers are universally *out*. Mr Chippendale [manager and part owner of the Alkrington collieries – he was Werneth Lees' son-in-law] writes that the masters have not the courage to proceed against them for combination or neglect – although the workmen's committee sits on stated days at a public house in Manchester as if on legal business.'[17]

The spinners' lock-out, 1826-7: The presence of large bodies of troops at Manchester five miles to the west, and at Rochdale a similar distance to the north, may make the lack of 'courage' referred to in the letter a little difficult to understand. What happened during the spinners' lock-out, if it does not offer a complete explanation, may at least make things more credible.

An outbreak of machine-smashing in early summer 1826 induced the authorities to give Oldham a temporary garrison of two hundred infantry. Foolishly the millowners took the opportunity to attempt a reduction of wages to the Manchester level and the result was a lock-out (involving over two thousand workers) by the nine largest mills and a ragged dispute that went on into the following spring.[18]

What is immediately significant is that the workers, despite the garrison, were able to keep up their illegal tactics. The clumsy mass of infantry proved worse than useless. Early in November, while escorting strike-breakers, it got surrounded and stoned. And when the local commander sent to Manchester for a 'small detachment of dragoons' to give him the necessary power of pursuit, his request was refused as dangerous. The officer there reported to the Northern Counties commander, General Byng, in justification that 'I thought you did not like to send out small detachments.'[19] By mid-November the unionists had got rid of the blacklegs and forced a complete stoppage. In the following weeks they attacked each mill in turn and destroyed the machinery. 'Such a state of affairs', the employers wrote to the home secretary, 'would seem incredible in any country under the rule of the law.'[20] In January the infantry again got into difficulties and had to be rescued by cavalry from Manchester.[21] The following week attempts were made on the lives of two leading employers, and the house of a third (the 'elegant' mansion of James Rowland) partially burnt. Rowland wrote to the home secretary:

I am the owner of an extensive cotton spinning and manufacturing establishment in Oldham employing about three hundred hands in which I have embarked a heavy capital besides devoting the whole care and attention of myself and sons . . . [and] respectfully entreat that some effectual means may be devised for our protection from violence – our very existence depends on the free and uncontrolled exercise of our trade without any restraint imposed by violence or mob government – in the prevelant state of affairs here neither our trade nor our property can be considered of any value whatsoever, saying nothing of our personal safety.[22]

Routine unionism, 1831-4: Activities of this kind were spectacular but exceptional. They occurred only when the undercurrent of union coercion had either lost its impact, or (as the employers mistakenly thought in 1826) been counter-balanced. Most extra-legal union activity – the perpetual background of small-scale violence and threats – has, by its nature, escaped record. But something of its scope may be suggested by listing a few actions that are recorded for the years 1831-4. *June 1831:* striking colliers stone off a party of Shropshire blacklegs.[23] *October 1831:* Whitehead, a large-scale jerry-builder, tries to introduce machine-cut planks: warehouse burnt.[24] *March 1832:* some handweavers take work from a blacked employer: looms slashed.[25] *March 1833:* violent picketing at Collinge and Lancashire's iron foundry: one man caught; five 'men unknown' get away.[26] *March 1833:* dispute over hours in the timber yards: Braddock's yard fired.[27] *June 1833:* same dispute: Cooper's yard fired.[28] *October 1833:* cotton pay dispute: Shaw Mill, Greenacres burnt.[29] *February 1834:* Whitehead (the jerry-builder) in pay dispute: building sites raided.[30] *February 1834:* master builders still holding out: acid attacks on Whitehead and his manager.[31]

Labour and local government

What made all this possible was not so much the government's

outright military weakness as its loss of control over local administration. The army by itself could do nothing. It might be able to
capture a few rioters, but not crack organization. The coercion
from below would go on. As long as the police, the inquest jurors
and the poor law officials (with their list of inhabitants) refused to
co-operate, there would be no arrests, no witnesses and no evidence.
The magistrates and army commanders were left to a dangerous
game of blind man's buff amid an overwhelmingly hostile population.

This was why the politics of local government became so important. It is not easy to give the struggle for control, a hard-fought
struggle that went on for forty years, concise presentation. It
involved a diversity of local administrative bodies – both 'popular'
and government-controlled – and it went on against a background
that was continually changing in step with the broader situation
and a legal framework which the government was in the process
of amending to its own benefit. Probably the best place to start is
with the parliamentary elections because, though outside the orbit
of local government itself, they provide a very useful example of
the way labour solved its basic local government problem: how to
win control when even the right to participate in the elected sectors
was restricted to property-holders and rate-payers.

Electing MPs: Oldham township and the out-townships of Royton,
Crompton and Chadderton were formed into a two-member parliamentary borough in 1832, and the registered electorate was limited
by the property qualification to one thousand out of a fifty thousand population. This electorate was, however, not solid. The
families who owned the town (with their henchmen, the clergymen,
lawyers and surgeons) made up only one-fifth. The remainder was
composed of small masters and, overwhelmingly, shopkeepers,
publicans and 'farmers' (smallholders with a few cows) who were
all dependent on working-class custom for flour, beer and milk.[32]

As was seen in the previous chapter, Oldham's radicals were
old hands at using food prices for political ends. Two instances
are recorded for the years immediately before the formation of the
borough. In April 1820 they mounted a campaign against high
prices, placarding the area with printed bills giving 'present prices'
and 'radical prices' and announcing a boycott of shopkeepers charg-
ing anything above 'radical prices'.[33] In July 1829 there was a
similar boycott of farm produce (milk and butter) with a series of

boycott meetings and at least one attack on a blackleg customer. The boycott placards were printed by the same printer who published the 'one man – one vote' placards in 1827.[34]

So in 1832 the plan of 'exclusive dealing' came naturally. A handbill of 1832 reads:

> The enemies of reform are everywhere alarmed at the non-electors adopting exclusive dealing. The nation and your enemies know the immense power of the working classes. . . . Therefore, workingmen, if you wish well to yourselves, lay out your money with those electors of Oldham who support . . . Fielden and Cobbett. . . . The electors' franchise is a trust to be used for your benefit; and not a right to be used against you.[35]

The job was very well organized. Before the election window bills were issued to compliant shopkeepers.[36] And the Oldham Political Association published a list of electors. The preface goes:

> When this trust was conferred on them, it was unjustly withheld from you who possessed superior claims to it; being the most industrious and intelligent part of the nation. . . . Who are they who do not earn their living by the sweat of their brow? . . . They are individuals who supported a system by which religion is disgraced, justice perverted, morality disturbed and the nation impoverished. . . . The people have awakened from the sloth of apathy; they have detected the nefarious and plundering schemes of their oppressors, knowledge has succeeded ignorance, frauds of every description are crumbling. . . . The Association issued a placard, announcing their determination to adopt a plan of exclusive dealing. . . . We are well aware it is in the interest of the shopkeepers to uphold the cause of the working classes – but the question is, are they resolved to do this? The great majority of this portion of society ranked themselves on the side of tyranny and corruption and opposed to the utmost the just claims and demands of the people. What guarantee have we for their future better behaviour? I'll tell you. We now possess an influence over them that we did not possess, and our suffering wives and children call upon us to exercise it whenever an attempt is made to continue the present system of oppression. . . .[37]

A breakdown of the way in which shopkeepers eventually voted shows how very effective this influence could be (table 3a).

Table 3 Parliamentary voting of traders exposed to exclusive dealing[38]

(a) December 1832	Cobbett and Fielden	Bright and Burge	Cross	Total
foodsellers	100	7	2	109
clothing	17	2	0	19
drink	49	0	0	49
farmers	131	9	5	145

(b) July 1852	Cobbett (and Duncuft)	Fox and Duncuft	Cross	Total
shopkeepers	256	155	84	492
innkeepers	104	14	20	138
beersellers	123	14	26	163
farmers	144	15	36	195

(c) July 1865	Cobbett and Spinks	Platt and Hibbert	Cross	Total
food	60	61	22	143
clothing	10	41	5	56
drink	75	15	7	97
farmers	108	34	13	155

In 1832 the radical candidates Cobbett and Fielden enjoyed tremendous majorities over their employer-backed Whig and Tory opponents. In the 1835 general election the employers did not attempt a contest. In the by-election of that summer (following the death of William Cobbett) there was, it is true, a setback. A split in the radical caucus between the supporters of Cobbett's son, John Morgan Cobbett, and those who wanted Feargus O'Connor, gave the seat by thirteen votes to J. F. Lees, the son of Colonel John Lees, late commander of the Oldham Volunteers.[39] But Lees' victory only lasted eighteen months. In the general election of 1837 the caucus united behind Feilden and W. A. Johnson (a radical general who had fought in the Peninsular War). 'Exclusive dealing', commented the Oldham journalist Butterworth, 'is an agent of terror when in the hands of the mass.'[40]

1839 saw the same methods used to a slightly different purpose. After the arrest of various members of the National Convention (the workers' Parliament) the Oldham Political Association started a subscription towards the National Defence Fund. A committee was set up which 'divided the town into districts and appointed collectors to each district who are to visit all shopkeepers, publicans and others of that class in order to ascertain their sentiments towards the working classes.'[41] In the 1841 general election there was again no contest. 'I thought it would be so', wrote Morgan Cobbett (now Fielden's son-in-law), 'but the principal reason I am glad that it ended *without opposition* is that that eminent rascal the *Manchester Guardian* had hoped and predicted that there would be one. I am glad that he and the League found it useless to attempt one.'[42]

By 1847 various local changes (to be discussed later) put the employers in a position to hit back. A broadsheet was issued signed by the representatives of all the borough's large firms:

> We the undersigned having been informed that language threatening exclusive dealing is being used to some of the electors to prevent them exercising their unbiased judgement in the election of members for the next Parliament hereby beg to express our disapprobation of such dishonourable and disgraceful proceedings and that we will use all means in our power to counteract its demoralizing and baneful effects.[43]

The employers ran John Duncuft (a local 'Tory' cotton spinner) and the 'Liberal' W. J. Fox (a freelance propagandist and *litterateur*). Fielden and Morgan Cobbett (who had now taken over Johnson's place in the team) were defeated by a few votes. The Political Association put out the following 'Address to the Industrious Classes':

> A blow has been struck at our liberties in this borough such as was never before attempted; our masters have entered into a compact for the purpose of . . . rendering us the mean-spirited, degraded creatures of their arbitrary purposes. Honest hardworking men have been thrown into the streets guiltless of any crime save only for having spent their sweat-bought wages as they thought proper. Factory overlookers have been stationed at the doors of those shopkeepers whom we consider worthy of our support to note down those who frequent their establishments.[44]

The employers, now with local government mostly in their own hands, had managed to beat the workers at their own game. Already by the late 1840s the organized working class had been deprived of its old, full-bodied unionist justification; and, without it, began to break up. A few leaders backed Morgan Cobbett in an alliance with the Tories, putting in a 'radical' lawyer beside those for the Tories and Liberals at the registration courts of 1847 and 1851.[45] However, though in 1852 Cobbett did get himself elected, he soon became, as the old pattern of allegiance and coercion dissolved, as Tory as his remaining backers.[46] The changed pattern of shopkeeper voting (table 3b and 3c) shows how this process went. Even so, twenty years later in 1871, the memory of the earlier control was still sharp enough to make Platt (the MP owner of the town's largest machine works) speak out for the secret ballot:

> At all contested elections in his own borough for many years the small shopkeeper, for fear of violence, had had to place in the windows of their houses the names of the candidates for whom they intended to vote, and sometimes pickets were actually stationed near a tradesman's shop to stop customers. . . . This was done by those turbulent and unscrupulous men who form a minority of the operatives in a large and populous borough and who were at the bottom of all strikes. . . . He [Platt] believed the ballot would have a conservative influence because . . . it would take away the power possessed by small sections of the working classes.[47]

Parliamentary elections, then, show that in favourable circumstances it was possible to sidestep the property qualification. How this was done also demonstrates another point of interest. The techniques used were carried over from the traditional methods of labour bargaining: boycott, picketing and reliance on *mass* discipline and allegiance. But while the unions used these methods inside a trade, their political application on behalf of labour as a whole put their operation in the hands of the community's essentially revolutionary nucleus of radical leaders.

Police: vestry and police commission: Having representatives in Parliament could be useful, but the basic social function of labour's organized strength was to control the police. If, beside the army, the authorities had a police force to provide *local* intelligence (and, in case of prosecution, witness and evidence) the practice of extra-legal unionism would be in grave danger. So whatever else the working-class leaders might do, their first duty was to keep hold of the police.

At the beginning of the century, responsibility for the enforcement of law and order rested with the vestry of each township (and was, therefore, divided in Oldham between the vestry of Oldham township and those of the out-townships of Chadderton, Crompton and Royton). Each October a vestry elected two constables who would be jointly responsible for police functions in the coming year: hiring and managing the police; appointing jurors at inquests; granting permission for public meetings. The vestry kept overall control by its right to refuse sanction to the expenses presented by the constables every quarter. Voting at the vestry was open to all who paid rates.

The constable was, therefore, in any circumstances, exposed to popular pressure. Even before the end of the eighteenth century the vestry was liable, on occasion, to break loose. During the wartime crises (when the 'direct attack' of the state on the people disrupted normal authority patterns) the constables seem to have been apt to disengage themselves from the state machine. In 1757 and again in 1796 the state failed to conscript its quotas of militia men from large areas of the country because the constables refused to supply lists of men for ballot.[48] It is also significant that in 1793 an Act was passed aiding the summary conviction of parish officers who failed to carry out magistrates' orders.[49] Once the ruling class had altogether lost control, the vestries were easily captured. In Oldham the working class seem to have first put in their own men in 1812. The 'Jacobinical' constables were reported to the home secretary as refusing to intervene in the attacks on flour warehouses which preceded the Middleton fight.[50] In 1816 the constables permitted the holding of universal suffrage meetings and one, Ashton Clegg, described as 'extremely disaffected' and 'violent', took the chair.[51] The first (surviving) evidence of disaffection in Royton's vestry comes from 1818 when the constable, Thomas Hardman, a working weaver, also spoke at universal suffrage meetings.[52]

The legislative reaction was prompt. In June 1818 an Act was passed for the 'Regulation of Parish Vestries', in which persons in arrears lost their vote while persons rated more than £50 gained an extra vote for every additional £25 (up to a maximum of six).[53] This, complained the Ashton radicals five miles south, was 'a death blow to their rights and privileges – that now what was called a gentleman would gain no less than six votes'.[54] But, in Oldham at any rate, the Act failed to alter the balance; and the government became painfully aware of this when the constables appointed hostile jurors for the inquest on a local man killed at Peterloo.[55]

The next government move was to 'revive' the right of the hundred court-leet steward (a crown nominee – in this case stipendary magistrate of Manchester) to overrule vestry elections altogether and appoint constables at his own discretion. In 1820 the radicals seem to have been taken by surprise and two large employers were appointed. In 1821 they fought the issue right through, from the vestry to the court leet, from there appealing to King's Bench – where of course their case was dismissed.[56]

The situation was now somewhat confused. Responsibility for law and order was vested in crown appointees; control of the expenses with the vestry. The conflict soon came into the open. In October 1821 the vestry refused to refund expenses incurred in hiring barracks for the temporary garrison of 1819-20.[57] The makeshift solution was for the town's big firms to underwrite expenses at the beginning of the year. The formula for 1826 was: 'We engage ourselves to reimburse the constables of Oldham any expenses they may incur in providing such accommodation as may be necessary for soldiers introduced during the present year and the same to be paid by us to them (in case such expenses not being allowed by the vestry) in the same proportion as we are respectively assessed to the poor rate.'[58] The long-term solution was to have another go at remodelling the legal structure. This process was set on foot in December 1824 by a meeting of 'inhabitants' petitioning Parliament that 'a general Police Act for the better regulation of the town had become absolutely necessary'; the parliamentary business was seen through by the county members, and in May 1826 the Oldham Police Act received royal assent.[59] The Act established a police commission levying up to two shillings and sixpence in the pound rates and mortgages to £20,000. The commission could build watchhouses, appoint night patrols and hire and arm watchmen – the watchmen given power of arrest and resistance made punishable by summary conviction. Qualification for commission membership was fixed at £60 rateable value, thus excluding all but the largest shopkeepers and employers.[60] The employers were enthusiastic about the immediate results. 'Mr Peel is glad to find', the Home Office replied in 1827 to one of the town's largest firms, 'that the workmen have returned to their labour and particularly that the provisions of the new Police Act have had so good an effect in accelerating that desirable event.'[61] But the initial enthusiasm proved misplaced. Either by outright coercion or exclusive dealing the radicals managed early in 1831 to get a majority on the commission and dismissed the police force. Doherty's *Voice of the People* saluted the victory thus:

> The Oldham police commissioners, conceiving no doubt that economy and retrenchment are highly necessary in every branch of public expenditure . . . have judicously dispensed with the aid of all the watchmen they previously employed leaving even the operative weavers to protect their property.[62]

The working-class hold over the commission could never be more than touch and go. In November 1831 the employers succeeded in reappointing a token force of five watchmen, and two months later secured the election of the lawyer to the Cotton Masters' Association as commission secretary.[63] But things were uncertain enough to make the police wary of interfering with the unions. In 1834 an example was made of two over-zealous policemen ordered by the magistrates to seize some trade union papers. After being manhandled by the mob, they were censured by the commission and dismissed from service. 'The unionists and their friends', commented the *Manchester Guardian*, 'had exerted themselves in an extraordinary manner to bring their party forward . . . small farmers . . . having been threatened with having their milk returned . . . shopkeepers with the loss of their customers.'[64] In October 1834 one of the constables (still ultimately responsible for law and order and barrack expenses) tried to refuse appointment on the grounds that 'the township of Oldham was sadly deficient in its police force; they had no military aid at hand in case of disturbance; and the town was completely in the hands of the destructives.'[65]

Again, there was obvious scope for legislative action. In 1834 a Municipal Incorporation Bill was introduced threatening compulsory incorporation. It is doubtful whether an elected council vested with police powers would have made much difference at this stage, but the radicals certainly saw it as a threat. A public meeting was called to correspond with other towns in opposition. 'The people present', claimed one radical, 'were all well aware that the townships in the borough were locally governed in an excellent way.' 'Instead of three hundred and fifty police commissioners', warned another, 'there would be only twenty of a committee . . . there had been crafty work over the Church and there might be about this.'[66] Though the Bill was passed, the authorities did not try it on Oldham till 1849.

The real answer was to abandon attempts at a 'safe' but still ratepayer-controlled police, and build up local police forces under direct crown control.[67] In the mid-1830s Acts were passed giving magistrates power to arm and direct special constables, and some use was made of these in Oldham during the winter lock-out of 1836-7.[68] Far more important was the County Police Act of 1839. This permitted lord lieutenants to recruit large permanent police forces paid for out of county rates. The radicals knew what this would mean. A public meeting was held to appoint a liaison committee to act with other towns. 'The evils arising from the said Act is the placing of such police under the immediate control of justices . . . the whole power of appointing police was taken away from leypayers and they were left to the tender mercies of a set of men from whom they knew what to expect when they had power . . . it was their duty to foil the magistrates in putting this Act into force.'[69] In autumn 1840 small parties of the new police entering the Oldham area were attacked.[70] But the following spring they arrived in force to protect blacklegs in the colliers' strike.[71] And after the unsuccessful general strike in 1842 the radicals' worst fears were realized. Between August and November the county police acting with military escorts arrested forty-nine local working-class leaders on sedition charges. They were picked off one by one usually in the early hours of the morning before the mill workers were on the streets.[72] In 1842 the government also passed a Bill transferring ultimate control of parish police from constables to magistrates.[73]

This massive counterattack did not finish the unionists overnight, and for some years yet they were to make their presence felt. The authorities, with their new powers over the police, allowed the appointment of constables to revert to the vestry. And the unionists still controlled the vestry and, less firmly, the police commission.[74] In 1843 barrack expenses were disallowed and had to be credited to the rates by special magisterial action.[75] In January 1843 the unionist police commissioners barred the military from the Town Hall[76] and in August only lost a motion to open the building to O'Connor by one vote.[77] In November 1846 they managed to block a move to increase the police force.[78]

The town police force itself seems to have been manned by hand-picked unionist sympathizers (as late as 1853 it went on strike for better pay).[79] In May 1847 the town police brawled with the county at the petty sessions.[80] And it was the partizanship of the police which eventually brought the whole question to a head. The August 1847 election sparked off a long period of rioting, with several anti-union wholesale tradesmen in the town centre badly beaten up. The town police, though asked for protection in advance. refused to intervene. In October the radicals failed to carry the police commission and Joseph Wild, the deputy constable, was struck off the commission payroll.[81] The union-controlled constables countered by reappointing Wild deputy.[82] Against this, the commission refused Wild the key to the lock-up, and the following May Wild was arrested by the county police and committed for rape by the coalowner magistrates.[83] This episode effectively ended the dualism of main-force power in Oldham.

In the twilight years of the late 1840s there was a half-hearted attempt at resistance when the employers decided to incorporate and get rid of the still potentially dangerous commission and vestry. The residual radical group that was running Morgan Cobbett for Parliament got up two counter-petitions, but failed to make much impact on the government commissioner.[84] In the first elections for the new council in 1849 Cobbett's supporters won only five seats out of twenty-four and lost those in the following years.[85] The rules of conduct for the new borough police force included the provision that a policeman should be non-political: 'He should abstain from any expression political or religious calculated to give offence and obey all orders of his superiors, and on no acount be allowed to vote in the election of Members of Parliament or any municipal officer on pain of dismissal.'[86]

Poor relief: select vestry and poor law guardians: Pretty well the whole purpose of Oldham working-class politics was control of the police – but as a means to this end poor relief could be very useful. For the years 1850-1 the expenditure of Oldham borough council was only £1,300; that of Oldham union £16,000.[87] And in previous years Oldham township poor relief had stood variously at £3,200 (1821), £3,500 (1831), £7,400 (1838) and £20,500 (1843).[88] If the working class wanted to build up a system of political influence, the obvious way to do it was through the manipulation of poor relief expenditure; the jobs, contracts and relief itself provided a body of patronage far greater than anything else in local government.

This, at any rate, seems to be why the working class clung so hard to the control of poor relief from the late 1810s till the take-over of the new poor law in 1847. And, till 1847, they succeeded far more completely than they did with the police. The Sturges Bourne Act of 1819 (following the cumulative voting act of the previous year) gave vestries the choice of completely surrendering poor relief to the magistrates or of annually electing a select vestry (maximum membership of twenty-four including rector, church-wardens and overseers) that would transact poor relief business by the week.[89] The Oldham unionists opted for the select vestry, confident (rightly it seems) that they could manage the annual elections. After this there was no further legislative action till the Poor Law Amendment Act of 1834; and for a dozen years this proved completely unenforceable in south-east Lancashire.

The evidence for working-class domination rests on the compo-sition and chairmanship of the select vestry. The overseers, carry-ing out the arduous day-to-day supervision but without any ulti-mate authority, were usually large employers (often only taking the post under duress). The select vestry, on the other hand, carried a permanent majority of radicals, and chairmanship seems to have been almost invariably reserved for ex-political prisoners (Haigh, Swire, Knight, Haslam, Yardley).[90] At the 1821 protest meeting over the constables and the court leet, Haigh (arrested for his part in the 1812 campaign) held up the select vestry as a model of demo-cratic efficiency: 'They [the authorities] had refused to concur in the nomination of the inhabitants because the persons nominated were what they called *radicals* . . . he wished these gentlemen would look at the radicals . . . who were now in office; let them look at the overseers and the committee, and say whether they would suffer by comparison with any of their own. . . .'[91]

It is difficult to determine quite how 'corrupt' the select vestry was (its books have disappeared). Two reports were made by government commissioners: Henderson in 1833 presented Oldham as an example of how things ought to be done; Clements in 1844 as an object-lesson in mismanagement.[92] Neither was in any posi-tion to get at the facts. The answer to the 1833 questionnaire seems too good to be true, especially as they were written by men involved in a national campaign against poor law amendment and in particular against the commissioners who circulated the ques-tionnaire. The 1833 vestry members represented themselves as scrupulously pairing down expenditure and doing so because they were, of course, all ratepayers. Eleven years later Clements accused the Oldham vestry of letting expenses get quite out of hand. Comparing the growth of relief costs between 1838 and 1843 in 'amended' unions with the increase in Oldham (an increase of 279 per cent against the 68 per cent average for amended Lancashire), he claims that the difference 'can only be attributed to superior management . . . under a board of guardians every item of expenditure is more strictly scrutinized and the real circumstances of every applicant more accurately ascertained'. It seems unlikely (especially in the touchy political climate of the 1830s) that the Oldham vestry ever dared use poor relief to augment strike funds – though on occasion they were under considerable pressure to do so.[93] On the other hand, the high expenditure in the early 1840s certainly shows (to say the least) a unique liberality, and the small shopkeepers on the vestry had every interest in maintaining labour's purchasing power during depression. Nor can there be any doubt about the use of poor relief for patronage. In 1838 the ageing John Knight (till recently secretary of the Oldham Political Association) was made salaried treasurer of the township poor relief fund.[94]

Whatever was going on, the authorities were very anxious to stop it; and the unionists equally anxious to keep things as they were. The government solution was, of course, the Poor Law Amendment Act. Though the great object of the Act was to reallocate the rural unemployed, many of its provisions seem aimed at towns like Oldham. The election of the board of guardians was to be by secret ballot with cumulative voting according to rateable value. County magistrates were to be *ex officio* board members (with full voting rights), and expenditure could be challenged by the central board in London. It is also significant that the Act provoked a greater barrage of popular opposition from the manufacturing districts than any other Whig 'reform'. When the poor law commissioners made their first attempt to get guardians elected for Oldham in January 1837 the overseers and rate collectors refused to deliver the voting papers.[95] The following year a visit by the area assistant commissioner was boycotted by the parish officers.[96] From then until 1844 no serious attempt was made to implement the Act. In November 1844 the magistrates and 'principal inhabitants' were reported as 'taking measures' to bring in the new poor law, but the only result seems to have been Clements' Report.[97] In November 1845 the poor law commissioners threatened, if elections for guardians were not held, to appoint the magistrates. After a massive series of protest meetings nothing more was heard.[98] The end came, as usual, in 1847. The poor law commissioners issued writs of *mandamus* against the overseers in May, an appeal to Queen's Bench failed, and in July the writs were served. The unionists did not contest the elections and the results gave the employers a monopoly.[99] At the first meeting the lawyer to the Oldham Cotton Masters' Association was appointed board secretary (at a salary of £150).[100]

The Church: Vestry and churchwardens: Though the Oldham radicals were not great churchmen, they discovered that it was unwise to neglect Church affairs. When the working class seized the vestry, they left the office of churchwarden to the employers. In 1824 the employers seem to have realized the opportunity this presented for creating patronage of their own. That year the churchwardens presented Parliament with a petition for rebuilding the nave of the parish church; a job, it was claimed, costing £6,000. An Act was passed naming forty-four large employers as trustees; further trustees could be co-opted – with the qualification fixed at £100 rateable value or £4,000 personalty. During building operations these trustees were given absolute power over the rates and vestry control was suspended.[101] When the rebuilding of the nave was completed, a second Act was passed continuing the powers of the trustees while they rebuilt the tower and chancel.[102] By the end of 1830 the entire church had been rebuilt and in 1832, with payment finished, control reverted to the vestry. The employer churchwarden refused to publish the accounts and the radicals put in one of their own men.[103] Total expenditure was found to have exceeded £30,000.[104] From then on, the radicals were careful to keep hold of the office.[105] A radical churchwarden, besides blocking employer patronage, also took over the useful power (held jointly with the constables) of being able to call public meetings.

The authorities

So far the story has been about how the unionists got hold of the 'popular' parts of local government. The focus has been on the working class, and the local opposition to it has remained shadowy. Legally, the men responsible to the crown for law and order were the justices of the peace. In practice, the local magistracy was only part of a much more high-powered organization. The real day-today decisions came out of a three-cornered dialogue between the Home Office, the local military command and the local Home Office intelligence network (operated by the stipendary magistrate at Manchester and, for a time, by Colonel Fletcher from Bolton).[106] Again in practice, the organized local opposition took in (besides the justices) the three-score capitalist families – who appear variously as yeomanry cavalry, special constables and 'principal inhabitants'. Taken together these made up what the unionists called 'the authorities', and by their interests and social composition they underlined at a local level the real nature of the confrontation between bourgeois state and working class.[107] From the point of view of 'the authorities' the confrontation can conveniently be divided into three phases: a defensive holding operation for the first years of the century; near paralysis by the end of the second decade; and from the middle of the fifth the reassertion of state power. These phases will be looked at in turn.

Though, of course, the law-and-order machine was in constant trouble from the beginning of the century, the authorities managed more or less to hold the line up until the middle of the second decade. They were able to operate a fairly effective intelligence network and, in the last resort, military commanders were still willing to billet troops in Oldham's public houses (Oldham, significantly, was not among the one hundred and fifty places in which Pitt felt it necessary to build barracks).[108] What happens in these years is the collapse of the mass acquiescence on which the authorities had previously relied and, as a result, the progressive crumbling of local para-military forces. Already by the mid-1790s it was thought dangerous to distribute arms to an indiscriminate sample of the general population and the local militia was consequently written off.[109] The alternative plan was to raise a 'Volunteer' force of picked men, in Oldham a troop of horse and six hundred infantry recruited in 1798 and kept on an active footing until 1810.[110] The twenty infantry officers were all employers and the colonel (John Lees) stored the muskets at the back of his factory.[111] By 1812 the Volunteers had gone the same way as the militia. During the guerilla campaign the muskets were kept locked up and the hastily barricaded and loopholed armoury (defended by two officers and a dozen NCOs) had to stand a two-day siege.[112] The following year the Volunteers were formally disbanded and the arms withdrawn to Manchester.[113] 1817 saw the authorities' last bid for a locally based military force: the Oldham yeomanry cavalry – forty-six employers on horseback armed with pistols and sabres.[114] This force was too small to be of much use and by the end of the decade the yeomanry corps over Lancashire as a whole had withered away (Colonel Fletcher blamed employer cowardice).[115] However, as long as it was possible to bring in troops from outside, the absence of any local military force did not matter much. In 1801 the East Norfolk militia were quartered in Oldham; in 1808 the Herefordshire militia and the 6th dragoons; in 1812 the Forfarshire militia; and continuously from February 1817 till late 1820 the 7th dragoons and detachments of the 54th and 58th foot.[116] It was when commanders became reluctant to put in outside troops that the first phase came to an end.

While this increasing reluctance to commit troops to a non-barracked town derived from a nationwide experience, the situation in Oldham by 1820 did nothing to make army commanders any more trusting. One big worry was fraternization. Billeted in public houses the troops were exposed to unionist influence; in autumn 1820 there was a fairly extensive campaign of subversion and the Home Office agent reported some soldiers ('bad characters generally') to have gone over, while in 1834 it was discovered that union funds were being used to induce troops to desert.[117] The other danger was the vulnerability of billeted troops to mob attack. 'Should a mob once find', wrote Bouverie in 1834, 'how very easily they [the troops] can be driven from a town or annihilated there is no saying to what extremities they might not be induced to go.'[118] In April 1820 this had very nearly happened. A radical-provoked beerhouse brawl sparked off three days of street fighting in which two people were killed, many injured and one military billet completely destroyed.[119] By the 1820s army commanders were imposing large restrictions on the supply of troops.

June 1821: the 'principal inhabitants' to the home secretary: 'In case of any . . . sudden disturbance it is to be feared the commanding officer in this district would refuse to send a sufficient military force to quell such disturbance unless the force so sent be provided with accommodation without being billeted in public houses – that having been the case upon former applications for the military.'[120] *July 1826:* the local commander to the magistrates: 'Sir John Byng writes to me . . . that he cannot allow a smaller force to remain in Oldham than 150 men . . . if the town does not assist in procuring buildings for barracks it might lead to the necessity of withdrawing the troops.'[121] *July 1834:* another memorial from the 'principal inhabitants' asking for a barracks and a permanent military station.[122] *June 1843:* another petition: 'The regulations of the War Office forbid the billeting of soldiers in the public houses during times of disturbance . . . and the inhabitants have frequently been deprived of the assistance and presence of the military at such times. . . .'[123] By 1843 the 'principal inhabitants' had, in fact, got what they wanted and the petition was for more money towards the temporary barracks already under construction.[124] But until December 1842 the barracks appeals had had no effect. Barracks were costly and the government was under constant pressure to ease the tax burden.[125] Barracks also represented a permanent military commitment to military commanders whose forces were already overstretched.

So for two decades (the paralysis phase) the ultimate military sanctions of class rule could not be properly applied in Oldham. The results show up in the failure of the magistracy and the breakdown of the spy system. Blatant combination went unpunished in 1818. General Lyon found in 1820 that 'there are . . . but few gentlemen about Oldham adequate for such a situation [the magistrates' bench] and they in general so intimidated that they are afraid to act with energy'.[126] In October 1826 when several factories were under open attack the newly appointed JP, James Lees of Clarksfield (himself an employer), refused to leave his house.[127] Of the six employers approached for nomination in 1838 three refused outright and, of the three appointed, only one took his seat on the bench; the second never took his oath and the third delayed till 1845.[128] Spying faced the same difficulties. The Home Office intelligence network suffered a severe jolt in 1817 when Captain Chippendale (the Oldham chief and son-in-law to Colonel Lees) discovered that the town postmaster was forwarding copies of his reports to the radical committee.[129] Even with a new postmaster things became progressively more difficult. In July 1819 Chippendale wrote that 'intimidation is in full operation and there is no getting people to come forward'. And 'the manner in which delegate meetings are conducted is a matter of serious importance – the delegates are summoned by the secretary with the utmost secrecy and dispatch. They are all regularly accredited.'[130] Later in 1819 Chippendale had to deny the home secretary permission to place his reports before Parliament because his informants were 'liable to persecution'.[131] In 1820-1 the system broke down altogether and the last letter contains a pension-plea for an informant 'forced to leave Oldham'.[132]

In this situation the authorities were left to makeshift expedients. Without advance knowledge of unionist plans they had to rely on a haphazard last-minute warning system. The borough reeve of Manchester wrote to the Oldham constables in April 1826: 'In the present disturbed state of the public peace it is of utmost importance that a constant communication should be established between the authorities of this and surrounding towns and for this purpose we particularly request you will by every post inform us of the state of affairs in your immediate vicinity . . . and in return we shall gladly state to you by every successive post what has been going on here . . . and shall any assemblage of people be collected in any part of your surrounding district . . . we should be obliged by your giving us by messenger the earliest information.'[133] Similarly, without military aid, individual firms had to fall back on self-help kits supplied by the Ordnance. The printed receipt forms in 1826 ran: 'I undertake to place [these arms] in the hands of confidential and respectable persons to be employed by me in the protection of my mill and factory. And I hereby engage to return the same.'[134] The *Manchester Guardian* commented in 1826 (with a smugness soon to prove misplaced): 'We believe that all the mills containing powerlooms are now in a state of defence so that if they should be attacked the rioters will have reason to regret their temerity.'[135] By the 1830s the big firms all kept up their own works' police.[136]

The beginning of the third phase of the confrontation is marked by the introduction of the county police and the establishment of a temporary barracks. Though these moves were made possible by changes in the wider, national situation, the reassertion of state power, once started, gained a momentum of its own. By mid-1842 the spy system was again in full operation, with regular weekly reports and with plain-clothes county police acting as agents.[137] On the basis of this intelligence it was possible to clean up the Chelsea Pensioners, striking unionist sympathizers off the pension list and putting the rest on a military footing.[138] The employers began to regain their nerve and by 1850, with nine more employer justices, the magistrates' bench was near to cluttered.[139]

In 1846 the garrison was withdrawn and from then on troops were only brought in when needed, which was in July 1847, June 1848 and December 1852.[140] By 1859, with the re-establishment of an employer-officered Volunteer Corps, the wheel had turned full circle.[141]

MPs in Parliament

If the authorities eventually won, it was because Oldham was only a smallish town in a country which remained throughout under bourgeois control. The government was able to alter the rules of the game as it went along, establish a state-controlled police force and expand the army. With this in mind, it is easier to understand the importance which the Oldham working class attached to having its own spokesmen in Parliament. Though, of course, the two MPs could not stop anything for long, they could (in alliance with other dissidents) make the job of the government far more difficult.

The mandate on which the Oldham working class 'elected' its MPs was that they should resign 'when requested to do so by a majority of their constituents' (*constituents* not electors).[142] The policies they followed, also, were hammered out in advance at mass meetings arranged by the Oldham Political Association. In Parliament Fielden always emphasized that he spoke on behalf of 'those who sent him there' and that he was 'a representative of the poor'.[143] And there was a continual liaison between the members in London and the dominent leaders in Oldham: John Knight (secretary of the Political Association), William Fitton (imprisoned with Knight in 1817) and later Alexander Taylor.[144]

Fielden, Cobbett and, after 1837, Johnson spent a good part of their parliamentary energies putting over the radical programme (one man – one vote, state control of hours, wages and investment, income tax, currency reform, etc.), which will be considered later. More relevant at the moment are their attempts to block the government offensive against extra-legal unionism. Any attack on the unions brought a quick response. In 1838, for instance, the government attempt to make capital out of the 'Glasgow outrages' was frustrated by a long series of procedural manoeuvres.[145] Similarly, all police Bills were fiercely opposed. Cobbett did a good job on the Suppression of Disturbances (Ireland) Bill of March 1833. 'He warned the people of England against the scourge which the government was preparing for them. It was nonsense to say that this was only a temporary measure. Ministers meant that it should be permanent; and they meant to introduce the same into England as speedily as possible. . . . Tyranny always comes by slow degrees.

... The system was spreading. Formerly it was confined to London, but the ministers had been smuggling it into the great towns; before long there would be a regular police force established in every village. ...'[146] Fielden gave the same treatment in retrospect to the Special Constables (1836) Act; in retrospect, because the government had (significantly) thought it wise to slip the Bill through the Commons during a half-empty midnight sitting. 'I little thought that the noble lord [Russell] would ... pass a law through this House at midnight which would establish an unconstitutional force so palpably for the express purpose of coercing the people. ...' And Fielden went on to quote from Russell's own *Essays on the English Constitution*:

> 'A standing army which destroyed the freedom of England would not march by beat of drum to Westminster. ... It would appear in the shape of the guardian of order; it would support the authority of the two Houses of Parliament; it would be hostile to none but mobs and public meetings and shed no blood but that of labourers and journeymen. It would establish the despotic power not of some king ... but of a host of corrupt senators and half a million petty tyrants.' I warn the noble lord against making us feel the abandonment of his own principles. I tell him it will be resisted and ... that I myself will, if necessary, be a leader in the resistance.[147]

On 10 July 1839 Fielden protested against the voting of funds for the metropolitan police, on 23 July against funds for the Birmingham police and on 24 July denounced the County and District Constabulary Bill as taking control from ratepayers, introducing a spy system and likely to provoke violent resistance.[148] In 1841 General Johnson backed Hedge's attempt to amend the 1839 Constabulary Act.[149] Predictably also, the army estimates came under continual fire. Johnson, together with Sharman Crawford (MP for Rochdale), wanted to know why the 1843 estimates allowed for thirty thousand more men over the 1822-4 average and fourteen thousand over the 1834 average.[150] In 1844, after a further increase, Fielden objected that 'the cry was always more force, the moment they got more force, they raised the cry of more taxes, and when they got more taxes then they wanted more force again. There must come an end to such a system.'[151]

When attempts were made to alter the legal basis of local government, reactions became even sharper. In 1837 Fielden attacked the

Collection of Rates Bill as taking 'from the ratepayers the control of the rates'.[152] And on the 1839 Highways Bill he warned that 'unless the House wished to perpetuate the present heart-burning and discontent it ought not to pass this Bill. It was nothing but an attempt to take local government out of the hands of those who contributed towards the repair of the highways.'[153] The great target was, of course, poor law amendment. On the one hand, the measure threatened, as Cobbett put it, to 'abrogate all the local government of the kingdom'.[154] And, on the other, quoting Fielden, 'to assimilate the wages of the labourers in the south to what they were in the north'.[155] Against amendment and the poor law commissioners, Fielden, Cobbett and Johnson waged non-stop war, with riots and mass meetings in the country and obstruction and exposure in the House. *February 1837,* Fielden: 'The commissioners are now trying to introduce this Act into Lancashire and Yorkshire, and I tell the noble lord he may as well attempt to conquer the world.'[156] *December 1837:* Bradford riot and demand for inquiry.[157] *February 1838:* motion for repeal.[158] *March 1841:* prolonged procedural campaign against the new amendment Bill.[159] *June-July 1842:* another procedural campaign against re-enactment, with a catalogue of scandals and exposures (Eversholt, Andover, Bridgewater, Sevenoaks, Keighly) and then a 'tale of folly and cruelty on the part of the poor law commissioners exceeding anything that has yet been heard of . . .' (the so-called 'migration scheme' by which the commissioners transported something over ten thousand pauper women and children from the south to work in the northern textile factories). Fielden demanded to know 'where the remnant of their victims were now to be found; how many had died; how many they had sent back; and the conditions of those that remained.'[160] Three days before the beginning of the July-August 1842 Lancashire rising Fielden delivered his strongest warning:

> If they continued in this way to grind the faces of the poor, acts of insubordination would follow, and though they might repress them for a while, they would find the spirit of resistance too strong for them ere long. If they attempted to carry out this Bill for another five years, they would find their own reign would be very short indeed. . . . He should be doing the greatest injustice to himself and those who sent him there, if he did not do all in his power to oppose this Bill . . . they treated the poor

worse than dogs – worse than the animals they kept in their stables.[161]

It would be easy to follow the story on. But the basic point should already have been made. Whether one looks at industrial bargaining itself, at labour's role in local government, or at central government reactions, it should now be clear that a labour community did exist. It should also be obvious that its growth was closely related to extra-legal unionism and involved a massive cultural reorganization of the working population. To this extent the claim made at the beginning of the chapter is borne out. While this labour consciousness may have stopped short of class consciousness it nonetheless played an important (and in European terms perhaps a unique) part in the *development* of a working class. Merely by providing labour as a whole with an immediate cash incentive for preventing the reassertion of establishment control, it served to insulate working people from outside control for over a generation and so provided the vital bridge between the crisis years of the 1800s and those of the 1830s. Had it not existed it seems likely that the development of new cultural controls (like Brougham's adult education and Place's Combination Act repeal) would have effectively restabilized the situation in the 1820s. As it was, this process (at least in many areas) was aborted and the road left open for the development of a deeper political awareness. Quite *how* deep is something that we must examine next.

4 Economics of class consciousness

Labour is the source of all property; and without a surplus of labour has been performed and of property produced no accumulation of property can take place . . . the primary object of all legislation ought to be to secure for the labourer the entire fruit of his labour . . . the various classes of capitalists have the sole power of making and administering the laws which is almost uniformly done for their own benefit. . . . Until they [the working people] lay their hands and hearts together their condition (bad as it is) will grow gradually worse till they are actually starved or worked out of existence' (resolution passed by a mass meeting of Oldham workers in March 1838).[1]

The words just quoted pose what is perhaps the central problem that has to be tackled in this study. They could be just rhetoric. They could also reflect a wider class consciousness. And on the answer depends the whole perspective of capitalist development presented here. Only if they can be said to reflect a wider political consciousness, a *mass* class consciousness, can one go on to argue for the concept of liberalization; that the economic and social changes of the 1840s and 1850s were indeed part of an overall social system response to anti-capitalist ideas having gained mass acceptance, and so become a 'material force'.

What follows cannot hope to provide a complete answer. Few things are more difficult to establish than class consciousness. Leaving aside the initial difficulty of defining something whose ideological content is always historically relative and specific, there is the still bigger problem of distinguishing the leaders and the led. The leaders may well have been using historically correct slogans. But what about their followers? It could be argued (very plausibly, in view of the timing of the various upsurges in working-class

activity) that any wider support was not much more than a spontaneous reaction to intolerable conditions. Or – granted that there
may have been some deliberation, some cultural base – that this
never went beyond the type of occupational solidarity examined in
the previous chapter. How does one establish the difference?

Simple comparison between areas can certainly tell us something. By looking at towns with markedly less militancy one can
at least see whether there was any direct relationship between militancy and the sheer badness of conditions. And this is why Northampton and South Shields are now brought into the study; both of
them towns which were, as will be seen, very much less militant
than Oldham.

However, for anything more positive, the comparison has to go
a good bit deeper. Obviously one cannot make the same tests for
class consciousness as one could for a living population. But one
can get some measure of the *process* by which, if it was class
consciousness, it must have come about. If Oldham's militancy was
indeed of this nature – the result of a mass realization of demands
for a total change of the social system – then it could only have
developed in very special circumstances; those in which the community's revolutionary vanguard was able to break out of its
structural isolation, get access to labour as a whole, and convince
people that radical political change was the only solution to their
problems. And this, to an extent, is something we are able to test.
If it really is class consciousness we are dealing with, then obviously we ought to be able to show that variations in militancy between
towns was directly linked to the differing scope each offered to
developments of this kind.

This is what this chapter will be attempting. It will start by
looking at each town's pattern of economic development, then
compare living conditions, and finally assess the differing scope
each offered for the realization of radical ideas.

Three industrial towns

Just looking at the overall figures for the three towns together
there may not seem very much between them. In 1851 all three
had the majority of their labour force working in industrial occupations (see figure 4). Occupational composition was also very
much the same, with between 70 and 80 per cent of all families
dependent on a wage income (figure 5). And in terms of population

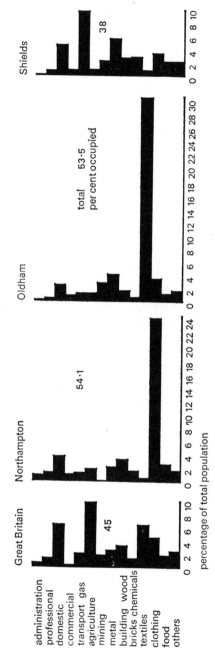

Figure 4 Labour forces, 1851: three towns [2]

size and growth, they all fit into roughly the same range – though Oldham was bigger than the other two and had many less immigrants (figures 6 and 7). Finally, they were all one-industry towns. Northampton, despite its rural hinterland, was dependent on the shoe trade. Oldham was equally dependent on cotton. And South Shields, while having some jobs in glass and chemicals, was essentially a shipping town (figure 8). It is only when one leaves the overall figures and looks at the concrete development of each town (and its industry) that the real differences start to show up.

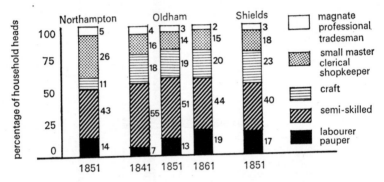

Figure 5   Occupations of household heads: three towns[3]

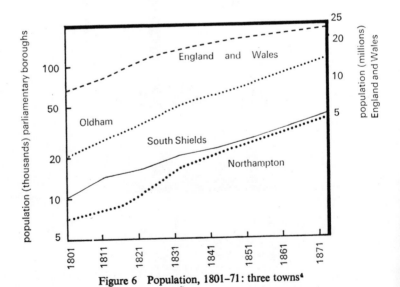

Figure 6   Population, 1801–71: three towns[4]

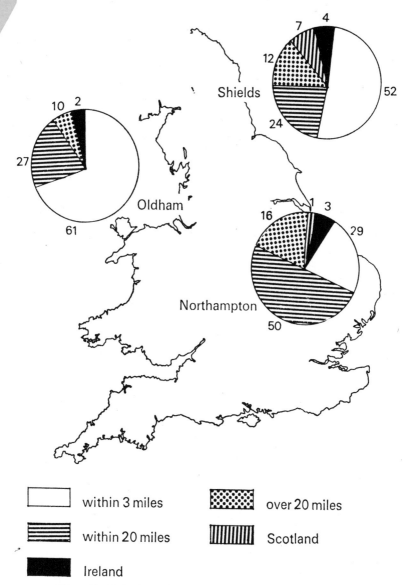

Figure 7 Birth places of household heads, 1851. hree towns[5]

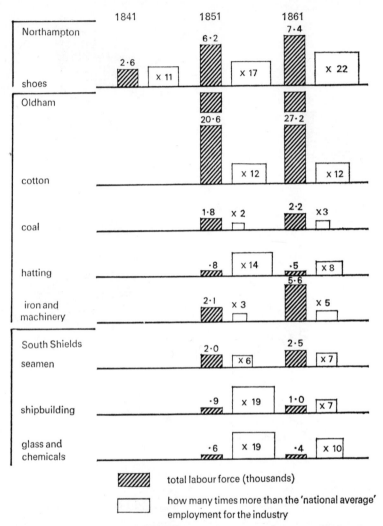

Figure 8   Leading industries by labour force: three towns[6]

Oldham: In common with other south Lancashire cotton towns Oldham's development can be divided into two periods. The first, already partly examined, was marked by the growth and crisis of handloom weaving. This itself represented the life and death of a whole economic system.

To begin with, there were the years of boom. In the late 1770s the cotton industry was localized round Manchester. By the early 1790s it had overrun the whole of south Lancashire and was reaching through the Pennines to Yorkshire and Derbyshire. For a largely unmechanized industry – and one which overwhelmingly depended on outwork labour – growth inevitably meant geographical expansion. It also demanded the creation of a costly economic infrastructure (turnpikes, canals, the encouragement of ancillary industries) by which all the branches of this complex, extended and highly profitable industry could be concentrated into the hands of the great Manchester merchants and cloth finishers. This was the situation in 1792-3; and Oldham, lying across one of the main routes to the untapped labour reserves of Pennine Yorkshire, was right in the middle of it.

Then, before the process was half completed, came the crisis years of the mid- and later 1790s. These crises did not stop the industry's expansion. But they did radically change its nature. The growth of continental competition in the market for finished goods (and the impact of this on profit margins) broke the dominance of the merchant houses and placed the whole weaving sector and the areas dependent on it in a state of protracted crisis. Conversely, machine spinning (using comparatively little labour and concentrated around Manchester and its immediate neighbourhood) enjoyed a period of accelerated growth. In Oldham it was these years that saw the establishment of specialist spinning firms working mainly for export.

Yet despite this change in the industry's balance, handloom weaving remained, and had to remain, by far the largest employer for another two decades. In the 1820s Oldham's rural out-townships, almost entirely dependent on handloom weaving, still contained nearly half the chapelry's population. Though their growth slackened after the 1800s, they did not suffer outright depopulation till the introduction of effective weaving machinery in the late 1820s and early 1830s (see figure 2, page 27). Even in the second decade of the century handloom weavers comprised between three and four thousand of the whole area's seven thousand adult male workers, with only about five hundred men in the factories and the rest either hatters (also domestic workers), miners, machine-makers or building workers.[7] And while the factories may have provided work for as many as two thousand women and children, their wages could only have slightly moderated the impact of weaving's repeated and deepening crises. In these circumstances it was only to be expected that the first period of Oldham's development would be, as we have seen it was, a forcing-house for radical social change.

The logic behind Oldham's *second* phase was quite different. While the earlier troubles stemmed from technological imbalances within the cotton industry itself, those that now followed were far more the result of having a completely mechanized industry operating within an otherwise technologically underdeveloped economy. As was argued in the larger treatment of industrialization, this created precisely those conditions which made for a long-term decline in the rate of profit. While in the cotton industry itself there was a rapid succession of technological advances (and heavy capital investment), the effect was merely to reduce the exchange value of the industry's output without any balancing reduction in the labour cost of inputs from other sectors, especially food and machine goods. And the result was a deepening series of crises which were clearly (as people said at the time) the consequences of a social system organized for profit and not social need. Indeed, in Oldham this conclusion must have been almost unavoidable.

During the 1830s the whole scale of industry within the town was visibly transformed. Though a few hundred handloom weavers struggled through to the 1840s, the great bulk of weaving production was mechanized well before the end of the decade.[8] By 1841 the cotton mills (fifty great steam-powered factories and a mass of smaller concerns) employed an outright majority of the area's labour force: fourteen thousand out of twenty-six thousand. And the scale tended to be large. In 1841 over three-quarters of the cotton workers were employed in mills with over a hundred workers, while most were in mills with considerably more (figure 9a).

Yet matched against this spectacular growth in productive power was an equally spectacular experience of crisis (and crisis which this time could not be blamed on a failure to mechanize, or foreign competition). The overall figures for the national industry show how serious the situation was. While the physical amount of cotton processed between the late 1820s and the late 1840s trebled, the actual *value* of output rose by little more than one-third and prices fell by over a half.[12] And what figures we have for production costs makes it pretty clear that profit margins were under heavy pressure throughout. Against a situation in the 1820s when there was only one year of really bad depression (1826), there were four in the 1830s (1831, 1836, 1838-9) and five in the 1840s (1841, 1842,

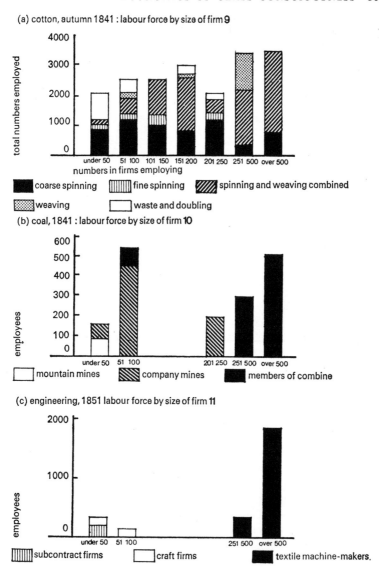

(a) cotton, autumn 1841 : labour force by size of firm 9

coarse spinning | fine spinning | spinning and weaving combined

weaving | waste and doubling

(b) coal, 1841 : labour force by size of firm 10

mountain mines | company mines | members of combine

(c) engineering, 1851 labour force by size of firm 11

subcontract firms | craft firms | textile machine-makers.

Figure 9   Oldham's industrial structure

1846, 1847-8). During these periods anything up to 30 per cent of the labour force would be out of work. More immediately to the point, the two decades saw an almost uninterrupted drop in the real wages of the largest section of adult male mill workers, the cotton spinners (figure 10). Having fought their way to a position not far short of skilled earnings during the 1810s and 1820s, they now found themselves the principal victims of the industry's almost suicidal economics.

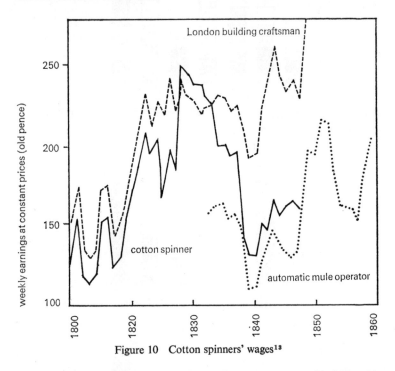

Figure 10   Cotton spinners' wages[13]

Just how far the employers themselves were trapped within this process is shown in figure 11. It reconstructs the income pattern of one of Oldham's big spinning and weaving factories (in this case owned by the Jones family), and though it unfortunately misses the pre-1844 crises it still makes two things eminently clear. First, the overwhelming degree to which the industry was dominated by the crisis cycle, and secondly the key place that labour costs occupied within it. At the height of a boom – as in 1845 – a 5 per cent wage rise could go almost unnoticed. Once prices started to collapse, however, wage costs immediately became the basic problem. In 1847, when profits scarcely matched interest rates, nearly 85 per cent of income went to labour. And in these circumstances the only way the employers could regain profitability (and full-time working) was to find some way of cutting their labour costs.

(a) Net income (wages + profits)

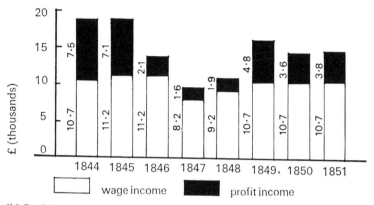

(b) Profit income as percentage of capital employed

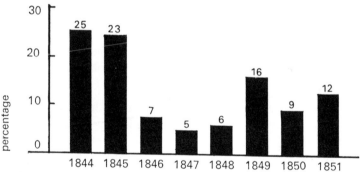

Figure 11   Wages and profits in an Oldham cotton mill, 1844–51[14]

Outright cuts in wages were, of course, the immediate response. But more dangerous in the long run (because they represented losses which could not be regained) were attempts to dilute the labour force, cut down the number of well-paid jobs, and substitute women and children for men. This was the real threat to the spinners' position. The 1830s and early 1840s saw a protracted struggle against the attempts to introduce an 'automatic spinning mule' which would do away with the need for skilled labour altogether. And though, as will be seen, this threat was eventually averted, it was not before the spinners' position had been critically weakened and the proportion of skilled workers much reduced.[15]

This, then, was the experience of the 1830s and 1840s: deepening crisis; repeated employer attacks on living standards and conditions; lengthening periods in which the whole basis of industrial society appeared to be breaking down. Certainly the spinners' experience (at least in terms of absolute losses) was worse than most, but the pressure on the earnings of other factory grades and the mining population was also heavy.[16] Within the labour force as a whole there was a sharp increase in the number of men having to make do with casual jobs in transport and labouring (see figure 5, page 76). Moreover, Oldham in the 1840s was no longer the semi-rural area it has been two decades before. The great bulk of its sixty thousand population was now crowded into the unsewered slums of the town centre and those unemployed no longer had the alternative of work on their own potato patch or allotment.

Instead there was the continuing spectacle of employer opulence – for though the *rate* of profit was under pressure, the absolute size of profits continued to increase. The great employer mansions still remained in well defended enclaves around the edge of the town and the fifty families inhabiting them can be estimated to have received up to half the community's entire income.[17] For the other 99 per cent of the population the reality is described by a *Morning Chronicle* journalist:

> The whole place has a shabby underdone look. The general appearance of the operatives' housing is filthy and smouldering. Airless little backstreets and close nasty courts are common; pieces of dismal wasteground – all covered with wreaths of mud and piles of blackened brick – separate the mills . . . melancholy clusters of gaunt unshaven men lounging on the pavement . . . dogs of all kinds abounded.[18]

Northampton: At first glance, Northampton might seem a total contrast. It was county town to one of the richest agricultural regions of the midlands and its dominant figures were the lawyers and tradesmen who competed for the custom of the surrounding gentry. Though its ancient walls had long been demolished, it still possessed areas of narrow medieval streets, a vast cobbled market square and its freemans' commons bordering the river Nene to the south. Along the main street there were big Georgian houses (once the town houses of the county gentry) and a massive yellow sandstone parish church fronted by a statue of Charles II. It was also somewhat smaller than Oldham. At the beginning of the century it had only seven thousand inhabitants and orchards grew within the limits of the old town walls. Yet anyone concluding from this that the town was somehow immune from the processes of capitalist exploitation would – even for the 1800s – be badly off the mark. Leaving aside Northampton's part in the regional development of large-scale commercial farming (a process spelling exploitation in any language), the town was already a national centre for the production of cheap, ready-made shoes, an industry which came near to handloom weaving in the grimness of its nineteenth-century experience. Like handloom weaving, shoemaking was unmechanized and, as most of its output went abroad, directly exposed to foreign competition. Unlike weaving, however, shoemaking *remained* unmechanized until well into the second half of the century, and though its wages never fell as low the industry's size and geographical spread (both much larger than one might at first imagine) gave it a leading place among the country's sweated trades.[19]

It was the economics of this industry which formed the real background to life in Northampton, and the pattern of the town's development was largely determined by the role it played in successive attempts to solve what was always the industry's biggest problem: how – in the absence of machinery – to achieve a sufficient reduction in labour costs to keep production profitable.

The first of these attempts came in the 1800s with the efforts of the great London contractors (for long the controlling power within the industry) to sidestep the effects of wartime wage inflation. Relying principally on export orders and fixed-price purchasing from the army and navy, they were particularly vulnerable to rising labour costs.[20] Their solution was to divert an increasing proportion of their orders from London (whose shoemakers had been uncomfortably militant long before the great 1812 strike) to the industry's provincial centres in the north and midlands.[21] These centres offered not just cheaper subsistence but a labour force that was unorganized and probably open to covert subsidy from the poor rates. Northampton was one of the main areas chosen for the new expansion. During the century's first two decades the number of shoemakers in the town doubled to nearly six hundred and the proportion of families dependent on the trade rose from perhaps one-fifth to one-quarter.[22] The increase for the *whole* Northampton hinterland (at this stage much of the work was still carried out in the surrounding villages) was probably much bigger. Certainly there seems little doubt that it was this blacklegging diversion of work from London that explains the first big spurt in the town's nineteenth-century population, as well as the increasing influence of the two or three dozen shoemasters (agents for the London contractors) in the town's political set-up.

In the following decades this type of blackleg growth intensified. The reserve of rural unemployed kept unionization restricted to the very small group of skilled men in the bespoke trade,[23] and 'Northampton' quickly became a by-word in the trade for shoddy work and sweat-shop conditions.[24] The mid-1830s saw the local industry employing about fifteen hundred shoemakers mostly on overseas work (Australia was already important), army contracts and ready-mades for the home market.

However, the underlying problem of labour costs was never far away. While the town's trade continued to expand (and enriched some of the middlemen to the point where they were able to start marketing on their own account), foreign competition was now beginning to make itself felt in the home as well as overseas market.[25] Once again, therefore, with no help from machinery, and wages already down to subsistence level, some further way had to be found of maintaining profitability. The new solution – a division of labour within the hitherto 'one shoe-one job' production process – largely explains the second major phase of Norhampton's nine-teenth-century growth.

Two things marked this phase: a massive expansion in the *town's* shoemaking labour force to over six thousand by 1851, and an equally massive expansion in the proportion of women and children employed in it (over 50 per cent by 1851).[26] The women and children were, of course, the new source of cheap labour, now employed direct by the shoe manufacturers to do the 'closing', lighter stitching work on the upper parts of the shoe.[27] The larger social importance of this was not so much their employment itself (they had to some extent been employed at home before) as the fact that they were now employed together, under supervision, in the town centre workshops. It seems to have been this (though there were also other factors like the increasing severity of the poor laws) that accounts for the second big development of the period: the mass influx of rural immigrants and the overall increase in the shoe labour force. Where previously shoemaking families had been able to work without difficulty in quite distant villages, they now had to be within daily reach of the town closing shops. By 1851 Northampton's population had reached twenty-six thousand and almost one in every two of its families were dependent on the shoe industry.[28]

There was, then, more similarity between Oldham and Northampton than might have at first appeared. By the 1840s the medieval streets were slum streets and the freemen's commons a breeding ground for cholera. True, Northampton was still not entirely industrial and proletarian. It remained the market and administrative centre for a very aristocratic farming county, a function underlined by the large proportion of shopkeepers, lawyers and tradesmen (see figure 5, page 76). Like most other country towns it also had its schools, a couple of banks, a brewery and enough wealthy patronage to maintain a few score coachwrights and goldsmiths. But it was certainly not this side of the town's life that explains the pattern of its nineteenth-century growth. The determining reality was far more the region's labour surplus and the ease with which it could be exploited. If for Oldham there is room for doubt about the overall trend of living standards in the first half of the century (though not about the reality of the decline in the 1830s and 1840s), for Northampton's shoemakers there can be no doubt at all. In the earlier 1790s and before the worst of the wartime inflation, the earnings of the cheap shoemaker – the custom trade did better – were put at between ten and fifteen shillings a week.[29] For the 1830s and 1840s no observer put earnings much above ten shillings, and the odd shillings from wives and children could only just have made up the difference.[30] Indeed, if we take into account the sharply increased proportion of shoemakers in the total population, the purchasing power per head for the whole community could very easily have fallen.

South Shields: Physically, the third town, South Shields, presents a further contrast. It stood on what was then a treeless wedge of land cornered by the Tyne and the North Sea. The Durham coalfield lay behind it. Two miles upstream there was Newcastle, and immediately opposite across the river North Shields and the garrison town of Tynemouth. Its hinterland – long blackened by smoke from the town's chemical works – was criss-crossed by railways running down to the Tyne. And dominating its straggling half mile of waterfront were the great mounds of Thames gravel ('ballast hills') that had been accumulated during a century in the Tyne-London coal trade. Most of the town's poorer inhabitants (the population was slightly larger than Northampton's) were housed in a warren of back-to-back terraces built more or less on top. The better-off lived further inland: the bankers and shipowners at Westcoe; the trades-men round a small market place erected (as a property speculation) by the local landowners, the bishops of Durham, in the later eighteenth century. Nowhere, however, was very far from the sea.[31]

This physical contrast is maintained when one looks at economic make-up. Unlike the other towns, Shields' dominant occupation was not manufacturing but transport. By the late 1840s its four thousand seamen were responsible for shifting a million tons of coal a year down to London.[32] Though there was also some work on the Baltic and Atlantic timber routes, it was this London trade, involving about one-third of the city's total supply, which provided Shields with its basic employment. On its prosperity depended the dockyards (employing seven hundred apprenticed shipwrights and another thousand labourers and subcontract metal workers), five hundred dockers (the loading was done direct from railway coal-drops) and two hundred sailmakers and provisioners. More imme-diately dependent on the seamen themselves were the town's two hundred public houses, a hundred and fifty prostitutes and a slightly larger number of crimps and shipowners (who also owned most of the pubs).[33] Otherwise, employment was limited. There were jobs for some five hundred miners in Shields' one big colliery, St Hilda's. The chemical works employed perhaps three hundred labourers (mostly Irish), and Cookson's glassworks a few dozen women and a couple of hundred men. But that was about all.

Mostly, therefore, Shields was a seaport town and the factors controlling its development tended – again contrast with North-ampton and Oldham – to be directly political. When change occur-red, it generally did so in response to alterations in the elaborate framework of formal and informal constraints by which the town's trade was governed. First, there were the laws regulating shipping. For the previous century and a half the merchant marine had acted as official peacetime reserve for the navy and as such had to carry a specified quota of apprentice seamen, to enforce near-military discipline and pay pensions. In return, British shipping got a monopoly of empire trade, and empire trade was itself boosted by a system of preferential tariffs. The key feature of the post-Napoleonic War period was the slow dismantling of this system, beginning with the reciprocity treaties of 1822-4 and ending with the repeal of the Navigation Acts in 1847-50. Second, and almost as important, there were the less formal constraints controlling the quantity of Shields' main shipment, coal. For centuries the great Northumberland and Durham landowners, sole suppliers to the London market, had been able to operate a system of restricted quota production. In the 1830s this monopoly, the Great Vend, started to break down, and in the 1840s collapsed. For the coal industry the result was inevitably a decline in prices. For the shippers, on the other hand, it meant a big increase in the amount of coal carried.[34]

The third political factor in Shields' development (ana also one of the main factors behind the breakdown of the coal monopoly) was the coming of the railway. Railways, involving a monopoly of cheap land transport, determined which of the Tyne-Wear ports would get the lion's share of the Durham coal. In the 1800s it was the construction of horse-drawn waggonways (and of facilities for direct railway drop-loading) which enabled the two ports of North and South Shields, in alliance with the surrounding gentry, to bypass the traditional coal port of Newcastle.[35] In the 1830s the new steam-and-iron railways, now being driven deep into the Durham coalfields, brought a hard-fought and only partly successful struggle with Sunderland over who should get the terminus rights.[36] Finally, in the 1840s, Shields inevitably lost its battle to prevent what seemed the ultimate disaster: the creation of a north-south rail link with London.[37]

Taken together, the combined result of these changes (all ultimately reflecting the previously heavy dependence of the northeast on the old mercantilist system) was to produce a sequence of economic growth markedly out of step with that in most other parts of the country. The 1795-1815 war period seems to have been one of unprecedented prosperity. Nationally (there are no figures for South Shields) these years saw a 56 per cent expansion in shipping tonnage.[38] The Navigation Acts remained in full force and foreign shipping was physically displaced from many of the routes it previously held. The immediate postwar years may also have been fairly prosperous, or at least profitable, as the discharge of naval manpower brought wages down faster than freights.[39] The 1820s, on the other hand, were bad. An existing overcapacity situation was made worse when the first of the reciprocity treaties threw much of the shipping previously on empire routes back on to the home market.[40] And if the 1820s were bad, the early 1830s were disastrous. In 1833 ten of Shields' sixteen shipbuilding berths had been idle for more than a year and one dock bought for £16,000 in 1806 was now unsold for £5,000.[41] Yet conversely, the following period, 1838-41, bad almost everywhere else, was good in Shields. Completion of the east-west coal railways and the breakdown of the vend brought a sharp increase in freight rates and a three-year burst of shipbuilding in the shipyards.[42] Then, when the tide was beginning to turn elsewhere, shipping again began to suffer from serious overcapacity. Freights fell 25 per cent below their previous lowest level, and both shipping and ship building went into a decline only partially relieved by the demand for foreign timber and corn in 1846-7. For shipping nationally the whole postwar period seems to have been one of chronic depression. Total British tonnage increased by only 24 per cent up to 1849 and in the twenty years 1815 to 1835 remained almost stagnant.

Indeed, the fact that it increased at all seems, in Shields' experience, to be only accounted for by the partly rentier nature of the investment and the ease with which new capital could enter the industry during the very brief periods of prosperity. Coal boats cost only two or three thousand pounds and one was as efficient to operate as ten.[43] Still in 1850 almost 70 per cent of Shields' shipping was controlled by men owning two boats or less and the great majority of owners seem to have been primarily engaged in other trades: fitting, provisioning, building.[44] Moreover, there seems reason to believe that in the coal trade itself the actual money was made more on the side: in docking, carting and what was referred to in shipping circles as 'our public house property'.[45]

Wages, if anything, fared even worse than the freight rates. Again there was the problem of a technologically underdeveloped industry in direct competition with cheaper-fed foreign labour. At no time in the second quarter of the century did the seamen's purchasing power (and seamen made up more than one-third of Shields' male wage-earners) reach that enjoyed at the height of the Napoleonic War. Very occasionally weekly earnings (including rations) may just have pushed above the twenty shillings mark. But far more usual was the thirteen shillings average experienced in 1832 – the combined result of low rates and 25 per cent unemployment.[46] Unemployment was also a big problem in the shipyards, Shields' second largest employer. Here, militant unionism was able to hold actual wage rates steady at fifty-four pence a day throughout the first half of the century. What altered was the amount of work available. Unemployed loggers in Canada could be got to build ships for twelve pence a day. In August 1842 the *Northern Star* reported that the average earnings of skilled men had not been above nine shillings a week for the previous year.[47] This was probably only an extreme example of a fairly general situation.

Those, then, are our three towns. Now to get down to the real problem of discovering why Oldham was so much more radical than the other two, and to start by looking at explanations that would make this *not* the result of class consciousness, of ideas become a material force, but purely and simply a matter of spontaneous reaction to intolerable physical conditions. If Oldham's radicalism was indeed no more than this, one would have expected labour's situation to have been in some way markedly worse than in the other two towns. Was it?

Work, poverty, family

To get even a partial answer at least three distinct aspects of working-class existence need taking into account: the physical nature of the work itself, the relative sufficiency of the earnings received for it, and finally the combined effect of both on the larger structure of people's lives.

First, conditions of work. For Oldham's twenty thousand mill workers undoubtedly the biggest burden was the sheer intensity of the labour itself. And this, despite the slight shortening of hours in the 1840s, got worse rather than better as the century went on. Each wave of innovation also meant a further speed-up. In mule spinning the number of motions that had to be completed in a minute more than trebled between 1814 and 1841, and the daily distance walked by the piecer went up from twelve miles to nearly thirty.[48] The same applied to most other departments, and it is the impact of the work on a badly fed and mostly female and juvenile labour force that emerges as easily the worst aspect of mill life. Accident rates (a traditional accompaniment of overworking) were high by any standard. Every year in the early 1850s more than fifteen workers in every thousand were either killed, lost limbs and fingers or suffered severe laceration.[49] From the 1830s there are frequent reports of workers over forty-five being paid off for lacking 'the necessary bodily vigour', and the familiar (but no less real) descriptions of physical deformities among the children.[50] Most telling of all, however, are the death and disease rates (figures 12 and 13). In the early 1850s deaths in Oldham from tuberculosis, the characteristic disease of overwork, were more than double the national average. The group worst affected, with treble the national rate, was women aged between twenty-five and thirty-four – the same group that also supplied the greatest share of millworkers. One in eight of Oldham's women died while in this age group, and over one-third worked in the mills.

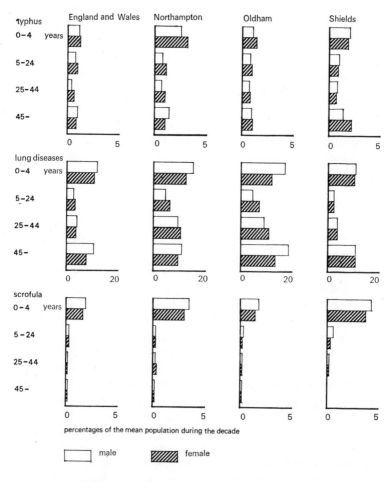

Figure 12 Deaths from disease, 1851–60: three towns[51]

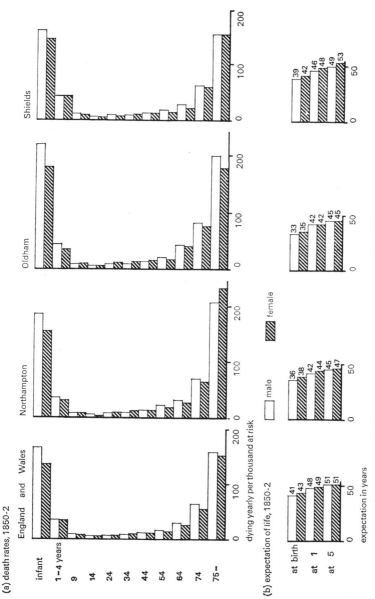

Figure 13 Death rates and the expectation of life, 1850-2: three towns[52]

Yet if things were bad for Oldham's cotton workers, it would be difficult to claim that they were any better for shoemakers in Northampton. Overworking can be found there too – and of women and children as well as men. Indeed, though we lack precise information, overworking could well have been worse than in Oldham. One Northampton shoemaker remembering back from the 1870s talks of some men working a sixteen-hour day in the early 1830s and described what was in effect the human side of the industry's new division of labour as 'the detestable custom of compelling women to do men's labour and taking children from their pap to work. . . .'[53] Another shoemaker writing in 1852 described Northampton as a place where 'no single-handed man can live; he must have a whole family at work, because a single-handed man is so badly paid he can scarce provide the necessaries of life. . . . As soon as they [the children] are big enough to handle an awl, they are obliged to come downstairs and work.'[54] And, inevitably, this use of children for the work of 'stabbing' the leather in preparation for sewing brought a high incidence of eye injuries and blindness.[55] Nor did the domestic nature of the work make it any more pleasant. For men it involved sitting the whole day cramped with lungs compressed, and – for the tough work of sewing the soles – considerable exertion: 'loins and shoulders, elbows, wrists and finger-joints all being strained to the utmost as stitch succeeds to stitch'.[56] Predictably, Northampton's tuberculosis rates for men were more than double the national average.

For the four thousand seamen in Shields the great killer was not disease but the ships they sailed in. Each year between the 1830s and 1870s Tyne-registered ships were sinking at a rate of between five and seven out of every hundred.[57] In the four years 1832-5 two hundred and seventy boats were lost on the North Sea coal run at a cost of 682 lives; just under 5 per cent of the Tyne's total sea-going labour force.[58] At the height of the battle with the railways in the 1860s North Sea colliers were going down at the fantastic rate of between six hundred to a thousand every year, generally accounting for half the total losses in British waters.[59] The reasons are easily found. As freights collapsed (first in the face of over-capacity and later railway competition) owners cut down on repairs and increased the size of cargoes. Between the second and fourth decades of the century there was a standard 20 per cent increase in loads that had to be carried – carried in ships that were almost always old and often derelict and over-insured.[60] With the result that, as the secretary of Shields' seamen explained in 1836, a vessel meeting a gale 'has not the buoyancy sufficient to lift her, and she goes under more like a raft of timber or a half tied rock than a vessel'. And while not every wreck meant the loss of an entire crew (generally four men and a boy) the mortality rate among South Shields seamen seems to have been pretty terrible. The relief books of its seamens' society show that 41 per cent of members dying between 1825 and 1835 were drowned.[61]

So, whatever the problems in assessing this type of evidence, it would seem very difficult to explain the relative lack of militancy in Northampton and Shields just by reference to better working conditions. Next, therefore, we must go on to examine the other side of the coin: the relative sufficiency of the wages people got in return.

Simply in terms of wage levels there can be little doubt that it was Oldham's workers who were least badly paid. Wage rates for labourers and building craftsmen appear to have been respectively 10 and 20 per cent higher than they were in Shields and Northampton. And average wages for men in cotton were certainly higher than those in shipping and shoemaking. This, however, tells us very little. To get the relative *sufficiency* of wages we need to know how income was distributed among families in the community as a whole and this is a problem which can only be solved by matching wage material with a sample of families taken from the census schedules. Consequently our answer has (unfortunately) to come from the very end of our period – 1849 – a year for which there is both enough information on wages and a nearby census from which to take samples of families.[62]

Even so the results make three things clear. First, and above all, they show just how uniformly appalling the poverty situation was, even in the relatively prosperous year of 1849. Taking the subsistence minimum used by the late nineteenth-century poor law authorities (and assuming that all occupied members of census households were in fact in full employment) one finds that the incomes of an outright majority of working families in all three towns were either already too low for them to buy all the food they needed or would be if they had to support just one extra adult member (figure 14). Moreover these figures refer merely to primary poverty. The larger reality of additional (secondary) poverty caused by illness, unemployment or debt was certainly very much worse.

The second thing that emerges concerns the distribution of

poverty. In all three towns poverty was not so much the special experiences of a particular group within the labour force as a regular feature of the life of almost *all* working families at certain stages in their development, especially in old age or before young children could start earning (figure 15). At some time or other it came to almost everyone. The third and final thing we can get from these results is an answer to our initial question about the relative sufficiency of wages. They make it clear that – with certain large qualifications – it was in Northampton and Shields that living standards were worse. While in Oldham the proportion of working families below the subsistence line at any one time was about one fifth, the proportion in Shields was over one-quarter and in Northampton over one-third (figure 14).

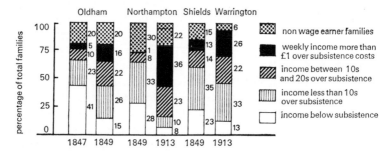

Figure 14   Family income and subsistence costs: four towns[63]

However, the qualifications are important. To a considerable extent Oldham's low figure was only achieved by serious sacrifices in other directions, and to understand these we must go on to the final section of this comparison: the combined effect of work and poverty on the larger structure of people's lives – how, in certain circumstances, families could avoid the worst results of low wages and malnutrition by choosing *alternative* forms of impoverishment: economizing on living standards, sending mothers and children out to work, and forming combined households with relatives.

These alternatives – and the scale on which they were adopted – provide perhaps the clearest indication of just how serious the plain problem of hunger was in early Victorian Britain (figure 16). In both towns where there was industrial demand for female and juvenile labour, Northampton and Oldham, over one-third of mothers with children aged eleven and under, and at least one-quarter (and probably considerably more) of children aged eleven and under went out to work – work that, as we have seen, exacted a terrible toll of its own. On housing the proportion of families economizing was even larger: one-third in Northampton, one-half in Oldham and in South Shields (with the prolonged absences of seamen husbands) over two-thirds. Besides the immediate effects on health, this sharing of accommodation must also have imposed considerable (though not easily measured) strains on family relationships.

The same probably applies to the type of economy that specially marked Oldham (and which goes a long way to explain its low poverty figure): the forming of combined households with relatives. Partly Oldham families were better able to do this because, in a locally born population, there were far more relatives about. But partly it was also because the combination of child labour with slightly higher wage levels meant that the original child-poverty period was itself somewhat shorter. As a result, a young couple with children could be 'carried' by parents or brothers and sisters for the worst three or four years; and later, when their own children were earning, help out themselves. In Northampton and Shields the child-poverty period was generally so long that combining households would have made much less difference. Figure 17 shows the impact of this on family structure, and figure 15 the effectiveness of Oldham's 'huddling' (as it was called) in reducing exposure to primary poverty, especially among labourers.

To end with, the ultimate results of all these various forms of impoverishment can be summed up by a glance at the registrar general's mortality statistics (figure 13). The effect of overworking on tuberculosis rates has already been noted. For working mothers an equally striking index is the rate of infant mortality. In Oldham 204 of every thousand children died before their first birthday, in Northampton 173, but in Shields (and the country as a whole) only 153. On the other hand, when one turns to disease associated with malnutrition and destitution – scrofula and typhus – it is predictably Shields and Northampton that come out worst. For most age groups the death rates are nearly double those for Oldham and the country as a whole. Finally, when one looks at the expectation of life for males at the age of five (and takes into account the heavy loss of life among Shields seamen) one finds that the situation was almost exactly the same in all three towns: a prospect of ending one's life before the age of forty-two.

(a) All wage-earner families : percentage in poverty by life cycle stage

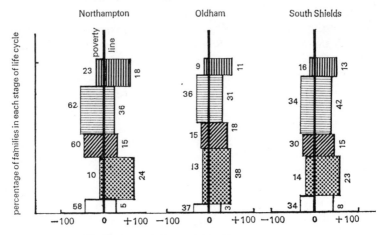

percentage of families in poverty (figures on left of axis)

(b) Labourer families : percentage in poverty by life cycle stage

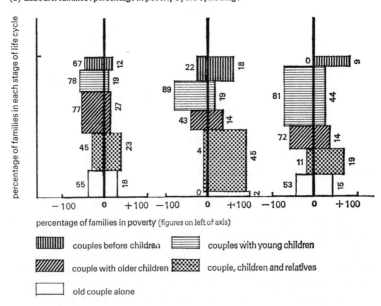

percentage of families in poverty (figures on left of axis)

Figure 15   Poverty and the family life cycle, 1849: three towns

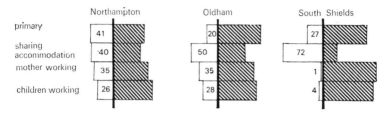

percentage of labour families in each type of poverty

Figure 16   Types of poverty, 1849–51: three towns

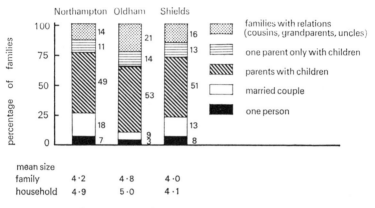

Figure 17   Family structure, 1851: three towns[64]

Conditions alone, therefore, will hardly explain the differing politics of the three towns. And although we have certainly not disposed of all the explanations which would make Oldham's exceptional militancy the result of something other than class consciousness,[65] it might now be more fruitful to test the argument that it *was*.

Radicals and the labour movement

At the risk of oversimplifying, two stages may be distinguished in the process by which the proletarian vanguard is able to achieve a mass realization of its ideas: first, the securing of mass leadership itself (and thus access to labour as a whole), and second, the *use* of that position to convince people of the need for a total change in the social system. Obviously, in real life the two stages cannot be completely separated. A vanguard group is only likely to gain mass leadership in conditions where its larger social orientation (and particularly its willingness to use extra-legal, anti-system tactics) has an immediate relevance. And conversely a vanguard group that attempts to sustain its leadership in a period where such tactics are no longer relevant (and fears to use its position to further its wider aims) always runs the risk of prejudicing its principles. But for present purposes a temporary distinction may usefully be made, and this section will be looking at the three towns in terms of the first stage of the process, the winning of mass leadership: how far there existed the basic preconditions for any form of mass leadership, an organized labour movement, and (if so) the relation of the radicals to it.

Oldham: The size and organization of Oldham's labour movement has already been well enough demonstrated, as has the base of radical influence within it: extra-legal wage-bargaining. It was the immediate relevance of such tactics that originally enabled Oldham's radicals to break out of their structural isolation and displace the old loyalist leaders. It was the continuing relevance of those tactics that enabled them to maintain their leadership long after the original wartime crises. Granted, such tactics were limited. They could not safely be taken to the stage of full-scale confrontation with the state. Nor could they do more than moderate the local incidence of overall market forces. But they did demand a profound reorganization of the working population. Quite apart from the emergence of a new collective discipline, the gains were quite sufficient to give every worker good reason to see state power (and any local extension of it) as an immediate threat to his living standards.

Looking at particular trades, it is difficult to single out any as somehow more 'radical' than the rest. In the 1830s all occupations (with the partial exception of the weavers) were organized.[66] All – from spinners and machine-makers to hatters and shoemakers – used extra-legal tactics. All contained within them at least some radical leaders, and all came out in support of the political general strikes of 1834 and 1842.[67] Nonetheless, two trades, cotton spinning and (for a period) mining, do seem to have held a special place. Besides dominating the two principal industrial sectors of the local economy, their particular patterns of development do seem (to go outside the limits of this section for a moment) to have enabled radical mass leaders to *use* their position of leadership for wider political ends.

The spinners formed a friendly society as early as 1796, only a few years after emerging as a distinct occupation.[68] By 1811 (at a time when they could not have numbered much more than four hundred) their militant tactics were already forcing the local authorities to take special countermeasures, and main force methods were again used in 1815 and 1818.[69] In the radical campaign of 1816-17 at least two of their members took a leading role and in 1818 Chippendale claimed that the union itself was under the direction of the 'reform orators'.[70] From that year also (if not before) there was close cooperation with the Manchester spinners.[71] Joint activity took place on wages, short-time and in support of the wider syndicalist movement of 1818 – the 'Philanthropic Hercules' – which Fletcher considered 'as a little dangerous when it is considered that from that body [the Spinners Union] the greatest share of pecuniary support to the [radical] blanketeers in 1817 was derived'.[72] This cooperation was revived in 1826 (and probably for the short-time campaign of 1824-5), and in 1829 formalized by the founding of John Doherty's National Spinners Union.[73] In Oldham it seems to have been the radicals (particularly John Knight) who played a leading role in cementing this amalgamation and in winning local support for Doherty's wider schemes for trade union unity. In September 1830 Knight was canvassing support for the National Union of the Working Classes, and in October 1830 chaired a meeting of spinners and piecers that called for a 'stronger and more efficient union of trades'.[74] It was Knight, too, who initiated the local branch of the Ten Hour Association in 1833.[75] By 1834 there was considerable overlap between the committees of the Oldham Political Union (of which Knight was secretary) and the local branch of the Regeneration Society (the political wing of Doherty's union) and, indeed, later that year the *Manchester Guardian* accused Knight of also being secretary of the spinners.[76] Following the failure of the general strike plans in 1834, links with Doherty's Manchester headquarters may have loosened, but locally the radical allegiance of the spinners seems to have continued uninterrupted till the great confrontation with the government in 1842.

The miners' radicalism never seems to have been quite as marked as this. Certainly in 1818 the radicals were deeply involved in the industry (Chippendale at the time described the miners' leaders as 'revolutionaries')[77] and there was also considerable radical activity during the massive conflicts with state power which marked the strikes of 1831 and 1841.[78] But most of the time union activity, however illegal, did not take on an openly political character. It was only after 1842, during the brief career of the Miners' Association of Great Britain, that one starts to get the miners emerging into the mainstream of local politics. Then – just at the time when cotton's militancy was dying down – the miners do seem to have done something to raise the political level of the surrounding community.[79]

In Oldham, therefore, one can find most of the preconditions one is looking for: an organized labour movement, the use of extra-legal tactics, a degree of radical leadership, and in two industries at least a situation where leadership was (or became) political in the wider sense.

Northampton: Turning to Northampton, one can also find plenty of radicals. Not unlike Oldham, there was an anti-state dissenter tradition going well back into the previous century.[80] From the 1800s a more strictly proletarian perspective makes its appearance, reinforced after 1820 by refugees from Cato Street.[81] By the 1830s and 1840s there existed a small but well organized Chartist movement closely in touch with national developments.[82]

What Northampton did not have, however, is anything resembling a labour movement. True, there were periodic attempts at union organization but only a small minority of workers joined for very long and from the 1830s to the 1850s every single strike in the shoemaking industry seems to have ended in disaster.[83] Given the nature of the local economy, this of course is just what one would expect. The whole pattern of Northampton's growth depended on the cheapness of its labour, its lack of militancy and the constant influx of new workers from the surrounding countryside. As a union organizer explained in 1834:

> There is no class of being in Christendom that more requires the aid of a well-conducted and properly regulated union than the operative cordwainers of the county; they having long been reduced to the lowest stage of poverty, privation and want and far sunk in the black night of ignorance. . . .[84]

Sixteen years later the situation was much the same. According to a *Morning Chronicle* journalist:

The society [of shoemakers] has endeavoured for some years to keep up the price of labour, but all their efforts have been ineffectual. 'Two or three years since', said the secretary, 'we struck in one of the shops in the town. It was no use our holding out for the scabs from the country went in and fetched the work for whatever price the masters liked to give'.[85]

Not surprisingly, therefore, the main Northampton shoemakers' society had only one hundred and sixty-six members out of a possible three thousand in 1845; and the society itself was principally a tramping organization which helped its members find work in other parts of the country.[86]

In all this the root problem was clearly a labour market that stretched far beyond the town itself and included (as a result of the rural clearances) a pauperized mass of labour willing to do almost anything to get work. But if this was the problem, it only proved insurmountable because it was not possible to use the same tactics as in Oldham. Unlike Oldham, Northampton had experienced little wartime radicalism and certainly no breakdown in law and order. A food riot in spring 1795 had quickly been smashed up by the Horse Guards and by the second quarter of the century there was an efficient police force and a permanent garrison.[87] Consequently without any tradition of anti-state labour solidarity and with strong-arm tactics ruled out, there was almost no way of imposing union discipline on the constant stream of immigrant workers. In terms of industrial coercion the boot was very much on the other foot. Savage punishments – flogging, imprisonment – were inflicted for work offences,[88] jailings were successfully used to break the trades movement of 1834,[89] and for the three elections of 1818, 1830 and 1842 (Northampton had household suffrage up to 1832) there is evidence of employer interference in voting.[90]

So, instead of a labour movement, all that existed were small islands of organized workers amid a labour force whose main cultural ties were still with the countryside (72 per cent were immigrants in 1851) and whose immediate lives were often controlled by the small employers who gave them employment.[91] Northampton politics reflect this situation closely. Though those workers who were organized tended to be radical,[92] the lack of a labour movement base left any who were genuinely class conscious with the bleak alternative of political isolation or an unequal alliance with non-labour strata. Indeed, it is this dilemma that holds the key to

Northampton politics right up till the ascendancy of Bradlaugh. When Peter McDouall stood as Chartist candidate in the 1841 election he did so with Tory support, and even then only got forty of the four hundred shoemaker votes.[93] And while the following year a self-styled Chartist was elected to the town council, it was with Whig support, and the new councillor was himself a tradesman closely linked to the temperance movement and radical dissent.[94] An alliance of a similar sort was formed again for the 1847 parliamentary election when the free trader and anti-state Church campaigner Epps ran with Chartist support, and in 1849 and 1850 a whole string of Nonconformist small employers stood for the council on a joint radical-Chartist ticket.[95]

Of possible alliances it was undoubtedly this one with the Nonconformist petty bourgeoisie that was the most dangerous – though also the most difficult to avoid. Politically, radical dissent had a considerable following. Its strength lay in the appeal of its rhetoric (anti-establishment and anti-clerical) for the great mass of dispossessed rural immigrants among whom, according to a Chartist observer of 1839, a hatred for their recent taskmasters, the rural clergy, was both 'strong and deep'.[96] Obviously, for the small employer such language played an important part in maintaining cultural control over his workers.[97] But equally for the working-class radicals any alliance with perspectives of this type made it almost impossible to carry through what should have been their basic task: to give overall political expression to the lessons of local industrial conflict. Indeed, it was probably this which prevented the bitterly fought (though unsuccessful) battle to stop the introduction of sewing machines in 1857-8 from having any wider political repercussions.[98]

All in all, therefore, Northampton bears out our argument quite well. The key role of extra-legal tactics is clearly demonstrated by the failure to organize labour, and the petty bourgeois, 'moral force' tendency of Northampton Chartism (especially in its later years) shows just what could happen to even genuinely working-class radicals who were not able to develop a labour movement base. The problem is summed up by a would-be radical union organizer of 1834: 'I would not retard the progress of the union by pressing any serious political question before its proper season . . . unity of numbers is the first essential object, and unity of sentiment the second to be obtained.'[99]

South Shields: If the example of Northampton demonstrates the importance of having a strong labour movement, South Shields' experience has an even more vital role to play in the argument by showing that neither labour movement nor extra-legal tactics was enough. For though both were eminently present in Shields, the town still failed to produce political militancy of the Oldham type.

In the later eighteenth century union organization seems to have reached a scale and maturity on Tyneside unequalled anywhere else in the country. Miners, keelmen, shipwrights and seamen had long possessed their own very effective forms of collective bargaining.[100] Even in South Shields – developing as it did outside the old restrictions imposed higher up the river – the seamen and shipwrights had organized themselves on a formal friendly society basis by the end of the 1790s and had been active industrially (together with other trades like carpenters and shoemakers) for some time before.[101] By the 1820s organization had spread to even quite minor trades like sailmakers, ropemakers and blacksmiths,[102] and by the 1830s glass and alkali labouring were probably the only occupations that remained ununionized. Moreover, on the law and order front the situation bears many similarities to that in Oldham. As early as February 1793 employers were being harassed and shipyards burnt.[103] In March of that year a local employer was writing to the Home Secretary to say that the port of Shields would only flourish with 'such police as they have in Westminster . . . but without it, the few independent people we have amongst us must necessarily leave a place in which they cannot live, with safety or satisfaction'.[104] By 1803 attacks on press gangs had become so serious that the Admiralty was forced to suspend recruiting.[105] And though the full-scale confrontation which developed in September 1815 between the seamen and their employers (and involved a massive military intervention) brought defeat for the union and widespread arrests, strong-arm tactics continued.[106] In 1820 the 'principal inhabitants' were petitioning for the reinforcement of law and order and the appointment of a full-time police magistrate[107] and in the years that followed industrial violence seems, if anything, to have increased.[108] After a particularly bitter miners' strike in 1832, Shields' most actively anti-union magistrate, Nicholas Fairles, was assassinated.[109] In its editorial comment the *Newcastle Journal* called for new laws against the unions and used its boldest italics to emphasize 'the remark which comes from everybody's mouth – *something must be done*'.[110] Even in 1844 local shipowners were still campaigning for an 'effective river police'.[111]

So, whatever the differences of degree, there can be no doubt that Shields went through much the same experience of coercive occupational solidarity as Oldham. Yet, despite this, there was no *political* mass movement.

Shields' radicals, at least compared with those in Northampton, were hard men, disciplined by a wider regional movement which took its direction from the Durham miners. In Robert Lowery, legal adviser to the Tyneside pitmen, they possessed one of the founding fathers of north-east Chartism and round him there developed in the early 1830s a group which consciously defined itself against the shopkeeper adherents of Place and Hume.[112] They were also well organized. The establishment of the Newcastle *Northern Liberator* in 1837 placed at their disposal one of the finest working-class newspapers in the country. A local branch of the Working Men's Association was formed the same year and in 1838 this was converted into the South Shields Political Union.[113] From then on till the late 1840s a consistent level of political work was maintained: public meetings, education, and campaigning among the seamen, chemical workers and miners.[114]

Yet apart from the few dozen committed Chartists, the movement's larger support remained disappointing (Shields was one of the few places which the authorities regarded as safe in 1839 and 1848).[115] True, the north-east trade cycle was out of step with that in the rest of the country but this did not prevent the development of a powerful Chartist movement in other north-east districts. The really significant thing about Shields is that at no time did its movement receive any significant support from organized labour. And not from want of trying. In 1839, for instance, the Chartists inaugurated a campaign to keep open Cookson's chemical works. The only known response of the chemical workers was (a few months later) to supply four hundred special constables for possible use against them.[116] Similarly with the seamen. The opening address of the Political Union made specific mention of the seamen's grievances and demanded an immediate end to naval empressment and the lash. But still in January 1839 Lowery was unsuccessfully appealing for their support.[117] The sole exception was the town's small mining community – with George Charlton, the local delegate, the one recognized labour leader who appeared regularly on Chartist platforms.[118]

So, to return to the basic argument, Shields – like Northampton – does point in the right direction. It enables us to make a clear distinction between the *occupational* solidarity which Shields clearly possessed and the development of a wider political content, and hence to go on to argue that Oldham's mass radicalism did indeed involve a further element, the key one in establishing class consciousness, that of *intellectual conviction*. What has to be demonstrated next, therefore, is that there was something about Oldham's industrial experience – as against Shields' – that did enable its radicals, *as radicals*, to win the conscious allegiance of organized labour.

The politics of the cotton industry

In doing this the 1830s (and especially the early years) would seem to be the key period. It was then, as we have seen, that Oldham's labour leaders start to make radical political change an intrinsic part of their industrial programme, and this poses our first basic question. Why did such a development not happen before? Already for a good generation the traditional apparatus of bourgeois control had been locally inoperative. And for an even longer period labour had been exposed to a progressively unifying struggle against state power. Why, then, was it only in the 1830s (and more particularly in the cotton industry) that radical mass leaders felt able to put forward demands for an alternative social system?

The first attempt at an answer might point to the obvious fact that labour was then coming under attack on a completely new scale. 1830 saw the start of a marked decline in all wages, and of a precipitous one for the leading contingent of Oldham's labour force, the cotton spinners. There was the threat posed by the new poor law and the government's assault on extra-legal unionism and the larger political base which sustained it. Yet, granted the importance of these developments, they hardly seem enough by themselves to provide an answer. Many other areas (including Shields) experienced both a decline in wages and an attack on trade union rights. Moreover, in Oldham itself there had previously been periods when conflict was almost as intense. What seems to have been the really decisive factor was not so much the attack itself as the context in which it took place. We have already noted the closeness with which the economics of the cotton industry corresponded to the more classic feature of the industrial capitalist crisis. Added to this, and scarcely less important, was the fact that its workers had become accustomed – in the normal course of trade union activity – to see the industry's development in terms which highlighted just those contradictions.

Since at least 1816 the common objective of all Lancashire cotton workers had been to get Parliament to pass a short-time Act. Far more than immediate wage bargaining, it was this which provided the spinners with their one continuing base for organizational unity.[119] The campaigns of 1816-19, 1824-5 and 1829-31 all demanded concerted local petitioning and agitation.[120] In addition, the heavy legal expenses incurred at Westminster meant that regular collections had to be taken at workplaces and the purposes behind the campaign constantly explained: that shorter hours (and less produced) offset the competitive pressure on cotton prices; that shorter hours (and more employed) counteracted the loss of jobs from faster machinery. As John Knight put it in 1831:

> The only remedy for the evils inflicted on the working class was to labour fewer hours. He was older than most of the machinery now in use. When people laboured by hand they worked only eight hours a day and had a comfortable living; and if the machinery were now properly used they ought only to have occasion to work one.[121]

So, as part of the everyday language of cotton trade unionism, one has the emergence of an economic perspective which, though still phrased in terms of the existing order, radically challenged its assumptions. Nor was this all. Not only did the short-time campaign accustom workers to viewing their industry in overall politico-economic terms, it also showed them (albeit somewhat fortuitously) that political action could bring immediate industrial benefits. Because of splits among the industry's employers – stemming from the technological imbalance between spinning and weaving – a restriction in the working hours for spinning was *also* (up till about 1830) in the interest of the politically dominant cloth merchant sector.[122] And the result was a series of relatively effective Acts – 1819, 1825, 1829 and 1831 – in whose enforcement the working spinners played an active role. It was union members (working in close cooperation with Doherty in Manchester) who had the job of laying informations against overworking employers – and during the 1820s and early 1830s almost every area of Lancashire, including Oldham, had its quota of prosecutions.[123]

This, then, was the context in which the attacks of the 1830-4 period occurred: an industry whose economics displayed with unique force the contradictions of industrial capitalist production; and a labour movement that developed around those contradictions a campaign demanding a fairly high level of mass understanding. What the new capitalist offensive did was enable radical leaders to transform this existing understanding into a larger commitment against the system itself. With wages falling fast, Parliament now setting itself firmly against an effective Factory Act and the automatic spinning mule threatening widespread redundancy, the old language could easily be given an altogether more radical twist. To quote John Knight again, this time in April 1834:

It is high time for the working people of this country to awake. . . . In less than twenty years . . . the work performed in our cotton factories has lost more than two thirds of its value . . . no article ever loses its price in the market until it becomes redundant. . . . It is high time for all English workmen to awake and no longer be driven in the road to ruin by their blind employers. . . . We must . . . learn to look beyond the improvement of our own particular branch of business and improve the conditions of the whole body of English labourers. . . . With this in view we ought to ascertain the *intrinsic* value of labour; for until we have learned that it is impossible to ascertain to what extent we are robbed of the fruit of our labour.[124]

What, then, is our argument? Not that the material attacks were unimportant. Still less that purely linguistic factors were the determining ones. Rather that it was the coming together of both that enabled radical leaders to take advantage so quickly (in just three or four years) of the third and basic factor: the hard, intractable *trend to crisis* into which the cotton industry became locked after 1830. However, for our immediate analysis the actual role of language should not be underestimated. If it can be shown that the development of a mass movement was in fact closely linked to the careful, conscious process by which the radicals guided mass understanding from one level to another, then we will be well on the way to establishing the key element of intellectual conviction. Luckily, two fairly well recorded periods of mass action in Oldham,

1834 and 1842, are available for testing this – as are the arguments of the radicals themselves.

To start with the arguments. For the first period these are best taken from the propaganda of the Regeneration Society. This organization (formed in 1833 and taking its name from the parallel organization of French workers) brought together Doherty's trade union apparatus, the hard core of Lancashire radicals – including Fielden – and Robert Owen's more tenuous network of Socialist and cooperative societies.[125] The immediate aim was to use the short-time, Factory Act issue as a lever for fundamental political mobilization (quite how fundamental was probably only grasped initially by Fielden, Doherty and their immediate confederates).

The society's programme, published in November 1833, began with the obvious facts of everyday industrial experience: 'The strange anomaly of one part of the people working beyond their strength, another part working at worn-out and other employments for very inadequate wages and another part in a state of starvation from want of employment.' It pointed to even worse to come: 'The productive power of this country aided by machinery is so great and so rapidly increasing as from its misdirection to threaten danger to society from a still further fall in wages.' And proposed a general remedy: 'Properly devised arrangements to enable society to produce the greatest amount of wealth in the shortest amount of time, and with the greatest advantage to the producers, and to distribute this wealth most beneficially to society at large.'[126]

How all this was to be achieved was outlined progammatically by Fielden in an article in Cobbett's *Register*.[127] Its detailed proposals were at once eminently practical and totally subversive. Externally, the economy's great problem was the adverse trend in the terms of trade for factory industries. The solution: cut hours and output in such industries by one-quarter and set up democratically elected local boards of trade to control further investment. 'Manufactures made from wool, cotton, silk and flax rise in price, probably on the average about 25 per cent, this rise would give for the lessened production the present amount or sum for labour expenses and profit which the manufacturer now has, and also enable him to give the foreigner and others the same quantity of his manufactures for the same quantity of raw material'. But if this were done for export trades, the same measures would have to be taken for all industries. 'An advance of 25 per cent in our manufactures would be a very different affair to our home consumer, and unless all engaged in other trades effect a corresponding rise in the price of their productions by diminishing the quantity (and which for their own protection they ought to do), they would suffer from the change.' And so a universal eight-hour day – with the result that:

> The productive classes, both masters and workmen, would thus secure for themselves a greater proportion for their own use with working an eight-hour day that they now have for working a longer time. And the political economists of our day would be spared the mortification of having to complain any more of *distress* arising out of overproduction.

Moreover, this time the political instrument for this was to be the workers themselves, not Parliament. On the same day that the new, regressive (1833) Factory Act came into force all workers were to refuse to work more than eight hours. The role of a Regeneration Society was to direct the resulting struggle and unite the various industrial and political organizations involved. After some delays – largely the result of lagging support in Yorkshire – the call for action was finally put out by Doherty in his *Herald of the Rights of Industry* for the first week of April 1834:

> We are now arrived at a most important crisis . . . You are to be the artificers of your fortunes. Philosophers may write, politicians struggle and your friends labour in vain. Unless you yourself now put your hands to the work in good earnest all will prove unavailing. If you are not emancipated now, *immediately,* the fault is your own. We say solemnly and emphatically Strike! Not against some handful of greedy wretched employers as heretofore, but strike at once against the whole tribe of idlers of every grade, class or condition. It is your labour which enriches them, and enables them first to despise and then oppress you . . . We do not advise you to strike against all work. . . . But if you strike against working more than so many hours, these hours will provide food, and, at the same time, certain power. . . . Come, then, friends of the trades unions, join the National Regenerators; resolve that on 2nd June next you shall work only eight hours a day. . . .[128]

Or as the authorities saw it (in this case General Bouverie of northern command):

> I learn that thirty-four delegates of the trade unions met at or

near Blackburn on Monday 8 April and that their proceedings were conducted so secretly that it is impossible to ascertain what they were . . . [my informant] thinks that they are taking a turn decidedly more political, that this has thrown the Regeneration people and the trade unions more together and that the real aim of the trade unions is now to overthrow the government, and that if they are not stopped they will make the attempt. He considers that their aim is to have a general turn-out on 2 June, and that they may then try their strength . . .[129]

Whether the radical plans were well conceived is of little immediate relevance. What matters is the scale on which they were supported – and here the subsequent events in Oldham seem to provide fairly conclusive evidence.

On the evening of 14 April (very possibly as part of a direct government bid to forestall the Regenerators' plans) a lodge of the town's Cotton Spinners Union, then in dispute with one of the larger employers, was raided by the police.[130] Oath-taking documents were seized and the two secretaries arrested in what seemed to be the start to another Tolpuddle-type prosecution.[131] Immediately the Oldham Regenerators placed themselves on the alert and the following morning, to quote Butterworth, 'droves of people rushed in like a mountain torrent and the hands of all the mills for miles around on learning of the proceedings voluntarily abandoned their work and flocked into Oldham'.[132] The account is continued by a local magistrate:

This morning about twenty minutes before nine o'clock the two men who had been taken into custody were removed from the lock-up to go before a magistrate, and immediately they came into the street a crowd of several thousand persons assembled from the cotton factories in the neighbourhood. When they arrived opposite the factory of Mr Thompson of Bankside [the factory in dispute] they were rescued by the rioters . . . After the rescue the rioters . . . called upon the new hands to come out, and eventually used force to break open the mill . . . the men inside [armed works police] fired upon the rioters one of whom was killed. But the rioters succeeded in breaking into the house of Mr Thompson and the factory . . . information was given to me about nine o'clock and I sent an express to Colonel Kennedy for troops. . . .[133]

The troops duly arrived – but without the usual results. Instead of subsiding like the normal riot, the situation continued to move towards confrontation. The local Regeneration Society put out a call for a general strike and received total support, not just from the factory population put from the miners, engineers, bricklayers, weavers, hatters and tailors. The Manchester headquarters followed suit:

> The struggle between rich and poor, between capital and labour, is now arrived at a crisis. You must either triumph now or be crushed. The rich are resolved on destroying your unions, your real strength, in order that they may continue to plunder and oppress you with impunity. . . . Your honest neighbours of Oldham have been openly assaulted, their Lodge feloniously broken into, their books and papers carried away and two of their members arrested. Another of their brethren has been shot dead by their side in open day and their town crowded with military to overawe, or, if need be, to slaughter them. . . . The men of Oldham have struck the first blow against their and your oppressors. They have to a man ceased work, till justice be done to them, and when they do return to work they are resolved to work only eight hours a day.[134]

When on 18 April the Manchester leaders Doherty, Durran and Wrigley appeared at a mass meeting in Olham (Butterworth estimated the attendance at twenty thousand), there was more than a touch of revolution in the air. News of the French workers' rising was just beginning to come through. 'Doherty', reported the *Manchester Guardian*, 'read extracts from the London papers containing accounts of the proceedings of the workmen of Lyon and Paris, and he assured them that before the sun set every man in France would have his rights, and a democracy established.'[135] Motions of solidarity were passed and delegates appointed to win support in Birmingham, the West Riding and London.[136] While the meeting was still in progress the local commander sent an urgent request for reinforcements. During the night the entire depot of the Thirty-Fourth Foot and two companies of the Thirty-Fifth moved into the town; further troops were ordered up to Manchester from the Wigan and Haydock Edge garrisons.[137] By 20 April Oldham contained detachments of the Eighteenth, Twenty-Eighth, Thirty-Fourth and Thirty-Fifth Foot and the Twelfth Lancers.[138] And a couple of days later William Cobbett was writing to Fielden (both were down south for the parliamentary session): 'The *Revolution* has begun! . . . That "Great Change", which you anticipated, is certainly at hand!'[139]

In fact, of course, it was not. In other areas the strike call received only very ragged support and after two weeks the Oldham leadership decided on a return to work.[140] But – quite apart from the important subsequent developments in Oldham (which are examined in the next chapter) – the episode adds at least something to the argument. It plainly reveals the ease with which radical leaders could move from industrial to political struggle *without losing* their mass support and also gives an unusually sharp focus to their ultimate objectives. What it may not establish as fully as one would like is the element of mass conviction. In view of the sequence of events, it could quite plausibly be argued that the wider mobilization sprang more from the attack on trade union rights than any belief in a new social order. The great value of our second episode, the general strike of August 1842, is that it is precisely this element that stands out most clearly.

The strike, a political one to force the granting of universal suffrage, covered almost all Lancashire, much of Yorkshire and parts of the midlands, and represented the first major challenge to the government since 1839. At a national level its full story remains to be written and many details are still obscure. But one thing that has never been in doubt is that its motive force was essentially local. It was not imposed from above. Those on the Chartist executive who originally favoured such a strike – mainly Peter McDouall and his followers – were in a fairly small minority, and the only way they could get national backing was by first creating a rank-and-file movement capable of forcing the executive's hand. In the event it was strike action by the south Lancashire factory population that enabled them to do this, and in Oldham we can watch this crucial support being won.

Three things stand out. The comparative *length* of the proceeding discussion (the initial strike was in no sense a matter of momentary infatuation). The key role played at every stage by the *intellectual force* of the radicals' arguments. and the *mass* scale on which the discussion took place.

The actual stimulus for the Oldham strike was external: the arrival on 8 August 1842 of several thousand striking cotton workers from McDouall's stronghold of Ashton-under-Lyne.[141] But the arguments they brought with them were by no means new.

Ever since the onset of the great 1841-2 depression some twelve months before there had been a steady rise in the political temperature. Nationally, it was this period that saw the culmination of Fielden's parliamentary campaign against the new police and poor laws, and in Oldham itself there had been the great public debates on corn law repeal.

These debates seem to have been particularly important. Taking place before the whole community and in circumstances of dramatic confrontation between workers and employers, they gave radical spokesmen an unrivalled opportunity for demonstrating the intellectual bankruptcy of the existing order. The first took place in April 1841. It was attended by the town's employers and shopkeepers and a 'vast crowd of operatives' which Butterworth described as 'principally of Chartist opinions'.[142] The employers just repeated the usual platitudes of anti-corn law political economy: 'A repeal would enable commercial men to exchange their cotton goods for the corn of foreign countries, hence an increase of trade would ensue and the conditions of the operatives be bettered.' The working-class spokesmen, on the other hand, challenged the whole basis of the repealers' economics. Free trade, they argued, would make no long-term difference to the economic situation and might even raise the price of food. The real causes of distress were quite different: the 'oppressive conduct of capitalists' and their 'misapplication of machinery'. And the remedies were consequently political: law-making power for labour – the People's Charter. When the employers refused to accept this, the meeting broke up. A similar confrontation was re-enacted before an even bigger audience in February 1842.[143]

As the depression intensified so the force of radical arguments increased. In November 1841, when twenty-four of Oldham's fifty-seven big mills were either stopped or on short time, John Doherty was again in Oldham lecturing to the Socialists on the relation between improved machinery, speed-up and unemployment.[144] In January 1842 the Manchester Chartist William Leach had an audience of over a thousand for a speech in which he attributed 'the present distress to the misapplication of machinery by which means a vast extent of human labour has been superseded and wages greatly reduced. . . .'[145] The same message (and its political sequel) was hammered home at increasingly frequent meetings throughout the spring and early summer of 1842.

Remembering back to this period, Benjamin Brierley wrote in later life:

> The *Northern Star*, the only newspaper that appeared to circulate anywhere, found its way weekly to [our house] being subscribed for by my father and five others. Every Sunday morning these subscribers met at our house to hear what prospect there was of the expected 'smash-up' taking place . . . . A republic was to take the place of the 'base, bloody and brutal Whigs' and . . . ten thousand trained pikemen would sweep England through . . . I had to turn my father's grindstone while rebelliously inclined amateur soldiers ground their pikes.[146]

By June 1842 the numbers attending a Chartist meeting on Oldham Edge was over five thousand,[147] and among several similar meetings in July was one at which McDouall himself argued his case for the unification of industrial and political struggles. Only united strike action by labour as a whole could, he claimed, force the political changes that were needed.[148]

So on 8 August 1842 when the thousands-strong column of Ashton workers marched into Oldham, everybody knew what was at stake. For the town's official Chartist leadership (committed to the policy of the national executive) the situation was particularly difficult. On the one hand they knew only too well that a political strike of this kind could easily destroy the movement's hard-won national unity and – if unsuccessful – give the government just the excuse it needed to begin its final assault on the local bases of working-class power. Against this, there was the strength of McDouall's own local following and the knowledge that politically time was running out. In the event, the Oldham leadership stuck by the executive and their ultimately unsuccessful struggle to hold their followers in line provides – in its detailed course – what is perhaps the clearest test of how far Oldham's workers had passed beyond a purely trade union consciousness.

The struggle lasted for seven days. It started on the evening of 8 August after the Ashton men had successfully stopped the mills. The two sides argued out their cases before an audience estimated at over ten thousand (the total Oldham area cotton labour force was eighteen thousand) and were only stopped by the unexpected arrival of troops. When the debate was resumed the following evening the issue was put to the vote and the Ashton men narrowly won. Accordingly on the following day, 10 August, the town's mines, factories and engineering works all stopped, and during the next five days – with the streets crowded with workers and the whole of south Lancashire in turmoil – there followed a confused succession of meetings and counter-meetings. Unfortunately, we only know a very little of what was said but it is clear that as well as the two groups of Chartists the town's Owenite Socialists also found a ready response.[149]

The situation did not crystallize till a joint meeting on 15 August when all groups agreed to abide by the decision of the aggregate meeting to be held between the Lancashire trades' delegates and the Chartist national executive in Manchester the following day. The eventual decision – coming as McDouall had originally planned on the twenty-third anniversary of Peterloo – was announced that evening. Fittingly, it was Sam Yardley, leader of the previously hostile local executive, who made the final call for action in Oldham: strike for political power – no return till the People's Charter is law.

The outcome is well known. Despite its initial successes, the strike was broken by the beginning of September. By the end of the year the military had moved permanently into many Lancashire towns, fifteen hundred labour leaders were in prison (Yardley was among the first of the forty-nine arrested in Oldham), and radical leadership in the cotton industry was more or less at an end.[150]

However, seen purely as an object-lesson, the strike reveals almost all the features we are looking for. It was clearly a political one to gain what amounted to state power. Support had to be won on these terms beforehand and the process of achieving it plainly involved discussion and argument on a mass scale. What is more, it is also clear (as it should be if we are really dealing with class consciousness) that the success of such arguments was closely linked to the immediacy with which the cotton industry's economics reflected – and could be shown to reflect – the contradictions of the overall system. So, to return to where we started, if we want to explain the differing abilities of radicals in Shields and Oldham to win the allegiance of organized labour, the cotton industry can fairly be said to provide a good part of the answer. Not just was its development trapped within a sequence of specifically capitalist crises but its workers themselves had long been accustomed to see their industry in overall politico-economic terms. A variant of the same situation can also be found in the town's other main industry, coal.

The coal industry

Oldham's miners, it will be remembered, did not become actively radical till well after 1842. While they had previously taken regular part in solidarity actions and definitely possessed a well developed trade union consciousness, they had never taken the lead in radical activity. What has to be explained, therefore, is why – at just the time when the cotton workers had been finally knocked out of action – the miners should (for a short period) have done at least something to fill their place.

First, a look at the industry itself. Its local development falls into two fairly distinct periods. Up to the 1830s there was fast expansion. Cotton's mechanization brought steadily increasing demand and despite some competition from Bolton, Oldham was close enough to Manchester to secure a very profitable share in its market. The 1800s saw the Lees and Jones families rapidly snapping up remaining coal rights, heavily investing in deep pits going down over one thousand feet (now made possible by steam pumps and winding gear), and developing a whole network of railroad feeders to the Ashton and Rochdale canals.[151] By the century's second decade the area's mining activity had been largely consolidated into the three interlocking partnerships that were – in one form or other – to survive for the rest of the century.[152] (In 1841 the Jones's cashier told the mines' commissioner that 'Messrs Lees, Jones and Booth form in various combinations several companies working the coal of this district').[153]

The industry's second period was much less prosperous. In the early 1830s railways started flooding the Manchester market with cheap coal from south-west Lancashire and by the end of the decade prices had fallen by as much as 20 per cent.[154] Moreover, to make matters worse, even the still partly protected local market became increasingly uncertain as the cotton industry moved into crisis.[155] Predictably, therefore, the period sees progressively more savage attempts to cut costs. Money wages were forced down from twenty shillings in 1832 to fifteen in 1844, the employment of children increased, and quite lethal economies were made in the manning of winding gear and engines.[156] According to Oldham's pro-radical deputy constable (in evidence to the 1841 mines' commissioners):

> The inducement to employ these children where life and death depend on their momentary attention is merely that their services can be obtained for, perhaps, five or seven shillings a week instead of thirty shillings which the employers would have to pay [an adult engineer] . . . The coroners' juries have always expressed dissatisfaction with the masters' employing children in such service . . . Three or four boys were killed at the Chamber colliery of Messrs Jones three or four years since . . . a deodand of £100 was levied but never recovered . . .[157]

And on children in the pits one working miner claimed that 'poverty makes parents bring them down very soon . . . is certain that parents bring their children earlier into the pit since masters began abating their wages'; another that 'a child of six or seven had better to be transported than sent into a coal pit . . . His own son did not go into the pit till he was thirteen; but his grandchildren went into the pit between six or seven years of age because his son was very poor.'[158]

So, like the cotton spinners, Oldham's miners had immediate experience of capitalist crisis. It was, however, not until some time after the formation of the Miners' Association of Great Britain in 1842-3 that one gets the development of active radicalism and it seems that this body did much the same job in educating the miners as Doherty's national trade union organizations had done for the spinners before 1833.[159]

Up till the early 1840s bargaining perspectives in the industry had been local. Like cotton, it was only the pressure of emerging national competition (and overproduction) which forced the regional miners' associations to come together and work out common policies for the industry as a whole. The same process also went on among the employers but their only solution was a series of largely ineffective disincentives to further investment, the 1842 Mines Act.[160] The remedy worked out by the miners was far more immediate: an absolute restriction of production enforced either jointly by masters and men or, if need be, by the union itself. Where working half-stint had previously been a local expedient for running down coal stocks before a stoppage, it now became – in January 1844 – an attempt by the union to salvage the whole industry (and like the Factory Act campaign demanded a mass education in thoroughly anti-capitalist assumptions). When it failed (or began to look like failing) the political lessons were easily drawn. As W. P. Roberts told the Oldham miners in March 1845 only a national union of *all* workers and a joint fight for political change could really improve the miners' situation.[161]

What one has, therefore, was a sequence of development not dissimilar to that in cotton but running (in Oldham at least) a good decade later. Still during the 1841 coal strike the actions of the local Chartists look very much like those of a group trying to get access: holding sympathy meetings and organizing support from small shopkeepers.[162] By 1843 the district miners' leaders were themselves Chartists – Swallow, Leach, Dixon, Roberts – and the authorities were expressing fears that they would use their position to promote another 1842:

> It would seem [wrote the Oldham magistrate Mills] that the colliers are proceeding in very much upon the same plan that the operatives in the cotton manufactures did in their trades union about ten years since and which ultimately (in the year 1834) became so violent. . . . Then as now there was a most dangerous centre from which rules and regulations emanated . . . so extended a combination becomes more dangerous than one among any other class of workmen from the power which the colliers have over the supplies of coal to the factories. . . .[163]

It was, however, only towards the end of 1844 and in 1845 (after the failure of attempts to enforce an industrial solution) that these leaders were able to win support for the idea of a general union of trades and political action.[164]

Industrial politics in Shields

Finally, if the argument is to be made fully watertight, Shields' *lack* of radicalism still has to be explained on the same terms. Is it possible, therefore, to make industrial factors also explain the failure of the town's labour force (or at least its seamen and shipwrights) to develop beyond the narrowest form of trade union consciousness?

At first glance the answer might seem to be no. There were quite obviously directly *political* factors also at work. Shields was, it seems, one of those areas which responded to the generally abortive – and still hardly analyzed – restabilization attempt of the mid-1820s (associated with the Combination Act repeal and the various liberalizing schemes of Hume, Place and Brougham). The men who took over control of both the seamen and shipwrights in that period – Woodroffe and Rippon – were direct contacts of Place and supporters of his 'non-violent' collaborationist line.[165] Moreover (and this was probably the key factor) the local employers were sufficiently impressed by previous industrial violence to see the advantages to be got from lending support to the new 'moderate' leaders, even if it meant conceding the principal of union organization. This was particularly so in the case of Woodroffe and the Seamen's Loyal Standard Association. By 1832 the new local MP, Ingham, had successfully turned the union into part of the local machinery for distributing Trinity House pensions, and a prominent local shipowner became a trustee.[166] Full political collaboration soon followed. In 1833 there was a joint campaign against empressment, in 1833-4 against seamen's registration, and in 1836 joint action on the shipwreck select committee.[167] The same continued in the 1840s: against free trade, railway competition and Navigation Act repeal. Indeed, even in the 1850s the first major strike, although organized by a new and apparently independent union, was directed not against the employers but the government-sponsored Merchant Marine Act.[168]

However, this 'political' explanation cannot be taken too far. Given the fact that the restabilization effort of the 1820s was fairly general and that only certain areas, like Shields, responded, one is still faced with the question *why*. And at this more basic level industrial structure does seem to supply the answer. Just by themselves patronage and subsidies are highly unlikely to have enabled labour leaders to get away with collaboration. Far more important would seem to be the way collaborationist arguments were – or appeared to be – directly supported by the industry's pattern of development. In cotton (and later coal) the anti-capitalist logic was clear. Even employers found it hard to deny that internal competition was the main problem. But in shipping (as yet hardly touched by technological change) employers could very plausibly claim that the real causes of depression were beyond their control – more the result of the government's anti-protectionist policies and competition from abroad. And the obvious conclusion was that both masters and men should unite to defend their livelihood. So here, in contrast to cotton and coal, one gets labour not developing its own perspective but captured by that of the employers. Nor was this all. It seems clear that employers were well aware of the value of the resulting 'shipping' identity and deliberately manipulated it in the interests of industrial collaboration.

As in Northampton, the actual language of collaboration was generated by the small employers, this time mixing demands for social reform (and distrust of Westminster) with an old-fashioned mercantile imperialism. Its principal exponent was a local ship-broker and pamphleteer, James Mather.[169] In 1832 Mather chaired the election committee of Hume's local nominee, Gowan, and in 1841 played a large part in the election of E. T. Wawn, who went to Westminster pledged to the secret ballot, imperial preference and an aggressive foreign policy.[170] When he stood for election himself in 1852 he became the only Shields' politician to receive active support from organized labour – with the secretary of the seamen's union on his non-electors' committee.[171] His general line of policy can be quickly illustrated by a couple of quotations. The first comes from his 1846 pamphlet against the building of a north-south railway:

> If our position, our nation's integrity, past glory, present and future security . . . will not induce the legislature and the public to arrest the impending evils; if a monstrous, gigantic monopoly is permitted to iron-band the land . . . if Britain be determined to dispense with the services of her navy, she should immediately *continentalize* herself . . . she should at once organize her militia . . . keep up a standing army . . .[172]

The second is part of an appeal made in 1849 against the final ending of the Navigation Acts:

> Let every master, mate and seaman as well as every naval artizan in every port in Britain do their last act of duty – petition . . . to preserve his employment from foreigners and his country from destruction.[173]

Most revealing of all, however, are the speeches at a dinner given in Mather's honour by Tyneside shipowners – both Whig and Tory – in March 1848. Though the dinner was in general recognition of his services to the industry, its immediate pretext was a protest march of several hundred seamen which he had led in

London against the Navigation Act repeal. The chairman, a local magistrate and large shipowner, began by contrasting the troubled politics of France with domestic peace in England and then went on:

> He now came to the demonstration made in London by the sea-men – a demonstration arising from their own spontaneous feeling of the necessity of doing something for themselves, seeing that all the shipowners had attempted was without effect. . . . The demonstration made by the seamen the other day was the most remarkable thing which had recently occurred; and it was gratifying to think that it was under the able and prudent management of their honourable friend. . . . He believed there was never the spectacle of a more peaceful or orderly pro-cession . . . .[174]

And, with that, the difficulties faced by Shields' working-class radicals – in a town where over three-quarters of the male labour force was similarly employed – should require no further elaboration.

Finally, to sum up. The point of comparing the three towns was to get some bearing on the nature of Oldham's militancy. What then are the conclusions? Can we really say it amounted to class consciousness? Certainly, those explanations taking the opposite line have little to recommend them. And looking at Oldham itself there does seem to exist – at any rate to a greater degree than in Northampton or Shields – the necessary conditions for class form-ation: a vanguard group leading mass struggle and able to use that position to argue for a wider struggle against the system itself.

However, what stands out most clearly of all is the perhaps surprising importance of language: of the forms in which the arguments were carried on. At every stage the social perspectives inherited from everyday industrial experience seem to have played a key role. It was the sectional shipping identity that made things so difficult in Shields. It was the Factory Act experience that at any rate helped them in Oldham. And – of all the evidence – it is perhaps this which provides the most convincing proof that it is class consciousness we are dealing with.

While mass movements often have radical leaderships, few become socially radical themselves. The reasons are obvious. Struggles on purely immediate issues demand no direct challenge to existing sectional identities (and indeed usually develop in their material defence). On the other hand, for a movement to become radical, for dialectically new (and socially incompatible) ideas to be injected into it, those sectional identities have – however imperceptibly – to be broken down. It is in this crucial – and usually unsuccessful – process that language becomes so important. As Porshnev observes, it is language – the particular social codes which determine what information is (or is not) acceptable – which forms the key-stone of any culture.[175] Cause that to disintegrate and so will the larger culture. If, therefore, radicals are able to enter a group and express certain immediate aspirations in terms which (though themselves acceptable) ultimately become incompatible with the system itself, the overall fight for a wider consciousness will be that much easier.

This is why the developments in cotton and coal are so significant. The fact that in both some such bridging process does seem to have been present – and indeed to have been the *precondition* for the development of political militancy – indicates that it did indeed involve a fairly profound process of mass cultural change.

To say this is not, of course, to claim that language was the determining factor – only that it was the one which enables us to see the process going on. What *caused* it was rather the logic of capitalist development *as expressed* in particular industries. Had cotton not followed for so long the classic sequence of industrial capitalist crisis there could plainly have been neither the period of preparation nor the move to full political involvement. Had Shields' industry been technologically further developed the perspective there would have been much less unfavourable. And if it is class consciousness we are dealing with, all this is as it should be. Only when capitalism itself reveals its full contradictions will people begin to understand why and how it is to be overthrown – a point which Marx himself makes in the quotation that heads the following chapter.

5 Class struggle and social structure

'The question is not what this or that proletarian, or even the whole of the proletariat, at the moment considers as its aim. The question is what the proletariat is, and what, consequent upon that being, it will be compelled to do' (Marx, writing in 1844).[1]

Solidarity and fragmentation: some measurements

The previous chapter ought to have made it clear that some sort of move from trade union to class consciousness did take place in Oldham during the 1830s and early 1840s. It should also have indicated the importance of industrial factors in this process – a finding that would support the argument that the main *previous* social trend (during the period of coercive trade union solidarity) had been the formation – or at least strengthening – of industrially based occupational cultures. If this was so, and if a radical erosion and replacement of these cultures then took place, at least something of it ought to show up in terms of social structure. Compared with Shields (still in the stage of trade union consciousness) and the even less advanced Northampton, one would expect Oldham to reveal a markedly greater degree of social closeness between working people of different occupational backgrounds. Indeed, the mere growth of mass class consciousness ought to have brought with it a corresponding repudiation of any system of occupational hierarchy based on bourgeois values. What follows is an attempt to see whether this was in fact so.

Figures 18 and 19 show the principal measures that have been used: tests of how far working families with different occupational backgrounds (and particularly craftsmen and labourers) inter-married and lived next door to each other.[2] Obviously, marriage is a much more reliable test than housing because where people live also depends on what they can afford and its distance from where they work. Obviously, too, in making comparisons between towns, it is necessary to take into account the income differentials in each. If, for instance, the average incomes of skilled and labourer families are much closer in Oldham than Shields, they would – as a result of this alone – be more likely to live next door

(a) POVERTY (1849) 3
overlap of experience – distance (in pence) of the central cluster of craft and labour families from the poverty line

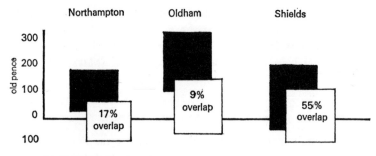

(b) HOUSING 4
likelihood of a labourer family living next door to a craft family. 100 per cent=number of expected housing relations, given relative sizes of the groups in the population

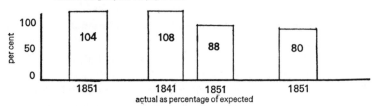

(c) MARRIAGE (1846-56) 5
likelihood of a labourer family intermarrying with a craft family. 100 per cent=number of expected marriages, given relative sizes of the groups in the population

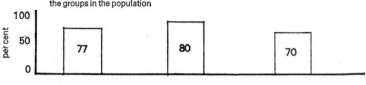

Figure 18 Social distance between craftsmen and labourers

to each other, possess similar ways of life and consequently inter-marry. So, to allow for this figure 18(a) gives the degree of income overlap between craft and labourer families in relation to the poverty line (calculated in the same way as the figures in the previous chapter). Taking this into account, the results are quite surprising. They show that it was Shields – the town that comes out as having the greatest income overlap – that also had least intermarriage or neighbouring, and conversely Oldham with the least overlap that had the most intermarriage. To this extent, the evidence supplies fairly striking confirmation for the overall argument.

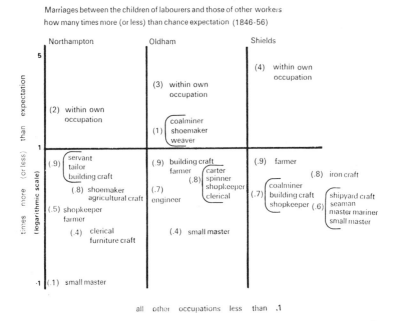

Marriages between the children of labourers and those of other workers
how many times more (or less) than chance expectation (1846-56)

Figure 19   Social distance within the labour force: three towns[6]

Plainly, the figures are not completely foolproof. Because of the deficiency of early marriage registration, they refer to a period considerably later than one would like: 1846-56 instead of the late 1830s and early 1840s. They are also mostly calculated from far too small a base (unfortunately even using the entire mass of several thousand marriages taking place in this period, the statistical likelihood of any two particular occupations intermarrying turns out to be quite small). Worst of all, the figures do not reveal trend. They show the position at the end of the 1840s, but not how it developed. As a result they cannot rule out the possibility (admittedly a small one) that the exceptional social cohesion of Oldham's working population was a cause – not a consequence – of radical political consciousness.

Nonetheless, whatever the qualifications (and there are a number of others), there can be no doubt that the figures as a whole are mutually consistent and fit in with the purely descriptive evidence. Shields, for instance, did have quite pronounced occupational cultures. The secretary of its improvement commission found it possible to list occupations by precise neighbourhoods when replying to the health of towns commission in 1842:

> The inhabitants may be classed and distributed as follows. First, the pilots living in parts of districts six and fourteen (The Lawe). Second, the sailors chiefly confined to the streets bordering the river. Third, the glassmakers. Fourth, the labourers in the alkali works. Fifth, the pitmen (Templetown). Sixth, the tradesmen and shopkeepers in the principal streets.[7]

And looking at the 'nationality' aspect of labour fragmentation (figure 21) one finds Shields' Irish families (mainly alkali workers) considerably more segregated in 1851 than Oldham's comparably sized Irish population in 1841 – when men of Irish origin (like John Doherty) occupied leading positions in the south Lancashire labour movement.

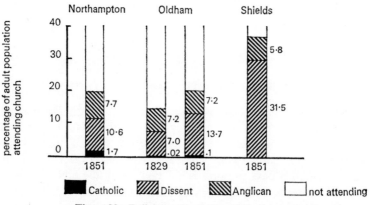

Figure 20 Religious attendance, 1851: three towns[8]

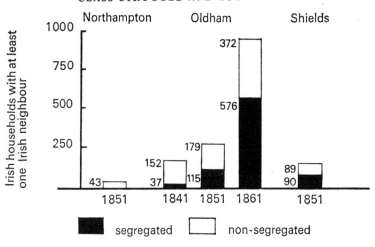

Figure 21 Segregation of the Irish population: three towns[9]

Moreover, if Shields' social structure was a reflection of trade union consciousness, the results for Northampton fit in with what one would expect from a population still under direct bourgeois influence. Simple occupation was clearly less important as a basis for culture. Indeed in 1851 (though not 1841) one finds more craft-labourer neighbouring than in Oldham. Far more decisive were divisions which transcended occupation and expressed themselves in terms of social behaviour and consumption: how far a family was (or was not) 'respectable and hard working' in the eyes of its immediate local task masters. It was such divisions that largely dominated the villages from which Northampton's population mostly came, and in the town itself one can definitely find such differences cutting across occupation. This was particularly so among the shoemakers. A good proportion were definitely not 'respectable'. According to a *Morning Chronicle* journalist in 1851 their 'principal source of amusement . . . appears to be the "Free and Easy" ',[10] and some years later another writing in *Good Words* noted a prevalence of drink and demoralization:

> In the lowest parts of London I have never heard such *general* superfluity of obscene naughtiness issuing from youthful lips as I heard during my stay in Northampton. After nightfall on week days the . . . Market Square is disgraced by scenes of juvenile depravity quite as shameless as those which may be witnessed . . . on Sunday evenings in Upper Street, Islington.[11]

Yet, against this, one finds among Northampton shoemakers a bigger segment of 'respectable' chapel families than among any group of workers in the other two towns. Table 4 gives places of marriage by occupation.

Table 4   Place of marriage by occupation of parents, 1846-56[12]

Northampton % marrying in	Anglican church per cent	Nonconformist chapel per cent	Registry Office per cent
professional	95	5	0
tradesman	71	29	0
small employer	59	35	6
shopkeeper	69	16	15
farmer	79	13	8
metal craft	84	4	12
furniture craft	80	10	10
building craft	71	12	17
shoemaker	57	11	32
servant	72	6	22
labourer	65	12	23

Oldham	church per cent	chapel per cent	Shields	church per cent	chapel per cent
large employer	80	20	large employer	89	11
tradesman	91	9	tradesman	86	14
small employer	95	5	small employer	89	11
shop	94	6	shop	90	10
farm	97	3	farm	94	6
supervisory	92	8	master mariner	83	17
metal craft	98	2	shipyard craft	94	6
building craft	98	2	building craft	96	4
spinner	96	4	seaman	96	4
weaver	98	2	coalminer	97	3
hatter	98	2	labourer	96	4
labourer	98	2			

The figures for church marriages are not strictly comparable. In Shields and Oldham it was the administrative custom for all but Nonconformist marriages to take place in church while in North-ampton Registry Office marriages were already common. But looking at Nonconformist marriages alone (and in Northampton itself at the spread between all three types) it seems clear that there were radically different social allegiances *within* individual occupations. And, as the last chapter showed, it was in Northampton also that a significant portion of the labour force still remained under the fairly direct cultural control of their employers.

Working-class leadership

By and large, therefore, the social structure of the three towns does seem to reflect their differing levels of political consciousness. What remains to be examined – at least for Oldham – is the process of interaction itself. If in the course of the 1830s a labour consciousness was heightened into class consciousness, if occupational consciousness was indeed transcended, the actual people who achieved all this still remain unidentified. To really prove our point, what still has to be established is the existence of some sort of real-life struggle between old and new types of labour leaders.

This poses a good number of problems. Some simply concern evidence. In themselves the sources are rich. Home Office and legal records, diaries and newspapers make it possible to name not just dozens but hundreds of people active in Oldham working-class politics between 1830 and 1850 – certainly quite enough to destroy any notion that the town's working-class activity was just spontaneous mob violence. What we lack is *complete* information. Only a small part of any individual's total activity is recorded and probably up to half of those active slip through the net altogether. Of the twenty-one people arrested on conspiracy and sedition charges in 1842 (and who unlike those held for riot might be expected to have been active previously), only ten are recorded as having been so. This means that any attempt to build up coherent groupings of working-class leaders by matching particular campaigns and slogans – as in table 8b at the end of the chapter – can really only be used as a rough backing for more impressionistic findings.

The other main problem is that posed by the facts themselves. At any rate at first glance, the existing material does not indicate any decisive change in leadership during the early 1830s. Indeed, almost the reverse. Comparing the lists of leaders for these years with those before 1830 (mainly from 1815-20) two things are immediately apparent. The key men remained roughly the same throughout: Knight, Fitton, Haigh, Mills, Swire. And at least in occupational terms the composition of the leadership becomes less (not more) proletarian as one moves on in time. It is only after 1830 that one gets the appearance of significant numbers of shopkeepers, publicans and small employers.

Table 5   Occupations of main working-class leaders[13]

	1795–1830	1830–50
magnate	1	1
small employer	0	5
small master	2	2
shopkeeper, publican	0	9
beerhouse, cookshop	1	3
schoolmaster	1	2
'doctor'	3	2
building craft	1	2
metal craft	1	1
other craft	0	3
factory skilled	0	2
spinner	1	9
factory semi-skilled	0	1
weaver	10	0
hatter	3	1
tailor, shoemaker	0	4
labourer	1	3
not known	8	10
	33	60

Partly, the explanation is simply a matter of definition. The figures we have refer solely to those who were *politically* active – not to industrial militants as such. So if there is continuity, it is that of the Jacobin hard core (the only group likely to have been politically involved in the semi-legal conditions of the early decades). But, even granting this, there still remains the problem of non-proletarian elements – shopkeepers and publicans especially – joining after 1830. One can see why they did not do so before. As men occupying a relatively public and exposed position (and until recently playing a key role in the old system of social control), they had every reason to lie low during periods of popular disturbance. Certainly, their absence is conspicuous in 1816 and 1819. But why did they come forward after 1830?

It is, in fact, this apparent contradiction that supplies the best clue to the precise nature of the changes then taking place. The situation was not so much that of radicals taking over any existing movement, but rather of drawing under their control a whole number of previously fragmented parts of the working population. This is why the changed position of the shopkeepers is so significant. Previously, their ability to keep out of politics at least partly reflected the survival of a narrow 'non-political' labour consciousness which as publicans and shopkeepers they had good reason (and opportunity) to sustain. Now, in the new situation, the sheer momentum of radical politics (particularly exclusive dealing and the control of local government) forced them to become part of the larger movement, and to do so, what is more, on terms largely dictated by the working-class radicals. If, therefore, one wants evidence for a decisive change in labour's leadership (and by inference for the erosion of the social bases which previously sustained 'non-political' leaderships), it will best be found by examining the nature of this new political unity.

Insofar as the evidence allows, three distinct social groupings can be distinguished within it: the continuing group of working-class radicals, the shopkeepers and publicans, and a number of small employers. On the committee of the 1831 Political Union their members were represented in the ratio of five, three and two, and this seems a fair weighting of their respective influence.[14]

The shopkeepers make their appearance during the later phases of the 1830-2 reform campaign (they played no part in the original attempt to establish a political union in June 1830 nor in the French revolution celebrations of August that year).[15] At times they attempted to maintain an independent course. They framed their demands in terms of the reform of a corrupt establishment (rather than class representation) and at the biggest of the mass meetings in October 1831 their acknowledged leader, Alexander Taylor, successfully intervened on the side of the employers, blocking a motion from Knight and Fitton in favour of annual Parliaments and the ballot.[16] Only during the election campaign which followed did they finally become integrated into the radical alliance. It was during these crucial months (July to December 1832) the working-class radicals at last found themselves in a position to focus, on this small but socially key group of two to three hundred people, the full force of popular opinion. It was, they argued, not just Oldham's representation that depended on shopkeepers' votes but the whole larger fate of what was then the central concern of all working people in Oldham: the new Factory Act.

It is indisputable [continues one of the Political Union manifestos already quoted in chapter 2] that the shopkeepers hold the power to separate their interests from the people, for if they vote for the return of Bright and Burge, who will not promise to reform one single abuse in the state, they identify themselves with that system by which you are injured, destroying at once that reciprocity of interest which should exist between you . . . and it is evident that your interest in their welfare is absolutely annihilated. . . .[17]

Under such pressures Oldham's shopkeepers finally capitulated. How far such enforced solidarity also developed a genuine commitment of its own remains unclear. Certainly, the shopkeepers were (in marriage terms) socially very close to the working population, as well as being uniquely well placed to understand the *generality* of economic distress. During the 1836-7 lock-out they demanded that the spinners be relieved out of the rates (and not by private subscription): 'The more they considered the causes of the affair the more evident would appear the obduracy of the employers. What advantage could there be in a subscription when every retail dealer and shopkeeper had been subscribing week after week to assist the sufferers, while the masters passed resolutions weekly to bring the men to compliance by starvation'.[18]

Yet against this has to be set the fact that the men who emerged as spokesmen (and mediators for a perhaps still less radical shopkeeper body) were not, in the last resort, reliable. Though Alexander Taylor, Knott, Stump and Stepney all spoke in favour of universal suffrage and the Charter, the campaigns with which they were particularly associated tended to be more aligned to the redevelopment of a limited labour consciousness: organizing aid to strikers and opposition to the new poor law and police (table 6). Moreover, whenever things came to the crunch – as in August 1842 – it was Taylor and his colleagues who appeared with the compromise solution and eventually in the later 1840s (when the force of working-class mobilization started to disintegrate) played a key role in forming a new alliance with the employers.[19]

The characteristic ambiguity of the group can best be summed up by a brief description of Taylor himself. Taylor (1800-53) began his life as a powerloom weaver and then sometime in the late 1820s set up as a retail flour dealer. Between 1830 and 1850 there was almost no public meeting at which he did not speak and by

Table 6 Oldham working-class leaders: shopkeepers and publicans[20]

Activity		Campaigns and Slogans	
active before 1830	0	1832 – reform	2
reform campaign	5	1832 – class	0
short time 1831-3	6	1842 strike	0
Regeneration Society	0	1842 compromise	2
Charter 1838-41	4	Owenite Socialism	0
active 1842	0	1840s factory campaign	2
arrest 1842	1	Anti-poor law	5
Holladay support 1847	2	Anti-police	4
Cobbet support 1847	2	Strike support	6
active 1848	0	Ireland protest	0

Total number for which *any* information: 16

the mid-1840s he had established a personal dominance over the popularly controlled parts of local government. At his death he was assessed on £5,000 personalty, giving some weight to the charges that he made a good thing out of exclusive dealing and the workhouse (which he ran till 1847).[21] His great strength lay in his ability to manipulate local government: he could intimidate the vestry and stage-manage crowds. He also understood the essentials of extra-legal unionism. From 1840 till 1847 Taylor led the fight against the new government-controlled rural police.[22] He moved the 1843 police commission motion against the use of the Town Hall as barracks; opposed the swearing of constables during the 1847 election.[23] In the poor law campaign his job was to produce crowd effects for Fielden's parliamentary campaign. This was how Fielden wrote to Taylor in November 1845: 'I have drawn up a few reasons in the shape of resolutions which you may either adopt or reject at your meeting tomorrow evening. You may in your speeches say much more severe things . . . but so far as resolutions go I think an appeal to reason is more likely to stay their proceedings'.[24] Fielden to Taylor, February 1846: 'If the overseers are [firm], why not re-elect them? If not, get others who will be firm to succeed them'.[25] Taylor could see to this without much difficulty. And to give an idea of his mob appeal (as well as his anti-establishment – rather than anti-capitalist – rhetoric), here he is haranguing a mass meeting held to protest against the coronation in 1838:

It was a most gratifying and delightful spectacle to behold such

an immense mass of human being met together, not like the
lords and the squires and the gentry and the rest of the small
fry that followed close upon their heels for the purpose of
filling their bellies with luxuries they could not, would not and
did not earn; and of exhibiting their embroidered coats and
lace hats which had to be paid for by the labouring millions;
they were not met for the purpose of exhibiting a loyalty they
did not feel like hundred of the nobility and gentry were doing
at that moment; and expressing an attachment to the queen
which was only inspired by their love of pensions and places
which had to be paid for out of the sweat and toil of an
industrious, insulted and plundered people. . . .[26]

But Taylor was also the man who gave Oldham radicalism its
formal death blow by concluding an electoral alliance with the
Tories in 1852.

Like the shopkeepers, the other main subordinate social grouping, the small employers, were only drawn into the alliance during
the final phases of the 1832 election campaign. Though somewhat
less vulnerable than the shopkeepers, they occupied (as will be
seen in the next chapter) an economically marginal position in
the town's economy and had certain common interests with
organized labour, particularly the statutory enforcement of short-
time. A considerable number were also engaged in wholesale
trading and so potentially exposed to popular pressure.[27] The
men responsible for handling their political affairs (it would
probably be putting it too strongly to call them leaders of the
small employers as a *body*) were largely dissenters – Holladay,
William Halliwell, Quarmby – and their politics markedly anti-
clerical and anti-establishment. (Indeed, the one occasion when
they broke ranks was when they put up O'Connor as a counter-
candidate to Morgan Cobbett in 1835 in a protest against his
record on disestablishment).[28] However, their most interesting
characteristic was their fairly sudden espousal of Owenite Social-
ism (table 8b shows four employers involved). This – at least in a
gutted 'union of industry' form – seems to have provided an
ideological let-out for the somewhat forced alliance in which they
found themselves. In the mid-1830s the group's principal spokesman, James Holladay, supplied much of the energy for setting up
Oldham's Socialist Society, and in 1838 acted as host to Owen
during his visit to Oldham.[29] Later on (after the collapse of mass

working-class pressure) it was also under the pseudo-Owenite slogan of a 'union of the industrious classes' that Holladay finally broke with the working-class radicals and attempted to stand as parliamentary candidate against Morgan Cobbett.

Looking at both these groupings, therefore, it does seem to have been the early 1830s that saw them largely abandoning any independent line of their own and being forced (for a time) into a one-sided alliance with the working-class radicals. To this extent one can legitimately claim the period as one of acute struggle between old and new forms of leadership: between an old structure that (in various ways) fragmented the working population and a new one whose strength derived from uniting it. All that now remains is to have a closer look at the working-class radicals themselves.

Table 7   Oldham working-class leaders active in 1832, 1842 and 1848[30]

Occupations		Activity		Campaigns and slogans	
large employer	1	pre-1830	11	Owenite Socialism	4
small employer	0	industrial	11	factory movement 1840s	3
small master	2	short-time 1831	7	anti-poor law	4
shop-pub	3	Regeneration	7	anti-police	6
beerhouse	4	Charter 1838–41	17	strike support	5
schoolmaster	4	active 1842	22	Ireland protest	10
'doctor'	1	arrest 1842	11		
building craft	3	Holladay 1847	4		
metal craft	1	Cobbett 1847	2		
other craft	5	active 1848	16		
factory skilled	3				
spinner	9				
factory semi	3	Total number on which any information: 57			
handweaver	1				
hatter	1				
shoe/tailor	4				
labourer	3				
not known	9				

Table 7 gives the occupations and campaign associations of those involved – from a radical standpoint – in three of the main struggles between 1830 and 1850. This time there can be no question about their proletarian composition. The great bulk were manual workers and even those listed as shopkeepers and beer-housekeepers were often (like John Haigh, Len Haslop and James Greaves) victimized industrial militants. The biggest single group are the spinners, the occupation which had now replaced weaving as the focus of industrial struggle. Moreover, it is also noteworthy that in contrast to the shopkeepers the most common campaign associations tend to be on larger national issues: not so much poor law, police or strike support (although quite a number were also active industrially) as the question of state power itself and – also significantly – Ireland.

However, the group's essential feature – its cohesion – does not show up in the figures at all. Though there were always tactical disagreements and a constant stream of new recruits, what strikes one most from the descriptive evidence is the degree to which members saw themselves as part of a continuing tradition. Radical allegiances tended to be inherited within families and associated with particular neighbourhoods. The Swires, Earnshaws and Warwicks were all families that produced at least two generations of radicals. And of neighbourhoods the best example is perhaps the 'Jacobin village' of Royton. In 1807 Chippendale noted that it was Royton which supplied almost all the audience and speakers at a peace meeting: 'Partington . . . a determined Jacobin . . . read the resolutions . . . he was attended by several of that family of Taylors whom I have often mentioned to you under the name of O'Calebs and others of the same kidney . . . particularly the schoolmaster Winterbottom'.[31] Again in 1812 he described Royton as 'a place in which every inhabitant (with the exception of five or six) are the most determined revolutionary Jacobins'.[32] And in 1818 Colonel Fletcher wrote to the home secretary: 'During the course of my correspondence I have more than once had occasion to notice the hostility of this village towards his majesty's government. Fitton . . . is an atheist, and so also is Kay, and probably most of the others. . . . The reformers decry religion under the name of bigotry and superstition and vow its utter destruction. . . .'[33] An effective summing up can be found in a speech by Fielden (himself an old Jacobin) at the celebration dinner following the 1832 election:

I know many persons in this borough who have been persecuted – persecuted, hunted down like wild beasts . . . . When I look at the company by which I am now surrounded, when I take a retrospective view of what they have done and suffered; when I consider the violence with which they have been abused, calumnated and persecuted; and when I consider the occasion we are now celebrating, it gives me a full conviction, if anything were wanted to give me that conviction, that the cause for which you have suffered is the cause of truth . . . .[34]

But if this community of experience and tradition was important, just as critical was the not unrelated ability to change and develop. It is this that provides Oldham's radicals with their strongest claim to be a genuine vanguard group. Because the main component of the tradition *was* radical opposition to the system itself, so one finds the members of the group stepping in to express each successive mass issue in terms of the overall political struggle. This is what brought the radicals into the leadership of the industrial struggles of 1794-1801. It was this which placed them in the forefront of the factory movement in the 1820s. And consequently one also finds their political analysis moving in step with (and expressing) the system's own emerging contradictions, as reflected in the changing nature of mass struggle. This is perhaps strikingly demonstrated by the career of John Knight.

Knight, born in 1763, was originally a small manufacturer in the hills behind Saddleworth.[35] Politically, he first appears as a 'determined Jacobin', imprisoned for two years following the 1794 clash at Royton. In 1801 he was on the county executive of the United Englishmen and in 1812 again arrested as one of the suspected organizers of the guerilla campaign.[36] After the war he was editor in turn of the *Manchester Political Register* (1816) and the *Manchester Spectator* (1818).[37] On both occasions the government suspended *habeas corpus* (1817 and 1819). Knight was one of the people they took care to put inside (on the Home Office index of suspected persons he is marked as 'violent' and 'one of the thirty-eight tried in 1812').[38] After some years away from Oldham in the early 1820s (in Burnley it seems) he reappears in 1827 and in 1831 he became secretary of the Political Union.[39] At the same time he also played an important part in the Spinners Union (and was accused in 1834 of being its secretary).[40] In 1836 he saw to it that the Oldham Political Union adopted the principles of O'Connor's London and Marylebone Radical Association. Five months before his death in 1838 he was appointed salaried treasurer of the town poor relief fund.[41]

Knight's greatest contribution, however, was his ability to keep thinking. For fifty years he went on trying to make political sense of what was happening. He started as a Tom Paine Jacobin. By the 1810s he had merged the struggle for political freedom with the larger struggle of labour against property.[42] When he saw the effect of machine production in the late 1820s and early 1830s – how wages fell as output rose – he worked out (or at least propagated) a primitive labour theory of value. And in the years immediately before his death, after watching the failure of one working-class movement after another, he was arguing that political activity would only be successful if it was by labour 'as a whole' – and if it was action for complete power. For the moment it will be enough to quote part of a speech he made, beside Alexander Taylor at the anti-coronation meeting, two months before his death. It is quite different from Taylor's and shows, if anything does, the way he thought and the close responsiveness of his leadership :

the ministers had settled upon the Queen an income of more than £1,000 a day while hundreds on thousands of her subjects were starving on 2½d, 1¾d and 1d per day. Something had been said about six shillings per day; he would like to see how many people there were before him who were earning six shillings per day. What, no one? . . . Well, how many of you get four shillings then? What, only five or six hands up yet? How many of you get three shillings and six pence? Oh, you can show a few now. [About twenty or thirty were held up for three shillings.] How many of you can obtain only two shillings per day? Ah, you put them up by hundreds now. But how many of you cannot obtain more than one shilling per day by reason of want of work and low wages put together? Ah, you hold them up in larger numbers than I expected you to.[43]

Mass action

We now reach the more or less final question. How far did this *ideological* development also express itself in mass activity? So far we have looked at the way the radicals won support in industry, at changes in social structure and labour leadership. What we have not yet tackled is the far more difficult problem of pinpointing the difference between revolutionary mass action in the 1830s and 1840s and the apparently just as revolutionary action of the 1810s. If we can answer this, we should be well on the way to getting some estimate of its overall social significance. Certainly, it is impossible to deny the very real degree of continuity. This shows up in both the popular response to crisis and in the tactics and strategy of the leadership.

On popular reactions in the later period we have already quoted descriptions from 1834 and 1842. But it would be just as difficult to make much immediate distinction between 'the near prospect was that of the monarch dethroned and all her followers . . . in headlong flight to escape the vengeance of an oppressed and vindictive people. This is no fancy sketch; it is a fair picture of the wandering day-dreams of the whole body of what were called the working classes forty years ago' (which is an ex-cotton worker remembering 1848) and Chippendale's contemporary description of Oldham during the earlier crises.[44] *April 1818:* 'A strange ferment was excited in the speeches and its effect spread through the country like wildfire . . . the strongest conviction exists that the grand struggle is approaching . . . an evident change in their habits in consequence . . . their minds are quite in an unsettled state and they are evidently engrossed in the contemplation of the great day. . . .'[45] *January 1819:* 'The delusion that prevails in this part of the country is lamentable. It is impossible to form any conception of it but by supposing an immense majority of both sexes throughout the working class to be the complete dupes of the indendiaries. . . .'[46] *July 1819:* 'The minds of the lower orders in these parts are exclusively occupied with political discussions and the expectation of an approaching explosion which is to produce a complete change in the present order of things'.[47] And if one wants evidence for the disintegration of 'value systems' and deference, here is Chippendale describing a mass meeting of two thousand Oldham workers in 1817. A journeyman mechanic had got hold of a loyalty declaration by the 'principle inhabitants'. He read the names over 'one by one with a considerable pause betwixt each of them. . . . This pause was filled up with some sort of indecent remark accompanied by a characteristic gesticulation . . . all the most respectable people for character and property in the town were made the subject of popular derision'.[48]

So, if (after Lenin) one describes these brief moments of revolutionary release as 'festivals of the oppressed', the earlier periods qualify just as fully as those that came later. And, turning to leadership, one again finds a continuity that goes beyond a mere overlap of personnel. By and large, the problems (and solutions) also stayed the same. It is important to remember that even in the 1810s one is dealing with men who *already* had great experience in handling proletarian mass movements. Another quotation from Chippendale makes this point very well. It relates to the very beginning of the postwar crises in September 1816:

> The work of disaffection is going on very rapidly in this neighbourhood, and the activity and industry of the malcontents is beyond conception. By their exertions meetings are established in every part of the country. There is not a village or hamlet or fold of houses anywhere but has its periodical meeting and committee. There is invariably one or more of the Royton agitators at these meetings. The activity of these people is to me most astonishing . . . . [Chippendale then goes on to give an account he had from an agent of one of these meetings at Miles Platting. The chairman introduced the meeting and then] inquired if there were any Royton people present. He was answered in the affirmative by three or four persons who stood together in the crowd. He requested some one of them to address the meeting and called upon Kay in particular. But Kay and the others declined saying it was more proper for some immediate neighbour to speak first. [There were then other speakers till one man made a 'violent' speech.] 'It is idle', said he, 'to expect anything from so vile and corrupt a source as the British House of Commons – let them proceed by force at once . . . we have only to unite and be firm. . . .' At this period he was interrupted by the Roytonians . . . . The Roytonians succeeded in silencing him . . . and he appeared to acquiesce. One of the Royton men, Fitton, then made a speech marked by great moderation. He said if they proceeded in the way recommended by the speaker who preceded him they would get stopped by the authorities at once. He concluded by recommending the formation of a committee. . . . [A committee was then appointed, future meetings fixed and the meeting ended.] The Royton people then returned towards home, and my informant mixed with them upon the road . . . in course of conversation upon the way they freely commented upon the speech of the violent man . . . they perfectly coincided with him in sentiment but the present was not the time for such opinions to be broached. They must wait a little longer.[49]

And this, of course, remained the dilemma throughout. However long they waited, whatever the period of mass mobilization, the confrontation ultimately had to come. As the radicals knew only too well, state power would not be conceded until the disenfranchised possessed (and were ready to use) an effective preponderance of outright force. So, although there were certainly changes in strategy, they tended to be variations on the same, basically insurrectionist, theme. Naturally, such strategy was evolved at a regional and national level, and this is not the place to go into it in detail. But because it was at the heart of so much radical activity, it is important to note its basic continuity.

1812, for instance, came immediately after the successful use of guerilla tactics in Spain and looked back to the failure of the London-based coups of 1802-3. It seems to have envisaged the use of industrial violence for mass mobilization in much the same way as peasant violence had been used in Ireland in 1798 (when, of course, many of the Lancashire leaders had been active in the United Englishmen). 1816-7 combined local insurrections with an attempt to overcome the weakness in London by marching south a mass of northern industrial workers. After the failure of this, 1818 saw a return to industrially based activity culminating in a general strike (during which one local spy reported that 'the main actors of 1812 have been heard to say that their projects have again been botched – and they fear that the different trades cannot be *roused* to the assertion of the people's rights . . .').[50] 1819 moved from a fairly sophisticated (and nationally concerted) plan of mass mobilization – in which the government was successfully cast as the initiator of violence – to an old-style insurrection in April 1820. 1830-2 saw a return to the 1819 mobilization plans (with Hunt again leading the action) while 1834 attempted to harness the rising momentum of extra-legal unionism to a more syndicalist challenge to state power. The various fiascos of 1839 are well known (and the north-west was probably wise to keep clear of them). But 1842 was largely a north-west affair and incorporated the experience of three decades in an attempt that came nearer to success than any other. After a month of confused hostilities the home secretary was still worried: 'We have had a very dangerous struggle, a sort of servile war, which is checked, but by no means overcome'.[51] The strategy involved the use of masses of armed, highly organized but ambivalently peaceful strikers to engulf and isolate troops – whose loyalty was uncertain.

This was tried again in May-June 1848. After its failure, August 1848 saw an almost straight repeat of the insurrectionist plans of 1817 and 1820: surprise midnight attacks in the big cities (with the Oldham contingent once more marching off to join others in Manchester).

Nor should it be forgotten that these radical strategies were put into effect and that some time or other during most crises badly armed men clashed with regular troops. It does less than justice to those involved not to take this as seriously as it was at the time. With the treason laws being what they were, detailed evidence is inevitably sparse. But enough survives to indicate that most mass actions were carefully and responsibly led. The drilling of 1819 was professionally organized by recently demobbed soldiers:

> This morning the number assembled on Tandle Hill was not less than two thousand. The order and regularity that prevailed among them astonished my informant as much as the progress they have made in discipline. The rifle company was very conspicuous as usual. The pivot men were discharged riflemen in uniform. While they stood in close column one of the buglers sounded the call. About twenty-eight drill instructors turned out and five adjutants were chosen out of them.

(General Byng's comment: 'It is an evil if not put down soon will grow to such an extent as to be eminently dangerous'; the Peterloo massacre came six days later.)[52] The mobs of 1842 at first seemed harmless, until it was discovered that they controlled Manchester.

> Applications have been received [wrote Colonel Warre requesting immediate reinforcements from London] from Oldham, Ashton, Staleybridge and Stockport soliciting the aid and protection of troops, which I am utterly unable to afford them, as I have but a very inadequate force in this town [Manchester] under the altered state of things from the organization among the working classes . . . I did not expect that a general turnout would take place . . . and that they should venture to march in bodies into Manchester notwithstanding the police and the garrison.[53]

General Arbuthnot later conducted an enquiry into the composition of these mobs and reported them highly organized and directed from meetings which his agents found 'impenetrable'.[54] Even a wild Oldham plugging riot of May 1848 turns out to be more than it seems. Mark Benson, an Irish labourer, was captured. From the evidence against him it appears at first that he was no more than a chance victim. One policeman: 'I went along with them [the crowd] . . . . I saw the prisoner . . . he had with him a long willow stick the upper part painted green with a small green ribbon at the top.' Another policeman saw Benson with his stick in the crowd that plugged Clegg's mill 'nearly in the front and there might be a thousand persons'. The manager of Greaves' saw 'Benson with his stick' in the mob which forced the mill gates. Another witness saw Benson in the crowd as it poured through Waterhead plugging one mill after another. But, then, as the crowd started back towards Oldham, the report makes clear that this was something more than random violence and Benson something more than a victim. 'They were off, and Benson had got five or six yards down the street when a man ran after him and said, "Come back, the other boiler is not off yet." Benson said, "We must have it off." He returned and said, "Come on, lads. We must have this other boiler plugged".' Another man then reported the arrival of police. Benson: 'We must stone the buggers off as we did the two at Tommeyfield. We must have it off.' That afternoon was fixed for a march on Manchester (along 1842 lines); every man had to be on the streets and every mill stopped. Four years before Benson had been imprisoned for taking part in an attack on the new (government-controlled) county police.[55]

After all this, therefore, the case for continuity would seem unchallengable. Whether in the tactics and strategy of the leadership or in the experience of crisis itself, the basic form of each successive bid remained much the same. It is against this background that we now have to pick out the differences.

Probably the best place to start is not so much the crises themselves as the periods between them. One would, in fact, expect the crises to be roughly the same. These were the moments when the whole objective basis of the social system seemed to be visibly breaking up and all that the radicals had to do was to point to current events themselves. John Haigh, April 1818: 'National bankruptcy was certainly at hand. He enjoined the people to persevere a short time longer and their deliverance would be obtained. Indeed, he said, it is already accomplished for nothing can prevent the arrival of the crisis. . . . By the natural course of events the great change must necessarily be brought about. . . .[56] Such circumstances would be bound to produce sudden shifts of allegiance away from any leaders intellectually implicated in the existing system (and this certainly included the 'non-political' labour leaders of the 1810s). Clearly, too, the resulting breakdown of sectional discipline would tend to produce just those bursts of social liberation already described. But equally clearly the great weakness of these earlier periods of radical consciousness was their lack of staying-power. Only a few months after the great upsurge of 1816-17 the *Manchester Chronicle* could congratulate itself on the state of domestic peace:

> In every direction, in the metropolis, in cities, in towns, in villages the call to insurrection was heard. The apostles of revolution swarmed over the land . . . . The partly unemployed . . . grew reckless of partial relief in anticipation of general amelioration. . . . It is impossible to contrast the present situation of the country with what it was twelve months ago, and not seem gratified for our deliverance. . . .[57]

As soon as the objective conditions of each crisis subsided (and a few military counter-measures had been taken), people seemed to slip back into their old attitudes remarkably quickly. Conversely, each time a new crisis developed, the radicals had to fight a new battle for supremacy in the movement with the 'non-politicals'.[58] Indeed, by 1818 this interior struggle was seen as so much part of crisis development that the government was deliberately intervening to strengthen the hands of the 'moderates' by getting employers to grant wage increases.[59]

It seems to have been this that marked the really key difference with the later period. In 1839 and 1842 the big struggles were not between 'politicals' and 'non-politicals' but between two lines of *political* action and (as was shown earlier) the whole nature of the change in working-class leadership during the early 1830s derived from the *permanent* subordination of all sections of the working population to radical control. It is here that ideological developments (linked, of course, to the development of capitalism itself) played such a key role.

It was not just that developments in the early 1830s made it possible to give long-standing industrial demands a radical content. Far more important, as was seen in the previous chapter, was the fundamental *intellectual* reorientation they demanded. In cotton and coal the form of struggle itself provided a constant re-education in anti-capitalist assumptions. It was now *economic* reconstruction that was seen as the ultimate goal, and political change only the precondition for it. Previously, things had been the other way round. 'National bankruptcy' was just one more step on the road to some ill-defined Jacobin republic. And reading the speeches of the earlier period, what strikes one most – despite the reference to changing 'the present order of things' and the undoubted spirit of radical egalitarianism – is the failure to make any long-term organic linkage between economic and political campaigns. 'Non-political' labour leaders could still present economic action as a credible *alternative* to political.

This difference also shows up in the cultural field. Although the evidence is somewhat scanty, there does not seem to have been any *sustained* rejection of bourgeois forms till well into the second period. When it came, however, it seems to have been sufficiently deep (and wide) to sustain something otherwise extremely rare: a distinctly new tradition of collective *class* expression. Putting on one side for the moment Oldham's own satirists of bourgeois manners (who will be quoted in the next chapter) there is the biggest and most undeniable development of all – a mass readership of the radical press. While this cannot be precisely measured, the descriptive evidence indicates that the London and Lancashire working-class newspapers achieved something near a monopoly in Oldham. The 1830s also saw church attendance falling to what was probably its lowest level of the century (figure 20), and atheist lecturers like Carlile and Hetherington collecting paying audiences running into hundreds.[60] And though one would certainly like much more evidence on the directly cultural side, the following assessment by W. J. Fox, Oldham's MP from 1847 and a leading proponent of liberalization, seems fairly realistic:

> There was one peculiar fact which could not but strike every reflecting person at the present day, and that was the number of writers springing up among the working classes – writers who did not like the authors of former days rest on patrons and patronage – writers who wanted no class above them, but who retained strong within them the feelings of the working class in which they were born and bred. Nothing like this was known

in former times . . . . Their works were animated by a peculiar
spirit – a spirit the result of the political circumstances of the
class to which they belonged. They had in them the rich racy
spirit of our old English writers . . . when the whole of this
literature was considered it would be found pervaded by a
spirit of indignation which would arise among men who felt
themselves reduced to a slave class, threatening the disruption
of that national unity which had hitherto constituted the glory
of this country. The stream of mind was separated into two
distinct courses; if they did not recognise its claims . . . the
genius of the country would become suicidal by the antagonism
of its elements.[61]

If, therefore, one wants to distinguish between the two periods,
it does seem to have been this permanence of intellectual commitment which was the really decisive factor. And while it is easy
to criticize the movement's theory – its somewhat unsystematized
economic analysis and its lack of Leninist rigour about state
power – the key point is that it worked. As far as the northern
factory population is concerned it passed the test of practice. It
succeeded in the most difficult task of relating the struggle for a
non-capitalist society to the immediate experience of working
people. It took the system's apparently most insoluble failings –
its inability to function without periodic bursts of overproduction
and wage-cutting – and turned them into political issues: political
issues whose solution was barred by the existing state-power set-
up. It was this which was the great achievement of the campaign
on poor law, police and above all factory reform, and it was
precisely this connection that John Knight made it his special task
to underline in the years immediately before his death:

> The making and administering of the laws is exclusively enjoyed
> by men of property, and, therefore, in the promotion of their
> own interests they are continually diminishing the rights of all
> the labouring classes. No plan hitherto laid for the benefit of
> the labourers has been successful; and so far as the legislative
> power remains exclusively in the hands of the men of property,
> no such plan will ever be effectual. In all disputes between
> employers and workmen . . . the magistrates almost invariably
> protect the employers. . . . Such is the phalanx of power opposed
> to the working class that until their influence does actively
> preponderate in the House of Commons, there is no possibility

of their circumstances being bettered. . . . No change favourable to the working class will be obtained unless for some object beneficial to the whole of them and for which they will unitedly, strenuously and perseveringly continue even to death itself.[62]

Which finally brings us to the most crucial question of all and the one that will occupy the rest of the study: why, if the movement was so effective in mobilising mass support, it ultimately collapsed so completely. A good many explanations have been suggested, and most blame the movement itself: the primitive level of its theory, the splits in its leadership, the failure to expand mass support beyond a few limited areas. All stress that it was the movement's own weakness that was the basic cause.

Here a somewhat different line is taken. The movement's eventual collapse was, it will be argued, in part the result of its earlier effectiveness: of its ability to force capitalist society to the point of crisis and then hold it there for a decade and a half. It is important not to be taken in by the professional pessimism of the academic historians. Compared with later proletarian movements this primitive English working class is remarkable for the long-sustained level its mobilisation (it should be remembered that even Lenin's revolutions required the external stimulus of war). As a movement it was perhaps unlucky not to find any such external stimulus itself. But even in its absence it was sufficiently powerful to bring about a profound modification in the structure of English capitalism. What destroyed it was, it will be argued, more its inability to maintain its offensive under the impact of these changes, and it is this larger process of crisis and restabilization that the remaining chapters will be concerned with. First, however, to back up what has just been said, one more case study needs to be made; this time to show the reality of Oldham's sustained mobilization in military state power terms. It comes from 1834 and concludes the story of the general strike begun in the previous chapter.

Working-class power in 1834

Our account left off with the massive influx of regular troops and the consequent decision to call off the strike. What followed demonstrates as well as anything the sheer weight of mass commitment which existed in the 1830s.

Even before the end of the strike the radicals were turning their control of local government to good advantage. The police who raided the union lodge were on the police commission pay roll. Three days after the raid an emergency resolution was passed 'that, deprecating as we do the conduct of our police constables in entering a trade union's lodge, an enquiry should immediately be set on foot to ascertain by whose authority our officers entered upon such an undertaking'.[63] Under pressure their sergeant named the magistrate Holme. Three weeks later, at a general meeting of the commission, a motion was put forward by Swire and Alexander Taylor that the constables who entered the lodge were 'not competant to fulfil their respective offices and that they be discharged'. It was passed by ninety-nine votes to seventy-five.[64] A local lawyer commented to the home secretary:

> I have already informed your Lordship of the violent and bar-
> barous outrage committed by the mob. . . . Ever since that
> day the radicals (for it is now entirely a political question)
> have been using every means in their power to deprive the
> constables of their situations and have at length succeeded.
> The police of the town of Oldham is governed by a certain
> number of commissioners who are qualified to vote by
> occupying property to the value of £30 per annum . . . a great
> number of these commissioners are shopkeepers depending on
> the working classes and such has been the feeling . . . that all
> kinds of threats and intimidation have been used by the
> radicals to compel these commissions to vote as they direct
> . . . .[65]

In this situation, the failure of the vestry to allow barrack expenses was predictable. When General Bouverie asked whether
'the delegates of the class of shopkeepers voted this way out of
hostility to the presence of the military, the answer was "they
darst not vote otherwise" '.[66] As usual the crown-nominated
constables received 'compensation from a number of inhabitants
who are engaged to indemnify them'.[67] Less predictable was the
success of the radicals in getting two members of the Bankside
mill works police committed for the manslaughter of the man
killed in the attack. The coroner's jury had sixteen members, four
from each township in the chapelry (with the constables making
the choice). In Oldham the constables were crown nominees; in
the three rural townships they were still elected by the vestry. This

gave the radicals just enough votes to get the two men committed to Lancaster castle.[68]

Far more important, however, was the struggle to prevent Oldham becoming a barrack town. From the moment the troops first marched into the town on 15 April it was this that was the basic issue. In May the employers got up a petition 'praying for the erection of a barracks in Oldham', and in mid-June 'a deputation of three large manufacturers . . . proceeded to London having been appointed . . . at a private meeting of the inhabitants to confer with the government'.[69] Against this the radicals staged a public meeting of their own. John Knight: 'It was the men of property who oppressed the labourers who wanted a band of fellows to coerce them.' Fitton: 'The barracks were demanded by the same party that instituted the building of the new church.

Table 8 Oldham working-class leaders: listings

(a) Main working-class leaders, 1795–1830[77]

'Main leaders' are those for whom activity is recorded three or more times in different years or who were arrested for sedition.

Andrew, James	weaver, Oldham, warrant for arrest April 1817, raided for pikes 1820.
Baker	Oldham delegate to 'four counties' meeting July 1801.
Bamford, Samuel	weaver, Middleton, active 1816-19, arrested 1819.
Beswick, John	Oldham, United Englishman, arrested 1801.
Binns, John	newsagent, Oldham, active 1817-18, warrant March 1817.
Buckley, John	Chadderton, United Englishman, transported 1801.
Browe, William	machine maker, Oldham, active 1816-17, warrant 1817, fled to America.
Clegg, Assheton	from magnate hatting family, active 1812-17.
Clegg, John	Assheton's cousin, active 1816-30; both seem to have become involved in the revolutionary movement in their late teens; neither was in the mainline of Clegg family (itself perhaps the richest in Oldham).
Cooper, Thomas	Heyside, United Englishmen treasurer 1801.
Earnshaw, John	(1779-1841) 'doctor' (served time in Manchester hospital), Oldham, Quaker, active 1816-19, warrant 1817, nephew (John Lees) killed at Peterloo.
Firth, James	weaver, Oldham, Methodist Connexion, active 1817-19, warrant 1817.
Fitton, William	(c. 1790-1840) weaver, son of 'doctor', Royton, active 1816-39, arrested 1817 and 1819.

Greaves, John	Crompton, secretary Crompton United Englishmen 1801, on county executive 1802.
Haigh, John	cotton spinner and later small shopkeeper, Oldham, active 1812-52, arrested 1812 and 1820.
Healey, Joseph	'doctor', Middleton, active 1816-19, arrested 1819.
Jackson, John	Chadderton, active 1797-1808, 1797 secretary Chadderton Friends of Liberty, United Englishman, transported 1801, returned 1808.
Kay, John	master weaver, Royton, active 1812-31.
Kent, William	Chadderton, active 1817-27, warrant 1817.
Knight, John	(1763-1838), Saddleworth manufacturer, later school master Oldham, active 1794-1838, arrested 1794, 1812, 1817, and 1819.
Lancashire, John	Middleton, active 1816-17, blanketeer organizer, arrested 1817.
Mellor, John	Oldham, active 1819-27, arms organizer late 1819.
Midgley, Isaac	hatter, Oldham, arrested as strike leader 1808, wounded and arrested Middleton 1812.
Newton, Joseph	cotton spinner, Oldham, Unitarian, active 1816-17, warrant 1817, fled to America.
Nicholson, Wm	master printer, Lees, active 1813-30, Cartwright contact.
Pilkington, Rob	weaver, Oldham, active 1816-18, weavers strike leader 1818, arrested.
Robinson	Hollinwood, 1800-1, United Englishman delegate 1801, contact of Cowdroy and Thelwall.
Rothwell, Wm	weaver, Failsworth, active 1817-20, warrant 1817, blanketeer, Moscow plot, post-Peterloo plot.
Shakeshaft	discharged artilleryman, Oldham, arms organizer late 1819, Harrison contact.
Schofield, James	hatter, Oldham, active 1817-19, warrant 1817.
Swire, Thomas	clogger (union leader), Oldham, active 1821-34.
Taylor	'doctor', Royton and Glodwick, active 1816-19, Hunt contact.
Taylor, Caleb	weaver, Royton, active 1801-27.
Taylor, James	spinner, Oldham, wounded and arrested Middleton 1812.
Taylor, John	weaver, Glodwick (father small farmer active 1816), Unitarian, active 1816-17, warrant 1817.
Taylor, Thomas	Royton, active 1797-1801, Royton secretary. Friends of Liberty 1798, United Englishman 1801, delegate to London 1801, 'four county' conference, died 1802.

They were in secret communication with the government.' Halliwell: 'The object can be no other than having a ready instrument to coerce and subdue the labouring classes in the event of any determination being manifested to keep up their wages at all higher than what the masters think proper they should give.' Holladay: 'When reductions of wages occurred barracks were wanted. The whole system is upheld by the bayonet, and if there was not a sudden change England would become another Ireland.'[70] The resulting radical petition was presented by Fielden.[71] But the radicals' strongest argument was the reality of popular control on the streets. It was this that was the real test. The more dangerous the situation could be made to appear (and the larger the garrison needed to control the town) the less likely was the government to commit itself. Within four days of his arrival Bouverie had reported radical attempts to infiltrate and win over his troops.[72] In July he asked Home Office permission to discontinue a dangerously exposed guard on the Bankside mill and, at the same time, advised the quick withdrawal of the whole force.[73] The Oldham employers and magistrates renewed their pressure for a permanent barracks and Bouverie was asked for a full report:[74]

The population of Oldham is in itself extremely numerous and in conjunction with that of Saddleworth forms a mass of people bound and connected together by unions that is altogether very formidable . . . the manufacturers and their men have at all time as I have heard and for the last six years as I have known been in a state of hostility, each having the very worst opinion of the other, and as far as I have been able to judge each side with good reason for its opinion. It is extremely natural that [the magistrates] should be most desirous to have at their command a body of regular troops nor can I conscientiously say in the face of the representations by the manufacturers that I conceive that property would be safe were the troops to be withdrawn. It is, however, to be considered whether the state of Oldham is ever likely to be at any future time better able to do without a military force than at present; and also, it being deemed desirable that such a force should be kept there, it is not highly expedient that the force should be such a one as under any possible circumstances would be able to act in an efficient manner, and act at all events to protect itself against such a body of people as might be poured upon it from all the reservoirs of such an immense district. The force now in Oldham I looked upon as

Table 8 Oldham working-class leaders: listings   (b) Working-class leaders active 1830–50[77]

Name	active pre-1830 (1)	1832 corruption (2)	1832 class power (3)	Short-time 1831-3 (4)	Regeneration (5)	Chartist 1838-41 (6)	1842 strike (7)	1842 compromise (8)	1842 arrest (9)	1847 Holladay (10)	1847 Cobbett (11)	1848 Charter (12)	Short-time 1840s (13)	Anti-poor law (14)	Anti-police (15)	Strike support (16)	Irish protests (17)
Andrew, John, shop				×													
Annan, Thomas, shop									×								
Ashley, James, not known									×								
Ashworth, James, n.k.									×	×				×		×	
Bailey, James, shop										×					×		
Bardsley, Robert, spinner													×	×		×	
Barstow, John, shop							×										
Beaumont, Mayall, spinner						×	×										
Bell, William, labourer							×										
Bell, Robert, shoemaker															×		
Bentley, George, shop											×	×					
Bentley, Joseph, spinner																	
Benson, Mark, labourer			×														
Bickley, Rowland, n.k.									×					×			×
Booth, John, shop														×			

Booth, William, n.k.
Brierley, James, basketmaker
Buckley, John, minister
Calvert, John, n.k.
Chadwick, Napoleon, doctor
Chapel, Henry, weaver
Chapman, Thomas, farmer
Cheetham, John, 'worker'
Chisenhall, John, n.k.
Clifford, Robert, n.k.
Collins, William, n.k.
Collinge, John, publican
Cooper, James, joiner
Cooper, Richard, lecturer
Cropper, E.C., n.k.
Crowther, John, painter
Dearden, James, spinner
Dixon, J. E, operative
Donovan, D., n.k.
Dyson, n.k.
Earnshaw, II, John, doctor
Fearns, Pat, n.k.
Fitton, William, doctor
Fletcher, Richard, employer
Garlick, James, 'worker'
Gartside, William, n.k.
Garside, John, spinner
Gifford, Robert, operative
Greaves, James, spnr-pub.
Greenhalgh, Rich., dresser

(b) Working-class leaders active 1830–50[77]

			Activity											Campaigns			
	active pre-1830	1832 corruption	1832 class power	Short-time 1831-3	Regeneration	Chartist 1838-41	1842 strike	1842 compromise	1842 arrest	1847 Holladay	1847 Cobbett	1848 Charter	Short-time 1840s	Anti-poor law	Anti-police	Strike support	Irish protests
	1	2	3	4	5	6	7	8	9	10	11	12	13	14	15	16	17
Hague, Benjamin, n.k.	·	·	·	·	·	·	×	·	·	·	·	·	·	·	×	·	·
Haigh, John, spnr-shop	×	·	×	·	×	×	·	·	·	·	·	·	·	·	·	×	·
Hallas, George, sm. master	·	·	·	·	·	·	·	·	·	·	·	·	·	·	·	·	·
Halliwell, John, small employer	×	×	·	·	·	·	·	·	·	·	×	·	·	×	×	·	·
Halliwell, Wm, small employer	·	×	·	×	·	·	·	·	·	×	·	·	·	×	·	·	·
Hamer, Wm, school	·	·	·	·	·	×	×	·	·	·	·	·	·	·	·	·	·
Hardman, Thomas, weaver	·	·	×	·	·	·	·	·	×	·	·	·	·	·	·	·	·
Hardacre, James, n.k.	·	·	·	·	·	·	·	·	·	·	·	·	·	·	·	·	×
Harrop, Benjamin, n.k.	·	·	×	×	×	·	·	·	·	·	·	·	·	·	·	·	×
Harwar, Charles, n.k.	·	·	×	·	·	·	·	·	·	·	·	·	·	·	·	·	×
Haslam, Richard, reedmaker	·	·	·	·	·	×	×	·	×	·	·	·	·	·	·	·	·
Haslop, Len, hatter-cafe	·	·	·	·	·	×	×	·	·	×	·	·	·	·	·	×	·
Hawkshead, J., lawyer	×	·	×	×	·	·	·	·	·	×	·	·	·	·	·	·	·
Hibbert, John, n.k.	·	·	×	·	·	·	·	·	·	·	·	·	·	·	·	·	·
Hirst, Ambrose, spinner	·	·	·	·	·	·	×	·	·	·	·	×	·	·	·	·	·

```
. . . . . . . . . X . . . . . X . . . X . . . . . . . .
. X . . . . . . . X X . . . . . . . . . . . . . . . . . . . X
. X . . . . . X . . X X . . . . . . . . . . . . . . . . .
. X . . . . . . . X X . . . . . . X . . . . . . . . . . .
. . . . . . . . . . . . . . X . . . X . . . X . . . . . .
. . . . . . . . X . . X . . . X . X . . . . . . . . . . .
. . . . . . . . . . . X . . . . . X . . . . . . . . . . .
. X . . . . . . . . X . . . . . . . . . . . . . . . . . .
X . X X . X . X . X . . . . X . X . X . X . . . X . X . X . . . X .
. . . . . . . . . . . . . . . . . . . . . . . . . . . . .
. . . . . . . . X . . X . X . . . X . . . . . . . . . . .
. X . . X . . . X . . X . . . . X . . . . . . X . . . . .
. . . . . . . . . . X . . X . . . . . . . X . . . . . . .
. X . . . . . X . X X . . X . . . . . . . . . . . X . . . . . X
. . . . . . . X . X X . . . . . . . . X . . . X . . X X . .
. X . . . . . . . . X . . . . . . . . . . . . . . . . . . . X
. . . . . . . X . X X . . . . . . . . X . . . . . . . X . .
```

(b) Working-class leaders active 1830–50[77]

Group	No.	Activity / Campaign	Pollit, John, pwr. weaver	Pollit, Geo., pwr. weaver	Quarmby, James, bookseller	Ratcliffe, H., unemployed	Riley, shop	Roberts, James, collier	Rushton, H., spinner	Simpson, Thomas, mechanic	Smethhurst, Henry, n.k.	Smith, Kinder, spinner	Spier, William, tailor	Stepney, grocer	Stump, Richard, shop	Sutcliffe, A., tailor	Swire, Thomas, clogger
Campaigns	17	Irish protests															
	16	Strike support		×	×	×											×
	15	Anti-police										×	×				
	14	Anti-poor law		×													×
Activity	13	Short-time 1840s										×					
	12	1848 Charter										×					
	11	1847 Cobbett															
	10	1847 Holladay			×	×					×						
	9	1842 arrest	×	×				×		×	×						
	8	1842 compromise														×	
	7	1842 strike						×									
	6	Chartist 1838–41						×		×					×	×	×
	5	Regeneration						×									×
	4	Short-time 1831–3		×								×		×			
	3	1832 class power												×			×
	2	1832 corruption											×				
	1	active pre-1830															×

Swire, John, clogger
Taft, Joshua, n.k.
Taylor, Alex, shop
Taylor, Ashton, spinner
Taylor, Augustus, beer
Taylor, Robert, turner
Taylor, Thomas, twister
Taylor, William, small employer
Tristam, Thomas, clogger
Tinan, Thomas, n.k.
Travis, John, n.k.
Ward, Barnet, n.k.
Warburton, Robert, spinner
Warburton, Paul, clogger
Warwick, father & son, cookshop
Watson, James, clogger
Whitehead, Eneas, twister
Wild, Jonathan, piecer
Wild, Thomas, n.k.
Williams, William, spinner
Wilson, Edward, n.k.
Wilson, Thomas, spinner
Winterbottom, J., shop
Wolfenden, Ralph, n.k.
Wolstencroft, John, n.k.
Wood, John, power dresser
Wright, John, n.k.
Yardley, Sam, shoemaker

totally inadequate. Two companies never exceeding 120 men would be placed in a very dangerous and trying predicament in such a town. . . . I am far from wishing to throw any blame on Mr Holme but he is impressed with the foolish notion that because the workpeople have hitherto refrained from attacking the soldiers and have generally given way when soldiers have been employed that such is always to be the case. I cannot divest my mind of the fear that sooner or later some disaster may be brought upon the troops and should a mob once find how very easily they can be driven from a town or annihilated there is no saying to what extremities they might not be induced to go. . . . I would most strongly impress upon the mind of the secretary of state the danger of keeping in such a town so small a force . . . and that if HM government should determine a force is to remain there that I should be empowered to have sufficient buildings to accommodate four companies of infantry.[75]

This, calculated the Home Office, would cost £9,000 (not counting the continuing cost of the garrison itself) 'which so far exceeds what the government would be justified in expending that he [the home secretary] cannot recommend the erection of such barracks. The difficulty of quartering the force now stationed in Oldham is so great and the inconvenience to the public service . . . of keeping so small a force in such a situation as Oldham is also so great that his Lordship thinks it will be necessary at the earliest opportunity to withdraw the present force'.[76] This eventually took place on 1 October 1834, and with the last army units retreating down the Manchester road we can now go on to examine the first stage of the process by which an establishment solution was found: the crisis of the town's bourgeoisie and the way in which the working-class challenge modified its culture and consciousness.

6 Crisis of the bourgeoisie

> Upon the different forms of property, upon the social conditions of existence, rises an entire superstructure of distinct and peculiarly formed sentiments, illusions, modes of thought and views of life. The entire class creates and forms them out of its material foundations and out of the corresponding social relations . . . . And, as in private life one differentiates between what a man thinks and says of himself and what he really is and does, so in historical struggles one must differentiate still more the phrases and fancies of parties from their real organism and their real interests, their conceptions of themselves from their reality (Marx, *Eighteenth Brumaire of Louis Napoleon*, 1852).[1]

This chapter will be mainly concerned to relate what Marx calls the 'phrases and fancies' of the bourgeoisie to its 'real organism' and in particular examine the way in which its attitudes were modified under the impact of working-class attack. First of all, however, we need to establish that a bourgeoisie actually existed in Oldham – as a coherent social grouping – and to identify its special characteristics compared with Northampton and South Shields. To start with, therefore, we must attempt a rough analysis of structure.

Sampling the bourgeoisie

It is not easy (or even very useful) to propose a tidy definition for a town's bourgeoisie. The main approach has been to take samples of individuals from all likely occupations and social groups – any that had (or might think they had) some stake in the system – and gather as much information on each as possible. The total sample covered employers of all sizes, merchants and tradesmen (though not small shopkeepers), members of the established professions, and magistrates, guardians and councillors. The lists used were collated from town directories supplemented by census schedules and refer to 1851. The samples for all three towns were stratified. Certain occupations of interest in their own right but too small to permit a significant sample (in Oldham coalowners, hat manufacturers and engineers) were taken complete. For other occupations, either large enough to admit a sample or of less strategic importance, a one-in-two (and in Northampton a three-in-four) sample was taken alphabetically. The complete sample attempts, therefore, to combine meaningful analysis of certain important occupations with a representative sample for a town's bourgeoisie as a whole.

In Oldham information was wanted for 341 individuals, in Northampton for 200 and in Shields for 293. The results varied very much with the type of information: politics and birthplace were identified for over three-quarters of the Oldham sample, but any indication of wealth (whether by probate, rateable value, numbers of servants or numbers employed) for only just over half. In these circumstances the number of people for whom we have a *complete* coverage is obviously small, and this limits the sample to a supporting role, indicating typicality and magnitude and not proposing casual relations. The biting edge of the analysis largely comes from elsewhere: the analysis of marriage frequencies between occupations, membership of trade, political and religious groups and above all the reconstruction of friendship groupings (all described in the note at the end of the chapter).

In practice, however, neither the untidy definition nor the low yield matters as much as might seem at first sight. There did exist in each town solid, consistent groupings of people, linked together by blood, friendship and common codes of religious and political behaviour. These groups stand out plainly despite the inadequate material, and it is these groups, not a generalized bourgeoisie, that formed the visible social reality.

How, then, did Oldham's bourgeoisie differ from that in other towns? Merely in terms of size there was no great contrast. In absolute terms Oldham's was of course bigger: perhaps six hundred against four hundred in Shields and three hundred in Northampton. But occupationally its components were more or less the same (table 9).

The big differences come when one looks at the internal structure of Oldham's bourgeoisie and its relations with the large sector of non-bourgeois (but also non-manual worker) occupations such as small shopkeepers and clerks.

Table 9 Estimated occupational make-up of elites, 1851: three towns

	Northampton	Oldham	Shields
professions	46	68	68
employers	96	400	250
tradesmen	75	98	96
	217	566	414

In Northampton and Shields these borderline occupations formed a massive social tail to the bourgeoisie proper, imitating (as far as they were able) its style of living and supporting it politically. In Oldham, on the other hand, one finds a definite break in social continuity at this point and it seems to have been this that led contemporary observers (including Horner and Engels) to believe that Lancashire towns like Oldham had a disproportionately small non-working-class element.[2] In fact, as we have seen, the size of the bourgeoisie proper was much the same and that of the borderline occupations considerably larger. The real difference was cultural. Whether willingly or not, the mass of Oldham's small farmers and shopkeepers voted for working-class candidates and this political identification seems to have been carried over into everyday life. Very few kept servants – only 3 per cent of Oldham's total families against 6 and 11 per cent in Shields and Northampton.[3] Most also lived in the same sort of housing. Again only 3 per cent of households paid window tax against 8 and 15 per cent in Shields and Northampton.[4] And most convincingly of all, fewer tended to marry into the bourgeoisie and more into the working population (figures 19 and 22). So structurally – and in comparison with Northampton and Shields – Oldham bourgeoisie can be marked out for its social isolation. This is the first big difference.

The second is that it was itself divided. There existed within it two distinct 'big' and 'petty' bourgeois groupings. Partly this can also be explained by the special political pressures to which its tradesmen and small employers were exposed. But partly it was the result of a different economic structure. Industry in both Northampton and Shields tended to be relatively small-scale and run largely to the profit of outside interests, quite unlike the earlier nineteenth-century cotton industry. Figure 23 shows the consequences in terms of private wealth. Oldham's cotton industry alone supported as many men leaving over £25,000 personalty as Northampton and Shields put together. And while in Northampton the owners of the brewery, the Phipps, and in Shields the resident owner of the big alkali works, Stevenson, were certainly very rich, they did not, as did their counterparts in Oldham, form a coherent social grouping running to seventy families and a hundred and fifty households. The difference shows up clearly when one looks at marriage patterns (figure 22). While both Northampton's professional families and the corresponding 'top' group in Shields, the shipowners, show a very considerable degree of internal marrying, neither approached anything like the degree of exclusive intermarrying shown by Oldham's over-£25,000 industrialists.

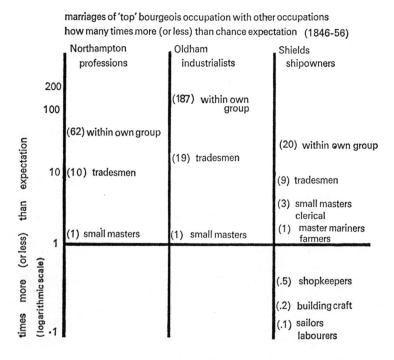

Figure 22   Social distance within the bourgeoisie: three towns[5]

proportion in each occupation estimated
as leaving more or less than £25,000

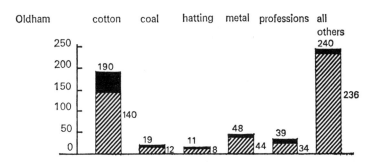

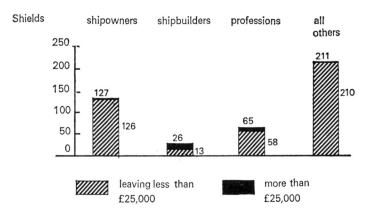

Figure 23 Wealth by occupation: three towns

These men were built on national scale and were seen to be by both local and outside observers at the time. In 1849 the London newspaper reporter already quoted (writing for the *Morning Chronicle*'s 'Condition of the People' series) devoted a good part of his report on Oldham to a description of the relative merits of what he called the 'larger' and the 'operative' capitalists.[6] And when in 1852 a group of Oldham Nonconformists, mainly town centre tradesmen, drew up a master plan for local missionary activity, they distinguished three major social groupings: eleven thousand 'operative families'; two thousand 'middle-class' families (composed of all those not directly involved in manual work: clerks, small shopkeepers, farmers, small masters, managers, but in which they included tradesmen like themselves); and finally a relatively minute group of two hundred households which they described as 'upper class'.[7] Though this particular evidence comes from the socially very fluid years of the early 1850s (when the Oldham bourgeoisie was rapidly developing the type of social 'tail' found elsewhere), the separation of 'upper' from 'middle' classes does seem significant. Moreover, as will now be seen, it also had very real political and social consequences.

The 'middle classes'

For the 1830s and 1840s – and before the development of any larger social 'tail' – the petty bourgeoisie numbered less than five hundred families. These were themselves divided into two further groupings: the tradesmen and small employers (totalling about a hundred and fifty families) and the 'little masters' who made up the remainder.

The tradesmen: The tradesmen group took in both small employers and large shopkeepers – food wholesalers, drapers, spirit merchants, printers, specialist metal manufacturers and some cotton spinners – and what seems to have distinguished them from the little masters was their common need to keep intact a relatively substantial working capital (usually around £2–3,000) and maintain credit with outside suppliers and customers. The greatest recurrent threat on both these fronts was a series of bad marriages: money thrown away uselessly on daughters; sons bringing back nothing in return. And socially the characteristic institutions of this group all seem designed to insulate its members from any contacts outside its own narrow circle.

To start with a description of a typical member.

> Let methodist Kooper – babe of grace –
> With formal mien and sanctimonious face
> Oppose Lyceum's dancing, draughts and chess
> And think of heaven the more, and earth the less.[8]

This was one of Oldham's working-class satirists describing Reuben Cooper. Cooper was an outsider, born in Derby in 1812. He came to Oldham in the early 1830s, set up his grocery business and joined the Manchester Street Methodist church (of which he was later to become a trustee). In 1837 he was a founder member of the Lyceum, in 1843 a subscriber to the anti-corn law league, in 1847 canvassed for Fox, and during the 1849 incorporation controversy voted for the supercession of the police commission (of which he was a member). He was also in the same year on the committee of the British and Foreign Bible Society, a year later on that of the Shopkeepers' Association and in 1853 of the Peace Society. His household in 1851 consisted of his wife and son, a female domestic, a journeyman grocer and four apprentices (all but one of whom came from outside). When he died in Oldham in 1883 he was assessed on £5,000 personalty, and named as his executors his son James, who carried on the business, and Matthew Hudson, a Manchester butter merchant and wholesale supplier.

Cooper had a hundred or so replicas in Oldham. They tended to come from outside, to prefer the company of their fellow tradesmen and be very careful to keep out of contact with the mass of the population. Statistically, it is not easy to find a satisfactory way of getting hold of them. The list in the town directories (drapers, grocers, metal manufacturers, etc.) mix tradesmen with small shopkeepers and little masters. But, for what they are worth, the lists analyzed under the heading 'tradesmen' in table 11 (page 199) do show a disproportionate number of immigrants, Nonconformists and voters for W. J. Fox. Again, the use of friendship clusterings is not altogether satisfactory. These tend to take in too few instead of too many. The geographical mobility of the group (and the partial nature of the sample) has meant that the largest clustering contains less than a score of families. All the same, the friendship groups do help slightly. Of the fifteen members of the 'Wainwright-Riley' group, five were immigrants and all voted for Fox.[9] The group also contained both small employers and traders: the Wainwrights doubled draping with bolt-making, and the Rileys draping with cotton spinning. More significant still, every member belonged to a church, and the group included Anglicans as well as Methodists and Congregationalists.

In this context, the churches seem to have been the most important artificial communities created to protect members from contact on equal terms with the population at large. Ninety-one servant-keeping traders had offspring marrying between 1848 and 1856. Eighty-two of them saw to it that the marriages were into other trading or professional families. Against this, of the two hundred and eighty little master marriages, all but fifty were with manual workers and small shopkeepers (and a good part of the remainder probably derive from the small employers – not little masters – who unfortunately cannot be separated off) (see table 20, page 268). And taking all employers and traders in the sample with less than £25,000 personalty (or its equivalent) and dividing them into Anglican, Nonconformist or neither, it seems pretty clear that it was the church members, and especially the Nonconformists, who were particularly careful not to live in houses next door to manual workers. Church members were also likely to be immigrants, not to employ their own families and to possess servants (see table 13, page 202).

From both sides, then, the link between church membership and tradesmen exclusiveness seems strong enough. In the working-class mind the separateness of the tradesmen was firmly associated with religiosity. It was 'methodistic' Cooper. A pro-Cobbett election squib of 1852 puts James Potter (an Anglican draper and president of the Shopkeepers Association) at the head of the Fox voters 'carrying in his hand the eighteenth verse of the ninth chapter of Lamentations followed by the shopkeepers of High Street and Market Street'.[10] And the tradesmen themselves also saw their apartness from the rest of the population in terms of 'religion'. The Manchester Street Methodists from the Wainwright-Riley group believed that 'we have thousands around us to whom the Gospel requires to be carried with the same urgency as to many of the heathen abroad. . . .'[11]

This protective function of tradesman religion is made all the more plausible by the way social exclusiveness was put before doctrinal soundness. The Methodist Rileys were quite ready to marry into the Congregationalist Suthers and the Anglican Fittons; both families had money. There is also an interesting fluidity between the three main tradesman congregations: St Peter's (Anglican), Queen Street (Congregationalist) and Manchester Street (Methodist). 'There has always been a tradition', write the historians of Queen Street, 'which closely connects the origin of Queen Street with St Peter's church . . . friendly relations have always existed between the two places. . . .'[12] Here again congregations moulded churches. Indeed, the same pressures seem to be behind such secular institutions as the Lyceum: the need for escape routes from the vulgar, levelling society of street and pub. The members of the Lyceum's 1838 provisional committee were John Riley (Methodist draper), Robert Green (Anglican printer and stationer), John Ogden (Anglican grocer), Thomas Mills (untraced), Reuben Cooper, Levi Holt (Anglican hatter) and John Taylor (Unitarian mill manager), and the Lyceum remained very much a preserve of what its historian calls 'the professional and trading classes'.[13] So, whatever the precise tradesman religion, the end-product is visible and impressive. The tradesmen, though incomparably less wealthy than the big bourgeoisie, managed to remain almost as exclusive. Only nine of the ninety-one marriages were into families of 'lower' social standing.

This was the structure of the group as it faced the troubles of the 1830s and 1840s: one hundred and fifty families; tightly intermarried; protected by a maze of prayer meetings, lectures, committees and Sunday Schools; educating its members in brands of behaviour which marked them off from the rest of the community; demanding a fierce group loyalty. The troubles came in on three sides. As manufacturers in cotton and metal the tradesmen were marginal. They had to rent plant, make expensive contracts for fuel, and were without the reserves that could tide them over the bad periods. Like the Hirsts, Methodist printers with money in cotton, they were apt to get their fingers burnt. More basically, the tradesmen were shopkeepers. Whenever mass unemployment set in, their goods became unsaleable. Frightened of losing custom, they had to give credit, and poverty, and especially the secondary poverty of drink and disease, made credit very risky. Worse still, perhaps, they were extremely vulnerable to working-class pressure. In parliamentary elections they controlled enough votes to swing the balance and exclusive dealing was devised with the town centre shopkeepers especially in mind. Even more unnerving than the loss of custom must have been the terror of isolation in a hostile community. For two days during the 1847 Oldham wakes the crowds burnt effigies of the anti-working-class candidates, Fox and Duncuft, and smashed in the boarded-up shop fronts of the tradesmen that supported them. Police protection was refused.[14] During the 1830s and early 1840s the situation had been – for them – even worse.

The reaction was partly in terms of practical self-help. For a time from 1838 the tradesmen managed to run their own bank, the Oldham Banking Company, with the drapers Potter, Byrom, Mulliner and Butterworth and the small spinners Holladay and James Wild among its partners.[15] The bank gave the group greater resilience during bad times but itself fell victim to the great 1847 depression. In 1845, in an attempt to cut transport costs, the tradesmen helped promote the Oldham District Railway Company and a direct link with Manchester. Two of the five promoters were James Potter and William Byrom (Potter's father-in-law with a wholesale grocery branch in Wigan). This also went down in 1847.[16] In the later 1840s the tradesmen cooperated with the big bourgeoisie to break working-class control over MPs, police and poor relief, voting almost to a man for Fox and Duncuft and in 1849 for incorporation.[17] A Shopkeepers Association was formed in November 1850 'for the purpose of protecting the general interests of the trade', with Potter as its president and fifteen of the most active tradesmen (Anglican and Nonconformist) on the committee.[18] Its first actions were to secure reductions in the price of gas to shopkeepers and freight charges on the railways, and to demand the suppression of unlicensed hawkers.[19] The tradesmen also seem to have been behind the establishment in Oldham of a County Court for Small Debts.[20] An 1852 propaganda sheet put out by the Cobbett faction warned the Irish about the town centre shopkeepers: 'These men are attempting to delude you. They are members of the Shopkeepers Association, who have entered into a conspiracy and pay their attorney to prosecute any poor Irishman . . . during the last two years upwards of thirty of your country men and women have been sent to the New Bailey Prison . . . .'[21]

Other tradesmen reactions were less closely calculated. Threatened from above and below they threw up some violent remedies of their own. One thing they fixed on was the establishment. Locally, it meant the 'upper class', the great property-owning families who, unlike the migrant tradesmen, had been in the area for generations, owned the land and had pews in St Mary's. Nationally, it was the cash-payment and corn-law government of the landlords and the big bourgeoisie; and the Church. The Church, apart from its role as an upper-class money spinner, represented the age-old threat to tradesman exclusiveness. As a blanket unit of administration, and one that theoretically subordinated the entire community to the same beliefs and habits, the Church struck dangerously at the whole logic of tradesman life. In the mind of an insecure minority, local injustice, national misgovernment and the Church easily merged into a larger conspiracy. Sometimes the language was extreme. At a disestablishment meeting in June 1834 the tradesmen applauded James Holladay:

> The American armies had triumphed over the armies of the English establishment. The American people were principally dissenters and fought hard for their liberty . . . an undeniable proof that a nation might be great without the union of Church and state. The Tories told them that if this Church was touched by their dissenting, impious, unhallowed hands all trade and prosperity would cease. The fact is . . . .'[22]

The tradesmen's fears were pandered to by the government education proposals: levelling operations, it seemed, under the eye of the Church. Birt, the Baptist minister, felt that the 1843 Factory Bill would mean the 'tyrannizing of British liberty' and give 'clerical trustees monstrous powers of extorting rates without consent of ratepayers'. At the same meeting (attended by Riley, Heap, John Taylor and Holladay), Brooks, Weslyan minister, allowed 'the desirableness of giving factory children a useful and religious education' but rather through 'Sunday schools than the established Church'.[23] Russell's 1847 scheme provoked similar reactions. 'The manufacturers and shopkeepers of Oldham', claimed Davies, Congregational minister, 'did not want government aid to educate their children; they could do it themselves; as for the working classes, they were amply provided for in the numerous Sunday schools and voluntarily supported schools'. To Quarmby, an immigrant Methodist bookseller, 'the government scheme appeared likely to create eighty-eight thousand teachers who would necessarily become instruments in the hands of the government'.[24] The anti-corn law league, of course, with its camp meetings and oratory, provided the ideal outlet; and in Oldham, while the money came from the big employers, most of the hysteria was supplied by the tradesmen.[25]

Towards the working class, tradesman attitudes were necessarily double-faced. At one and the same time the manual worker represented labour, principal customer, undesirable neighbour and political master. James Holladay, putting himself forward as parliamentary candidate in 1847 (backed by Reuben Cooper and Quarmby), presented a common front for the 'industrious classes': 'the Representatives of the People ought to force upon any government in power measures calculated to develop the resources of the Country and the industry of the People'.[26] But Holladay opposed the Factory Acts and had at least one conviction for breaking them.[27] Shopkeeper charity also had a double edge to it. Poverty in its various forms was a big threat to tradesman profits. In 1838 Riley, Cooper and John Dodge (Weslyan bookseller and printer) got up the first of a long series of temperance missions.[28] The Oldham Benevolent Society, founded in 1815, was run in the late 1830s by William Meek (immigrant Weslyan shoe-dealer) and a couple of Weslyan ministers.[29] In 1847 the Oldham Provident Loan Society appears in court prosecuting one of its clients.[30] The more informally organized shopkeeper credit also had, as the Irish discovered, a sting in the tail. Again with education, the tradesmen found themselves pulled two ways. Even without an Anglican bias, education for the masses may well have been felt as a threat to tradesman exclusiveness; and certainly for the country as a whole dissenter opposition blocked national education plans for a generation. On the other hand, the tradesmen had a very painful interest in what went on in working-class minds. It was in 1852, after the Cobbett mob had wrecked their shops for the second time in one year, that Wainwright, Riley, Hirst and their neighbours decided that 'we have around us thousands to whom the Gospel requires to be carried with the same urgency as to many of the heathen abroad. . . .'

All these contradictions find their most eloquent expression in the man who the tradesmen ultimately backed as MP in 1847, W. J. Fox. Here he is snug in Westminster:

> He had consorted with the working people . . . and he found in
> them that intelligence and those qualities which kept alive faith
> in human nature. . . . The working people would not elect

men of their own class as representatives unless under very strong inducements. . . . They would look to people of local importance, to local benefactors or else to men of national reputation. . . . Unite this class on such harmonious terms [Hume's Household Suffrage Bill] – disregard theological difficulties – spread education with a bold and free hand over the country – throw open the doors of the constitution – give the people an equalization of the burdens of taxation . . . do this, and they would have the millions no longer an alienated body, but the real and firm base of the social pyramid. By these means we should achieve far nobler conquests in other countries than our armies had ever yet won; for we should bring back voluntary tribute from every clime to which our commerce penetrated.[31]

But for his first three parliamentary contests in Oldham Fox had to be given military protection. Even his biographer, Garnett, finds it 'ironical that Fox, who claimed, "I belong to the people" should have gone in fear of his life at the hands of the Oldham operatives'.[32]

Yet it is important to do more than stress the contradictions. Certainly in the case of the tradesmen the contrast between 'their conceptions of themselves' and their social reality is particularly striking. But the really vital thing is not so much their false consciousness itself as the fact that during the 1840s it *changed*. This is where we come to the impact of the working-class attack. In the 1830s tradesmen politics had been defensive, if not passive. Insofar as they had contact with the working class it was on terms dictated by the latter, and their anti-establishment rhetoric was often little more than internal apology for collaboration. On the other hand, as working-class pressure declined in the 1840s, it was precisely the people who had borne the brunt of the earlier relationship – like Holladay – who now elaborated one of the most powerful of all liberalizing responses. What strikes one most about tradesmen politics in the later 1840s and 1850s is their *cultural aggression*. The missionary activity of 1852, the campaigns around temperance and voluntary education, and the new rhetoric about 'Industry' and 'the People' all assumed that it was the tradesmen who were now to be the leaders. 'The working class would not elect men of their own class . . . they would look to people of local importance'; and it was the Oldham Reform League (of which Holladay was first chairman) that was to play a critical role in achieving a real and firm base to the social pyramid in the two decades after its formation in 1848.[33] Moreover, their success in doing this provided them with more than a political following of their own. It gave them, as will be seen in the next chapter, a powerful bargaining counter in relations with the town's big bourgeoisie, and the 1850s would see them emerging to dominate many areas of local government. However, even then – when they were at last in a position to pass themselves off as the People and impose their culture on a good part of the community – it is worth remembering what a minute and unrepresentative part of the population they really were: just a hundred and fifty unpopular and still somewhat isolated families.

The 'little masters': The 'little masters' were quite different. The *Morning Chronicle* correspondent of 1849 had a close look at them:

> One of my first cares was to ascertain so far as I could the differences in the tone of relationship subsisting between the class of operative capitalists in Oldham and the workpeople as compared with that existing between the mill-hands and the larger and more assuming capitalists. . . . By two or three life-long residents in Oldham I was assured that the class of operative employers was by far the most popular with the mill hands. 'The masters', I was informed, 'are just the same as if they were the fellow workmen of those they employ. They dress in much the same way; their habits and language are almost identical, and when they go "on the spree" they go and sing and drink in low taverns with their own working men.' I enquired in what sort of houses the masters lived? 'In houses a little bigger and a little better than the common dwellings but managed inside in much the same way.' . . . My informants added that although masters and men often caroused together, yet on occasion of differences arising between them, the masters would get dreadfully abusive, and terribly bad blood would ensue.[34]

The little masters outnumbered the tradesmen by more than two to one. A proportion came from trades where craft was still dominant (building, brickmaking, clogging) but the great majority came from subcontracting in cotton and metal. Their activity was defined by their lack of capital. Without an immediate market, or even credit from the customer, they were helpless. Fielden described the effects of the 1846-7 depression: 'The weaker and poorer manufacturers suffer the most. Of necessity, they sell their goods as they are produced, and almost invariably at a loss in seasons of bad trade. The wealthier lay up stocks of goods in these times of depression, if materials and labour are low, and when demand revives . . . they bring their stocks into the market and undersell their poorer competitors.'[35] Many remained permanently in pawn to Manchester. 'Some wealthy agent in Manchester', wrote Samuel Andrew on commission spinning in the 1830s, 'would provide these firms with cotton, and for every eighteen ounces of cotton weighed to the spinner, sixteen ounces of yarn would have to be sent to the agent in return, or the spinner would be debited the difference.'[36] All the little master had was his skill. As master he remained part of the work group and his family worked beside him. He had no use for the exclusiveness (or religion) of the tradesmen.

Pinning down the little masters statistically is even more difficult than it was with the tradesmen. The little masters did not form a social group of their own. They shared the general working-class allegiance to neighbourhood and the communities within which they lived were those of street, beerhouse and trade. As a result, most little masters' marriages were into manual worker families (see table 20, page 268). When Frederick Bleasby (millwright employing ten men and four boys) married a second time, it was to the daughter of a cotton weaver; living in the same household was Bleasby's brother, a journeyman painter. Isaac Whitely (millwright employing his son as mechanic and hiring room in one of the Jones's mills) had his daughter marry a cotton operative. Social relationships like this make it impossible to isolate a specifically 'little master' friendship clustering. On the other hand, to take all the sample employers with less than fifty employees would mean including quite a number of tradesmen. The best approximation is probably got by reversing the logic by which the tradesmen were isolated and taking all non-big bourgeoisie employers who were not members of religious congregations (table 13, page 202). Here, the irreligious show up against the religious (and to some extent against the general run of small employers) as mostly living next door to manual workers, employing their own families as labour, being born locally, and possessing no servants. As little masters they had no reason to try to escape from the immediate community of their own street.

Politically, however, differences remained. As employers (however small), the great majority of little masters voted consistently against Fielden and the working-class caucus. And even the 8 per cent minority that did vote for working-class candidates seem to have been more allies than convinced supporters. Industrially, the only issue on which there was any real overlap was short-time working in the cotton industry. Here one does find the little masters on occasion lining themselves up with the working spinners to try and limit overproduction, and doing so in defiance of the major employers.[37] But even the men leading such action and cooperating with the working class more generally remained ideologically distinct and formed a potential base from which petty bourgeois ideas could spread out into the movement as a whole. In this they were not unlike their counterparts among the tradesmen. Where they differed was in their particular brand of ideology. Almost to a man the 'little master' radicals were proponents of the Cobbett tradition within Oldham politics, a tradition which in their hands tended to lose its radically anti-state character and increasingly become focused on the defence of traditional rights: the freedom of the beer trade and the small workshop to exist without outside interference. As soon as the organized working class started to break up in the late 1840s, it was this group that played a major role in leading one part of it into alliance with the Tories. The small spinners, John Halliwell and Richard Fletcher, both active in the radical movement of the mid-1840s, backed Morgan Cobbett in 1847, and by the early 1850s were closely identified with the Tories. John Schofield, a master mechanic, was the last member of the Cobbett faction to sit on the town council (doing so till his death in 1863) and in 1853 acted as executor to its last mass leader, Alexander Taylor. Another previously radical master engineer, James Mannock, also acted as executor to a Cobbett faction town councillor, Daniel Newton.

Those, then, were the two quite distinct cultures that existed within Oldham's petty bourgeoisie. Both – in their detailed make-up – appear to derive from a group's particular position within the relations of production. Both also seem to show distinct signs of response to temporary working-class mastery – the tradesmen in their anti-establishment radicalism and the little masters in their partial assimilation of working-class manners – and ultimately to have generated attitudes and language which would play an important part in the process of restabilization. When they did so, however, it was within a framework created by the big bourgeoisie and it is this we must look at next.

Structure of the big bourgeoisie

Though Oldham's upper class consisted of less than two hundred households (and many less families), its interior structure was almost as complex as the rest of the population put together. Despite its size and high degree of intermarriage, one can distinguish within it three separate cultural groupings. Among the families dominating the isolated mill communities which surrounded Oldham there survived the traditional Puritan-Evangelical way of life examined in chapter 1. On the other hand, in Oldham itself, where the big employers now drew their labour from a fluid and anonymous population running to fifty thousand, the old Puritan set-up altogether lost its relevance. Instead, there developed two basically outward-looking cultures: one aligned to the great merchant families of Manchester; the other to the county aristocracy.

To begin, however, with another look at the traditional 'Puritan' culture as it survived into the nineteenth century. Just as in the seventeenth century, one can define its basic characteristic as the attempt to tie the worker into the larger household of the employer. There was the same drive to minimize differences in way of life, to build up the moral authority of the family head and propagate an explicitly Calvinist (salvation by grace) theology. But (as with eighteenth-century Evangelicalism) it represented a continuity of experience, not tradition. The town centre congregation of St Peter's lost its Evangelicalism as soon as the working relationship with labour broke down. In the 1820s, after the rebuilding of the parish church, the big bourgeoisie moved out altogether, leaving St Peter's to the tradesmen and small employers. The 'Puritans' of the nineteenth century came from the out-townships: Royton, Crompton, Lees, Hey and Waterhead.

A glance at the 1848 ordinance survey shows the situation: the closed group of employer's house, the mill and workers' cottages repeated a score of times over.[38] Moreover, the out-township population was notably permanent: 77 per cent of all heads of family lived where they were born (and this was so for the employers as much as the general population).[39] The workers' existence remained precarious. Their employers became steadily richer. This reality had to be lived with at an intimate face-to-face level.

Of the seven major out-township congregations there is information about the ministers of five. All called themselves Calvinists of some kind or other. Two of the congregations were Independent-Congregational: Hope, Lower Moor (Davies) and Greenacres (Waddington). The rest were Anglican: St John's, Hey (Grundy), St James, Greenacres (Walker) and Holy Trinity, Shaw (Brammal).[40] The Church of England, gaudy in the town centre, became conscientious in the out-townships, merging in doctrine, as its congregations did in marriage and friendship, with dissent. Davies (Independent) wrote at the death of his friend Walker (Anglican): 'In politics he was a liberal; in theology he was a Calvinist ... he cooperated cordially with his Nonconformist brethren'.[41] This could not have been said of Lowe at the town centre parish church. Grundy, the Hey minister, used to tell his Sunday school children that it was their duty 'to learn and labour truly to get mine own living and to do my duty in that station of life into which it shall please God to call me'.[42] For all but two of the twenty-nine families (and fifty households) that made up the 'traditional' friendship groupings there is evidence of attendance at one of the out-township congregations.[43]

Measuring Puritan 'abstinence' is more tricky. The best surviving evidence would appear to be domestic servants. Possession of more than one resident domestic servant would exempt 'upper-class' mothers and daughters from routine household work. A decision by families able to afford two or more servants to make do with less meant a fairly conscious choice of a Puritan pattern. According to the 1851 census of the thirteen professional families in Oldham leaving less than £25,000, seven had two or more servants. Both the professional families with over £25,000 had more than two servants. But of all fifty-eight employer families whom we know left over £25,000 (or its equivalent) thirty made do with less than two servants.[44] And if one looks closer it becomes clear that this 'abstinence' is closely associated with the out-townships and even more closely with those employers who belonged to the 'traditional' friendship grouping.

Table 10   Servants among Oldham employers leaving over £25,000[45]

(a) *Servants by area*

	rural	town	total
less than two servants	21 (22)	9 (5)	30 (27)
more than two	6 (9)	22 (20)	28 (29)
total	27 (31)	31 (25)	58 (56)

(b) *Servants by friendship group*

	traditional	non-traditional	total
less than two servants	13 (17)	3 (2)	16 (19)
more than two	6 (3)	20 (28)	26 (31)
total	19 (20)	23 (30)	42 (50)

In each case the first figure derives from the sample (appropriately weighted) and the second (in brackets) includes all houeholds on which there is information whether in the sample or not.

A few examples will clinch these figures. Abraham Crompton (who was head of one of the oldest and richest families in the area and a benefactor of Holy Trinity Church, Shaw) ultimately left £50,000 personalty (in addition to considerable real estate). His money came mainly from cotton mills which drew their labour from the community living round the Crompton house. But the Crompton household – consisting in 1851 of two adult sons and a widowed father – had no servants at all and was run by his daughters. The same could be said of the Milnes, Travises, Holdens (in the village of Shaw), of the Hagues, Mayalls, Ogdens and Wareings (in Greenacres), all members of the big bourgeoisie, all living with less than two domestic servants, all listening every Sunday to Anglican Calvinist ministers. And, on the other side, it is easy to pile up examples of easy-going dissenters, members of the town-centre group: the Baptist James Cheetham with four female servants and a butler; Bankside Thompson, the owner of the mill involved in the 1834 dispute, a Quaker, with footmen as well as works police.

What moulded the traditional pattern of life was the need to maintain a working relationship with the small local population on which the employer families depended for labour; populations with faces, names and memories. Grundy felt this when he moved to his new parish at Lees. 'Whatever convenient or new refinement

any well-off person adopted, the worse-off nicknamed it "aristocratic" ... At Colton we had a small pony carriage. At Lees it
was treason to let a cab stand at the door.'[46] The same thing in
reverse, and reflecting the earlier disintegration of the 'working
relationship' in the town, is described by an Oldham working-
class satirist of the 1840s:

> The dames of old were trained to household toil,
> To brew and stew, to wash and bake and boil:
> Their daughters now in costly silks appear
> And study grace and manners by the year.[47]

But it is important to remember what lay behind it all. Puritanism cloaked the cleavage between capital and labour. Its net result
was to promote inequality. Any interpretation which leaves this
out of account is not going to get very far. As well as spreading
out spatially to engross labour, the out-township family had a
dimension in time which could stand as the essence of the whole
system: the inheritance of accumulated property. The employer
saw himself as son and grandson to an estate and judged himself
within this familial (still almost peasant) perspective. He was
successful if he increased the inheritance. The pattern of industry
itself made wealth more familial than personal. The capital
requirements of high-profit production meant that a firm's assets
could not be divided up every generation. Among the score of
firms in the traditional group all but a couple were run in 1851
by more than one head of household, a set-up in which the cohesion of the family was reinforced by the legal device of tenancy
in common.[48] At the very core of the traditional family was this
life and death struggle for wealth. Puritanism comprised the rules
of thumb passed on from generation to generation by which
labour, the source of it all, could be controlled.

The traditional way of life was, then, a special relationship
with labour. The relationship, while it worked, could be very
effective. But it was not pleasant. It meant a supervision of the
workman's life that went far beyond the mill. The quittance paper
was enforced to keep militants out of the area.[49] A close eye was
kept on politics. Mortimer Grimshaw, the power-weavers' leader,
described the situation at Greenacres in 1852:

> Every day brings to light some fresh deed of atrocity perpetrated
> by the Foxite employers .... The names of nearly fifty indi-
> viduals are before us who have been discharged by their

Foxite masters because they would not vote for their candidate at the late municipal elections . . . . Not content with discharging their workpeople who will not be their tools, they have withdrawn all their short-time workers from the school of John Dawson because that teacher has dared raise up his voice.[50]

Twenty years earlier Butterworth fairly shook with anger over what he called the 'tyranny of the cotton masters' at Shaw:

> We are astonished and staggered at the numerous instances of the inhuman conduct of these men . . . . They lately enforced an arbitrary attempt to delude [the factory commissioners] . . . by requiring all their work-people to throw away their comfortable clogs and even at the expense of a meal or sleeping on a cold hearth instead of a bed compelled them to buy shoes and procure dresses. . . . Were it not likely to prove injurious to several of the workmen we could adduce uncommon instances of hardship.[51]

Control as total as this paid its dividends. If Factory Act convictions are any evidence, there was far more systematic overworking in the out-townships than the town, with double the number of convictions per employer and only four of the twenty-five firms escaping a court appearance in the twenty years up to 1855.[52] While Grimshaw's interpretation of the relationship between religion and capitalism may be 'crude', at least he and his fellow-workers had their reasons:

> You may see them [he wrote of the Greenacres employers] wending their way to some chapel so demurely that you might imagine that the big saints had never done anything wrong, and no doubt their very thoughts at that instant are how another penny may be screwed from the hard-won earnings of their workpeople.[53]

The two non-'traditional' cultures developed wherever this household relationship had either collapsed or never existed.

Coal left little scope. The large scale of workings, a consortium of owners and the mystery of the miner down the pit only confirmed the obvious improbability of the Jones's passing themselves off as half-brothers to the pitmen. In hatting, some of the largest employers brought in the substantial capital needed from outside, and all recruited their labour from the town centre. This was also true of an increasingly large proportion of the cotton industry and the two great engineering firms which emerged in the 1830s.

At the middle of the century, non-abstinent households (and the accompanying friendship groups) included the five great hatting families (Clegg, Barker, Taylor, Gillham and Nelson), the coalowners not tied up in out-township cotton production (Jones, Lees of Upper and Lower Clarksfield and Werneth, Wrigley and Booth), the engineers (Platt, Hibbert and Eli and Asa Lees) and a dozen or so families whose money was mainly in town-centre cotton (Bailey, Barlow, Broadbent, Firwood, Cheetham, Collinge, Duncuft, Gledhill, Greenbank Lees, Mellor, Radcliffe, Rowland, Shiers, Tattershall and Wright). Tagging along hopefully came a dozen professional families: Church of England ministers (William Lees, Lowe, Holme, Hordern and Mills) and the lawyers (Ascroft, William Barlow, Bellot, Broome, Edward Brown, Kay Clegg, Littler, Henry Radcliffe, Redfern and Summerscales).

The professionals packed themselves into a short terrace of genteel houses in Queen Street.[54] Many of the employers themselves lived in the large-gardened mansions described by Butterworth in 1817: Pit Bank House, Bent Grange, Chamber Hall, Frank Hill, Orleans House. Others banded together to establish small 'upper class' enclaves. In 1841 the four large households of Collinge, Firwood Cheetham, E. A. Wright and Lancashire stood together on Greenhill. The Jones's with the banker Donaldson and R. J. Broome formed a smaller group at Mumps. And in 1847 the Platts, Hibberts, Eli Lees and Radcliffes combined to lay out an estate in Werneth Park.[55] Ultimately they moved out altogether. By the late 1860s none of the thirty-odd town-centre families remained permanently based in Oldham; for most the move had come considerably earlier.[56]

By residence, then, as well as economic circumstance, these employers were insulated from labour. The traditions of the mill household and the backward-looking familial tests of personal achievement lost their power. Instead the town-centre families looked to the ruling groups in Manchester and the country, seeing success in the present tense and relative to others with roughly the same income. Generally they had a much tighter order of peck, more sharply defined subgroupings and greater internal competition for precedence. Style and consumption became meaningful in themselves.

The group aligned to the country aristocracy contained the coalowners and the hat manufacturers and kept in close contact with the hierarchy of executive government: quarter sessions and lieutenancy, county MPs and cabinet. Both coalowners and hatters were in lines of business which had in the past rendered these contacts useful. In 1802, when Colonel John Lees of Werneth (lord of the manor) wanted to work the Greenacres coal measures, the Act of Enclosure appointed as commissioners his son-in-law Captain Chippendale (the Home Office agent), Colonel Fletcher (the Bolton coalowner and Chippendale's immediate superior) and John Clegg (a Manchester relative of Lees' business partners, the Cleggs of Bent).[57] Oldham's great hatting firms consumed a significant fraction of the beaver furs produced by the chartered Canadian monopolies. Buying direct in the London fur sales, and negotiating with the government over drawbacks and excise, the hatters also found these contacts useful.[58]

The 'county' group predictably supplied almost all the yeomanry officers.[59] The Home Office papers show them going about their duties: in March 1819 Captain Joseph Jones observing ('from a distance') a party of armed men drilling at Royton; in July Captain John Taylor tracking another party as they moved out to the moors; and on the morning of Peterloo Chippendale and his fellow officers watching the radical detachments assembling on Tandle Hill 'through a telescope in the garden of Mr Edward Lees'.[60] Half a generation later the same men can be seen following similar though less active paths: Jones entertaining Lord Francis Edgerton and the Hon. R. Wilbraham;[61] on the hustings at the 1837 election ('greeted by tremendous yells and hootings');[62] and in the conflict-ridden summer of 1834 sharing out the prizes at the prime 'county' gathering, 'Oldham floral and agricultural society', Taylor with the best red-laced pinks, John Lees of Clarksfield with the best basket of flowers, and Jones himself with early strawberries.[63] These, to quote Andrew, the working-class satirist, were the men

> Who just to show the world the time of day,
> Hunt, bet and swagger, drive their pairs and play.[64]

For men primarily interested in cotton the important links were those with Manchester. Two, even three, days a week they dined and bargained with the well-heeled merchants of the Exchange. In 1832, when the anti-slavery agitation seemed to threaten Caribbean cotton production, determined efforts were made to get Heywood Bright, the planters' Bristol agent, elected MP for Oldham. His backers included Mellor, Greenbank Lees, Barlow, Rowland, Radcliffe and Platt.[65] The same group appears again in 1840 (together with their bank manager Henry Tipping) to organize an 'Oldham British India Society' for the purpose of 'expressing the importance of improving British India'.[66] And regularly from 1840 the same names recur at the meetings of the anti-corn law league.[67]

This Manchester subgrouping contained the larger segment of the town-centre big bourgeoisie: Collinge, Barlow, E. A. Wright, Cheetham and Lancashire; Duncuft, Worthington, Radcliffe, Rowland and Mellor; Greenbank Lees, Shiers, Tattershall and Mellor; and the Platts, Hibberts and Eli and Asa Lees. The last group, the machine-makers, kept close to their customers, and the three families, besides themselves being interrelated, were linked by marriage with the Radcliffes, Duncufts and Worthingtons. The marrying was done in St Mary's and the whole group after signing the register (the page covered with florid signatures) would go off to feast: 'Trout in aspic, salmon, boned turkey, lamb, boiled fowls, tongues, roast fowls, ham, capon, ducklings, pheasants, guinea fowl, ptarmigan . . . .'[68]

The county's gold-laced epaulettes and aristocratic connections gave them (in their own minds at least) the edge over the Manchester grouping. This, plus the clash of rentier patronage and corn law repeal, made for a certain lack of sympathy. In the covert and sometimes open attacks which the Manchester group made on the county, the families which generally took the lead were the Hibberts and Platts – both engineers, very rich, 'modern and scientific' and soon to enjoy a toehold in the Crystal Palace. In the 1830s the challenge was mostly limited to anti-voting. When J. F. Lees (Colonel Lees's grandson) stood to win in the 1835 by-election, Elijah Hibbert, Henry Platt, Eli Lees, the Barlows and a scattering of traditionals voted the other way.[69] Sporadic attempts were made in non-critical churchwarden elections to put in a 'Manchester' list against the 'county'.[70] Later, John Platt was to make much more determined efforts, elbowing Joseph and William Jones off the town council and, in the parliamentary elections, getting his cousin Duncuft, then his brother, and finally himself, elected. The Jones's pulled out to become country gentlemen in the early 1850s, a good decade before the Platts.[71]

But the emnity must not be overstated. Both groups faced the common problem of living in the town and employing its mutinous population. The list of trustees appointed by Act in 1824 for the rebuilding of St Mary's stands complete as a roll-call of the town-centre bourgeoisie.[72] The same goes for the 1825 Gas and Water Act, an equally suspect piece of legislation.[73] Attempts to maintain or re-establish class influence over the general population were marked by an even broader co-partnership. The committee of the 1813 British and Foreign Bible Society contained, in addition to representatives of the county grouping (Clegg and Lees) and Manchester (Mellor) one from the traditional out-township families (Joseph Galland, the Greenacres minister).[74] The trustee lists for the elaborate system of charity patronage (which served the same ends) all contain representatives from each of the three segments of the 'upper class'.[75]

In more direct confrontation with the working class the same pattern persists. Signatures from every bourgeois family in the neighbourhood are appended to the 1821 barracks petition.[76] Whenever there was real danger the ranks closed: over the elections of constables in the early 1820s; on the vestry and police commission in the 1830s; against Fielden in 1847. On the magistrates' bench, controlling the ultimate sanctions of class rule, representatives of all three groups sat side by side.[77]

This, then, was the structure of Oldham's big bourgeoisie: seventy families, two hundred households, all ultimately related, immensely wealthy, sealed off by their economic function and concomitant capital from the petty bourgeoisie and the population as a whole. In isolating its internal structure the most important single method was the reconstruction of friendship groupings and the groups that emerged were, therefore, real enough, containing people who went to each others' weddings and funerals and acted as mutual executors. But though the friendship clusterings were used to isolate the groupings, the groupings themselves plainly derived from the common position of their members within the relations of production. The particular way a man used his capital modified his behaviour. It was the relationship with the factory village which had the wife of an out-township employer doing the cooking, and his son 'working his way through the mill'. In the town, men who had to make conversation with Manchester merchants or run errands for the Derbys developed different manners and allegiances. Families associated with those who had struck their bargains with economic reality on the same terms as themselves.

The big bourgeoisie and the working-class challenge

> The country was in the condition that . . . France was in just before the breaking out of the first revolution. Mr Arthur Young who was resident in France at the outbreak of the revolution which shook that country to atoms . . . wrote these words: 'It is impossible to justify the excesses of the people in taking up arms; they were guilty of certain cruelties. . . . But is it really the people to whom we are to impute the whole – or to their oppressors. . . . ? He who chooses to be served by slaves . . . must not in the moment of insurrection complain . . . [78]

This was Fielden delivering one of his periodic threats. The task of this final section is to assess the response of the big bourgeoisie to the challenge of working-class consciousness and (inasmuch as this involved a crucial change of course) its *crisis*.

The biggest problem, of course, is to disentangle the national and the local. With the big bourgeoisie so nationally orientated it is difficult to tell where one ended and the other began. But some obvious points may be made at the beginning. If one tries to pinpoint a decisive change in attitude to England's existing political economy (and social stability), one finds the tide of reassessment clearly starting in Westminster, not the factory districts. In Oldham, as will be seen in the next chapter, the turning point did not come till the onset of the 1846-8 depression. It is only then that one finally gets key figures within the big bourgeoisie coming out in favour of short-time and household suffrage.

Nationally, however, the critical period seems to have been the late 1830s and early 1840s. A whole string of crucial initiatives were made during these years. 1838 saw the beginning of moves which were to culminate in the 1844 Bank Act and the development of more informal (but no less important) Bank of England controls over industrial credit. Together these had vital implications for the stabilization of Britain's currency in the interests of overseas banking and capital export. 1841 marked the setting up of a select committee which would (in 1842) result in the lifting of the long-contested ban on machinery exports (and especially that on textile machinery). And in 1844 there was the passing of a Factory Act which at least partly reflected the home secretary's conviction – strongly reinforced by the events of 1842 – that the expansion of the factory sector somehow had to be brought under control.[79] Finally, and most significant of all, it was these years that saw an explicit reversal of positions by key figures in the intellectual establishment. In the early 1840s both McCulloch and Senior found reason to retreat from this previously unqualified endorsement of domestic industrial expansion.[80] In their place, the rising star of political economy was now J. S. Mill, an open proponent of capital export and domestic class collaboration.

Given this sequence of events, it would obviously be quite wrong to suggest any simple relationship between working-class pressures on the industrial bourgeoisie and a national switch in policy. The real process of change was obviously more complex. On the purely economic side there were the governmental and banking reactions to the increasingly severe economic crises of the 1830s and early 1840s (usually blamed on domestic industrial speculation), a recognition of the gains to be won by making London *the* international banking centre, and the emergence of the necessary technological conditions for large-scale capital export. Socially, there was the very real perception of the dangers presented by the existing economic course. And – as far as the industrial bourgeoisie was concerned – not so much a change of analysis as a loss of will to oppose changes which still cut across their basic interests.[81] It was the interlocking of all these factors that brought the national change.

Moreover, when one turns to the local change in attitude one finds it not so much addressed to the government as to the immediate social problem of resuming cultural control over the general population. As with the tradesmen and little masters, it marks a return to cultural expansion. (One thing that stands out from the Oldham evidence is the general lack of public statements on public issues before 1845 and their frequency after.) And also like the petty bourgeoisie, its language seems to have developed in response to the pressures of the earlier period and involved a thoroughgoing modification of bourgeois culture.

It is important to remember the starkness of the confrontation (and responsibility). Oldham's seventy big bourgeois families lived off twelve thousand working families in a most unpleasant way, getting their profit from child labour in the factories and mines and from the sweated labour of handloom weavers. The average income of a working family was around £75 a year, that of a bourgeois family over £5,000, and between them this minute group (far less than 1 per cent of the population) took over half the community's income.[82] Or to put things the other way round, if the bourgeoisie was expropriated, the income of each worker family could be doubled. As the constables warned in 1843, 'during the time that must necessarily elapse before military assistance could be obtained from the nearest military station an immense loss of life and property might be sustained'.[83]

Now obviously, this type of situation was not new. It had existed long before the 1830s and 1840s and not prevented the bourgeoisie making a spirited and intellectually effective defence of their position. Where the position now differed was in the collapse of this old 'intellectual' type of justification in face of economic crisis and working-class attack. Previously it had been possible to present inequality (and capital accumulation) as the necessary price of progress. Now capitalist inequality stood plainly in the way of further advance. And if the big bourgeoisie were to regain effective cultural control, it had to find other explanations for poverty and inequality that would divert attention from their own responsibility. Indeed, this was as much a necessity for their own cultural integrity as a precondition for social stabilization.

What strikes one most about the social perspective which resulted is the degree to which it marked a *retreat* from rationality. Its language was simplistic, its ultimate explanations founded on divinity, not economics, and its view of society reduced to that of the family. What follows can only provide the sketchiest outline of these emerging attitudes, but it should at least make clear that there was a basic departure from the dispassionate political economy of earlier generations.

To start by quoting an address given in 1848 by a local lawyer, Richard Broome, and later printed at the expense of the Oldham Lyceum:

The wealthy may be looked upon as the parents and guardians of the poor. . . . We would say to the masters – take a lively interest in the prosperity and well-being of the working classes. They are your servants; if faithful, respect them and encourage a continuance of their duties. Educate them and they will not be found, as before, listening with greedy ear to the insidious advice, the anarchical and revolutional dicta of facinerious demagogues either resident or itinerant . . . mentally sterile for any good work, yet displaying a wonderful superfoetation of mind to fructify the dissemination of Hydra-headed evil. . . . The ignorance of the people is the support of restless agitators – the prolific source of agitation. Food of hungry and designing knaves, who, having nothing to lose, care even less for the rights and property of others. Supply the mind with food. Leisure hours devoted to good and healthy instruction – and not to secret meetings, imbibing conventional principles, often ruinous to the men and prejudicial to the masters – will gradually produce a thirst for knowledge. . . . Your much-to-be-regretted turn-outs will be fewer in number. The enlightened and well-trained mind may listen to the voice of reason; but ignorance – dark, sullen, depraved ignorance, with all its inimical bearings, its evil concomitants – never. . . .[84]

Broome was a Tory and a friend of the Jones. But almost exactly the same language was used by the other wing of the big bourgeoisie. Here is James Platt, the liberal engineer, writing in 1850:

Ignorance is now regarded as the parent and perpetuation of error and misery, and no man in his senses looks for good from so evil a tree. The notion that men would more readily obey legitimate authority because they were utterly ignorant of its claims and their obligations, or that they would better discharge and fulfil the responsibilities that Providence had assigned them because they were kept in darkness as to the reciprocities of social life, will now be rejected as the most preposterous of fallacies.[85]

'Good', 'evil', 'Providence' were the pass words, and 'education' – cultural control by the bourgeoisie – the immediate solution. Indeed, 'education' represented the typical bourgeois response to the biggest intellectual challenge of all, mass poverty.[86] Not just was any independent working-class perspective seen as 'evil', the physical conditions in which working people had to exist were themselves attributed to 'immorality'. This is Kay Shuttleworth (brought up in a Rochdale banker household) trying to explain an increase in poverty in Manchester:

> The population gradually becomes physically inefficient as the producers of wealth – morally so from idleness – politically *worthless* . . . and noxious as dissipators of capital accumulated . . . morality would afford no check to the increase of population: crime which banishes or destroys its victims, and disease and death are severe but brief natural remedies which prevent the unlimited accumulation of the horrors of pauperism. Even war and pestilence when regarded as affecting a population thus demoralized . . . seem like storms which sweep from the atmosphere the noxious vapours whose stagnation threatens man with death.[87]

The disease metaphors are characteristic. In 1839 Shuttleworth was writing (as secretary to the Privy Council for education) that 'education' is to be regarded as one of 'the most important means of eradicating the germs of pauperism from the rising generation',[88] and Rickards, Oldham's local factory inspector, believed that without 'a sound moral and physical education the manufacturing population remained the slaves of vice, prejudice and passion'. Every child 'should be compelled to attend a Sunday school. It is only by systematic education that the vicious habits of this population can be corrected'.[89] For Broome the great function of education was to remove children from the 'prejudice of ignorant parents'.[90] And John Platt, speaking at the opening of the Oldham 'mission' in 1860, believed that 'if the children of the degraded and criminal classes are allowed to grow up untaught . . . they will become a source of great annoyance. Therefore it is better to grapple with the difficulty at once, and endeavour to nip the evil in the bud'.[91]

The pathology of all this is brought out by comparing the Shuttleworth's demand for more state-aided education with John Knight's verdict on Sunday schools. Shuttleworth:

> There are social disorders not attributable to defects in the physical condition of the people. The trade unions, which have long endeavoured to limit the number of workmen in the best-paid employments; to prescribe a minimum of wages; to impose a uniform standard of wages for young and old, the feeble and the robust, the industrious and the negligent, and

to withdraw workers from the control of their masters, have for long periods rendered the working classes . . . the victims of their ignorance. . . . Those who pretend that public liberty is endangered by the rewards which the government desire to give to efficient school masters . . . appear to forget how many thousand troops of the line are employed to protect the institutions of the country – how many thousand police to watch the houses and protect their persons – how many warders, gaolers and keepers of the hulks. . . .[92]

Knight:

He was not so ardent an admirer of the system upon which the Sunday schools were at present conducted. They were supported by the rich. . . . And, in the end, what was the substance of the instruction. . . ? Why, they were taught to toil as hard as they could and to live upon as little as they could – the doctrine of passive obedience and submission to those who possessed wealth and power . . . in a word, instead of teaching the poor, or endeavouring to excite a free and independent spirit among them, the conductors of these schools might be considered as preparing children for slavery and degradation.[93]

It seems fairly clear, therefore, that the need to resume broader cultural control did – in the new conditions of the 1840s – profoundly modify the social perspectives of the big bourgeoisie. The new world-view which they sought to project on to the rest of the population reduced social relationships to those of the family and only evaded the problem of class responsibility by blotting out key areas of social perception. In fact, it has been argued that it involved even more than this: that it was the need to maintain the credibility of this good-evil 'child world' which imposed the straight-jacket discipline of 'Victorian' manners.[94] Certainly it was only in the 1840s – after the bourgeoisie had begun their battle to resume wider cultural dominance – that Oldham's working-class satirists started to lampoon this particular aspect of their culture (and generally associated it with just those figures who took a leading part in this process). Here, for instance, is R. S. Andrew describing George Worthington, member of a family which played a major role in developing a popular base for Oldham Toryism:

> Let Worthington with many a simpering smile
> Reply to ladies' healths in honied style
> And call on heaven to shield the pretty doves
> That is – the Tory petticoated loves.[95]

Worthington was also the butt of another working-class writer, Benjamin Grime:

> The following is somewhat in keeping with the style of language in which [he] . . . often indulged on the appropriate occasions: 'The Ladies, Mr Chairman, Gentlemen – the conservative angels of this loyal town – delightful creatures – absolute divinities – cheek on which the rose and lily struggle bashfully into light – tender and gentle as fawns . . . .[96]

Greenbank Lees, the second major of Oldham, similarly provoked popular ribaldry. To quote Grime on Lees's part as returning officer during the 1852 election riots: 'His fine notions of propriety . . . flattered him that violent and rebellious spirits could be quieted by the utterance of cant phrases in an affected and pedantic tone'.[97]

Moreover, what the working-class commentators ridiculed in particular was the make-believe and prudery used to keep reality (with all its implications) at arm's length. This was what they found to attack in the Reverend Thomas Lowe (of the town-centre parish church) and his diminutive church schoolmaster, Langstaffe – both active in 'the erection of new churches and the extension of the principles of the established church'.[98]

First Andrew:

> Let Lowe, with soul inspired with godly zeal
> Seize 'Rochester's Memoirs' and 'Fanny Hill'
> And Langstaffe make his silly heroine sigh
> And place a tear on tip-toe in her eye.[99]

And Whitworth (journalist and friend of Edwin Butterworth):

> And Parson, Mary's matchless clerk, comes next,
> The sweet expounder of the hackneyed text,
> Adonis of the pulpit – king of hearts –
> High priest of Hymen – butt for cupid's darts.[100]

And while the ultimate drive behind the development of this 'polite' culture was clearly the need to resume a broader cultural mastery, its practical preservation seems to have involved a new element of class segregation. Andrew's comments on the manners of the rich have already been partly quoted:

> Their daughters now in costly silks appear
> And study grace and manners by the year;
> Expand their parasols on cloudy days
> That no rude son may bronze them with his rays
> Sing, waltz, chatter, parlez-vous francais.
> The purest porcelain of the Oldham clay;
> And curl their noses if a son of toil
> Perfume the air with shoddy dust and oil.[101]

More crudely, there were the iron railings put up in Lowe's neo-Gothic St Mary's; built, as Butterworth wrote, to the orders of 'opulent hatters, coalowners and cotton spinners' – 'that strutting, vain, egoistical crowd', but paid for out of a rate levied on working-class householders:

> The iron railings divide the free from the private pews or the honest rags of poverty from the rich attire of roguery . . . . 'Free' is inscribed as if to mock us for our absurdity – what should we think of the rascal who after dipping his hand in our pocket told us we were free . . . ?[102]

Finally, to sum up. The chapter began by examining the structural peculiarities of Oldham's bourgeoisie: the fact that it contained (in contrast to Northampton or South Shields) a large and distinct sector of extremely wealthy magnate families, that it was consequently divided politically and culturally into big and petty bourgeois sectors, and (also unlike Northampton and Shields) possessed no larger social 'tail' of intermediate non-bourgeois occupations such as small shopkeepers and clerks. The chapter also tried to show how the various component cultures within this bourgeoisie did ultimately derive – as the original quotation from Marx indicated – from differing 'material foundations' and their 'corresponding social relations'. However, the chapter's main task was to define the response to working-class challenge and here the evidence was much less satisfactory. There was again the problem of disentangling national and local. Going by the dates it seems unlikely that the industrial bourgeoisie of south Lancashire played much part – except by default – in determining the fairly decisive change in national economic policy that took place in the early 1840s. What happened locally seems to have been a more gradual, though no less fundamental, process of cultural modification. Under the impact of working-class challenge, profound changes occurred in the attitudes of all three major components of Oldham's bourgeoisie. Among the two petty bourgeois sectors, the tradesmen and the small masters, the period of working-class alliance produced new ideologies which would play a key go-between role in creating a new bourgeois-dominated alliance in the late 1840s. And for the big bourgeoisie itself, whose intellectual change of front ultimately made this alliance possible, the abandonment of orthodox political economy demanded the substitution of a new world-view which (as has just been noted) appears to have involved a big step back from rationality. What has to be tackled next is the overall process of liberalization in which these changes found full expression.

Note on methods

Two main methods have been used in the analysis of the bourgeoisie: a sample (based on 1851) and the reconstruction of friendship groupings.

The sample: Its basic outline is described in the text and the principal results are given by occupation in table 11. The sampling fraction adopted for each category is stated at the foot of each column. The sample framework comes from *Slater's Directory of Manchester and Salford, 1851*. 'Cotton' includes manufacturers, spinners, candlewick, rope and twine. 'Coal' all proprietors. 'Engineers' millwrights, machine makers, bolt makers, iron founders, gas-meter manufacturers. 'Surgeons' qualified medical practitioners. 'Tradesmen' builders, drapers, timber merchants, shoe dealers, lime merchants, hosiery manufacturers, wine and spirit merchants. 'Other fixed capital' dyers, curriers, millers, printers, brickmakers, chemical manufacturers, tanners, bleachers. 'Employing own family as labour' refers to routine manual labour only, and is an attempt to distinguish little masters. 'Tory': voters for Duncuft, Heald, Morgan Cobbett after 1852, Spinks, J. F. Lees. 'Whig': Bright, Fox, Platt, Hibbert. 'Radical': Fielden, Cobbett, Morgan Cobbett in 1847, General Johnson.

Table 12 is an attempt to approximate *social* groupings within the bourgeoisie. In addition to members of the occupational sample it also includes magistrates (Oldham petty sessions 1851), town councillors (also 1851) and poor law guardians (1851). 'Traditional' and 'non-traditional' groupings are based on friendship clusterings. 'Sub-£25,000 small employers': all sub-£25,000 employers with less than fifty workers. The groupings combine members drawn from both 1 : 1 and 1 : 2 samples. The results are, therefore, weighted estimates. The figures in brackets are the contributions from each sample (the 1 : 1 figure comes first). 'Magistrate/councillor' also includes poor law guardians. 'Vestry/police' denotes active members of the vestry and members of the police commission. 'Lyceum' includes membership of any trade, political or social organization of which there is a record.

Figure 23 (page 165) includes comparative material on wealth from similar samples made for Northampton and Shields (using *Slater's Bedfordshire Directory for 1850* and *Ward's North of England Directory for 1851*). For Northampton and Shields the evidence is entirely drawn from probate personalty and the proportions worth more or less than £25,000 are estimated from those cases on which there is information (the detailed results can be found in Foster, PhD, pp. 214-5). For Oldham the probate material has been supplemented by evidence on rateable value, numbers of resident domestic servants and numbers of workers employed. As is shown in table 13, it is possible to make certain minimum assumptions about the relationships: that a man with more than one resident servant (who is also an employer) is likely to be worth more than £25,000 – as is a man with more than a hundred employees or rated at over £250. These assumptions, however, only apply to Oldham.

Friendship groupings: For living communities fairly sophisticated techniques have been developed for reconstructing friendship groupings. Generally, these make group membership depend on friendship with at least half the existing members. Here *any* link with an existing group member (by marriage, executorship or business) has been taken as indicating membership. In practice, the groups which emerge are internally fairly consistent and show 'network' rather than 'chain' patterns (though this, of course, varies with the completeness of the sample and the yield of information). The individuals involved are mostly drawn from the 1851 sample (itself covering over half the total bourgeoisie members) but others not included in the sample selection have also been used. The groups set out below are neither claimed as complete nor altogether mutually exclusive.

'Traditional employers' (some marriage links with 'non-traditional')

Lees (Waterhead), John*: cotton, Greenacres moor Presbyterian, Whig, born locally

Moss, Edward and Elkanah: Cotton and property, Anglican, Whig, father immigrant

Wareing, John and John*: cotton, Anglican, Whig-Tory, local

Mayall, Edward and John: coal and cotton, Greenacres Presbyterian/Anglican, Whig, local

Greaves, John, James, Joseph*: cotton, Anglican, Whig-Tory, local

Hague (Acre), John and Jonathan*: cotton, Anglican, Tory, local

Hague (Vineyard), Samuel*: cotton, Anglican, Tory, local

Newton, James*: cotton, Greenacres Presbyterian, Whig, local

Taylor, Samuel Marlor: cotton, Anglican, Tory, local

Andrew (County End), John and Samuel* cotton, Anglican, Tory, local

Booth (Lees) John: cotton, Greenacres Presbyterian/Anglican, Tory, local

Taylor, G. B.: cotton, Greenacres Presbyterian, Whig, local

Schofield, Jonathan, John, Andrew: wine merchants, Anglican, Whig, local

Holden, John*: cotton, Anglican, Whig, local

Walker, W. F.: minister St James, Anglican, Whig, immigrant

Davies, R. M.: minister Hope Chapel, Congregational, Whig, immigrant

Crompton, Abraham*: coal and cotton, Anglican, Tory, local

Cocker, J. T. and Thomas*: coal, Anglican, Tory, local

Milne, John and Henry Travis*: cotton and coal, Anglican, Tory, local

Seville, Isaac, Joseph, Thomas*: cotton and coal, Anglican, Whig, local

Travis, George*: coal and cotton, Anglican, Whig, local

Cheetham (Clough), James, James and Joshua*: cotton, Weslyan, Whig, local

Stott, James*: coal, Anglican, Tory, local

Evans, Edward: coal, Anglican, Tory

* Employer worth over £25,000 with less than two servants

Non-traditional big bourgeoisie (county)
Jones, Joseph and William: coal, cotton, banking, Anglican, Tory, local, Volunteer officers
Lees (Clarksfield), John, James and Joseph: coal, Anglican, Tory, local, officers
Lees (Werneth), Edward, J. F., George and Chippendale: coal, Anglican, Tory, local, officers
Barker, Thomas and James: hatting and coal, Anglican, Tory, local, officers
Taylor, John and James Myers: hatting, Anglican, Tory, local, officers
Redfern, Richard: lawyer, Anglican, Tory, local
Bailey, Frederick: cotton, Anglican, local
Clegg (the Bents), James and Abraham: hatting, Anglican, Tory, local, officers
Gillham, Charles and Joseph: hatting, Anglican, Whig, immigrant
Brown, Edward: lawyer and coal, Anglican, Tory, local, officer
Bellot, Abraham and Owen: surgeons, land, cotton, Anglican, Tory, local, officer
Littler, Henry: lawyer, Anglican, Tory

Non-traditional big bourgeoisie (Manchester) – several marriage links with 'county' group
Lees (Greenbank), James: coal and cotton, Anglican, Tory, local
Lees (Primrose), John: cotton, Anglican, Tory, local
Becker, Hannibal and John L.: chemicals, Tory, German
Wright, E. A.: cotton and coal, Anglican, Tory, local
Collinge, James: cotton, coal, iron, Anglican, Tory, local
Mellor, Jonathan: cotton and railways, Anglican, Tory, local
Wrigley, William: coal, Anglican, Tory, local
Livesey, Thomas: coal, land, Anglican, Tory, local
Cheetham, James and John Taylor: cotton, Baptist, Whig, local
Barlow, George and William: cotton, lawyer, Anglican, Whig, local, father officer
Dunkerley, Enoch: surgeon, Greenacres Presbyterian, Whig, local
Rowland, James, Joseph and John: coal and cotton, Anglican, Tory, local
Clegg (Schoolcroft), Kay: lawyer, (secretary to cotton masters), Anglican, Whig, local
Radcliffe, Samuel, John, Joseph and sons: cotton, Anglican, Whig-

Tory, local (father immigrant from Saddleworth where family were manufacturers)

Platt, Henry, John, James: coal and iron, Greenacres Presbyterian /Anglican, Whig, father immigrant from Saddleworth

Lees (Count Hill), Samuel, Eli, Asa: coal, iron, cotton, Greenacres Presbyterian, Whig, local

Hibbert, Elijah, John, Thomas: coal, iron, Anglican, Whig, Ashton

Whitehead, William: land and coal, Anglican, Whig, local

Emmot, George and Thomas: civil engineering, cotton, Quaker, Whig, immigrant

Schofield, Andrew: timber merchant, Anglican, Whig, local

Duncuft, John, John and James: coal, cotton and railways, Anglican, Tory, local

Worthington, John, George, Nathaniel, John: coal and cotton, Anglican, Tory, local

Lees, William: Anglican minister (St Peter's), Tory, local

Lowe, Thomas: Anglican minister (St Mary's), Tory, immigrant

Broome, Richard: lawyer, Anglican, Tory, local

Shiers, Richard: cotton, Anglican, Tory, immigrant

Broadbent, Samuel: cotton, Anglican, Whig, local

Tradesmen

Riley, Joseph, John and Samuel: drapers, Weslyan, Fox, local

Wainwright, George, John and Joseph: drapers, Weslyan, Fox, immigrant

Beard, John: small cotton spinner, Weslyan, Fox, immigrant

Turner, Charles: hosiery, Congregationalist, Tory, immigrant

Fitton, Richard and Robert: small cotton, Anglican, Fox, local

Suthers, Spencer: small cotton, Congregationalist, Fox, local

Mellor, Hague: leather dealer, Weslyan, Fox, local

Fielding, Samuel: corn merchant, Weslyan, Fox, immigrant

Charlesworth, William: small cotton, Fox

Clegg (Mumps Mills): small cotton, Anglican, Fox, local

Hirst, John: printer, cotton, Weslyan, Fox, local

Hamilton, George: corn merchant, Anglican, Fox, local

Cooper, Reuben: grocer, Weslyan, Fox, immigrant

Dean, Samuel: shoe dealer, Fox, immigrant

Table 11 Oldham bourgeoisie by occupation, 1851

	cotton	coal	hatting	engineers	surgeons and solicitors	Anglican clergy	dissenting ministers	cotton waste	tradesmen	other fixed capital
Birthplace										
Oldham	58	13	7	22	11	2	2	21	18	4
within twenty miles	8	1	0	6	8	0	1	3	7	2
over twenty miles	2	0	1	13	8	11	8	3	10	3
total known	68	14	8	41	27	13	11	27	35	9
Servants										
none	22	3	2	24	5	1	3	16	18	4
one	19	2	3	8	6	5	4	8	10	2
two or more	11	4	2	3	10	5	0	0	2	1
total known	52	9	7	35	21	11	7	24	30	7
Employing own family as labour	7	0	2	7	—	—	—	8	6	0
total known	31	9	7	15	—	—	—	13	18	6
Politics										
Whig	54	3	7	34	11	1	10	28	25	9
Tory	27	15	2	8	14	9	4	8	6	4
radical	1	1	1	3	5	0	0	2	4	3
total known	85	19	10	45	30	10	14	38	35	16
Religion										
Anglican	30	8	5	6	18	—	—	2	1	3
negative Anglican	47	9	4	30	13	—	—	31	27	9
dissenter	18	2	2	11	3	—	—	11	21	4
total sample	95	19	11	48	34	20	24	44	49	22
fraction	1:2	1:1	1:1	1:1	1:1	1:1	1:1	1:2	1:2	1:2

Table 12   Oldham bourgeoisie by groupings

	over £25,000 Traditional	over £25,000 non-Traditional	sub £25,000 small employer
Birthplace			
local	(3+11) 25	(13+6) 25	(14+25) 64
non-local	(0+1) 2	(1+2) 5	(10+16) 42
total known	27	30	106
Servants			
none	(0+1) 2	(0+0) 0	(19+27) 73
one	(1+5) 11	(1+1) 3	(5+11) 27
two or more	(0+3) 6	(6+7) 20	(0+0) 0
total known	19	23	100
Neighbours			
Manual workers	(0+3) 6	(0+1) 2	(15+27) 69
not	(0+4) 8	(7+2) 9	(8+7) 22
total known	14	11	91
Activity			
magistrate/council	(1+1) 3	(9+1) 11	(0+2) 4
vestry/police	(1+5) 11	(2+3) 12	(2+7) 16
Lyceum, etc.	(1+4) 9	(0+0) 0	(6+7) 20
inactive	(0+0) 0	7	(16+28) 66
total known	29	30	106
Family as labour			(8+21) 50
total known			106
Politics			
Tory	(1+4) 9	(11+3) 17	(7+9) 25
Whig	(1+6) 13	(3+4) 11	(13+25) 63
radical	(0+1) 2	(0+0) 0	(3+4) 11
total known	24	28	99
Religion			
Anglican	(3+8) 19	(10+4) 18	(2+4) 10
negative Anglican	(0+1) 2	(1+3) 7	(19+27) 73
dissent	(0+4) 8	(3+1) 5	(3+10) 23
Total sample	29	30	106

Table 12 Oldham bourgeoisie groupings (contd.)

	sub £25,000 Anglican	sub £25,000 dissenter	sub £25,000 no church
Birthplace			
local	(6+15) 36	(7+18) 43	(16+37) 90
non-local	(2+4) 10	(4+14) 32	(12+18) 48
total known	46	75	138
Servants			
none	(3+9) 21	(9+15) 39	(20+33) 86
one	(4+5) 14	(5+10) 25	(4+15) 34
two or more	(0+0) 0	(0+0) 0	(0+0) 0
total known	35	64	120
Neighbours			
manual workers	(3+5) 13	(4+0) 4	(7+8) 23
not	(2+5) 12	(4+9) 22	(18+33) 84
total known	25	26	107
Activity			
magistrate/council	(2+2) 6	(1+2) 5	(0+3) 6
vestry/police	(0+5) 10	(2+10) 22	(3+9) 21
Lyceum etc.	(3+0) 3	(2+17) 36	(3+17) 37
inactive	(5+10) 28	(9+15) 39	(31+71) 173
total known	50	102	237
Family as Labour	(1+3) 7	(0+5) 10	(6+13) 32
total known	61	102	237
Politics			
Tory	(3+7) 17	(2+4) 14	(12+22) 56
Whig	(5+13) 31	(12+36) 48	(19+51) 121
Radical	(1+1) 3	(0+1) 2	(2+7) 16
total known	51	64	193
Incorporation			
for	(4+4) 12	(4+21) 46	(8+15) 38
against	(1+1) 3	(1+1) 3	(1+2) 5
total known	15	49	43
Total sample	54	102	237

Table 13   Oldham bourgeoisie: wealth equivalents
(all figures are weighted estimates)

(a) *Probate and servants*

	below £25,000 personalty	£25,000 or above	total
one servant	24	30	54
two or more	2	28	30
total	26	58	84

(b) *Probate and employees*

hundred or less	5	3	8
more	0	19	19
total	5	22	27

(c) *Probate and rates*

£250 or less	3	12	15
more	0	16	16
total	3	28	31

7 Liberalization

The international split within the entire working-class movement is now evident. . . . What is the basis of this world-historical phenomenon? It is precisely the parasitism and decay of capitalism, characteristic of its highest stage of development, i.e. imperialism. . . . Capitalism has now singled out a *handful* of exceptionally rich and powerful states which plunder the whole world simply by 'clipping coupons'. . . . Obviously out of such superprofits it is possible to bribe the labour leaders and the upper strata of the labour aristocracy. And this is precisely what the capitalists of the 'advanced' countries are doing: they are bribing them in a thousand different ways, direct and indirect, overt and covert. . . .' (Lenin, Preface to the French edition of *Imperialism*, 1920).[1]

Of the working men, at least in the more advanced countries of Europe it may be pronounced as certain that the patriarchal or paternal system of government is one to which they will not again be subject. . . . Whatever advice, exhortation or guidance must henceforth be tendered to them as equals. . . . The prospect of the future depends on the degree to which they can be made rational beings. . . .'

'Improvements in production and the emigration of capital are what we have chiefly to depend upon for increasing [the gross product and the demand for labour at home].'

'It is only in the backward countries of the world that increased production is still an important object; of the most advanced what is economically needed is a better distribution of which one indispensible means is a strict restraint on population' (J. S. Mill, *Principles of Political Economy*, 1848).[2]

For Lenin, imperialism, the existence of a labour aristocracy and the apparent stability of advanced capitalist countries were inseparably linked. It was, he claimed, only the development of a new form of empire – that based on foreign investment – which made it possible for the bourgeoisie to buy off and neutralize a key section of the working class. If this argument is correct, the period of English history that should bear it out most conclusively is the mid-nineteenth century. It is at this particular point that one gets a massive switch to capital export, a general increase in wage differentials and the rapid disintegration of a previously powerful working-class movement. What this chapter will be trying to do is establish a *connection:* to show – as far as can be done locally – that these developments were indeed part of an overall politico-economic process of social restabilization.

Oldham provides clear examples of all the developments mentioned. It possessed an engineering industry which supplied machines for many foreign textile industries and which had expanded to employ over 20 per cent of the town's male labour force by 1861. Over the same period (and not unconnected with this development of engineering) there was a marked increase in economic polarization within the working population. As a combined result of increasing wage differentials and a sharp rise in the number of low-paid jobs (see figure 5, page 76), the real earnings of the bottom half of the labour force actually fell slightly between 1839 and 1859 at a time when those higher up the scale enjoyed quite a sharp rise.[3] And finally, and as noted in an earlier chapter, there was a significant increase in social segregation between skilled and unskilled and English and Irish, all coinciding with the collapse of a previously strong ·working-class movement.

Now obviously these developments could be quite unconnected. What has to be demonstrated is that Oldham's bourgeoisie consciously *used* its industrial power (and the economic and psychological reality of empire) to split the labour force and bribe its upper layers into political acquiescence. Indeed more than this. If one wants to specify the historical *content* of this restabilization – as well as perhaps that of the previous class consciousness – it is just as important to be able to establish *which* of the bourgeois responses were the really effective ones: which of them, that is, were dialectically adequate to the job of restabilizing capitalist society at this particular stage in its development. Only then will one be able to identify what was essentially new about the social formation that resulted.

The breakdown of the working-class movement

First, therefore, an attempt to date and describe the disintegration of Oldham's working class itself.

While it is not easy to be precise, the main part of this process – the re-isolation of the working-class vanguard – seems to have been complete by 1850. 1846-7 marked the end of working-class control over police, poor relief and parliamentary representation and also the secession of the main non-working-class elements from the radical alliance. And while 1847-8 did bring some revival in mass support, this never reached the proportions of 1839 or 1842. An attempt in October 1847 to impose short-time working by strike action failed to win the support of more than two thousand workers.[4] And the revolutionary feeling among the factory population – apparently quite considerable in March-April 1848 – was neither sufficient to stop the mills in May nor push the number of Oldham men who actually went out (armed) on the night of 14-15 August beyond a hundred.[5] By 1850 even the partial repeal of the Ten Hour Act failed to rouse industrial action and by 1852 many previous working-class leaders were themselves in the process of being absorbed by one or other of the bourgeois parties.

So, if 1850 can be taken as the date by which the mass influence of the working-class vanguard was fairly conclusively broken, what changes in circumstances can account for it?

The most common explanation is 'economic recovery'. Undoubtedly the period did see a lessening of unemployment and a major shift in the basis of economic activity. Matched with the changes in economic policy there was the development of a new heavy industry technology which ultimately did much to reverse the trend to crisis that had brought previous trouble.

What is less certain is that these changes acted quickly enough to effect a process already largely complete by 1850. Wages remained low in Oldham till the end of the decade and the 1846-8 depression seems to have been the worst of the series.[6] Moreover, when one looks at the long-term trend in the rate of profit, it seems that neither the capital-cheapening effects of the new technology nor the price-inflating effects of cheaper gold (nor even foreign profits and cheaper food) had much impact till some time later. Certainly in the cotton industry the pressure on wages was not relaxed till the early 1850s. The only development which *might* have had some effect was the lifting of the ban on machinery exports in 1842. In the years that followed Oldham's engineering industry did experience very fast expansion, creating a relatively large sector of well-paid jobs as well as a labour force which was occupationally split into skilled and unskilled.[7] But even here the real dividends in terms of labour collaboration could only be drawn after the breaking of the old craft unions, and this did not take place until the engineering lock-out of 1851. Up till then, the industry's rapid growth probably tended to intensify conflict.

So, if economic recovery can only stand as a very partial explanation, what about law and order?

Here at least there can be no doubt about the deliberation. As was seen earlier, the authorities had been trying to break radical control in the labour movement (and local government) since the beginning of the century and by the 1840s the build-up of local military and police forces was at last starting to take a grip. The county constabulary acted as a political police from its introduction in 1841 and as early as May 1842 the area military command could report a systematic watch on local leaders.[8] Though arrests on the 1842 scale were not repeated, the memory of the imprisonment, the presence of the army and the reality of industrial victimization (used openly in the 1847 election) must have done a good deal to weaken further resistance.

Yet even taking into account the cumulative effects of all this (especially for the use of extra-legal tactics in the trade unions), the reassertion of law and order does not, by itself, seem to supply an altogether adequate explanation. It is not just that police repression of a far worse order has failed to destroy working-class movements elsewhere (or even that the Oldham movement itself had beaten off attacks that were almost as dangerous only a decade before). What really turns the argument is the movement's quite striking loss of initiative in 1846-7. For the first time it failed to rally mass support during a period of unprecedented industrial depression. Still worse, its own leadership started to disintegrate. A significant number of previously loyal working-class leaders now moved into alliance with certain sections of the bourgeoisie. It was this that really confused and dispirited the movement; and did so precisely because it resulted from a new plausibility in arguments for the existing order, not from outright repression.

Which brings us to the final explanation: active attempts by the bourgeoisie to win back mass allegiance, and the fairly dramatic change which these underwent in the middle years of the 1840s at just the time when the working class seemed to be preparing its final assault.

In January 1846, when it was becoming clear that another industrial depression was imminent, two leading members of the (Tory) town-centre bourgeoisie, Nathaniel Worthington and Jonathan Mellor, publicly came out in favour of a Ten Hour Bill.[9] This support, apparently involving open acceptance of the working-class case against orthodox political economy, marked a massive break in the hitherto solid front of bourgeois opposition. Yet precisely because it did so, it also presented the working-class movement with an almost impossible dilemma. Either the proffered alliance was rejected, and the support mobilized round the ten hour issue placed in danger. Or if some kind of pact with the local Tories was made, it would be at the risk of losing other elements of support within the movement. It was eventually this second alternative which was adopted, and coming on top of the proposal of the pro-Anglican Morgan Cobbett as successor to the retiring General Johnson as MP, it proved too much for both the Nonconformist tradesmen and a proportion of the atheist 'old revolutionaries'. Within three months, in March 1846, there were attempts to promote a counter-candidate, James Holladay. Support came not just from the tradesmen but several hardline Chartists (Haslam, Haslop and Yardley, the latter two both imprisoned in 1842).[10]

Twelve months later this split was widened still further. Another section of the big bourgeoisie now made a bid for the group gathered round Holladay. The prime movers seem to have been the Platt family: cousins to the Worthingtons, owners of the biggest engineering works, once Congregationalists but now Anglicans. With their backing, W. J. Fox – a Nonconformist publicist – was put up for Parliament on a platform of disestablishment and household suffrage.[11] Richard Cooper, a spokesman for the Fielden group (and one of Oldham's early Socialist theorists) warned that he was 'a stalking-horse to gull people out of the real fruits of the Ten Hour Bill' and that he was being put up by those who were 'doing the best they could to split the borough into the utmost division'.[12] Nonetheless, by early July Fox had succeeded in getting the support of Holladay, most of his original following and even one or two additional Chartists (John Swire, Ambrose Hirst, A. F. Taylor).[13]

Within little more than a year, therefore, two major slogans of the working-class movement had been appropriated (or at least undermined) and its leadership split. In their new guise as 'parents and guardians' of the poor, the big bourgeoisie now presented a face of humanity and concern; and the approach was all the more effective because it was made by two apparently rival factions. How far this itself was deliberate is difficult to tell. It would seem likely that it was originally a genuine projection of existing rivalries within the big bourgeoisie. But if it began accidentally, its advantages must soon have become apparent and the suspicion of complicity is given further support by what happened next.

At the very last moment before the July 1847 election – and with sizable groupings detached from the radical alliance – the 'left' and 'right' factions within the bourgeoisie formed an electoral pact. The Worthington group now put up its own competing candidate against Fielden (and Cobbett) and ran him in harness with Fox. The man chosen was John Duncuft, cotton manufacturer, railway promoter and mutual cousin to both the Worthingtons and the Platts.[14] Against this the radicals, with their organization shattered and faced with systematic victimization by the employers, went down to fairly easy defeat. As Fielden put it afterwards, 'a more foul coalition never existed'.[15]

The closing moves began a year later. With the Nonconformist tradesmen (and quite a number of ex-Chartists) drawn firmly into the orbit of the 'Liberal' employers, the 'Tory' employers – the Worthingtons, Mellors, Jones – now made another bid for what remained: the small masters, working-class shopkeepers and trade union radicals who had remained loyal to Fielden and the ten hour campaign in 1847.

The slogan adopted was the one with which the small masters and shopkeepers had been most closely identified in the past: no state interference. Already in February 1848 the Tory Jonathan Mellor was giving support to protests against the recently imposed new poor law and in March joined the opposition to the Health of Towns Bill.[16] The main issue, however, was incorporation. This had been taken up by the 'liberal' employers at the end of 1848 and involved the transfer of police from control of the police commission (and ultimately the county magistrates) to a town council under direct Home Office supervision.[17] As things stood, this would probably have made little difference either way to trade union activity but a majority of the remaining radical leaders came out in opposition (Alexander Taylor, Kinder Smith, Richard Cooper). For a campaign which lasted much of the following year these men worked in harness with the Tories to get up counter-petitions and meetings.[18]

The final takeover came after the defeat of this opposition and during the subsequent town council elections in September 1849. In these the Tories and the pro-Cobbett radicals put up a joint slate of 'rate-payer' candidates. Though five radicals (including Alexander Taylor) were returned, their position was entirely dependent on Tory support.[19] Three years later both sides in the two parliamentary elections of 1852 – Fox and the now openly pro-Tory Cobbett – were under firm bourgeois control. By then only a small and isolated group of Chartists survived.

So on this evidence the case for a deliberate bourgeois attempt at restabilization would seem fairly strong. Whether or not the bourgeoisie collectively set out to split labour in two, they certainly attempted to win it away from the working-class vanguard and did so only too effectively. In terms of a revolutionary bid for power the defeat was complete and irrevocable.

Yet the process of restabilization involved far more than just this. The bourgeoisie had survived, but only by making concessions. And though these concessions were made on their own terms and lacked their old destabilizing force, their total and eventual sum – nationally, across the country – profoundly altered the internal bargaining balance within capitalist society in England. In any future 'trend to crisis' the room for bourgeois manoeuvre had been significantly reduced and the level at which legitimate expectations had now to be met – the trigger for any future destabilization – raised one step nearer the level of (capitalist) economic intolerability.

The strength of the new pressures can be demonstrated by the extent to which ex-working-class leaders actually became incorporated into the new parties. Many, of course, disappeared altogether (presumably moving out of the area or becoming non-political). But of those who remained politically active an outright majority can be found continuing their activity *inside* the new Tory and Liberal parties. And not entirely as stooges. Though the material in tables 15 and 16 can only be approximate, it is quite obvious that each of the factions contained within them not just isolated individuals but coherent groupings.

Table 14 Politics of ex-working-class leaders by occupation[20]

	Tory	Liberal	total
tradesmen	0	3	3
small masters	4	3	7
shopkeepers	4	2	6
trade unionists	3	4	7
not known	0	3	3
total	11	15	26

Table 15 Politics of ex-working-class leaders by previous campaign identification[21]

	Tory	Liberal	total
factory reform	5	1	6
disestablishment	0	4	4
charter	2	8	10
anti-state (police)	4	1	5
not known	0	1	1
total	11	15	26

Moreover, any reading of the local press also makes it plain that it was the continuing identification of these groupings with their original slogans which enabled the two parties to win mass support. Repudiation could easily have thrown local politics back to its position in the mid-1840s. The joint Tory-Cobbett manifesto of 1852 affirmed its support for a ten-hour day and opposition to the poor law and then declared its intent to 'preserve a just balance between capital and labour, and especially to protect the labouring classes against the cruel machinations of a false political economy'.[22] On the other side, Fox was equally committed to suffrage extension: 'Spread education with a bold and free hand over the country – throw open the doors of the constitution – give the people an equalization of the burdens of taxation – do this and they would have the millions no longer an alienated body. . . .'[23]

The process was plainly two-way. But if some sort of deliberate restabilization process can be admitted, how far does it go to answer our original question? Can it be claimed as a sufficient cause for the collapse of mass class consciousness?

Obviously in terms of both dating and demonstrable effect it fits a good bit better than either 'economic recovery' or 'law and order'. But as a complete explanation one again has to admit reservations, or at any rate reservations about 'restabilization' as so far defined. Apart from anything else, a mere bourgeois take-over of working-class slogans explains far too little about the detailed content of Oldham's mass politics as they emerged in the 1850s: the anti-Irish racism, the brash imperialism and (most significant of all perhaps) a pattern of labour politics which, by the 1860s at least, was quite out of step with what one would have expected in terms of the original factional bidding in the 1840s. The spinners, for instance, did not eventually link up with the Tories, the original champions of factory legislation, but became the main labour movement base for the Liberals. Conversely, the miners, originally with Liberal links, were far more identified with the Tories by the late 1860s.

Finally, therefore, we come to an area not yet tackled at all – the whole larger dimension of class struggle and social structure: of how people reacted to the collapse of their revolutionary hopes, and the way in which the bourgeoisie actively attempted to re-construct the community in ways which would minimize anti-system (or vanguard) influences.

The actual quantitative indications of labour fragmentation – deficient though they are – have already been described. For the decade 1841-51 there is evidence of a significant increase in housing segregation between both Irish and English and craft and labour.[24] And for the period 1827 to 1851 (but presumably occurring in the later 1840s) there is evidence of a small but significant increase in church attendance.[25] But neither this nor the larger mass of descriptive material is at all easily related to the larger political disintegration of Oldham's working class. Once again there is the problem of disentangling cause and effect. The growth of sectional consciousness could equally well have been the consequence of a large number of factors: local political col-lapse itself, disillusionment at the repeated national defeats, direct social intervention by the bourgeoisie. Indeed, in this case it seems likely that all these factors (and several others) were all working simultaneously. So, as far as the original question goes, a conclusive answer is unlikely.

Nonetheless, the area remains one of central importance. Even though there seems no way of assessing the relative weights of the factors involved, some treatment of the process by which new forms of sectional consciousness emerged is essential if we are to tackle the other great range of problems posed at the beginning of the chapter: those referring to the development of a labour aristocracy and its relation to the politico-economic changes of the middle of the century.

Authority systems

To tackle these problems it is necessary to be more general for a moment and return to the argument in the opening chapter.

The development of sectional consciousness was presented as a *response* to exploitation: to the denial of people's equal control over their society's development. Its essence was defined as the restriction of social contact to those with a roughly equal command over resources, thus creating a series of subgroups *within* which people can *appear* to possess an equal control over the social product.

Two points about this process are of immediate relevance. The first concerns its historical *relativity*. The particular levels of material and cultural consumption around which groups define their identity are not arbitary but historically determined and *concrete*. In trying to analyze a particular social formation (like the labour aristocracy) nothing could be more dangerous than attempting to do so in terms derived from experience elsewhere. It is not just that each particular set of wage differentials and occupational roles generates its own pattern of sectional consciousness. Nor even that the dimension of inequality governing their mutual relations is apt to shift disconcertingly from (for instance) simple income to authority at work or access to technical information. What really rules out the possibility of any long-term regularity is the degree to which subgroup cultures are geared into particular sequences of historical change.

This is particularly true of the labour aristocracy. Torn away from its historical context, the term 'labour aristocracy' means almost nothing. By definition almost any subgrouped (or stable capitalist) social structure will reveal groups of higher paid workers attempting to distinguish themselves socially from the rest. And politically the bourgeoisie have been attempting to split, bribe and hoodwink labour leaders ever since capitalist society first developed. On the other hand, *in its context* (and referring to the politico-economic function of a specific social formation) it denotes a unique stage in capitalism's social development. And to define this even concrete description is not enough. The essential starting-point must rather be a *historical* perspective that enables one to isolate the dialectically *novel* elements and then in turn to use these discontinuities to help define its specifically new relationship to the development of the system as a whole.

The second point follows on from this and concerns the *way* in which this has to be done. As was argued earlier, subgroups themselves are neither static nor monolithic. They exist (and develop) as a tension between two *poles* of leadership, between two centres of influence and discipline (and even to some extent as a balance between different attitudes within the same individual). On the one side, there is the need to filter out disruptive contacts from outside, to maintain and reinforce the group's particular codes of social recognition and rejection. On the other, if a group is to survive in a socially changing environment, there is the continual need to change and 'modernize' its identity. And it is precisely by examining the rather special groups of people who perform these functions that one is best able to pinpoint the key discontinuities and changes. This is particularly so in analyzing – as we are here – the development of an entirely new subgroup formation after a long period of class consciousness.

So far only one side of this process has been examined: the way in which the old working-class leadership was broken up and absorbed into the political apparatus of the bourgeoisie. This was of course important. It made it possible to identify the basic elements of the post-1848 restabilization, exemplified in the slogans taken over by the bourgeoisie, and to get some idea of the groups of labour leaders who would ultimately be responsible for defending them. But for present purposes it is the other pole of labour leadership which is the key one. If one wants to discover what was specifically new about the relations between labour and the post-1848 production system, then naturally the leaders one must be most concerned with are those who directly represented the system's changing demands – acted, so to speak, as its messenger boys and interpreters in the labour community. By seeing how far the old (pre-class consciousness) system of labour control was, or was not, implemented in the old way, and how far altogether new forms were added, one should be able to get at least a preliminary indication of what new, distorting factors were at work.

To start, therefore, with a look at the old traditional forms of control as they survived into the mid-century.

The churches: First, the churches. Although church attendance always remained very much a minority activity among working people, probably never involving more than 10 per cent, there does seem to have been a definite increase between the 1820s and 1851. Comparing the returns for the two periods, the percentage of the adult population as a whole (including non-worker sections) seems to have risen from about 14 to 21 per cent (see figure 20, page 128). Still more interesting, the increase was very unevenly distributed (table 16).

Table 16   Oldham's church attendance, 1821–9 and 1851[26]

	1821–9		1851		percentage share in increase
Anglican		1,900		3,255	24
Nonconformist and Catholic		2,108		6,343	76
Methodist	605		3,555	51	
Congregational	440		1,015	10	
Baptist	63		855	14	
total		4,008		9,598	100

The Anglican Church received a disproportionately small share (of the seven churches put up in the 1840s three remained almost empty in 1851 and only two had secured congregations of a hundred or more). The 'old dissent' sects (Congregational, Baptists Unitarians, Quakers) did only slightly better. The denomination which took the lion's share (over half the total increase) was the Methodists. And going by the censuses of 'sittings' or seating accommodation made in the decades after 1851, this trend appears to have been maintained till at least 1871.[27]

This, then, is our first discontinuity. Although church attendance increased (and this itself is of course significant), it did not do so in the old way. It was precisely those congregations in which the big employers no longer played a socially dominant role – those of the Methodists – which expanded fastest. By the middle of the century their occupational composition was distinguished from that of other Nonconformist (and presumably Anglican) churches by their lack of big employers and the large numbers of tradesmen, clerks and supervisory workers (table 17). Conversely, the old-style mill churches – the 'Puritan' communities dominated by their elders – though surviving in the outlying villages, were clearly obsolescent in the areas of expanding population. If, therefore, the churches still played a part in tying labour to the existing order, they now did so in a very different way.

Table 17   Nonconformist marriages by occupations of fathers[28]

	old dissent per cent	Methodist per cent	all marriages
big employers	4	0	—
tradesmen	2	5	1
small masters	8	6	7
shop, supervisory	15	30	10
skilled	18	13	24
semi-skilled	48	41	49
labourer	5	4	9
total	100	99	100

Sunday schools: The same could be said of the Sunday schools. Unlike church attendance, going to Sunday school was definitely a mass experience. On census day in 1851 almost 40 per cent of Oldham children aged between four and fourteen must have spent some part of the day at school, and on these figures it seems reasonable to assume that a large proportion of the working population attended Sunday school at some period of their childhood or other. It also seems likely (on the evidence of the visitation reports and Butterworth's census) that the proportion remained more or less constant from the beginning of the century.[29]

On the other hand, the character of the schools certainly did not. In the 1790s and 1800s the bulk were run directly by mill-owners as fairly crude instruments of labour control (to some extent even in defiance of more traditional Anglican practice). They were, however, still religious in content, and so very much in contrast to the dominant form emerging in the 1820s and 1830s: entirely secular schools devoted to teaching reading, writing and accounts. Giving evidence in 1841 the curate of St James, Waterhead claimed that the 'majority' were still of this character, and that 'formerly all Sunday schools were of an entirely secular nature . . . and generally the children went to no place of worship'.[30]

In view of this, the trend back to religious control in the 1840s and 1850s is all the more striking. Only one or two schools (with an insignificant number of pupils) are recorded as 'non-sectarian' or 'independent' in the 1851 census. All the rest, having under their control something over six thousand children, were directly linked to various religious denominations. Which is where we come to our next discontinuity. Not just were these schools now under direct church control (rather than that of a millowner who hired his own chaplains) but the nature of the churches was very different. It is again those controlled by the small masters and tradesmen which appear to have been dominant. Less than one-third of the children went to Anglican schools. Over 40 per cent were taught by the Methodists alone (table 18). And the potential social influence which went with this control was made all the greater by the almost complete lack of any other form of mass education for working children till the establishment of compulsory primary education in the 1870s.

Table 18 Sunday school attendance, 1851[31]
(percentage of population aged from four to fifteen)

			per cent
Anglican		2,040	13
Nonconformist		4,620	27
Methodist	2,660		
Congregational	720		
Baptist	460		
total		6,660	40

The friendly societies: Beside the Sunday schools the only other really mass institution surviving from the beginning of the century was the friendly society.

Quite how far this can be seen as an active part of the social control apparatus – either in the early or middle years of the century – is not easily determined. But there can be no doubt about its potential importance. The friendly society was the one social institution that touched the adult lives of a near majority of the working population. Numerically, friendly societies seem to have been about as strong at the beginning of the century as later on. In 1794 Rowbottom reports over twelve hundred people, members of fifteen Oldham friendly societies, attending St Mary's church as part of the sick club feast (which would have given the attenders alone about a one in two ratio to the adult male population).[32] By 1877 the Oldham membership of the five main affiliated orders – United and Independent Oddfellows, Druids, Gardeners and Forresters – neared six thousand.[33]

Unfortunately – apart from the organizational side – very little evidence has survived on the friendly societies' larger social orientation. We know that their component lodges generally contained four or five dozen members, that membership tended to come from roughly the same age group (with each new generation entering in early manhood – probably at the same time as receiving full wages) and that recruitment was on an area rather than trade basis.[34] We also know that lodges met at monthly intervals with elaborate ceremonial (usually in the club rooms of public houses) and that a good part of the time was spent drinking and singing popular songs. And more practically, of course, the friendly society handled four of the situations in which working people might otherwise be forced to seek help outside their immediate circle: unemployment, sick pay, medical attention and death.

But on the leadership and wider political links of these vital institutions, and whether any changes took place, information is very scant indeed. Two scraps of evidence might suggest direct loyalist connections: the already mentioned church service of 1794 and the appearance of a group of Oddfellows (along with Masons and Orangemen) in a procession to mark the founding of a church school in 1843.[35] Yet against this could be set the sustained failure of *any* Oldham sick-club to register with the appropriate authorities between 1795 and 1862, and – in sharp contrast to the much smaller groups of Orangemen and Masons – the lack of any further evidence to suggest active establishment links.[36] Indeed, it is perhaps the more general negative evidence that has most to tell us. It is significant, first of all, that as institutions the friendly societies actually *survived,* during a period when so much else did not. It is also significant that they remained exclusively organizations of, and for, working people. Despite periods of great financial difficulty, they never resorted to outside help; they remained free of the otherwise pervasive influence of the clerical establishment and the tradesmen petty bourgeoisie. Further, unlike the Masons they developed no tail of middle- and upper-class membership – no noble patrons. Indeed, if anything, the increasing complexity of their ceremonies and language must have served to insulate them still more from outside influence.

All this, of course, cannot be taken to mean that the friendly society did not indirectly serve the purposes of social control. But their precise position is probably best left undefined while we look at what was undoubtedly the most important area of all: the public houses.

The public house: In the 1790s loyalty in the pubs was ensured by a fairly vigorous application of the licensing laws. While by the middle of the century control of this crude type seems to have lapsed, the returning loyalty of the publicans is one of the most marked features of the period. In the 1830s the drink trade was the mainstay of the radical vote. By 1865 nearly 80 per cent of its members were voting Tory (see table 3, page 54). What is interesting, comparing the situation with that earlier, is the degree to which this new Toryism seems to have been voluntary and self-sought. Already in 1848 when the Oldham Licensed Victuallers Association was reorganized, the trades' central figures seem to have been John and G. B. Nield, members of a family with a long record of support for the Operative Conservative Association.[37] And at the licensed victuallers' annual dinner the following year the guests included two central figures of Oldham Toryism, William Jones (now mayor) and the MP John Duncuft.[38]

However, there was probably more to publican Toryism than a purely organization takeover. Also at the 1849 dinner were two leading Cobbett radicals, Alderman Alexander Taylor and Councillor John Earnshaw, and the ultimate adhesion of the publicans to the Tory Party would seem to have been as much as anything a product of the overall process by which labour was reabsorbed into the system. The really important thing is that in this process the publicans (and presumably most of their customers) seem to have identified themselves not with the liberal 'free trade' and 'suffrage' slogans but with the factory reform and anti-state campaigns adopted by the Tories.

Masons and Orangemen: The final sets of old-style organization which need examining are the Masons and the Orangemen. The number of Masonic lodges in Oldham expanded from ten in 1820 to twelve in 1850 and fifteen by 1870 (when their membership probably neared a thousand).[39] In the absence of any occupational breakdown it is difficult to tell how far these later lodges maintained the characteristics of their predecessors in 1799. But going by newspaper obituaries the bulk of members seem to have come from the petty bourgeoisie: lawyers, accountants, publicans and shopkeepers. A majority seem to have been Anglican and Tory but there was also a significant mixture of Liberals and Nonconformists. They were certainly still anti-Catholic and probably continued to serve as an important focus of loyalism and social cohesion (all the more important because it was the petty bourgeoisie which now began to monopolize civic office). But with the passing of immediate revolutionary fears it seems likely that they were now more strictly convivial groupings than their predecessors at the beginning of the century.

The Oldham Orangemen held their first parade in July 1803 (ending with a service in St Peter's).[40] Their 'chief member', according to Rowbottom, was the Reverend William Winter, chaplain to the Volunteers, curate at St Peter's and the main clerical handyman to Oldham's big employers. The same associations were to continue for the following two generations. Representatives of the Jones family, the Clarksfield Lees and the Duncufts (plus the Neilds and the curates of St Peter's) duly reappear year after year.[41]

What changed was the organization's level of success. In the 1830s Butterworth makes the Orangemen (together with the Operative Conservatives) little more than a joke, made up entirely of flunkeys, foremen and mill managers.[42] In the 1850s, on the other hand, there was a rapid expansion of activity. By 1855 there were already at least eleven lodges and in the following years a small fortune appears to have been spent on anti-Catholic literature and lecturers.[43] An anti-Catholic 'Pastoral Aid Society' was formed in 1855 with St Peter's as its organizational base and two years later St Peter's also provided the main focus for the activities of the Oldham Protestant Association.[44] Nor can there be any doubt about the development of a mass following. 1861 saw serious anti-Catholic riots (to be examined in detail later). And by the mid-1860s the Orange Order seems to have achieved a fair stranglehold over the colliery labour force (where the main employers were of course the same families – the Joneses, Leeses and Duncufts – which supplied the financial backing for St Peter's and the order itself). Nonetheless, it also seems clear, particularly in view of statements by the authorities (and newspapers) during the 1861 riots, that by the 1860s this popular momentum had taken the Oldham movement to a stage when it no longer responded automatically to the directives of its original promoters.

That, then, brings us to the end of the *old* institutions as they survived into the mid-nineteenth century and the discontinuities they reveal are – in sum – quite considerable.

As was seen in the second chapter, two main varieties of social control existed at the end of the eighteenth century. In the still isolated mill villages the principal form remained the 'Puritan household': an attempt to integrate labour *directly* into the cultural orbit of the employer. Where this was no longer possible, and labour had developed separate institutions of its own, attention was focused on those who acted as leaders within them. Legally, the loyalty of these men was ensured by a very rigid system of licensing, later buttressed socially by the formation of exclusive 'NCO' groups like the Masons.

Originally, all the institutions examined performed one or other of these functions. By the middle of the century, on the other hand, none can be said to have done so, at any rate in the old way. While labour's typical mass institutions, the pubs and friendly societies, seem if anything still more distanced from direct control, the political loyalty (or more precisely non-class consciousness) of their leaders seems to have been far more spontaneous. There was clearly less need to rattle the licensing laws or provide artificial loyalist environments. And when one turns to other areas, like the churches and Sunday schools, where labour was previously placed directly within the employers' cultural orbit – made to adopt the same language and concepts – one now finds in control members of the petty bourgeoisie who employed only an insignificant fraction of the labour force. Moreover, the congregations themselves now tended to be limited to a small minority of largely supervisory and skilled workers.

Significantly, it is also the same group of workers that is associated with all the new institutions that appear in the middle of the century: adult education, temperance and the cooperative movement.

Adult education: This seems to have found its fastest growth in the years 1848 to 1855. While the Lyceum, founded in 1839, certainly had four hundred or so employee members (including a large slab of clerks and managers) its social composition remained dominated by tradesmen and manufacturers.[45] What distinguished the dozens of small education clubs which sprang up after 1848 is that they were run by working men themselves. Though many had financial backing from religious denominations and employers, their essence was *mutual* improvement.[46] Some (like the Oldham branch of the National Engineers Association) were directly vocational but all seem to have seen education as immediately relevant to occupational advancement.[47] And socially their orientation was strongly Liberal and Nonconformist. In 1852 William Marcroft, a Unitarian engineering worker, presented a testimonial to W. J. Fox signed by five hundred members of thirteen educational institutes.[48] By 1855 overall membership included perhaps one in ten of Oldham's younger workers.

Temperance: This also only seems to have found an independent base within the working population in the 1850s (in the 1830s and 1840s it was largely the Nonconformist tradesmen who had manned the committees and missions).[49] When workingmen did take the lead, they were largely the same people as those who also dominated the cooperative movement and adult education. All those speaking at the 1855 United Kingdom Alliance meeting (John Schofield, William Marcroft, John Neild) were active in one or other of these fields.[50] By the 1860s the Oldham Temperance Society (operating from its own Temperance Hall) was holding an average of two large meetings a week and had nearly three hundred people attending its annual celebration in 1861.[51] The total proportion of workers involved was probably – if one includes the smaller denominational societies – roughly the same as that in adult education.

The cooperative movement: This was certainly bigger than both, but was dominated by the same men. Again its development was very much a phenomenon of the 1850s. Simple shopkeeping along cooperative lines was, of course, a much older form of working-class organization (in Oldham the first example seems to have been in 1808).[52] The difference between the many small ventures of previous decades and the societies established in the 1850s is that the latter lasted, became successful business institutions able to draw on a continuing stream of eager recruits. What was previously a simple convenience now became a movement in its own right. By the end of the decade the two Oldham societies (the King Street society formed in 1850 and the Greenacres formed in 1851) each had near a thousand members.[53] What is more, they were active members (not just purchasers), with nine hundred turning up for the King Street annual meeting in 1858.[54] The really interesting thing, however, is the degree to which this large membership remained controlled by (and maybe subordinated to) a relatively small group of semi-permanent officials: William Marcroft, John and William Booth, James Schofield, Edward Ingham and a few others. It was these men also (and particularly Marcroft and Ingham, the president of the local Engineers Association) who played a leading role in developing the wholesale production side: the Sun Mill Company (from 1858) and, with colleagues from other Lancashire towns, the Cooperative Wholesale Society in 1861.[55]

Finally, a couple of points can be made about these men in general. First, on their politics. Though all were young, most in their late twenties and early thirties, they were also old enough to have taken part in the working-class movement of the previous decade. As far as one can discover, none did. They are, therefore, to be clearly distinguished from those other labour leaders who ended up in the Liberal camp – the ex-working-class leaders committed to campaigns and slogans taken over after 1846. The second point concerns their future careers. The leaders, the small minority who controlled the organizations, tended to be notably mobile. A sample of the town elite for 1890 (when these men would have reached the climax of their careers) showed one in seven of businessmen (mostly small) and one in five of councillors and magistrates to have come from manual worker backgrounds.[56] In absolute figures this meant about forty men for the whole town. Of these almost all began their careers within the adult education, Sunday school, temperance orbit (itself of course very much a minority group within the labour community). And as many as ten seem to have owed their advancement not to industrial promotion or setting up on their own but directly to positions held (and capital acquired) in labour organizations, particularly the co-op.

Now to relate all this to our basic question about social control and how it changed over the previous half century.

At first sight there might seem to have been two apparently contradictory processes at work. Among the great mass of the population – that identified with the pub and the friendly society – the old active forms of control appear to have completely died down. Though the publicans certainly did still act as leaders and linkmen, there was no mid-century counterpart to the previously elaborate system of formal controls. And yet while this section was, if anything, still more distanced and insulated from polite society, its loyalty (or at least non-class consciousness) was far more real and spontaneous. On the other hand, it was precisely the much smaller group remaining within the cultural orbit of the bourgeoisie – the attenders at church and teachers at Sunday school – who were the focus of the specifically new (but apparently unnecessary) integrating institutions of the middle of the century: adult education, and the temperance and cooperative movements.

Instead, therefore, of a fairly monolithic labour subculture tied and penetrated at all its key points (pub, school, sick-club) what one seems to have are two mutually exclusive groupings with all the authority systems concentrated round the smaller one and no apparent connection between the two. While the social base of the mass subculture was the public house, it was a rejection of public house society – temperance – which was virtually a condition for entry to Sunday school teaching and adult education. While the self-educators spoke the language of their betters, the mass took pride in an aggressively opaque dialect. And while the social life of the smaller group was spent almost entirely within an intimidating complex of formal institutions, the free-and-easy friendly society remained the only – and exceptional – organizing element for the majority.

So, if there was some overall, integrating authority system, it must have taken a very different form to what had existed previously. The solution that will be argued here is that its form had indeed changed and that the crucial dimension was now authority *in industry*.

It should already have been sufficiently demonstrated that whatever the characteristics of the temperance-education group, it was not – in contrast to the publican NCOs of the 1790s – an effective exercise of authority in the community. Nor *culturally* is it easy to explain the distinctive features of either grouping in terms that might be used today: a simple matter of different forms of socially orientated consumption. On the other hand, if one assumes for the moment that the industrial developments of the middle of the century demanded an altogether new labour force structure – a segment of *production* workers (not just foremen) willing and able to implement technically phrased instructions from above – then many of the characteristics of the 'labour aristocracy' group begin to make sense. Temperance brought with it a direct rejection of labour's traditional controls and sanctions. Education – especially adult education – entailed a continuing receptiveness to employer instructions. And the cooperative movement (and tradesmen Nonconformity) provided the necessary social buttressing against direct, unmediated contact with both non-aristocrat labour and the employers.

Moreover, if such an explanation is indeed correct – if authority in industry *was* the key orienting dimension of labour subculture in the mid-century period – then it might also explain the riddle noted earlier: why the politics of trade unions, of the small organized elite, switch over from opposition to identity with those of the employers between 1840 and 1870.

For the moment, however, all this must remain supposition. What still has to be done is establish whether developments in industry will indeed supply the missing link we are looking for.

Industry

Engineering: To look first at an industry that up till now has been ignored almost completely, engineering. As far as the 1830s were concerned its omission did not matter much. It employed no more than a few hundred workers in small scattered workshops. By mid-century, on the other hand, engineering was in many ways Oldham's leading industry and its development is directly relevant to the question we are now tackling. It was technologically advanced, geared to foreign markets and with a labour force that demanded not just the creation of a whole new grade of supervisory taskmakers but the simultaneous elimination of an old grouping which has often been mistaken for a 'labour aristocracy': the highly paid, autonomous craft elite.

This destruction of craft was an essential part of the industry's transformation. Up to the 1830s the organization of machine-making was very similar to that in building. And for much the same reasons. Though some components could come in from outside, the job of fitting up and servicing the primitive machinery of the early days was something which could only be done locally.[57] In Oldham the score of small machine-shops lived almost entirely off the surrounding mills.[58] Coupled with contemporary police conditions and a lengthy apprenticeship, this created just the situation needed to give labour an almost impregnable bargaining position. As a result, the millwright and mechanic enjoyed a power and autonomy that was unrivalled even among craftsmen. Throughout the first decades of the century their local closed shops supported regional and national unions that were able to guarantee sick and unemployment benefit and enforce a uniform sixty-hour week, overtime pay and general wages 50 per cent above the adult male average.[59] Conversely the machine-making employers were as little likely to accumulate capital as the jobbing builder and certainly none in Oldham came near to rivalling the coalowners or cotton manufacturers.

The only exceptions were the iron founders who supplied the cast-iron components – rollers, spindles, boilers – which had been mass produced since the beginning of the century. And it was consequently these men, not the craft machine-makers, who were able to take advantage of the technical advances of the 1820s and 1830s (the slide lathe, accurate planing, standardization) to produce ready-made, all-metal textile machinery. In Oldham there were three firms of this character: Samual Lees (already producing cast-iron spindles in the 1790s), Hibbert and Platt, and Seville and Woolstenhulme.[60] By 1851 they had reduced the craft shops to subcontract work and together employed over 80 per cent of the town's two thousand metal workers.[61] The key period of this development came with the mechanization of weaving in the early and mid-1830s. Already by 1841 Oldham machine-makers were claimed to have the second highest concentration of horsepower in Lancashire and capital worth £200,000.[62] And it seems to have been the slump in home orders following this heavy initial investment which brought about the decisive drive to eliminate craft control and cut labour costs to a minimum.

This happened across Lancashire generally. 1844 saw the introduction of a quittance paper against shopfloor militants and two years later the general secretary of the largest engineering union was held on a conspiracy charge.[63] There were also open attempts at dilution. Several firms succeeded in using non-craft labour on the new, semi-automatic boring and slotting machines. And in the less mechanized departments the piecemaster system was introduced.[64] This gave certain skilled workers an incentive to boost production by subcontracting for the labour of others (both skilled and non-skilled). By 1851 the census figures for the Oldham industry indicate a considerable increase in the proportion of juvenile and non-skilled workers over 1841.[65]

The final confrontation came with the formation of the Amalgamated Society of Engineers in 1850 (uniting previously separate regional and craft unions) and the countrywide lock-out of engineering workers beginning on 31 December 1851. Both developments were explicitly related to the issues of craft control and industrial authority. Four months after the founding of the ASE, John Simpson told a mass meeting of Oldham engineers that 'he knew how much depended upon the union, and that attempts would be made to destroy it. . . . We have everything to gain by this agitation; we have lost so much we have little further to lose; and now that a greater union exists among us, now let us say we will be free. . . .'[66]

The subsequent lock-out stemmed fairly directly from events in Oldham. The town's main firm, Hibbert and Platt, was – with thirteen hundred workers – well on the way to becoming the country's largest textile machine-maker. Already it had taken the lead in several attacks on craft autonomy. Now in summer 1851 Platt's engineers twice got ASE backing for successful (though limited) attempts to win back lost ground. On both occasions the areas in dispute were the piecemaster system, use of non-craft labour and systematic overtime. The Oldham leader, Edward Rye, claimed during the first of the strikes that 'they must either regain these machines for the mechanic or improvements would go on until all skilled work was done by labourers, and the avocation of skilled mechanic would be entirely lost in their trade. . . .'[67] Newton, for the national executive, declared that 'it was a question upon which depended the future of our trade. . . . The executive was prepared to assist them to the utmost of their ability'.[68]

The reply of the firm's head, the future MP John Platt, was to unite the employers' associations of Lancashire and London behind a joint threat of national lock-out. Either Platt's workers surrendered their demands or all engineering workers would be locked out on 31 December. The issue was squarely one of industrial authority. The employers' ultimatum denounced the men's demands as 'totally inconsistent with the rights of employers of labour, and would if acceded to preclude the exercise of all legitimate authority by the masters in their own workshops. . . .'[69] In the event, fifteen thousand men were locked out, and by April 1852 the ASE was broken. To get his job back each man had to sign a declaration that 'I am neither will . . . become a member or contributor to a trade union which directly or indirectly . . . professes to control or interfere with the arrangements or regulations of this or any other manufacturing establishment. . . .'[70]

With this, independent craft autonomy in the engineering industry more or less came to an end. In 1866 Platt told the Commons that 'during the last fifteen or twenty years an advance had been made by the trade unions. Formerly many of them had very restrictive laws; but since then some of the most important of them, and among them the ASE, had abolished all their restrictive laws, and converted themselves into single benefit societies; after which their employers had no further trouble'.[71]

The results can be seen in the changing structure of the labour force. Between 1841 and 1861 the proportion of skilled workers in the Oldham industry declined from about 70 to 40 per cent (with equivalent increases in the number of labouring and semi-skilled jobs). The number of juvenile jobs also went up from about one-seventh to one-quarter.[72] According to Platt's manager in 1863, 'the system of apprenticeship had been very generally abandoned'.[73] By then, too, the automatic machines were altogether out of skilled hands: 'By far the greater part of what may be called preparatory work, drilling, planing, slotting, turning and the like is done by lads under eighteen'. And in skilled work the piecemaster system was universal: 'As a general rule all work that is susceptible of measurement is paid by the piece. In such work the workman usually hires and pays the boys who assist him'.[74]

This piecemaster system was particularly important. In many ways it represented the central institution of the new type of labour force and went considerably beyond the old type of foreman supervision. It meant that the skilled engineer was now actively involved – as pacemaker and technical supervisor – in the work of management. Indeed, it is significant that the Oldham system received its final shape at the hands of the temperance-cooperative leader, William Marcroft. As a mechanic at Platts in the 1840s and 1850s, Marcroft took a leading part in evolving a system of profit-sharing piecework which extended the piece-master incentive to all skilled men in a workgroup.[75] Adult education served a very similar purpose. At one and the same time it enabled this new generation of engineers to carry out technically phrased instructions from above and supported their rejection of surviving craft practices and discipline. Most of the thousand or so young workers involved in adult education in the 1850s seem to have come from engineering and Platts certainly gave large support to both the independent mechanics institutes and the School of Science and Art established under the provisions of the Technical Education Act of 1864.[76]

The clearest expression of the collaborationist attitudes that result comes from the new 'vocational' body for skilled engineers, the National Engineers Association. Its Oldham branch was set up in 1854 with the mechanic Edward Ingham (Marcroft's colleague in the cooperative movement) as its president. Its first move was to offer its services to employers in the work of boiler inspection, giving at the same time its 'best thanks' to 'those employers who have favoured them with their approval, and that they be assured that the aid which they have given will be duly appreciated'.[77] Seven years later in 1861 the association's role was made still plainer by its Oldham secretary, John Lees. He described the association as:

> . . . the principal means by which engineers must elevate them-selves either intellectually or socially or pecuniarily. He could point to several instances in their own lodge where these meetings had been the principle means of enabling several of their members to become qualified for, and obtain, their £2 per week; two instances in particular where two of their members had received their £3.10s. a week, one having gone to Russia, and the other to Holland, the former having received a further advance of £1 per week making his wages into £4.10s. per week, in addition to other prerequisites and occasionally very handsome presents.[78]

Which provides an almost word for word illustration of the opening quotation from Lenin.

Developments in engineering do, therefore, give considerable support to our basic argument. The industry's technological growth really did demand a new structure of authority, one in which the skilled top third of the labour force acted as pacemakers and taskmasters over the rest. And the struggle that was necessary to achieve it provides the clearest possible demonstration of the difference between the new labour aristocracy and the old craft elite. While the self-imposed work routine of the craft worker served to insulate him from employer control, that imposed by the technological demands of the new industry equally firmly identified the skilled worker with management. For the new generation of engineers fulfilment was to be very much in terms of career achievement at work.

Finally, a more general point should be made about engineering's new (and rather special) status as an industry. If the cotton industry can be said to have acted as the high-profit sector of the early industrial revolution (when engineering was still the preserve of the small master), the positions of the two industries were certainly reversed by mid-century – with the crucial differences that while cotton had been genuinely competitive, engineering was dominated by a mere handful of giants. Only the biggest and most stable firms, able to install and service machinery on an international basis, could hope to maintain themselves in the new circumstances. By 1860 just two Oldham firms, Platts and Asa Lees, were employing nearly 90 per cent of the six thousand strong labour force (figure 9c gives the 1851 situation). By 1867 Platt's capital alone was worth £900,000, compared with £300,000 for the entire Oldham coal industry.[79] Moreover, their scale of operation was international in a quite new way. From the 1840s Platts were themselves installing abroad (and servicing) up to half their machinery output.[80] Much of it was going to build up entirely new cotton industries in places like Italy, Russia and Brazil. So in this respect also – in terms of the overall structure of British capitalism – Oldham's engineering industry was indeed a true representative of the new era.

The cotton industry: Cotton provides an example of the other side of the coin: an industry declining into a low profit, petty bourgeois sector. Yet, just as much as engineering, cotton also reveals the development of a labour aristocracy.

On both counts the critical period seems to have been the two decades after 1845. It was these years that saw the drastic regrouping of the cotton industry into geographically separate weaving and spinning areas, and the consequent decline of the old type of integrated firm which had dominated the Oldham industry since the 1830s.[81] While the local evidence does not allow us to chronicle this decline in detail (examining profit rates, investment and so forth) there is quite enough to provide a broad outline of how, and why, it occurred.

The key factor (in addition to the general deterioration in profitability) seems to have been the growing shortage of female and juvenile labour in south Lancashire. Already by the late 1840s this had raised the wages of these grades significantly over the level in the north, and by the 1850s had placed any firm employing a large proportion of women (as did all weaving firms) at a marked disadvantage.[82] The consequences are easy to see. From the mid-1840s one gets a perceptible shift in industrial conflict from spinning to weaving. There were long weavers' strikes in 1843-4, 1945-6 and 1850.[83] By 1856 the situation was serious enough for twenty-four of Oldham's largest firms (sixteen of them combines) to sign an agreement indemnifying any one of them for losses incurred in resisting wage demands.[84] And by the late 1850s some of the biggest firms were beginning to give up the struggle altogether (it is during this period that the Jones family sold out its cotton interests to the Radcliffes).[85] By 1869 the proportion of combined spinning-weaving firms in Oldham had dropped to one-fifth of the total (as against a third in 1851).[86]

Exactly parallel to this comes the rise of the small spinners. Up to the 1840s these had formed a totally subordinate sector: hiring premises, employing no more than a few dozen workers, operating entirely on credit. By 1851 at least six of these firms had pushed their labour forces over the hundred mark.[87] Others followed in the course of the decade and when a new employers' association was formed in 1866 its leadership was drawn largely from this group. The man to receive most votes in the first committee election was John Riley, a long-standing leader of Oldham's Nonconformist tradesmen.[88]

Yet if the mid-century period saw the rise of the small spinner, this rise was not to the affluence and power of the firms they displaced. They remained very much a petty bourgeois sector. The market for yarn was increasingly flooded with output from the new limited liability companies (largely funded out of local petty bourgeois savings).[89] By the 1870s the return on investment was scarcely above the interest payable on bank loans,[90] and it is no doubt as a result of this that one gets a switch from labour- to capital-saving investment in the Lancashire cotton industry as a whole during these years.[91]

Turning to developments in the labour force, three things stand out: the new militancy among women and juvenile workers, a drop in militancy among the adult spinners, and – more organizationally – the survival (indeed perhaps *re*vival) of adult male control in spinning. The first two developments are fairly easily explained by the changed labour market situation. What may seem more difficult to explain is the survival of the adult male spinner at all. The original purpose of the automatic mule (a purpose to some extent realized in the early 1840s) was to replace male labour altogether.[92] And yet despite the decline in the adult workers bargaining position (and despite the fact that in all competing industries overseas the automatic mule *was* ultimately run with female labour) the old traditional unit of adult spinner and piecer survived into the second half of the century with renewed strength and authority.[93]

In fact, what seems to have happened was not so much survival as transformation. Between the late 1840s and the early 1860s the role of the skilled spinner underwent a change quite as radical as that affecting his counterparts in engineering and it is this change which would also seem to provide at least part of the explanation for the spinners' new political orientation and the increasing militancy of other grades.

The situation offers several parallels with engineering. In cotton also there had been an elite of workers who maintained their position by various union controls (some illegal) over the conditions of work: principally labour supply and hours. And, in addition, at more or less the same time that it became possible for employers to destroy these controls, the industry's own developments made necessary the creation of a new pacemaker grade *inside* the labour force. On the one hand, there was a technological (and perhaps economic) situation which demanded the speed up of existing labour rather than its replacement by new types of machinery; on the other hand, a labour situation in which the majority of semi-skilled (juvenile and female) workers – all paid on time rate – found a new bargaining strength. The obvious solution was, therefore, for the spinners (paid by piece) to become pacemakers for the rest. Instead of enforcing discipline against the management they were now to do so on its behalf.

The way this was achieved does not seem to have involved

anything as dramatic or clear-cut as the 1851 lock-out in engineering. It was rather a lengthy process of defeat, victimization and
compromise which stretched over a decade. Already in the mid-
1840s there are signs of weakening in the all-Lancashire Associated
Cotton Spinners to which the Oldham union was affiliated in
1844-6. Though its leadership contained at least some hard-line
militants, its general membership seems to have remained cowed
by the experience of 1842. It vacillated over affiliation to the
National Association of United Trades for the Protection of
Labour and eventually turned down the appointment of W. P.
Roberts as legal adviser.[94] Its balance sheet for 1845 congratulated
members on 'the good feeling which has arisen and is existing
between the employer and employed, and the better understanding
of their mutual interests', and applauded 'the social meetings
which have been held in the several districts to celebrate the
existence of the improved state of feeling'.[95] In 1846 these attitudes
seem to have been consolidated by the repeal of the corn laws.
The slogans carried on what is reported as a 'millworkers' ' procession in Hollinwood (Oldham) included 'May the cultivator,
spinner, manufacturer and operative through free trade principles
make a blessing to the world' and 'Free trade with all the world –
yarn for the India and China markets'.[96] Even during the depression of 1847 there was no return to the spirit of 1842. At a
meeting in October 1847 which called for strike action to enforce
short time, the chairman Thomas Wilson (a working spinner)
described this course as in the best interests of 'the employers as
well as the employed', and John Wood (then secretary of the
Operative Spinners' Association) expressed regret that the association's earlier advice had not been voluntarily adopted.[97] And
even after this the association failed to muster sufficient support
to enforce its decision.[98] By March-April 1848 the union was
trying to solve its unemployment problem by buying land and
developing market gardening.[99]

   Following this, the Oldham spinners seem to have dropped out
of activity altogether (certainly no references were found for the
1850s), and when they were reorganized on a regional basis in
1864 their make-up was clearly collaborationist and aristocratic.
The new union's officers took a large part in setting up the Oldham
Trades Council in 1867 and both bodies were closely associated
with the Oldham Workingmen's Liberal Reform Association
established in 1872.[100] In 1868 the man appointed to become the

union's full-time secretary was Thomas Ashton, a liberal Non-conformist who had previously been a pupil teacher at a mill school.[101]

However, by far the best way of clinching the argument is to look at what happened over the Factory Acts. This provides a direct test for any transformation in the spinners' attitudes. In the 1830s the restriction of production had been at the heart of the old unions' strategy, and obviously if the spinners were to take on their new pacemaker role, this 'restrictionist' psychology would have to be broken. Three pieces of evidence suggest that it was. The first is the clear decline in support for the short-time movement in the late 1840s and early 1850s. Though the 1847 Ten Hours Act was first systematically broken and then (in 1850) replaced with a weaker Act, the short-time leaders failed to mobilize anything like the old support. Indeed, that section of the movement most closely associated with the organized spinners seems to have supported Ashley in his compromise agreement with the millowners.[102] On the other hand, if short-time commitment among the spinners declined, it definitely increased (as one would expect) among the time-rate piecers whom the spinners employed on subcontract. Already in the late 1840s employer newspapers were trying to disparage local short-time supporters as 'mostly young lads'.[103] And during the campaign for a more stringent Act in 1853 the piecers emerged as a distinct group organizing (with Chartist support) what the newspapers described as a 'piecers' strike' which lasted a couple of weeks and involved mass pickets two or three hundred strong.[104] (And on at least one occasion there was direct conflict with the older spinners.) Here, therefore, one has definite signs of a rejection from below of the spinners' new role as pacemakers for management.

The third and final piece of evidence is the acute sensitivity of local employers to any reopening of the factory issue. It was on these grounds that Oldham's employer-backed MP Fox opposed Ashley's amendment in 1850. It would, he believed, tend to revive 'an agitation that was much worse than a political struggle because it struck deeper into the social system, and inflicted serious wounds on the interests of society'.[105] And again in 1855 when the factory inspectors attempted to tighten up safety regulations and instituted proceedings against local factories, much of the violence of the employer reaction would seem to stem from the damage they feared it would do to their carefully nurtured system of labour control. Dickens' description of the employers' defence organization as 'the national association for the protection of the right to mangle operatives' was attacked by the editor of the *Oldham Chronicle* as 'literary incendiarism'. His 'misapplied philanthropy' only served to 'feed the green-eyed monster which preys upon the vitals of our manufacturing industry. Engineers, manufacturers and even operatives united in condemning certain useless, impractical and almost unenforceable clauses in the Factory Acts. . . .'[106]

Taking all the evidence together, therefore, it seems clear enough that cotton did develop a labour aristocracy, and – as in engineering – it was the introduction of a new dimension of authority at work which was the key factor. In all, the industry's twenty-seven thousand workers probably supplied another three thousand 'aristocrats' (mainly spinners and adult male carders) to the two thousand already accounted for in engineering.

Coal: Finally, a look at the coal industry. Coal is particularly worth examining because it presents some very marked contrasts to the other two industries. Strike action remained just as frequent – and bitter – in the late 1850s as it had in the 1840s, and took place under roughly the same leadership. And *politically*, while engineering and cotton moved from radical to liberal, coal went the other way about: maintaining radical-liberal links well into the 1850s and then switching to the Tories. By the early 1870s a local Oldham miner was writing that 'the miners as a body have been accustomed to vote for the Tory Party'.[107]

Yet, despite these differences, the ultimate explanation still seems to lie with the same basic issue of industrial authority. Indeed, it would appear that the longer survival of militancy in coal and the late switch in its politics (into line, it should be remembered, with those of the employers) stemmed directly from the much greater difficulties which the industry presented to the development of an appropriate work structure: one in which a body of skilled workers could be set against the rest.

There seem to have been two main problems. The first was economic. Unlike cotton or the new engineering industry, current wages comprised almost two-thirds of production costs. Consequently, in a period of overproduction and fluctuating prices (and with railways eroding local monopolies) labour often came under very heavy pressure indeed. Though wages in Oldham rose fairly rapidly in the war years of the mid-1850s, they suffered severely in the period that followed. They were cut by one-sixth in 1856 and by another sixth in 1858, the second reduction setting off a strike which lasted most of the winter. Similarly, sharp fluctuations were experienced in the 1860s, and with movements either way generally accompanied by strike action, mining militants were provided with a firm base for continuing influence.[108] The second problem derived from the organization of the work itself. Payment, as described in an earlier chapter, was by the piece – which left the miner very much at the mercy of the management's weighing of the coal at the pithead. The daily disputes which resulted inevitably produced a very different pattern of union activity to that in cotton or engineering. While in the two latter industries the principle aim had been to maintain a privileged position for the craft worker, the issues in coal affected all workers equally and remained just as acute after 1850.

What is significant for our argument is that it was only after these blocks had been fairly consciously removed that one gets the development of collaboration and pro-employer politics. The biggest breakthrough, the introduction of a sliding scale which automatically tied wages to prices, did not come till the 1870s. But the statutory appointment of checkweighmen certainly had an important effect in the mid-century period. By the 1860 Mines Act workers were given the right to elect one of their own number – subject to employer approval – as a full-time pithead observer. This provision, enacted with employer support, seems to have done more than anything to lay the foundation of a new authority structure in coal. It was not perhaps aristocratic in the full sense. But it undoubtedly gave the man responsible for handling grievances very good reason not to fall out with the employers, and together with the spread of Orangeism seems to have had a large part in bringing about the change in mining politics which occurred in the 1860s.[109]

In Oldham this change is not easily pinpointed, and seems anyway to have been ragged and incomplete. But enough evidence survives to make it plain that a fundamental shift did occur. In 1858 the miners' political links were clearly Liberal. In the strike of that year (when at least three of the leaders were veterans of 1843-4) a sympathy committee was set up whose leading members came from the reform association, and the food distribution it organized was supported by local shopkeepers and the *Oldham*

Chronicle.[110] The Liberal petty bourgeoisie (who as small spinners were also coal consumers) were obviously using the opportunity to embarrass their Tory opponents (and it is perhaps significant that it was also this year that saw a big increase in Tory support for organized anti-Catholicism). A decade later the situation was very different. Despite the slump in wages during the cotton famine and strikes in 1867, the leaders of Oldham's miners were now much more closely linked with the Conservatives. At a miners' demonstration in May 1867 – headed by the rifle corps band – one has the national union leader Alexander MacDonald praising the Tories Lord Elcho and Morgan Cobbett (Oldham's Tory MP from 1872) as champions of the mining population. Five years after this there is still firmer evidence in the local correspondence of the Liberal candidate, E. L. Stanley.[111] The letter already quoted on the Toryism of the Oldham miners went on to denounce the Lancashire union leadership for being hand in glove with the coalowners. Another letter at the same time came from a Liberal supporter who had been expelled from his Orange lodge, and describes the lodge members as being mostly employed by the 'Lees family at Clarksfield . . . as underlookers and colliers'.[112]

So there can be no doubt that there was a considerable, if not complete, change in the political attitudes of the mining population. The real question is whether it amounted to the development of a labour aristocracy. In the strict sense the answer is probably no. There was no creation of a distinct grade within the labour force (like the piecemasters or spinners) exercising authority on behalf of the management. It was more the development of an understanding with the *bargaining representatives:* an understanding which led them – in a way that was to become more familiar in the later stages of new unionism – to exercise discipline against 'agitators' and militants. Moreover, it was also an understanding which had to be supported by more traditional forms of control: by vesting coercive authority in the under-lookers (foremen), by continually driving out militants, and by exploiting the fear of Irish competition among what was a relatively unskilled labour force. Yet it also has to be recognized that something more was involved than just the old-style control from above. In time there does seem to have developed a *cultural* receptiveness to employer attitudes among certain sections of the labour force, most typically expressed in the development of

Wesleyan Methodism. In 1861 Allen Tetlow, the local miners' agent claimed that

> ... when he took [the miners'] cause in hand, he tried to his best ability to lay down plans that would raise them in the scale of social intelligence and worth, so as to fit them to become useful members of society, and lead them to enjoy a future inheritance when the world's cares and anxieties were done with.[113]

Indeed, it seems likely (on evidence from other areas) that such attitudes did ultimately result in the formation of a culturally insulated group of 'stint-breakers' within the coal labour force not unlike their counterparts in engineering and cotton. And for Oldham it is at any rate worth nothing that the two *Tory* ex-workingmen in the 1890 elite sample were both originally miners who had attended Anglican and Wesleyan Methodist adult education institutions.[114]

Finally, to sum up the whole section. The aim was to discover whether changes in *industrial* authority would explain otherwise inexplicable developments in the population at large. On balance, at least for the major male-employing industries of cotton and engineering, it would seem that these changes do indeed supply the missing link we are looking for. Both industries show the development of a stratum of production workers exercising authority on behalf of the management. By the 1860s about one-third of all workers in engineering and about one-third of all *male* workers in cotton were acting as pacemakers and taskmasters over the rest; and in doing so made a decisive break with all previous traditions of skilled activity.

For the population as a whole this meant perhaps five or six thousand adult male workers out of the town's total of twenty-five thousand, a proportion which would more or less correspond to the sizes of the two major groupings identified earlier. It would, moreover, also explain their relationship. It would account for the apparently complete *social* (extra-industrial) insulation of the two groupings, since in the new situation the key dimension of inequality (the experience that had to be socially eclipsed) was the exercise of authority at work. It would also explain why it was the smaller 'labour aristocrat' grouping (and not the general mass) which was surrounded by a cocoon of formal institutions. It was, of course, the labour aristocrats who would otherwise be exposed to the constant ridicule reserved for bosses' men. William Marcroft, for instance, the acknowledged leader of the adult education movement (as well as developer of the piecemaster system) had great difficulty with his neighbours. In one of the volumes of his autobiographies he writes that 'on several occasions I had to suffer much personal abuse. . . . To be released . . . I removed my place of living several times'. What his neighbours found most objectionable was apparently the 'system of household management' which he imposed on his wife (and which he claimed was the secret of his subsequent rise to become a small-time businessman and landlord).

Correspondingly, the essence of the non-aristocrats' culture was a rejection of everything associated with their work-time taskmasters: discipline, subservience, abstinence. Its most characteristic expression was the public house – where no free-born Englishmen need call any man his master. And protected by dialect, a defence the labour aristocrat had to do without, it needed no formal institutions beyond the friendly society to handle the most unavoidable contacts with the authorities.

If there *was* any social connection between the two groupings, it was more through the corner shop. The small shopkeepers held a key position in the working community and seem to have been fairly closely associated with the 'labour aristocracy'. Many were themselves retired spinners and engineers (or members of their families) and judging by marriage patterns close links were maintained.[115] What gave them their very considerable *social* influence was their control over credit. Often a family's survival depended on their estimate of its 'respectability and steadiness' and to this extent they could exercise a very powerful cultural control over the general population. Indeed, one explanation for the sharp distinction between men and women (and their respective cultures) within the non-aristocratic family could well be the wife's need – as purchaser – to maintain a respectable 'labour aristocratic' image with the shopkeeper.[116]

Liberal society in action

To end with, three tests can be given to this analysis by looking at the new subdivided (or pluralist) labour community in action.

The first concerns reactions to the Crimean War and shows the degree to which imperialist assumptions were by then embedded in both main labour groupings. The second derives from the anti-Irish movement of 1861, and demonstrates the link between pluralism and racism. The final episode is meant as a corrective: a warning against seeing the new structure as permanent and monolithic. It describes the temporary breakdown in relations between the big employers and petty bourgeoisie which occurred in 1861, a breakdown that highlights at least some of the contradictions within the new structure which were eventually to bring it down.

The Crimean War: In looking at the local reactions to the Crimean War, the first thing that strikes one is the intensity of pro-war sentiment among sections of the big employers. In 1853 the Platt family had been associated with the Peace Society.[117] By October 1854 James Platt (John's younger brother) was attacking it in no uncertain terms:

> If the experience of the last eighteen months will not satisfy Englishmen of the folly and danger of leaning upon arbitration for our own security instead of replying upon the skill, courage and indomitable energy of our soldiers supported by the blessing of Almighty God – I say if this experience is not enough for us, we may find when it is too late that when a nation thinks more of its ease and luxury, and of buying and selling to its advantage, than it does of its independence, then it is the time when, according to all history, the decline of that country begins. . . .[118]

Over the following months the same line was repeated many times over by the *Oldham Chronicle,* and by February 1855 John Platt was organizing a local branch of the New National Movement to call for total mobilization.[119] It is not easy to be sure about the reasons for this sudden turn-about. There are some indications that it could have been associated with the recession in textile orders and the hope (among engineers) for armaments orders instead.[120] On the other hand, there is also considerable evidence that the strongest motives were social and political: above all, the desire to use the opportunity to reassert leadership over the labour population. Special arrangements were made to sell James Platt's pamphlet 'Observations on the Policy of the Czar' at half price to 'workingmen', and much of the movement's rhetoric was clearly populist.[121] According to the *Oldham Chronicle,* the New

National Movement was 'simply a movement against aristocratic monopoly in every official department of state. It is the natural consequence of a breakdown of the monopolists in the discharge of the national work they choose to assume at the expense of the People.'[122] At one of the Movement's meetings William Woolstenhulme, partner in the town's third largest engineering works, made the message even clearer, as well as linking it with the new ideology in industry: 'The principle of promotion from merit was one of the chief elements of success in all commercial undertakings . . . the greatness of England as a commercial nation was due to a steady adherence to these principles. . . .' His partner, George Seville, went on:

> The greatest secret of Napoleon's success was that every private soldier when he entered the army had a marshal's baton in his knapsack. . . . No nation could be truly great unless it possessed this inherent principle of determination and courage to maintain its rights and privileges. . . . He thought that they were all agreed that our military system was rotten to the core . . . the people had allowed it go to decay for the aristocracy from the time of Cromwell had had the whole power of the army and navy. . . .[123]

The really interesting thing, however, is the degree to which local labour leaders failed to challenge this language. The sole support for the Peace Society (whose anti-war resolution was defeated six to one at a public meeting) came from certain sections of the tradesmen petty bourgeoisie.[124] The ex-working-class leaders – just because they accepted industrial (and political) partnership as genuine – seem to have been pre-empted from doing anything but echo the new identity of interest. James Quarmby had once been a supporter of O'Connor and McDouall. In 1847 he had been prominent among those who defected to the Liberals on the suffrage issue. Now he was in full support of the war:

> We are in the war. It matters not who provoked it, how it was provoked, or who brought it about. What we have to do is fight it out. The people of this country live by trade and commerce, and the interests of England – the trade and commerce of England – the well-being of the working classes of Oldham and the British empire would not tolerate a universal monarchy in Europe.[125]

Still stronger evidence of the same process comes from the other (Tory) side of the political spectrum, and within the non-aristo-cratic grouping. In September 1855 there was a full-scale con-frontation between Bronterre O'Brien and John Schofield who had been a radical vestry member in the 1830s and was now leader of what remained of the Cobbett faction on the council. O'Brien came to Oldham to lecture on the war but was apparently unable to find a local man even to chair his meeting. His analysis linked the war to loan-mongering and empire:

> If battles and victories could do us good we ought to be the most prosperous people in the world (*a voice:* 'we are') . . . the sun never sets on our dominions. . . . All these we had got by our victories and he should like any man to tell him how much richer they were in consequence. . . . The people had been made to believe we are fighting for the liberty of nations, for progress, for a spread of free institutions; and that if it had not been for the war the Russians might come by and by and rob us of our civilization and liberties. . . . He would like to know what liberties they had to be robbed of. They could not take their public parks or pleasure grounds because they had none to take; they could not take their houses or land because not three or four in a thousand had houses to take. Nor could they take the franchise from them. But they could take the privilege of working twelve hours a day to produce wealth for other people. Napoleon had murdered two republics, one in his own country and one in Rome; and Lord Palmerston connived at this, and England allowed him to do so because it is governed by the aristocracy, by capitalists, by merchants, by millowners and usurers. There were many well-meaning spirited men in England who fancied that England and France had gone to protect Turkey from being victimized by a power-ful and rapacious Russia (hear, hear). There was never a greater mistake. They had not gone to save Turkey but to dispute with Russia who was to have a bigger share of the carcase; and they had done more injury to the Turks in one year than the Russians had in fifteen. Since they had gone to Turkey they had abolished the fundamental law of Turkey, for it was contrary to the Koran for the government to contract debts with foreigners; but France and England had got the Sultan to contract two loans in England, the first of which they

made him mortgage his tribute in Egypt, and for the second they made him mortgage the customs revenue of his empire. . . .

O'Brien was not allowed to finish his speech. Schofield expressed the mounting hostility of the audience:

> Now when a gentleman came to Oldham with one lie in his mouth and told them they were stupid fools, and had no more sense than children who had left their mother's apron strings, he felt justified in questioning whether his other facts were not equally wrong (loud cheers). . . . Mr O'Brien had told them that their conditions were as bad or worse than Russian serfs, but he would ask him to point to a page in history where Russian serfs could meet and discuss public questions as they were doing that night (hear, hear and cheers) – where Russian serfs could eat white bread and good and wholesome food. Mr O'Brien might talk about the slavery and oppression of the people in this country, but when the time had come for their freedom they would get it. Look at the enlightenment they could obtain by a liberal press, and by the right of public meeting obtained by their brave and noble fathers (cheers). It was a shame for a man to stand on a public platform and compare them to Russian serfs . . . and it was high time to scrutinize and watch carefully men such as these (hear, hear). . . .[126]

Here, therefore, we have an excellent example of false consciousness at work: the blocking out of a class analysis just because it posed such a devastating challenge to protective assumptions so carefully built up over the previous years. Two things are especially noteworthy about Schofield's reply. First, the way in which he rephrases the dispute in nationalist terms – the free Englishman against the Russian serf. But second – and remembering back to the argument earlier in the chapter – that despite the deference shown to authority ('freedom' when the time had come) Schofield's language also encompasses the class gains of the previous period (the 'rights' obtained by their brave fathers). As one would expect from an ex-working-class leader, Schofield represented that *pole* of leadership (within the non-aristocratic grouping) responsible for defending existing rights from outside attack. So even among the semi-skilled and labouring population (who had gained little or nothing materially) one finds a new level of consciousness emerging from the mid-century restabilization.

The anti-Irish movement: The next episode was a logical outcome of this 'English' false consciousness another six years further on: the anti-Irish riots of June 1861. To begin with an on the spot description from an *Oldham Chronicle* reporter:

> For some time past the feeling of antipathy between the English and the Irish has been increasing in intensity . . . threats have been made on the one hand that the Irish should be driven out of the town, that their chapels should be destroyed and that they should be treated as they were in Stockport . . . on the other hand, foolish boasts have been made respecting the increase of the Irish in the town. It has been stated that they intended to have all Oldham to themselves before long. This feeling has gone on rising with greater intensity, and, as is usual, taking hold of the young of both nations with greater force. . . . The clan spirit has been powerfully aroused among them, and for some days past crowds of English boys containing from fifty to three hundred have perambulated the town, insulting and, in some cases, maltreating any Irish people they meet. . . . How the spark caught on Thursday night is not certain. Suddenly there appeared to be some general commotion which no one could account for satisfactorily. One gentleman states that he was at Greenhill at the time, and heard the cries, yells and shouts coming from various parts of the town, which convinced him there was every prospect of an intense riot. It seemed to be the gathering cry preceding battle; and soon the streets were filled with excited crowds, while that peculiar roar known to all those who have ever noticed the rising of a disturbance was heard mingled with the heavy clatter of clogs on the pavement as parties moved rapidly from one part of the town to another. . . .[127]

Before the police had brought the situation under control, two widely separated Catholic chapels had been attacked (one was more or less gutted) and many people injured.[128] In the Priesthill district Irish resistance was sufficiently strong to drive back the rioters without assistance. The following day (Friday) attempts were made to resume the attacks. On this occasion there is definite evidence of prior organization. The *Oldham Chronicle* reports that 'notices were passed from hand to hand in some factories calling upon the hands to assemble in force that evening, and near Messrs Platts . . . written notices were affixed upon walls calling for them to assemble'. In the event, police dispersed the crowds – several thousand strong – before trouble could occur and after some weeks the tension declined.

But while these Oldham riots were not as severe as some elsewhere, the question remains why they should have occurred at all. It is not enough to point to the mere build-up of the Irish population. True a big increase had taken place. Estimates from the census suggest a rise from perhaps three to eight thousand between 1851 and 1861.[129] But even in 1861 the Irish did not comprise more than 7 per cent of Oldham's population, and if increasing numbers were themselves the determinant one would rather have expected the riots to have accompanied the much more noticeable incursions of the immediate post-famine period. Instead, as will be remembered from an earlier chapter, the late 1840s saw at least a measure of Anglo-Irish political solidarity and individual Irishmen taking quite a prominent part in working-class leadership.[130]

A more plausible explanation is the long-term social effect of political restabilization and the build-up of anti-Irish propaganda. The development of Orangeism and the founding of the Pastoral Aid Society and the Protestant Association have already been described. Still in the 1850s anti-Catholic sentiment had to be prodded and fanned by the Anglican establishment. At the 1855 annual meeting of the St Peter's Pastoral Aid Society the Reverend T. Walsh was urging a new Protestant offensive: 'They knew the power which the priesthood possessed over the people . . . they had most of them emigrated from Ireland, they were employed in our mills, mixing with our population and they would injure us or we must benefit them'.[131] By 1861 anti-Catholicism had taken on a very much more popular tone. In March and April of that year speakers from the London Protestant Association were lecturing to massed audiences, audiences that shouted down any Catholic attempt to reply.[132]

To make matters worse, as English hostility increased the Irish community solidified and turned in on itself. Distinct Irish neighbourhoods developed; in the area round St Peter's six hundred out of a thousand households visited were described as Catholic,[133] and in the aftermath of the June riots the *Oldham*

Chronicle could describe the Irish as 'remaining very commendably in their own quarters'.[134] And while in the 1840s the Oldham Irish had defied the priesthood in order to join trade unions and support the Chartists, the 1850s saw a definite increase in clerical control.[135] Church-controlled friendly societies and Catholic young men's associations made their appearance to parallel those among the English.[136] Indeed, it was the religious embodiment of racial attitudes – among both English and Irish – which provided the immediate pretext for the June riots. For years before 1861 the focus for sectarian rivalry had been the Whit processions of Sunday school children. On the Whit Sunday of that year the Catholic procession happened to cut across the tail of the Anglican, and in the ensuing melee – in which many bystanders took part – several children were trampled on and injured.[137]

But not even this, neither the slow build-up nor the Whit Sunday incident, explains why relations should finally have reached breaking point in the spring and summer of 1861. For the final explanation it seems that one has to go to the economic situation: to the steady deterioration in employment prospects which marked the opening months of 1861 and seriously affected both the Irish and the semi-skilled non-aristocrat English. Certainly it was the jobs issue that was seen as the main one by the rioters themselves. The central speaker at a meeting of English in July claimed that he 'would send all the Irish out of the town, drive them down to Liverpool and insist on their departure for Ireland. He complained they would not stand up for a fair wage: they would work at any price, and he averred that plenty of them were doing the same kind of work he had to do at seven pence per day less than what he got'.[138]

Such an explanation would also fit in with what was said earlier about subgroup structure. If labour false consciousness had been solely the result of one-sided manipulation from above, it is highly unlikely that the riots would have occurred at all. What the authorities wanted – both Catholic and Anglican – was not mob violence but the strengthening of cultural ties over their respective labouring populations. If, on the other hand, one sees a subgroup as defined by the tension between two different *poles* of leadership, then the occurrence of race riots at a time of rising unemployment makes a bit more sense. While loyalist publicans and Catholic priests might have had some previous success in winning acceptance for the ideas of their controllers, unemployment meant a decisive threat to the existing standards of both groups. And in this situation, the *other* pole of leadership – that defending existing expectations and rejecting disruptive contacts from outside – would inevitably tend to link the new threat to the principal alien group.

In the present case there is at least some evidence that this is what happened. On the Irish side it seems to have been the same groups which would later – as Fenian supporters – be in persistant conflict with the hierarchy which now organized the defence against the English. The priests themselves, according to the *Oldham Chronicle,* had been 'advised to do all in their power to keep them from showing themselves in the busier parts of the borough, and they had gone round trying to impress them with the importance of paying attention to this necessary precaution'.[139] Similarly among the English. The magistrates and clergymen all expressed pious horror at the riots, and were fairly prompt at putting them down. The real impetus clearly came from within the semi-skilled population itself: particularly the young English labourers working at Platts.[140] Indeed, there could even have been links with organized labour. It is significant that the lawyer defending the English arrested during the riots was the miners' advocate, W. P. Roberts.[141]

The 1861 split: The final episode concerns the split that occurred in 1861 between the big employer and tradesmen elements in the Liberal Party. Though this mainly relates to the emerging tensions within the bourgeoisie itself, it is also (like the anti-Irish riots) at least partly relevant to the leadership structure of the labour population. It might therefore be useful to start by summing up what has been said so far.

Two things at least should have been fairly well demonstrated. First, that there did exist three distinct poles of mass identification – the Irish, the temperance aristocrats and the non-aristocrat English – and that their relationship was primarily determined by the introduction of a new dimension of authority at work. Second, that politically (as was seen at the beginning of the chapter) the old working-class leadership had been split in two and each half been at least partly integrated into the dual Liberal-Tory structure of bourgeois politics – with the Tory-oriented leaders generally identified with the non-aristocrat grouping and the Liberal-oriented with the aristocrat. But despite this, and despite their general bourgeois orientation, it is also clear that the role of the ex-working-class leaders within the new sectional cultures was not entirely on ruling-class terms. Indeed, quite the reverse. As was seen in the dispute between Schofield and O'Brien, and hinted at in the case of the Irish, it seems to have been the ex-working-class leaders who formed the *counter-pole* within each grouping to those leaders who simply retailed commands from above. In their role as defenders of their own (sectional) culture against alien influence, they were also potential champions of rights and standards won in the past. The significance of the 1861 split in the Liberal Party is that it helps reveal this duality of leadership in considerably clearer focus.

Long before the final rupture in January 1861, there had been trouble brewing between the big employers and the tradesmen. On top of the antagonisms inherited from the 1830s, there were now the tensions introduced by the new orientation of the economy as a whole. The tradesmen saw themselves penalized by policies ultimately geared to the interests of others: a Bank Act that restricted liquidity, and an expansionist foreign policy for which they had to pay. Still nearer home they feared that the introduction of a state-run education system (demanded by the big industrialists) would finally destroy their one great engine of political influence, the Sunday school. However, despite rumblings on these and other questions (especially an extension of the franchise), the issue fixed upon for the final break was an infringement of local byelaws by Platt's engineering works. For several weeks following the January meeting of the town council the *Chronicle* came out with editorials like the following:

> Even in a borough which boasts of having within it more of the democratic element than any other town in the empire, it is a fact that standards of criticism vary very much with a man's social status. . . . Our municipal authorities consider that when they have instituted regulations they must be obeyed however ignorant a man may be of their nature. A very different thing it is when the regulations are broken by one of our magnates. . . . He stands distinct from the herd. He makes laws for others to obey, but claims something of an immunity from strict observance of them. . . . At the risk of encountering the potent indignation of the great *power* in Oldham for merely hinting that in all cases strict justice ought to be meted

out, and that an Alderman and a shopkeeper should stand upon precisely the same ground, we must contend that the case made against Mr Alderman Platt at the last council meeting was a very serious one.[142]

And two weeks later:

> The mighty potentate of our own day [binds] an iron girdle across the heart of the town. . . . If any solitary unfortunate could be discovered depraved enough to refuse to bow down and worship the remotely cold iron image with its face of gold and its carefully covered feet of miry clay, there would be nothing for him but dire punishment. . . .[143]

At the time the *Chronicle* was owned and run by the Hirsts, Nonconformists related to the main tradesmen families, and the attack was an open challenge for the leadership of the Liberal Party. The previous year there had been a clash with Platt over the price of gas (an important source of subsidy for the big employers). Now the aim was to force Platt's resignation altogether.[144]

On their side, Platt and his big employer relatives, the Radcliffes and Lees, were well prepared. In the mid-1850s the Platt family had been subsidizing the *Chronicle*. In the late 1850s these subsidies stopped and in 1860 Platt and his friends established a rival paper, the *Oldham Times*.[145] According to Platt, the *Chronicle* had

> . . . always selected him as an object for attack. But latterly it had been done under the pretence of making an attack upon him about those celebrated waterpipes . . . the spleen accumulating for a number of years was hurled against him. . . . The Liberal Party had long seen it would have to do battle with the *Chronicle*. It was necessary, therefore, for the Liberal Party to have an organ of their own, and hence the origin of the *Oldham Times*. . . . The purpose of the editor of the *Chronicle* was clear enough. He thought he had gained sufficient position and eminence in the town to dictate terms to the Liberal Party. . . .[146]

For the immediate argument, however, the importance of the incident is not so much that it split the Liberals as that it temporarily disrupted the institutional framework of the labour aristocrats. It set the big employers against the Nonconformist organizers of the aristocrats' life *outside* the workshop. This is why it is so revealing. It forced a choice. In February 1861 a ward meeting was got up to support Platt. The prime movers were the big employers but all three mechanics institute leaders present came out firmly in favour of Platt.[147] The only trouble-makers were two ex-working-class leaders who four months later were also to attack the Lancashire Cotton Spinning Company (a business venture of the Oldham cooperators) as a sell-out to employer procedures.[148] As one would expect in a social formation where the main dimension was authority at work, those leaders who usually took their orders from above sided with the big employers while the counter-pole of ex-working-class leaders supported the tradesmen. This pattern recurs when one looks at the activities of the anti-Platt faction. Though its principal support came from members of the shopkeepers' association and some of the Nonconformists, its most interesting feature was the alliance that was formed with the ex-Chartists. The previously orthodox *Chronicle* started to attack Bright and Gladstone (as well as Platt) as sham radicals and to give backing to the universal suffrage demands of the Reform Association (a body which included the rump of Liberal ex-working-class leaders and had the qualified backing of the now minuscule Oldham Chartist Association).[149] Indeed, the *Chronicle's* policy went even further than this. It included an attempt to reunite the two rival groups of ex-working-class leaders around the 'middle classes' and against both 'Whiggery and Toryism'. Morgan Cobbett for instance, who had previously been the *Chronicle's* standard target of attack, was now presented along with the town's other MP Fox as a champion of 'radical Oldham'.[150]

Predictably, however, the 'masses' (as the *Chronicle* called them) failed to respond. By late February 1861 the paper was lamenting the decline in their 'political earnestness': 'they appear to have retrograded at a fearful rate over the last years, and a political demonstration in their favour meets with but little support from them. If they are not prepared to do their own work, no one else will'.[151] And disappointed in this support the petty bourgeoisie more or less capitulated. Within a few months Platt was able to close down his costly *Oldham Times,* and the *Chronicle* returned to its old subservience (by 1868 it was describing him as a 'benefactor of the species who makes two blades of grass grow where one grew before').[152]

Yet despite the no-change outcome, this last incident is perhaps the most significant of the three. It exposes the two counterposed poles of leadership within the Liberal-aristocrat group: the old working-class leaders whose slogans had been appropriated in the 1840s and the new generation of industrial taskmasters (above all the self-educators) who actively disseminated the culture of their employers. Still more, it underlines – in the ultimate victory of the big employers – the basic dominance within this tension of *industrial* authority. And finally (and most important of all) it reveals the *potential* instability of the new social formation. Though the economic and social pressures of 1861 were only slight, there would be others within the next two decades quite strong enough to rupture the mid-century set-up and open the way to a new class consciousness.

How far, then, has this chapter answered our original questions? On the deliberation of the local bourgeois response there can be few doubts. There *were* deliberate attempts to reconstruct the labour force in ways which would isolate the working-class vanguard, and obvious use of imperialism and racism to do so. Nor can there be any doubt that the process also required fundamental concessions: that it *was* restabilization, not merely a return to the old conditions. Without the original process of outbidding the vanguard in 1846-8, and the subsequent honouring of the promises made, it seems unlikely that class collaboration would have returned so quickly. (On this count it is significant that the national pressure for liberalization within the two bourgeois parties came from just those areas where class consciousness had previously been most intense.) What cannot be demonstrated as easily is that this *local* restabilization was indeed part of an overall change in the nature of English capitalism, part of the switch to a new capital export imperialism. To establish this, work is needed at many different levels. But one piece of evidence no one can deny is that the engineering orders which sustained Oldham's prosperity in the 1850s came largely from Russia. In these years machinery for something over a hundred entire cotton factories was exported. And it was these machines (and the form of exploitation they embodied) which helped lay the basis for a proletariat which ultimately broke the first links in the chain of imperialism.

8 Postscript

Finally, to sum up and consider wider implications.

The study began with two sets of questions. The first concerned the problem of 'liberalization': the specific nature of the process which lay behind the new developments of the middle of the century. These first questions all involved the inside workings of a particular slice of English history (did it represent a process at all? Was it related to the preceding class consciousness? Why did it occur then and not later?) The other questions were more designed to place these developments in a larger perspective: to specify the changing content of mass consciousness against what came before and after; to reconstruct concrete forms as a basis for comparison elsewhere.

Within the limits of the evidence, some of the answers should already have become clear.

In Oldham at least the changes associated with liberalization (the extension of the vote, the development of mass parties, the legal recognition of trade unions) were quite obviously part of a process by which specifically capitalist authority was reimposed and the working-class vanguard pushed back into isolation. Obviously, too, it was the earlier development of some form of mass class consciousness which originally made this necessary.

Of course, these answers refer *only* to Oldham, and in the present state of knowledge one can only speculate on wider applications. Looking no further than Northampton and Shields there is ample evidence of quite different developments and it seems unlikely that many other towns followed exactly the same road as Oldham. On the other hand, remembering the principal milestones of national working-class development, it also seems that the general *trend* in Oldham was by no means unique. The rise of trade unionism (and the adoption of extra-legal tactics) was much more than a purely local episode in the 1800s. And quite a number of towns with industries similarly exposed to a declining rate of profit in the 1830s and 1840s (textiles, coal, iron) show signs of a parallel class consciousness. Moreover, it also seems to have been just those areas where class consciousness was previously strongest (and restabilization presumably most thorough-going) that eventually formed the political bases for liberalizing pressures in the country at large. The West Riding, the Black Country, North Staffordshire and industrial Lancashire all offer a number of likely candidates. However, at the moment (and within the limits of available research) one can only guess.

More immediately to the point is the problem of assessment and placing: not *how much* of any particular mode of consciousness (or even what such consciousness 'is' in general) but what *kind* in particular. Within a dialectical perspective, it is this establishment of difference and direction which must be the key objective. What follows is not a direct attempt to do this. (As far as can be, this has already been done in the body of the study itself.) The purpose is more to examine the problems of wider, *external* comparison, and in doing so to revisit the theme of overall 'incompleteness' opened up at the very beginning.

In particular, this means trying to clarify the position of Oldham's experience within the theoretical perspective sketched in the introduction. Intentionally, this was left very general. Capitalism was presented as a 'class society' – systematically unequal – and 'alienation' the resulting disruption of people's full development as 'social beings'. It might now be useful to be a bit more specific, especially about people's 'social being'. No more than technology or social organization can this be seen as standing still across history. And if it is something of a platitude to say so, it still remains true that we know very little about the evolution of human personality, about the actual processes by which new areas of social potentiality and need are opened up. Concepts like 'social injustice' and 'exploitation' can be traced back to the beginning of history. But we do not really even know *why* human beings should perceive social inequality as affronting their own existence, let alone have any precise idea of its changing realization and effect.

Here we have been concerned with just one particular phase of human development: early industrial capitalism. It would be foolish to pretend that anything much has been added. One might point in general terms to the destruction of socially closed formations – of fixed castes of craftsmen, merchants and peasants –

and the role of the family as their hereditary bearer; to the changing balance between commodity exchange and subsistence production; even to the use of 'education' (instead of its deliberate restriction) as a method of social control. But while all these must have done at least something to intensify the range and complexity of human interrelationship, it is not easy to devise ways of charting the actual results. All that this study can claim to have done is provide evidence on two *related* developments. Not the changing level of human potentiality itself but how people *themselves* became conscious of new areas of potentiality blocked by the existing system, and, as the converse of this, the subsequent changes in the concrete forms of false consciousness. Both developments reveal something.

The class consciousness examined in this study had a number of special features beside the mere fact that it was chronologically first. It was essentially local and generated *inside* the labour movement; it was not the product of a nationally (or internationally) organized revolutionary party. And though, as we have seen, this was largely because the labour movement possessed its own inherited core of Jacobin revolutionaries, it is also noteworthy that the precipitating factors were heavily industrial and (perhaps confirming a one-sided industrial base) the leadership included no women at all. True, in 1905 Russia (as in Oldham in 1834) it was an industrial slogan – 'The immediate realization in a revolutionary way of an eight-hour working day' – that Lenin made the principal basis for mobilizing the factory population. But even on that occasion, as in 1871 or 1917, the actual creation of a mass movement derived from a whole multiplicity of factors of which the majority were directly political. So, if one is looking for the opening up of new potentialities, it is tempting to suggest that the origins of the class consciousness of the mid-1830s did involve something more than just the simple injection of anti-capitalist ideas during the period of sharp ruling-class attack. Historically, these years were marked by two rather special developments. There was the peak expression of an altogether new type of *social* relationship: the collective, cooperative strength of labour solidarity. And *economically* one had (in cotton) an industry which combined the most advanced and complex of production forms with the worst consequences of unplanned, competitive organization. At one and the same time workers experienced a new strength and a new weakness. And accordingly, if the pioneer class consciousness of these years was peculiarly industrial in origin, it could well be because it was the worker's experience inside industry that still provided the most powerful reflection of these two new (and essentially antagonistic) areas of human dependence. As yet bourgeois democracy was unknown. It was only as a *result* of these struggles that one gets the development of mass parties, and only then would the need to maintain the illusion of participation (on occasion) express this contradiction in immediately political terms.

The same conclusions also seem to stem from an examination of false consciousness.

Unfortunately, the treatment of labour's social structure before the industrial revolution remains one of the weakest parts of this study. Whole areas still need to be defined. But it seems possible to establish at least one or two points of difference with the situation in the 1860s. The pre-industrial revolution systems of authority (the controls over publicans, teachers, religious societies) seem to have been far tighter than they were later, the discipline exercised more stringent and monolithic and – above all – the base of that discipline in the community rather than industry. Moreover, if one turns to the process of restabilization itself and compares it to those which have taken place subsequently (either in England or on the continent), one can hardly fail to notice the degree to which its social resolution was *worked out* in terms of industrial organization. Its key component was the creation of a privileged grade within the labour force – the labour aristocracy – and it was around this dimension of inequality that social structure later crystallized. Granted there were differing politico-economic contraints in each case. Not all ruling classes had the same wide opportunities of overseas expansion or technological innovation. But there does seem to be some justification for seeing the structures of the 1850s as arising partly in response to (and partly to incorporate) new potentialities which had been generated by specifically industrial development – and struggle – over the previous two generations. To this extent, the class consciousness we have been examining does bear the marks of being *first*.

Appendix 1: Poverty

Poverty and the prospect of poverty were the biggest problems which working families had to face. The survey made here (and presented in figures 14, 15 and 16), attempts to compare its impact in the three towns, and in particular to examine the experience of different occupational groups within them. It deals with households (not individual wage earners) and the labour population as a whole (not particular occupations), and does so by marrying information on wages, prices and employment with a sample of working households taken from the 1851 census. The principal definition of poverty (or subsistence minimum) derives from the surveys which Rowntree and Bowley made at the turn of this century.[1] For the immediate purpose of *internal* comparison (either between towns or different groups within them) it does not matter much whether the Bowley minimum is an absolute minimum, or whether its translation into mid-century terms involves slight inaccuracies. Nevertheless, if poverty is seen as a specific lack of food and clothing (and not in terms of overall well-being), there seems no reason why the results given here should not be broadly comparable with those of Bowley and Rowntree, especially as the methods and assumptions are almost identical. If the definition is expanded (as in figure 16) to include overwork and overcrowding, then wider comparisons are obviously less reliable.

Minimum food and clothing

Rowntree's minimum was based on the local government board's estimate of the weekly food requirements of an adult male workhouse inmate.[2] These were: 118 ounces of bread (25 per cent of total budget cost); $21\frac{1}{2}$ ounces of cheese (17 per cent); 48 ounces of oatmeal (12 per cent); 34 ounces of potatoes (12 per cent); $4\frac{1}{2}$ pints of skimmed milk (11 per cent); 9 ounces of bacon (10 per cent); minute amounts of tea, coffee, cocoa, sugar, treacle and margarine (13 per cent). In 1899 this cost 3s. 3d. In 1849 (with one ounce of butter instead of one ounce of margarine and in Manchester retail prices) the cost would have been 4s 3d.[3] What mid-nineteenth-century budgets there are show considerable similarity.[4] The one big difference was a bias against cheese: the poorest families tended to leave it out altogether and the better-off to substitute the equally expensive but less nutritious butcher's meat. This preference they shared with actual working families of the early twentieth century and Bowley specifically amended the local government board's vegetarian minimum to include two pounds of meat (his own 'new standard' minimum). Two pounds, at least for the middle of the century, seems an overcorrection, and here one pound of meat has been added and cheese reduced to eight ounces. Otherwise Rowntree's minimum stands, and in total the minimum food for an adult in 1849 would have cost 4s 6d (Bowley used both standards in his surveys and found no significant difference between the results). The weights used to relate a family's size to its food requirements are Bowley's: man over eighteen = 100; boy over fourteen = 85; woman over sixteen = 80; girl over fourteen = 70; child over five = 50; child under five = 33; all over sixty = 60. For clothing,[5] Bowley makes an additional allowance of 8d for each adult man (taken as 8d in 1849 prices),[6] and here this has been weighted in the same manner as the food requirements.[7] A total allowance of 5s 2d (in 1849 prices) has, therefore, been made for the food and clothing requirements of each man.

Minimum fuel and rent

The weekly rent of almost 90 per cent of Oldham's working-class housing (that rated at under £10) was between 1s 9d and 2s 9d.[8] Northampton's rents were slightly but not significantly higher, and while the level in Shields is not known it is unlikely to have been very different.[9] Fuel costs were around 1s 6d.[10] Fuel and rent were fixed costs on each household which bore little relation to the household's size. But, on the assumption that the poorer families lived in the cheaper housing, 4s is subtracted from the income of households with a total income of less than 20s (an arbitrary division), and 5s from those with more (this also allows a little for sick club contributions). The remaining income matched against minimum food and clothing requirements give a family's relation to the poverty line.

Wages and prices

Wage sources are far better for the Manchester area than for Northampton or Shields. For 1849 Chadwick (*JRSS* 1860) supplies Manchester area earnings for a wide range of occupations which he obtained (as secretary of the Manchester Statistical Society) by circularizing local employers and then having their figures vetted by local trade unionists. These figures can also be supplemented by those in E. Butterworth, *Oldham* and G. H. Wood, *History of Wages in the Cotton Industry*. For Northampton and Shields information is largely restricted to staple trades, and earnings elsewhere have had to be estimated either from rates in the same area (in Shields' case Newcastle) or even more crudely by modifying national rates in terms of the local differentials revealed by other trades. Generally, the earnings of both craftsmen and labourers in Northampton were *assumed* to be 90 per cent of the rate in Manchester,[11] and in Shields 80 per cent for craftsmen and 90 per cent for labouring occupations.[12] For seamen in Shields an annual average weekly income of 17s 6d was credited to all households with a seaman member (whether present or absent on census day). This assumes ten months employment a year at 60s a month with an additional 30s a month in food.[13] For Shields coalminers (who got housing with the job) a wage of 19s was credited but no deduction of 4s made for rent and fuel.[14] Retail prices were assumed to be the same in all three towns.[15] In fact, even if all these estimates are as much as 10 per cent out it would make little difference to the results. The really important variable is occupational composition by household.

Household composition

Information on household size and occupational composition is taken from samples of the 1851 census schedules (and is thus liable to sampling error), and – as with Bowley and Rowntree – restricted to wage-earning households.[16] All lodgers who were obviously related to a family were included as members. All not, were regarded as contributing 1s profit on their keep to the family income, but otherwise excluded from the survey.[17] Lodging *families* were regarded as paying 2s fuel and rent to the landlord family and included in the survey as separate families.[18] Because material on earnings and prices is so much better for summer 1849 than for March 1851, the occupational structure for 1851 has been taken as that for 1849.

Primary and secondary poverty

This survey deals solely with primary poverty – those families unable to afford the minimum however carefully they spent their income. It does not measure the number of families in the community who did not, in fact, get the minimum: having fore-gone it to buy medicine, education, drink or to pay off old debts. In human terms there was no difference between this 'secondary' poverty and primary poverty. Charles Booth in his London survey lumped the two types together. Rowntree estimated that the number of persons in York living in secondary poverty was just short of double the number in primary poverty.[19]

Unemployment and poverty in Oldham in 1847

For Oldham in 1847 there is sufficient information on unemployment to simulate its effects on household income. This enables one to get some idea of the incidence of poverty during industrial depression compared with the relative prosperity of 1849. April 1847 combined high prices – food and clothing minimum (with fuel and rent constant) at 6s 4d – with heavy unemployment. For the week ending 28 April 1847 the *Manchester Guardian* (the cotton market paper with a firm financial interest in accuracy) gives precise unemployment figures for Oldham's cotton industry: two thousand in full employment, sixteen thousand working two-thirds time, and two thousand laid off; and a more general des-cription of the hatters' position as 'even worse' with a 'large number entirely without work and those employed with only two or three days work a week'. The picture given by Alexander Taylor (*Manchester Advertiser*, 26 June 1847) corresponds closely and the situation does not seem to have improved until well into the following year.[20] Other industries, in the absence of evidence to the contrary, have been assumed to be working full time. All the same, in coal, engineering and above all building, there was bound to be more unemployment than usual and the survey errs on the side of optimism. To simulate the incidence of unemployment among cotton workers a rota of one employed, three on two-thirds time and one unemployed was followed from household to household; for hatting a rota of one employed, seven on half time and two unemployed. Occupational composition was based on the same sample of 1851 census schedules as the 1849 survey. In this case the assumption that household composition remained the same over the period is considerably less safe. Not only is the period longer but families may well have modified their structure in face of hardship. The main results are given in figure 14, but other tables (breaking down the incidence of poverty by occupational grade) can be found in Foster, *Oldham* (Cambridge PhD, 1967) pp. 340-1.

Life cycle stage (figure 15)

The stages are defined as follows: (1) man, woman or both, aged below sixty and without children; (2) man, woman or both aged below sixty with half their children aged ten or below and no earning relative; (3) man, woman or both aged below sixty with half children aged over ten and below nineteen with no earning relative; (4) family in either stage (2) or (3) with *in addition* an earning relative or earning child aged over eighteen; (5) man, woman or both aged sixty or over without earning child or other relative. Stage (4) is meant to indicate how far families gained support from *potentially* independent kin. The definition of 'labourer family' is the same as that used in figure 18.

Overworking and overcrowding (figure 16)

'Sharing accommodation': all families *either* sharing accommodation *or* with lodgers *or* with a working relative present *or* with a son over eighteen at home. 'Mother working': percentage of families *with children under eleven* where the mother worked. 'Children working': percentage of families with children aged over six and under twelve where *any* child in this age group worked.

Appendix 2: Marriage and neighbouring

Historically the degree to which people of different occupational backgrounds married together, or lived next door to each other, provides one of the best indications of how far a population was *socially* subdivided by occupation and (to some extent) income.[1] This appendix describes the use made here of the registrar general's marriage certificates (available from the 1840s) and the census schedules (available for 1841, 1851 and 1861).[2]

Both sources provide opportunities which have so far been only very partially exploited, and certainly the methods adopted here are experimental and primitive. The biggest *limiting* factor appears to be the problem of significance. Even if one uses an overall population of several thousand marriages (or neighbouring relations), the likelihood of interrelationships between particular occupations like shoemakers and bricklayers remains too small (at least by the significance test outlined below) to permit a significant comparison between towns. Either one has to group together a whole number of occupations (as is done in figure 18) or extend the survey for so long a period – in the case of marriages – that it becomes historically unfocused. So although most of the intermarriage between individual occupations shown in tables 19, 20 and 21 differs significantly from random expectation it does not do so sufficiently to establish a significant difference from the pattern in other towns.

Intermarriage: material and methods

Marriage certificates: The information used comes from the registrar general's marriage certificates deposited in the local Registration Offices (which for the first time asked for the occupations of both parents to each marriage). This state registration did not begin until 1838 and did not become properly effective till the mid-1840s. Consequently, the years used come *after* 1845 and not (as would be more relevant to the problem in hand) immediately before. For Oldham 5,550 marriages were analysed for the eleven years 1846-56 (including over a thousand marriages of Oldham residents in St Mary's, Prestwich – Oldham chapelry's mother church – which were registered in Bury); for Shields 3,180 marriages for the same eleven years; and for Northampton 3,146 marriages for the twelve years 1845-56. The number of marriages was limited by the space limits of the town and the time limits of the period under study; any period much longer than the decade used would (in the rapidly changing conditions of the middle of the century) have been dangerous. So the number of marriages used here represents a maximum. To increase the number in each cell of the contingency table, the marriages of sons and daughters have been combined (taken separately, the preferences of sons and daughters seem to show no important differences).

The marrying and the marriageable: The analysis assumes that the population marrying over the decade was near-identical to the marriageable population from which it was drawn. For England as a whole in 1949 Berent found that among women the proportion of those who married increased with decreasing social prestige; the difference between the proportion at the top and bottom being 10 per cent.[3] There are no comparable figures for nineteenth-century towns but the trend was probably the same. This bias might slightly increase the indices of preference between lower-category sons and higher-category daughters.

Use of parents' occupations: The occupations of the male parents to the marriage have been used, and not those of the marriage partners. Even if all women marrying were occupied, their occupations would not have been comparable with their husbands'. Nor would the occupations of their husbands at the time of marriage have been comparable with those of their fathers-in-law. It seems fairly realistic to assume that socially the marriage partners were defined by the families out of which they were marrying. For widowers, their own (and not their father's) occupation has been used.

Marriage outside the registration district: Registration Offices only recorded marriages in their own district. Some marriages of local people may have been elsewhere (and vice versa) and these people may, socially, have been recruited unevenly. It seems likely that the higher the social prestige of a category the greater the probability that it is underrepresented in the local marriage certificates, and that those marriages which are represented were downwardly mobile to a greater degree than those that are not.

Exclusion of Catholics: All marriages in Catholic chapels were excluded. These were almost all between Irish, whose choice of marriage partner was limited by ethnic and religious pressures. Catholic marriages never exceeded more than 2 per cent of the total.

Work and marriage: Using marriage frequency to estimate social distance assumes that *social* similarity is the only factor liable to produce preference. It seems likely, however, that there are other factors involved, especially the purely *work* characteristics of the occupation. Men in trades where the wife helped the husband (e.g. shoemaking) would prefer to marry women brought up in shoe-making households. Similarly, the concentration of certain industries in particular areas of a town (e.g. farming on the edge or mining along the coal seams) would produce a geographical barrier to marriages that were otherwise socially similar. This bias, though probably not too important, does give a partly spurious three-dimensional effect to social distance within the labour force; coalminers and cotton spinners may show themselves equally distant from both labourers and foremen but still show no significant mutual interrelation.

Marriage of the big bourgeoisie in Oldham: In St Mary's, Oldham the occupation columns of marriage certificates were not filled in until the end of 1849 and consequently marriages taking place in St Mary's for the years 1846-9 have had to be excluded from the survey. But because the number of marriages from the big bourgeoisie for the whole period was much smaller than one would have liked (and because those taking place in St Mary's could be identified by name), it was decided to include these marriages by themselves. The marriages of thirty-five sons from the big bourgeoisie (and the marriages of a similar number of daughters) have, therefore, been weighted against a total of 6,977 marriages (not 5,550).

Specific manual worker occupations in tables: Tables 18, 19 and 20 are abstracts from two sets of tables given in full in Foster, *Oldham,* pp. 327-9: those for general (grouped) occupations and those for special individual manual worker occupations (i.e. cotton spinner rather than 'factory skilled'). Hence the tables given here cannot (because they separate out certain individual manual worker occupations) conveniently provide meaningful 'general' categories for those remaining occupations too small to permit useful comparison. Such 'general' categories (including both the individual occupations used here and those excluded) can be found in Foster, *Oldham,* pp. 330-3, as can the absolute figures from which the indices themselves are calculated. For *specific* manual worker occupations the indices are calculated (as a result of the way the information was collected) solely on the basis of *sons'* marriages.

Index of association: This measures how far the number of marriages which actually took place between different occupations exceeded (or failed to reach) the number that might have been expected had marriage between occupations been entirely random. The 'random expectation' of intermarriage between occupations A and B is calculated by multiplying the incidence of all occupation A sons and daughters in the total marrying population by the incidence of occupation B sons and daughters (e.g. $1/10 \times 1/5$) and then multiplying up by the total number of marriages for all occupations. This gives one the expected figure. The *actual* number of intermarriages is then divided by this. If precisely the same number of A sons and daughters married B sons and daughters as the 'random expectation', then the index stands at unity (100 in the tables).

Neighbouring: material and methods

Census schedules: These have been used for 1851 (and in the case of Oldham for 1841 as well). Entries run by streets and with the use of a map it is usually possible to identify neighbours. The sample was based on *households* (not houses or families, though generally a household would be made up of only one family and be the sole occupant of the house). In each case it was the relationship with the preceding household in the enumerator's book that was used (and only if no such household acted as neighbour was the subsequent household taken). The occupations were those of household heads or eldest male earning relation. Irish households were included in the survey.

Samples: For Northampton (1851) a 1 : 1 sample was taken to produce 5,100 neighbouring relations; for Shields (1851) a 1 : 3 sample (2,074 relations); for Oldham (1841) 1 : 4 (2,748 relations); and Oldham (1851) 1 : 2 (5,889 relations). The index of association (and test of significance) is the same as that used for the marriage survey. The material presented in figure 18 is abstracted from contingency tables covering the same range of occupations as those used in the marriage survey.

Significance test

A simple chi square test will establish whether or not the distribution of marriages for any particular town (or occupations within it) differs significantly from random expectation. What it cannot do is measure how far the deviation in one town differs from that in another. The following test has been kindly supplied by Dr R. Blackburn of Cambridge University Department of Applied Economics.

To test the null hypothesis that differences in the distribution of marriages in two towns are due to opportunity only (i.e. that all marriages are from the same population with respect to the propensity for the distribution of marriages). The general distribution for a town is given by:

		women			
		A	*B*	*C*	
	A	*aa*	*ab*	*ac*	α
men	*B*	*ba*	*bb*	*bc*	β
	C	*ca*	*cb*	*cc*	γ
		α	β	γ	*t*

where (for instance) A = craft, B = labourer, C = rest. For Oldham use suffix o (e.g. aa_o), for Northampton n. Let E be expected frequency purely on the basis of opportunity, then $Eab = \alpha\beta/t$ etc. For the two towns combined, $E = E_o + E_n$ (e.g. $Eab = Eab_n + Eab_o$).

We wish to test the null hypothesis that differences between towns are due to opportunity only (in other words that the factor of deviation from opportunity present in each is *constant* between them) and that all marriages are from the same population with respect to propensity for distribution. This would imply that the sum of observed frequencies for the two towns equals the sum of the expected, e.g.

$$Uab_o + Uab_n = ab = ab_n + ab_o \text{ (where } U \text{ is expected).}$$

The resultant expected frequency U for any town depends on two factors: (i) the opportunity structure which gives E, and (ii) the propensity for types of marriage regardless of the opportunity structure. This is given by the index I for the two towns combined, e.g.

$$Iab = \frac{\text{observed } ab}{Eab} = \frac{ab_o + ab_n}{Eab_o + Eab_n}.$$

Thus

$$Uab = EabIab = ab.$$

$$Uab_o + Uab_n = \frac{ab_o + ab_n}{Eab_o + Eab_n} \cdot Eab_o + Eab_n = ab_o + ab_n = ab = Uab.$$

Now, taking

$$x = ab + ba$$

$$Ex = Eab + Eba = 2Eab \text{ (because } Eab = \frac{\alpha\beta}{t} = \frac{\beta\gamma}{t} = Eba)$$

$$Ix = \frac{x}{Ex}$$

$$= \frac{ab + ba}{2\,Eab} = \tfrac{1}{2}\,Iab + Iba$$

therefore

$$Ux_o = Ex_oIx_n = 2Eab_o\,\frac{ab_o + ba_n + ab_n + ba_n.}{2\,(Eab_o + Eab_n)}$$

We may now derive the following 'observed' and 'expected', (U) tables comparing towns:

	observed marriages				expected marriages		
	x	rest			x		rest
Oldham	$ab_o + ba_o$	r_o	t_o	O	$Eab_o\dfrac{ab + ba}{Eab}$	Ur_o	t_o

North/tn $\quad ab_n+ba_n \quad r_n \quad t_n \qquad$ N $\quad Eab_n\dfrac{ab+ba}{Eab} \quad Ur_n \quad t_n$

$$ab+ba \quad r \quad t \qquad\qquad ab+ba \qquad r \quad t$$

The form of the table gives one degree of freedom. The values of r and Ur come from $t-x$. The important point is that $Ux_o+Ux_n = ab+ba = x_o+x_n$. An ordinary chi square test can now be applied.

Note: The expected table may also be written.

	x	rest	
O	Ux_o	Ur_o	t_o
N	Ux_n	Ur_n	t_n
	$ab+ba$	r	t

The full expansion of Ux_o is

$$Ux_o = Eab_o . \frac{ab+ba}{Eab} = \frac{\frac{\alpha_o\beta_o}{t_o}}{\frac{\alpha_o\beta_o}{t_o}+\frac{\alpha_n\beta_n}{t_n}} . \; ab_o+ba_o+ab_n+ba_n .$$

Table 19 Northampton marriages (1845-56): indices of association

index = $\dfrac{\text{actual}}{\text{expected}}$ 100 = unity   * = expected cell frequency below 5

	(1)	(2)	(3)	(4)	(5)	(6)	(7)	(8)	(9)	(10)	(11)	(12)	(13)
(1) big employer/professional	6,200*												
(2) tradesman	1,000*	8,000*											
(3) small master	143*	812*	965*										
(4) clerical	—	83*	235	475*									
(5) shop	—	26*	147	176	258								
(6) farm	—	52	210	266	185	398							
(7) building craft	—	—	46	125	103	54	113						
(8) furniture craft	—	—	95	100*	140	50	108	331					
(9) agricultural	—	—	—	66	105	229	100	195	182				
(10) shoemaker	—	—	48	76	76	38	89	73	85	160			
(11) servant	—	—	—	96	114	75	71	24*	112	92	412		
(12) tailor	—	—	—	60*	161	101	97	39*	80	76	94*	200	
(13) labourer	—	—	17	50	54	64	92	39	82	83	95	93	218

total marriages used 3,146

Table 20 Oldham marriages (1846–56): indices of association

index = actual/expected   100 = unity   * = expected cell frequency below 5

	(1)	(2)	(3)	(4)	(5)	(6)	(7)	(8)	(9)	(10)	(11)	(12)	(13)	(14)	(15)
(1) big employer	18,700*														
(2) tradesmen	1,860*	11,560*													
(3) small master	126*	200	600												
(4) clerical	—	53*	186	435*											
(5) shop	—	38	251	251	320*										
(6) farm	—	23*	68	97	200	246									
(7) supervisory	—	40*	175	175	103	94	317								
(8) building craft	—	—	35	185	140	159	79	162							
(9) metal craft	—	—	56	89	112	76	150	98	200						
(10) Spinner	—	—	75	63	97	82	130	101	117	165					
(11) weaver	—	—	48	59	81	107	108	87	62	86	170				
(12) coal	—	—	60	71	72	73	62	195	72	99	105	300			
(13) hatter	—	—	55	41	60	65	75	43	61	117	42	41	115		
(14) carter	—	—	32	25	130	156	350	109	117	141	106	130	75	200	
(15) labourer	—	—	36	50	88	92	75	89	141	85	106	117	47	84	200

total marriages used: 5,550

Table 21   South Shields marriages (1846-56): indices of association

	(1)	(2)	(3)	(4)	(5)	(6)	(7)	(8)	(9)	(10)	(11)	(12)	(13)
(1) big employer	2,028*												
(2) tradesman	924*	1,000*											
(3) small master	340*	400*	616*										
(4) clerical	278*	180*	273*	412*									
(5) shopkeeper	47	95*	200*	143*	187								
(6) farm	97	293	143*	74	215	324							
(7) master mariner	23	25*	43	81	177	161	259						
(8) shipyard craft	17*	—	29*	98	88	35	66	200					
(9) building craft	19*	91*	66*	72*	78	154	113	96	100				
(10) metal craft	—	—	87*	21	100	77	230	64	123	246			
(11) seaman	11	25	67	40	93	50	62	127	103	71	189		
(12) coalminer	—	—	—	—	100	21	100	47	80	126	60	810	
(13) labourer	—	—	28*	57	73	123	50	60	68	76	52	68	405

total marriages used: 3,180

Appendix 3: Sources on the Oldham bourgeosie

Secondary

James Butterworth, *History and Descriptive Account of Oldham* (1817).

Edwin Butterworth, *Historical Sketches of Oldham* (1856).

G. Shaw, *Local Notes* (1887).

G. Shaw, *Oldham Annals* (1904).

J. Brierley, *Jubilee of Oldham Incorporation* (1899) (often inaccurate).

C. Higson, 'Pedigrees' (series of bound ms. volumes in OPL dated 1913-14).

C. Higson, 'Cotton Mills of Lees' (ms. volume).

H. Wilde, 'Mills and Millowners of the Last Century' (volume cuttings from *Oldham Chronicle*, March 1934).

Edwin Butterworth, 1812-48

Butterworth is the most important single source for earlier nineteenth-century Oldham. He was the son of James Butterworth, town postmaster and author of the 1817 history. From the mid-1820s he acted as assistant to Edward Baines (then writing his history of Lancashire), and from 1830 was correspondent to Baines' *Leeds Mercury*. Later he wrote local notes for a number of Manchester papers including the *Manchester Advertiser, Manchester Times* and *Manchester Examiner*. In 1836 he was appointed registrar of births and deaths for Busk, and died of typhus in April 1848. He published a *History of Ashton under Lyne* in 1842, and posthumously *Historical Sketches of Oldham*. He also left a mass of ms. material (now in OPL) including a day-by-day account of life and politics in Oldham from 1829 to 1844 which he used as a basis for his press reports.

Family origins

Bishop's transcripts of births, deaths and marriages: LRO DRM
2/ 237a, 237b, 238, 238a, 238b, 239, 239a, 240, 240a, 240b, 251,
251a, 253, 254, 259, 261.
Census schedules (PRO): HO 107 BDL, HO 107, RG 9.
Hairpowder duty: 1795 LRO QDH 1/1; 1796 QDH 1/2.
Yeomanry correspondence: PRO HO 50 and 51.
Newspaper obituaries in *Oldham Chronicle*, 1854-90.
Directories: E. Raffald, *The Manchester Directory* (Manchester
1773 MPL); *Scholes' Manchester and Salford Directory* (Man-
chester 1794 Guildhall); *Scholes'* (Manchester 1797 Guildhall);
Pigot's (Manchester 1811 Guildhall); *Deans'* (Manchester 1813
BM).

Wealth

Probate records: Somerset House and LRO. These give a valuation of personality, but not real estate. A total valuation of all
wealth (for death duty purposes) was not introduced until 1894.
Between 1815 and 1894 the basis of valuation remained virtually
unchanged: G. Griffith, *Digest of Stamp Duties* (eleventh ed.
1894) and S. Buxton, *Finance and politics*, vol. II, p. 293 (1888).

Rateable value: Petitions for and against incorporation in 1849
give the sworn rateable value of each petitioner (PRO PC 1/851
and 852). This material has been used in preference to the township poor rate assessment book for 1850 (LRO PR/1126) where
rates are listed by street and occupier, making the calculation of
any one man's aggregate liability almost impossible.

Servants and employees: From census schedules.

Land: Land tax 1780-1830 LRO QDL (of very little value).

Companies: Files in Companies' House, Old Street and PRO BT.

Politics

Poll books for 1832, 1835, 1847, July 1852 (both pro-Cobbett
Remembrancer and pro-Fox *Poll book)*, December 1852 (pro-
Cobbett and pro-Fox), 1857 and 1865 (all in OPL).

Police Commission minute book (1843-9) and town council minute book from 1849 in Oldham town clerk's office. Poor law guardian's minute book from 1849 (LRO). Oldham Lyceum membership book 1847 (Oldham Lyceum, Union Street).

Statutes (for commissioners, trustees and proprietors). Enclosure: 42 Geo III c 59; 43 Geo II c 44; 7 Geo IV c 67. Church: 5 Geo IV c 64; 9 Geo IV c 99. Gas and water: 7 Geo IV c 17; 6 Geo IV c 171. Roads: 45 Geo III c 7; 46 Geo III c 63; 52 Geo III c 59; 54 Geo III c 171; 6 Geo IV c 83; 7 and 8 Geo IV cc 54 and 55; 10 Geo IV c 89. Police: 7 Geo IV c 117.

Religion

Except where otherwise stated all material is in OPL. *St Mary's*: Register of pews 1820-94 (church safe), petition of vault owners, G. Perry Gore, *St Mary's* (1896). *St Peter's:* Consecration deed 1768 (Giles Shaw ms. VII MPL), Churchwardens' accounts 1769-1830 (Shaw ms. LXXVIII), *Church and Parish of St Peter's* (1868). *St Paul's, Royton:* Churchwardens' accounts 1806-34 (Shaw ms. XI), *Grand Bazaar Handbook 1896*, G. Shaw, *Local Notes* 180. *Holy Trinity, Shaw: Oldham District Churches and Clergy* (n.d. c. 1902). *St John's, Hey:* H. Bateson, *Hey Chapel*, S. Andrew, *History of Hey* (1905), G. Shaw, *Annals*, vol. III, p. 112. *St James', Waterhead:* G. Shaw, *Local Notes*, 116. *Holy Trinity, Waterhead:* G. Shaw, *Annals*, vol. II, p. 196. *St Thomas's, Werneth:* S. Deem, *St Thomas'* (1937). *St John's, Werneth:* W. Westley, *St John's* (1945). For St Margaret's, Hollinwood and St James's, Shaw, no separate information was found, but for these, as well as the other early foundations, lists of 'principal residents' can be found in the 1779-1821 visitation reports (Chester RO EDV 7). *Baptist, King St:* Manual for 1903 (Cloxton, 305 Windsor Road, Oldham), *Sunday School Union Report 1890*. *Greenacresmoor Congregational:* church record (vestry), British day school minute book (vestry), Sunday school minute book (vestry), G. Waddington, *Independent Church at Greenacres* (Manchester 1854). *Hope Chapel, Congregational:* minute book 1894-1920 (vestry) and grave stones (now in school yard over road). *Queen Street, Congregational:* Annual record 1885-1900 (vestry), J. Mansley, *Queen Street Chapel* (1955). *Methodism:* G. Shaw, *Annals*, vol. III, p. 42, J. Marrat, *Wesleyan Sunday Schools* (1855), *Oldham Monthly*

Remembrancer and Workingman's Friend, 4 March 1848. *Manchester Street, Wesleyan:* Trustees' cash account 1811-27 (Shaw ms. LXXXII), *Centenary Celebration 1890,* B. Dunkerley, *Wesley Past and Present* (1832). *Northmoor Wesleyan:* F. Kelly, *Northmoor Church* (1955). *Middleton Junction: Middleton Junction Methodist Church 1800-1951.* *Hollins' Wesleyan:* 'A Century of Wesleyanism', *Oldham Chronicle,* 21 May 1937. *Royton Wesleyan: Wesleyan Methodist Sunday School* (1898). *King Street Methodist Free: Church Record* (1891). *Wesleyan Association* (1834, Stephens' secession): list of signatories to deed with Unitarians in J. Taylor, *Unitarian Chapel* (1913). *Primitive Methodists:* W. Farndale, *Primitive Methodism in Lees 1822-1911* (1911), W. Walker, *Builders of Zion Chapel* (1914). *Quakers:* J. Ward, *Oldham Meeting of the Society of Friends* (1911). *Unitarians:* J. Taylor, *Unitarian Chapel* (1913), A. Gordon, *Dob Lane Chapel* (1904). *Moravians:* Register of births and deaths from 1827 and membership list 1835 (Manse, 325 Lees Road, Oldham).

Notes

Chapter 2: Industrialization and Society

1 The first quotation comes from William Radcliffe, *Origin of the New System of Manufacturing Commonly Called Power-loom Weaving* (Stockport, 1828). The second is from the diary of the Oldham handloom weaver, Rowbottom, for 11 August 1793. The ms., covering the years 1788 to 1830, is in Oldham Public Library (henceforth OPL). Some assessment of it as a source can be found in T. Ashton, 'Standard of living', *Journ. Econ. Hist.,* supplement IX, 1949.

2 S. Chapman, *The Early Factory Masters* (Newton Abbot, 1967) demonstrates the predominantly mercantile origin of the factory builders in Derby and Notts.

3 The list of millowners used comes from the following sources: *Builders 1776–1811:* E. Butterworth, *Oldham* (Oldham, 1856) pp. 117–60. *1811 spinners:* Crompton's census of mule and twist spindlage taken from the typescript in Manchester Public Library (henceforth MPL) collated from the original lists in the Crompton Papers. Chadwick Museum, Bolton. G. Daniel discusses this source in 'Crompton's 1811 Census', *Econ. Jour. Hist. supplement,* 1930.

   Survivors are those firms listed as in business by trade directories throughout the period 1825 to 1851: Pigot and Dean, *Directory for Manchester* (Manchester, 1825) ; J. Pigot, *Directory* (Manchester, 1836) ; I. Slater, *Directory of the Manufacturing Districts* (Manchester, 1844) ; Slater's directory of Manchester (Manchester, 1851). *Founders* are those of firms employing four hundred workers or over in 1846 (E. Butterworth, *Oldham,* p. 118) checked against the 1851 census schedules. The sources for information on origins are discussed in appendix 3.

4 The first three steam engines were brought in by Jones (coal), William Clegg (hatting) and John Milne (coal) (E. Butterworth, *Oldham,* p. 134). The hatters were probably the wealthiest of the late eighteenth-century Oldham manufacturers. Henshaws had a capital of £154,000 in 1807, and one of the partners was a brother of the Manchester banker William Allen of Byrom, Allen, Sidgwick and Place (E. Butterworth, *Oldham,* p. 154, and L. Grindon, *Manchester Banks and Bankers,* Manchester, 1877).

5 1811 Crompton Census, *Wroe:* E. Butterworth, *(Oldham,* p. 152. *Duncuft:* Werneth Colliery partnership deed 1794 (Lancashire Record Office DDRe/6) and 1776 land survey (LRO DDRe 15/1)). The dozen spindle jennies of the 1770s and the early mules could be driven entirely by hand. By the 1790s the widespread adoption of powered mules had pushed the competitive size towards two hundred spindles per mule (G. Daniels, *The Early English Cotton Industry,* Manchester, 1920, p. 125). *Dean's Manchester and Salford Directory, 1813.* On powerloom factory, Butterworth, *Oldham,* p. 152.

6 *Coal:* three of the four main mining concerns (Werneth, Fairfield, Greenacres Moor) were dominated by four families. Werneth Colliery partners in 1794 included William Jones, (Col.) John Lees of Werneth and James Lees of Clarksfield (who was also William Jones' son-in-law): LRO DDRe/6 and DDX 614/19. The Fairfield partners at the beginning of the century included John, James and Joseph Lees of Clarksfield and Joseph Jones Senior (William Jones' son): LRO DDx 614/16. And among the Greenacres Moor partners (by the 1803 lease: LRO DDRe 6/3) were William Clegg, James and Joseph Lees of Clarksfield and John Lees of Fairfield (eldest of the Clarksfield brothers).

Cotton: estimates of size are difficult, but some indication can be got from the fire insurance records. For 1792 those of the Royal Exchange show the cotton business of John Lees of Werneth insured for £3,500, that of James and Joseph Lees of Clarksfield for £3,500 and the partnership of John Lees of Fairfield with Locke and Hindley for £4,200 (Guildhall Library RE 7523 vol. 23 ff 97 & 99 and vol. 24 f 1). This puts them way ahead of the smaller cotton manufacturers insured for only fractions of these figures (like James Hardman of Royton insured for only £200 in 1791 – RE 7253 vol. 22 f 96). Because the records are incomplete, no final estimates of magnitude can be made but it would seem likely that two Lees families, the Cleggs and the Jones's, between them employed something near half of the area's approximately two thousand handloom weavers in the 1790s.

Canals: John Lees of Fairfield, James Lees of Clarksfield and William Jones were the local committee members of the Ashton Canal in 1798 (the major channel for Oldham coal): British Transport Historical Records AC 1/1, Minutes 27 July 1798. Representatives of the Clarksfield/Fairfield Lees and the Werneth Lees were among the proprietors of the Peak Forest Canal (a southern projection of the Ashton Canal: 34 Geo III c 26), on the committee of the Huddersfield Canal (which took the Ashton Canal over the Pennines via Saddleworth: BTHR HUC 1/1 26 June 1794) and among the proprietors of the Rochdale Canal (which cut across the western edge of the Oldham area and ultimately crossed the Pennines via Todmorden: 34 Geo III c 78).

Land: information on landholding for the late eighteenth century is very poor. The land tax returns (LRO QDL i/6 59) are scrappy, and the only extensive material is a 'survey of housing and land' originally made in 1776 of which a copy exists among the Jones family papers (LRO DDRe 15/1). The general impression is of a considerable degree of fragmentation both in terms of land area and the components of ownership (chief rent, mineral rights, leasehold occupation and housing). In 1776 the principal proprietors in Oldham township appear to have been the Cleggs, the Clarksfield Lees and the Hopwoods but with a wide dispersion among two dozen or so other families among whom the Jones's and the Werneth Lees were prominent. *Enclosure 1802/3* 42 Geo III c 59 and 43 Geo III c 44 enabled the division of three hundred acres of common land among a number of owners (including the Cleggs and the Clarksfield Lees) with John Lees of Werneth getting the mineral rights by virtue of his 'lordship of the manor' purchased a few years previously.

7 C. Higson, 'Pedigrees' (1913-4, ms. volume in OPL). E. Butterworth, *Oldham*, p. 182.

8 Membership is available for the main dissenter congregations but not for all the Anglican – which allows at least the negative statement that the fourteen of unknown religion were unlikely to have been dissenters (appendix 3 for detailed sources).

9 J. Butterworth, *Oldham* (1817), pp. 51-165.

10 For a list of the officers: Derby to Dundas, 18 September 1803 (HO 50/76).

11 In addition to the descriptive evidence from select committees (like that on manufacturers in 1833 or the exportation of machinery in 1840), the overall figures for the industry itself – however inadequate – point in the same direction. Taking the total 'value added' minus wages within the cotton industry (P. Deane, *British Economic Growth*, p. 187) and holding it against the current value of the industry's fixed capital (from Blaug, *Econ. Hist. Rev.*, 1961) plus the annual bill for wages and raw materials, one finds that, even allowing for a fairly drastic cut in coal, gas and transport charges and a faster rate of turnover, there was a steady and marked deterioration between 1830 and 1844-6. Though the fall then appears to have steadied, the gross rate of surplus for all sectors of the industry together, seems to have dropped from over 50 per cent. in 1830 to nearer 30 per cent in 1844-6.

12 *Victoria County History* (hereafter VCH), Lancashire, vol. V,

pp. 95-115. H. Bateson, *Oldham*, p. 17, lists the services demanded by the Taylors and the Tetlows.

13 Tetlow and Chadderton. Bateson, *Oldham*, p. 37. VCH, vol. V, pp. 96, 99. The 1611 will of Thomas Tetlow could well serve as an epitaph for his class – 'a caliver, two great bills, a yew bow, a broken cross-bow; also a pair of playing tables valued at one shilling'.

14 VCH, vol. V, pp. 95-115. The Radclyffe's steadily sold away their land during the eighteenth century. A series of 999 year leases is preserved in DDRe 9 (LRO).

15 W. Jordan, *The Social Institutions of Lancashire 1480–1660* (Manchester Cheetham Society, 1962) for the sudden trade expansion 1600–50 and the London link-up. W. Howson, 'Plague, Poverty and Population in Parts of North-West England 1580–1720', *Trans Lancs and Ches. Hist. Soc.*, 1960. Bateson, *Oldham*, p. 42. E. Butterworth, *Oldham*, p. 100.

16 Yeoman purchasers: the Lees bought Clarksfield from the Cudworths and the Cleggs, Bent from the Chaddertons (VCH, vol. V, pp. 99–113). The outside merchants (*ibid.*, and deeds in DDX 614/14, LRO) became the area's gentry for the eighteenth century.

17 1 Anne c 18 (and others recited in preamble to 6 & 7 Vict c 40).

18 Wadsworth provides a count of Oldham baptisms: 1725-7 (571), 1745-7 (640), 1765-7 (902), 1779-81 (1,056). Already in 1725-7, 49 per cent of the fathers were weavers (the proportion in 1779-81 was 53 per cent). Wadsworth emphasizes that most of these were also cottagers or husbandmen. A. Wadsworth, *The Cotton Trade and Industrial Lancashire* (Manchester, 1931), pp. 315-6.

19 Defoe travelled across the northern tip of the chapelry in the second decade of the eighteenth century and noted the swollen population: 'Among the manufacturers' houses . . . scattered an infinite number of small cottages' and that 'neither, indeed, could one-fifth part of the inhabitants be supported without the [manufactures]'. D. Defoe, *A Tour of the Whole Island of Great Britain* (London, 1962) vol. II, p. 195.

20 Wadsworth, *op. cit.*, p. 344.

21 *Linen and Broad-ware Weavers' Apology* (1758) quoted by Wadsworth, p. 317. Wadsworth also makes an analysis of urban and rural apprenticeship on p. 333.

22 For the use of south-east Lancashire's cheap labour in hat-making, see P. Giles, 'The Felt-Hatting Industry 1550–1850', *Trans Lancs and Ches. Antiq. Soc.*, 1959, and 'Report Upon the Petitions Relating to the Manufacture of Hats (1752)', *Reports from Committees of the House of Commons,* vol. II, pp. 371 ff.

[23] Rowbottom makes regular mention of the August rushbearing throughout his diary.

[24] L. Schuecking, *Die puritanische familie* (Bern, 1964) ; C. Hill, *Puritanism and Society in pre-Revolutionary England* (London, 1964) ; N. Birnbaum, 'Zwingli and Zurich', *Past and Present, 1959*.

[25] Bateson, *op. cit.,* p. 42.

[26] W. Shaw (ed.), *Minutes of the Manchester Presbyterian Classis* (Manchester Cheetham Society, 1890).

[27] Copy of bond dated 16 April 1716, Giles Shaw ms. LXXXII (MPL) ; G. Waddington, *The Independent Church at Greenacres* (Manchester, 1854).

[28] Schuecking, *op cit.,* p. 9, makes the important point that 'Puritanism' existed as much inside as outside the established Church of the earlier eighteenth century.

[29] St Peter's consecration deed 1768 (Giles Shaw ms. VII). St Peter's churchwardens' accounts 1769–1830 (Giles Shaw ms. LXXXVIII).

[30] Chester diocese visitations – replies from St Peter's in 1778 and 1821 (Chester RO EDV 7/1 & 6). Fawcett, curate of the parish church, expressed his disapproval of the Thursday lectures at St Peter's in his reply for 1789 (EDV 7/2).

[31] G. Shaw, *Oldham Annals,* vol. III, p. 42. J. Butterworth, *Oldham,* p. 47 Manchester Street Weslyan Methodist Church trustee steward's cash account 1811–27 (Giles Shaw ms. LXXXII). Among the St Peter's men backing the Methodists at this date were William Jones (coal), Edmund Whitehead (hatting), George Hadfield (coal and hatting), Thomas Cussons (cotton)́, Thomas Cooper (cotton) and Daniel Mellor (cotton).

[32] Salem Moravian Chapel register 1825–1900 (The Manse, 325 Lees Road, Oldham). The congregation was linked to that at Fairfield four miles to the south and similarly dominated by the senior branch of the Clarksfield Lees (E. Butterworth, *Oldham*).

[33] E. Butterworth gives figures of 1,737 and 1,892 for Oldham township and the townships of Crompton, Chadderton and Royton respectively in 1714 based on a count of hearths, and again for 1792 the figures of 9,480 and 6,296 (report in *Manchester Advertiser,* 29 December 1838). In *Oldham,* p. 132, he gives 8,012 and 5,904 for 1789. Other material in figure 2 comes from the census.

[34] Reply from Fawcett, curate of St Mary's, for 1804 visitation (Chester RO EDV 7/3).

[35] The figures refer to *regular* communicants, the average number of people to whom the sacrament was administered monthly, not

the Easter communicants. Blanks indicate no reply. (Chester diocese visitation reports: Chester RO EDV 7/1, 2, 3, 4, & 6).

36 26 Geo II c 31, 29 Geo II c 12 and 32 Geo III c 59. The 1792 Act tightened restrictions on the transfer of licences between the annual licensing sessions. Also S. and B. Webb, *History of Liquor Licensing 1700–1830* (London, 1903).

37 Rowbottom diary, 12 January 1793.

38 *Ibid.*, 22 September 1792.

39 *Ibid*, 22 October 1794. 'Upwards of twelve hundred members from the different societies' attended the service.

40 33 Geo III c 54.

41 Protestant Dissenting Ministers Act 1779 (19 Geo III c 44).

42 Returns of members' names and occupations made to the clerk of the peace under 39 Geo III c 79 by Friendship Lodge (Oldham), Philanthropy (Hollinwood). and {St Bernard \ (Chadderton): LRO QDS 2/1/ 16, 25 & 26. According to F. Pick, *The Lodge of Friendship No. 277* (Manchester, 1934, OPL) six lodges existed in 1800. Of the fifty-nine members of the lodges making returns fourteen were innkeepers, fifteen craft masters and sixteen small employers. However, there was no representation of the big employers or gentry as defined by payers or hairpowder duty (LRO QDH 1/1 (1795) & QDH 1/2 (1796)) or those exempted from the duty as holders of commissions (Derby to Dundas, 18 September 1803, PRO HO 50/76).

43 A. Gordon, *Dob Lane Chapel* (Manchester, 1904), and J. Taylor, *Unitarian Chapel, Oldham* (Oldham, 1913).

44 D. Bogue and J. Bennet, *History of the Dissenters* (London, 1808), vol. III, pp. 213–49. *The Manchester Socian Controversy* (Manchester, 1825, MPL).

45 J. Wesley, *Journal* (London, 1910), vol. IV, p. 59.

46 Bogue and Bennet, *op. cit.*, vol. III, p. 213 and vol. IV, p. 241.

47 Wadsworth, *op. cit.*, pp. 345, 349 (*Apology* quoted at length).

48 J. Taylor, *op. cit.*, p. 12, and G. Shaw, Annals, vol. III, pp. 2, 45. Supporting evidence for the subversiveness of these congregations comes from the later period. Dob Lane was attacked as 'Jacobin' in 1793 (Gordon, *op. cit.*, p. 48), and Lord Street had six of its fourteen trustees active leaders of the working-class movement in 1816-7 (Taylor, p. 12 for trustees). State warrants were issued for William Browe (machine-maker), Joseph Newton (cotton spinner) and George Wilson. All three fled to America (Taylor, p. 38 and A. Marcroft, *Landmarks of Local Liberalism*, Oldham, 1913, p. 36). The chapel was used as a distribution centre for seditious

K*

pamphlets, and described as 'extremely disaffected' by Chippendale, the local Home Office correspondent (Chippendale to Sidmouth, 7 October 1816, PRO HO 42/153).

49 19 Geo III c 44 and 21 Geo III c 49.

50 S. and B. Webb, *Liquor Licensing,* appendix 1.

51 Sunday Observance Act 1781 (21 Geo III c 49), and Seditious Meetings Act 1795 (36 Geo III c 8).

52 Rowbottom diary, 12 June 1789.

53 *Ibid.,* 18 February 1788, 26 January 1792 and 29 March 1792.

54 *Ibid.,* 16 June 1794.

55 The lists of officers (Derby to Dundas, 18 September 1803, HO 50/76 and for 1808 HO 50/196) show the same men as the lists of churchwardens for the Evangelical stronghold of St Peter's (see note 29): the Cleggs, Jones's, Clarksfield and Werneth Lees, Duncufts and Mellors. The incumbent of St Peter's, William Winter, was company chaplain. For the local activity of the yeomanry, 'Return of dates during the last ten years at which any volunteer of yeomanry troop was called out for actual service', PP 1828 XVII (273).

56 Gordon, *op. cit.,* p. 48.

57 Rowbottom, 22 September 1792 and 12 January 1793.

58 G. Shaw, *Annals,* vol. III, p. 181.

59 Rowbottom, 4 January 1794.

60 This is a minimum. The evidence presented in figure 3 (see note on handloom wages) would suggest an even heavier fall in real income. Rowbottom (8 December 1793) described the hatters as having 'dropped half of their wages' and appears to present the fustian trade in an even worse position.

61 Rowbottom, 1 June 1793, 11 August 1793 and 8 December 1793.

62 *Ibid.,* 6 May 1793.

63 *R. v. Thomas Walker:* brief for the prosecution (10 August 1793) PRO TS 11/892/3035.

64 Rowbottom, 21 April 1794.

65 *Ibid.*

66 *Ibid.,* June 1795 throughout.

67 *Ibid.,* 30 May 1795.

68 *Ibid.,* June 1795.

69 *Ibid.,* 30 July, 1 August and 4 August 1795.

70 36 Geo III c 8 and 36 Geo III c 7.

71 Rowbottom, 31 December 1794.

72 Wall slogans (Bayley to Portland, 23 March 1801, HO 42/61). Armistice celebrations (identifying the radicals with peace and plenty) organized by the 'patriot' Thomas Buckley (Rowbottom, 8 November 1801). *Petitions:* peace (Rowbottom, 17 December 1795), minimum wage (Bancroft to Portland, 29 April 1799, PC 1/44/A 155). 'Fair price' campaigns (Rowbottom, 4 August 1795). *Press:* in June 1801 the Oldham district United Englishmen resolved to set up their own press. Previously most of their printing had been done by Cowdroy (Volney's *Les Ruines* was a favourite): Hay to Pelham, 7 June 1801, HO 42/62, and Fletcher to Portland, 6 June 1801, HO 42/62. In 1797 the government had imposed severe penalties not only on unlicensed printers but unlicensed manufacturers of printers' type.

73 Fletcher to Ryder, 24 December 1805 (HO 42/83).

74 Rowbottom, 23 July 1794, 8 November 1801 and 13 July 1803.

75 For the 'gentlemen-mechanic' split in the Manchester movement see prosecution brief *R. v. Thomas Walker* (TS 11/892/3035) and 'Examination of James Dixon 5 May 1798' (HO 42/45). For the links between Oldham and Manchester groups: letters of solidarity from the secretaries of the Friends of Freedom, Royton (Thomas Taylor, 20 June 1797) and Friends of Freedom, Chadderton (J. Jackson, 22 June 1797) to the Manchester group enclosed in docket 10 January 1798 (PC 1/43/A 152). Thomas Taylor (the Royton secretary) went down to the London corresponding society in July 1801 to collect the new type of membership card (substituted for the old oath): Fletcher to Pelham, 31 August 1801, HO 42/62, and Fletcher to Pelham, 28 July 1801, HO 42/62. Table 8 (at the end of chapter 5) lists the main working-class leaders of the period.

76 See especially Chippendale's description of the Royton family of Taylor enclosed in Fletcher to Hawkesbury, 27 December 1807 (HO 42/91).

77 Each township had a directory acting as liaison committee between its own districts and the area delegate meeting – which in turn sent delegates to Manchester. In 1801 the authorities cracked part of the network and transported three Oldham leaders (Stansfield, Buckley and Jackson). The most important sources for organization (including some captured documents and the fragment of a subscription list from Crompton) are: Hay to Pelham, 18 May 1801 (HO 42/62); Hay to Pelham, 8 July 1801 for the link-up with Thelwell (HO 42/62); Fletcher to Pelham, 31 August 1801 (HO 42/62); Fletcher to Pelham, 28 July 1801 (HO

42/62); Fletcher to Pelham, 7 January 1802 (HO 42/65); Fletcher to Pelham, 2 April 1802 (HO 42/65).

78 Fletcher to Pelham, 31 August 1801 (HO 42/62).

79 Again this is a minimum – see note on handloom wages (p. 43).

80 R. F. to Privy Council, 8 August 1799, PC 1/44 A 161. Correspondence from local magistrates shows a peak of concern during the following eighteen months. Perhaps most worrying of all was the formation of a common front of 'labourers, mechanics and artificers' at Manchester in November 1799 against the Combination Acts with the treasurer of the society of fustian cutters supplying funds: Bayley to HO, 16 November 1799 (PC 1/45 A 164).

81 Fletcher to Portland, 6 April 1801 (HO 42/61), and W. R. Hay to Portland, 6 May 1801 (HO 42/62).

82 Thomas Ainsworth to Sir Robert Peel, 12 March 1801, and 'a magistrate' (the name is illegible) to Peel, 14 March 1801 (HO 42/61).

83 Chippendale, enclosed in Fletcher to Hawkesbury, 27 December 1807 (HO 42/91).

84 E. Butterworth, *Oldham*, p. 158. Farington to Hawkesbury, 24 March 1808 (HO 42/95). Farington to Hawkesbury, 28 May 1808 (HO 42/95). Silvester to Hawkesbury, 2 June 1808 (HO 42/95).

85 *Leeds Mercury*, 25 April 1812 (quoted E. Thompson, *Making of the English Working-Class*, p. 568).

86 Chippendale to Fletcher, 23 April 1812 (HO 40/1).

87 Rowbottom, 20 April 1812.

88 Chippendale to Fletcher, 23 April 1812 (HO 40/1).

89 J. Cartwright to J. Shuttleworth, 24 February 1813 (scrapbook of J. Shuttleworth, MPL).

90 Lancashire militia minute book 1800-24, 15 May 1812 (LM 1/2 LRO).

91 This process will be examined in more detail in chapter 5.

Chapter 3: Labour and State Power

1 First report RC county constabulary, p. 82 (PP 1839 XIX).

2 Report RC handloom weavers, p. 113 (PP 1841 X).

3 So far there have been only two countrywide surveys: F. Mather, *Public Order in the Age of the Chartists* (Manchester, 1959) which makes little reference to industrial violence and provides no detailed community studies, and A. Aspinall, *Early English Trade Unions* (1949) which restricts itself to the purely industrial.

More useful are the local studies, but as yet only a few areas
have been tackled: G. Williams, 'Radical Merthyr', *Welsh Hist.
Rev.*, 1961 ; D. Rowe, 'Tyneside Keelmen', *International Rev.
Social History*, 1969 ; A. Rose, 'Plug Riots', *Trans. Lancs and
Chesh. Antiq. Soc.*, 1957 ; and E. Midwinter, *Social Administra-
tion in Lancashire 1830-60* (Manchester, 1969).

4 Mather, *op. cit.*

5 Compare, for instance, the figures given for cotton spinners
working on similar counts in G. Wood, *Cotton Wages* (1910).

6 For the 1820s Eckersley to Hobhouse, 19 September 1826 (HO
40/21 f 523): 'Wages of spinners have for a long time been
higher in the town [Oldham] than elsewhere, and the masters are
now determined to be regulated by the general average wages
. . . ' For 1839, Chadwick (*JRSS*, 1860) gives medium self-actor
spinners in Manchester eighteen shillings and Butterworth (diary,
21 April 1839) makes the Oldham spinners in the same grade
receive twenty-two shillings. For two/three loom power weavers
the respective earnings were nine and twelve shillings.

7 Aspinall, *op. cit.*, pp. xii-xviii. D. George, 'Combination Acts',
Econ. Journ. Hist. Suppl., 1927. R. Hedges, *Legal History of
Trade Unionism* (1930), p. 29.

8 Section 13 of 39 & 40 Geo III c 106.

9 *Lost* (not lacking because there were no convictions). For these
years *all* summary conviction copies (a very substantial bulk of
parchment) are missing from the recognizance bundles. Obviously
they were filed elsewhere (a search of other Quarter sessions
series, Order books, Indictments and Petitions, failed to locate
them).

10 LRO QSB 1/192-196.

11 *Rochdale:* 6 July 1818, J. J. Drake and Entwisle: three cotton
spinners sentenced to two months' hard labour. *Manchester:* 13
August 1818, J. Norris: two Manchester cotton spinners. *Burnley:*
3 October 1818, J. J. Hargreaves and Whitaker: five cotton
spinners. *Chorley:* 14 October 1820, J. J. Ridgeway and Silvester:
two cotton spinners. *Blackburn:* 12 June 1821: four cotton spinners. *Preston:* 4 August 1821, J. J. Parker and Addison: two
cotton spinners and their publican organizer. *Colne:* 6 July 1822,
J. J. Parker and Clayton: five shoemakers.

12 Chippendale, 9 July 1818 (HO 42/178). Fletcher to Hobhouse, 26
April 1823 (HO 40/18 quoted by Aspinall, *op. cit.*, p. 368) names
Oldham spinners' Union among the subscribers listed in the
captured books of the Bolton spinners. Also Rowbottom diary, 5
June 1815: 'About the middle of July they [the spinners] mostly

returned to their employ having subdued their masters by compelling them to give the usual wages'.

13 Chippendale, 25 July 1818 (HO 42/178). Chippendale, 4 August 1818 (HO 42/179).

14 'XY' (Chippendale) to Byng, 3 August 1818 (HO 42/178). Norris, 13 August 1818 (HO 42/179).

15 Chippendale, 25 July 1818. Chippendale, 4 August 1818 (42/179).

16 Chippendale, 9 July 1818.

17 Fletcher, 4 September 1818 (HO 42/180).

18 Eckersley to Hobhouse, 19 September 1826 (HO 40/21 f 523).

19 Eckersley to Byng, 11 November 1826 (HO 40/21 f 639).

20 Memorial to Peel signed by John Lees and Sons and eight other firms, 21 December 1826 (HO 40/21 f 771).

21 Eckersley to Byng, 20 January 1826 (HO 40/22 ff 103 and 113).

22 Joseph Rowland to Peel, 21 January 1826 (HO 40/22 f 125).

23 Voice of the People 18 June 1831.

24 Manchester Guardian 1 October 1831.

25 Butterworth diary 7 March 1832.

26 Ibid., 7 March 1833.

27 Ibid., 23 March 1833.

28 Ibid., 16 June 1833.

29 Ibid., 17 October 1833.

30 Ibid., 13 February 1834.

31 Ibid., 21 February 1834.

32 The registered electorate was 1131 in 1832 and 1890 in 1847; Dod, Electoral Facts (1847). Composition: A list of the voters in the borough of Oldham who elected the first members (John Knight, Oldham 1832).

33 'XY' (Chippendale) to Byng, 30 April 1820 (HO 40/13).

34 Butterworth diary, 7 to 17 July 1829. The printer of the placards was D. Evans who also printed the one-man one-vote bills in 1827: Eckersley, 13 March 1827 (HO 40/22).

35 'Power of Exclusive Dealing' by 'Plutarch', 22 November 1832 (quoted in full in B. Grime, Memory Sketches, p. 14).

36 Grime, ibid., p. 15.

37 William Spier, member of Oldham Political Association, A List of Voters in the Borough (Looney, Manchester, 1832).

38 Table 3 gives the voting of all traders in the categories listed for

the three elections for which information is available (the poll books used are listed in appendix 3). It does not seem possible to provide a meaningful 'general population' which might act as a control for these figures. The election results were, however: *1832:* Fielden (radical) 645, Cobbett (radical) 677, Bright (Whig) 145, Burge (Tory) 101 ; *July 1852:* Morgan Cobbett (radical-Tory) 947, Duncuft (Tory) 869, Fox (Liberal) 777 ; *1865:* Hibbert (Liberal) 1,103, Platt (Liberal) 1,074, Morgan Cobbett (Tory) 896, Spinks (Tory) 844. As Oldham was a two-member constituency each elector had two votes and those splitting them between parties are listed under 'cross'.

39 E. Butterworth, *Oldham,* p. 207. O'Connor withdrew from the poll after an hour.

40 Butterworth diary, 28 July 1837.

41 *Northern Star,* 27 July 1839.

42 Morgan Cobbett to S. Fielden, 2 July 1841 (in the Fielden letters collected by the late Professor David Owen of Harvard, to whom I am indebted for providing transcripts).

43 *Exclusive Dealing* (John Hirst, Oldham, 21 June 1847) in OPL.

44 *Oldham Monthly Remembrancer and Workingman's Friend* (31 July 1847) in OPL.

45 *Manchester Guardian,* 23 October 1847 and 29 October 1851.

46 Grime, *op. cit.,* p. 65.

47 Hansard CCVII c 602, 26 June 1871.

48 J. Western, *The English Militia in the Eighteenth Century* (1965), pp. 290-302.

49 Parish officers Act, 33 Geo III c 55 (21 June 1793).

50 Chippendale to Fletcher, 23 April 1812, forwarded to HO in Fletcher, 26 April 1812 (HO 40/1 f 1).

51 Fletcher to Becket, 26 September 1816 (HO 42/153). Chippendale to Sidmouth, 10 February 1817 (HO 40/10).

52 Chippendale to Fletcher, 23 March 1818 (HO 42/175).

53 58 Geo III c 69 (3 June 1818).

54 Thackeray to Fletcher, 16 May 1818 (HO 42/177).

55 Chippendale to Sidmouth, 12 December 1819 (HO 42/200) ; Hobhouse to Chippendale, 7 March 1820 (HO 41/6).

56 *Manchester Guardian* 20 and 31 October, 3 and 24 November and 1 December 1821. *Exchange Herald,* 23 October 1821.

57 *Manchester Guardian,* 24 October 1821.

58 James Rowland and Sons (and twenty-nine other firms) to Rev.

James Holme (magistrate), 17 July 1826 (Duncruft transcripts, Giles Shaw MSS XCII MPL).

[59] *Commons Journal* LXXX, 7 and 11 February 1825; LXXXI, 8 February 1826.

[60] 7 Geo IV c 117.

[61] Hobhouse to Collinge and Lancashire, 26 February 1827 (HO 41/7).

[62] *Voice of the People,* 19 February 1831, p. 64.

[63] Butterworth diary, 2 November 1831 and 13 January 1832.

[64] *Manchester Guardian,* 17 May 1834.

[65] *Ibid.,* 11 October 1834.

[66] Butterworth diary, 12 February 1834. First speaker William Fitton; second William Knott.

[67] Russell to Derby, 11 January 1839 (HO 43/56). Russell, obviously under pressure from the army, asks Derby to build up a *county* constabulary under the provisions of 3 and 4 William IV c 90 and 5 and 6 William IV c 43.

[68] *Manchester Advertiser,* 17 December 1836 and 4 February 1837.

[69] Butterworth diary, 2 January 1840 (the speaker quoted is Alexander Taylor). Also broadsheet *Rural Police* (Daniel Mellor, Hirst, Oldham, no date – OPL 35 PO).

[70] *Manchester Advertiser,* 12 and 26 September 1840.

[71] Butterworth diary, 5 March 1841.

[72] *Manchester Advertiser,* 27 August to 19 November 1842.

[73] 5 and 6 Victoria c 109.

[74] In 1843 the radicals put forward their own list in the vestry and carried it, but the court leet appointed two employers (*Manchester Advertiser,* 14 October 1843). In October 1847 the radicals won in the vestry and their list was not challenged by the court leet (*Manchester Guardian,* 13 October 1847).

[75] *Manchester Advertiser,* 12 July, 30 September, 21 October and 18 November 1843.

[76] Minute book Oldham police commission, 1843-9 (Town Clerk's Office, Town Hall, Oldham), 4 January 1843.

[77] *Manchester Advertiser,* 12 August 1843.

[78] Commission minute book 18 November 1846. Also *Manchester Guardian,* 9 January 1847.

[79] H. Bateson, *Oldham,* p. 132.

[80] *Manchester Guardian,* 22 May 1847.

81 *Manchester Advertiser,* 7 August, 4, 11, 18 September, 9 and 23 October 1847.

82 *Ibid.,* 30 October 1847.

83 *Ibid.,* 6 November 1847 (refused lock-up key) and 13 May 1848 (committed).

84 PRO PC 1/851, 852, 853, 855. *Manchester Guardian,* 5 August 1848, 19 August 1848, 17 and 21 February 1849.

85 *Manchester Guardian,* 7 April and 4 August 1849.

86 Jackson Brierley, *Oldham Jubilee* (Oldham, 1899) p. 10.

87 Union expenditure: PP 1852 XXIII (1461). Borough: PP 1852 LIII (411).

88 RC Poor laws 1834, appendix B 2 town questionaires (PP 1834 XXXV & XXXVI). C. Clements, 'Report', in *Official Circular* (No. 41), 30 September 1844 (Charles Knight for Poor Law Commissioners – LSE 42 A 247).

89 59 George III c 12.

90 To take the 1833 annual vestry meeting (Butterworth diary, 3 April 1833). The overseers were all employers (Greaves, Lees, Brideoak, Braddock, Bradbury and Radcliffe). The new chairman was John Halliwell who in 1821 had been the radical candidate for constable and in 1832 proposed Cobbett as parliamentary candidate. Of the select vestry members Butterworth writes 'some members of the old vestry were re-elected and numerous lists of new ones consisting chiefly of shopkeepers adopted'. At the 1843 annual meeting (Butterworth diary, 29 March 1843) radical dominance was particularly blatant, with the chairman (Lawless) and both auditors (Haslam and Quarmby) members of the area Chartist executive (Butterworth, 6 November 1838; *Northern Star,* 20 November 1841 and 17 December 1842).

91 *Manchester Guardian,* 3 November 1821.

92 G. Henderson, 'Report', First report RC poor laws (PP 1834 XXVIII p. 909a); Clements, 'Report' as cited in note 88.

93 During the 1836-7 spinners' lock-out the pro-union shopkeepers convened a meeting demanding relief for the spinners out of township rates (Butterworth diary, 30 December 1836).

94 *Manchester Advertiser,* 31 March 1838. William Fitton's obituary of Knight, *Northern Star,* 22 September 1838.

95 *Manchester Advertiser,* 4 February 1837.

96 Butterworth diary, 6 March 1838.

97 *Manchester Advertiser,* 21 September 1844.

98 *Ibid.,* 15, 22 and 29 November 1845.

[99] *R.* v. *Overseers of Oldham,* 10 QB 700, *English Law Reports* (1910), XLV KB division pp. 266-7. *Manchester Advertiser,* 10 July and 4 September 1847.

[100] Minute book Oldham poor law union 1847-50, 22 September 1847 (LRO). Nine magistrates attended the first meeting as *ex officio* members. Kay Clegg was elected the first secretary (see 'articles of agreement 5 November 1856', LRO DDR e 14/12 for Clegg as lawyer to the Oldham Cotton Masters Association).

[101] *Commons Journal,* LXXX 16 and 27 February, 11 and 19 March, 12 and 14 May. 5 Geo IV c 44.

[102] 9 Geo IV c 99.

[103] Butterworth diary, 8 April 1833.

[104] *Ibid.,* 10 February 1834 for a detailed account of the whole affair.

[105] *Manchester Advertiser,* 21 April 1838.

[106] The dialogue takes place in the Home Office files HO 40, 41, 42, 43, 45, 50, 51, 52 & 79. For a discussion of this source see H. Davis, *Lancashire Reformers* (Manchester, 1936) and E. Thompson, *Making of the English Working Class* (1963) pp. 591-5. Captain Chippendale acted as Home Office correspondent in Oldham from 1801 till 1821. He was a half-pay regular, son-in-law to Colonel John Lees of Werneth and managed the family's Alkrington colliery. For the identification of Chippendale as 'XY' see Fletcher to Sidmouth, 27 February 1819 (HO 42/184). He was thought of sufficiently highly to get £71 expenses for the period June 1818 to April 1819: Fletcher to Sidmouth, 30 April 1819 (HO 42/186). In 1827 the previous undersecretary at the Home Office wrote to his successor to ask for a pension for Chippendale's widow: 'She is the widow of *the* man who (as I know Lord Sidmouth and Sir John Byng will both be ready to testify) obtained for the government far more useful information than any other individual. . . .' (Hobhouse to Herries, 5 June 1827, HO 79/4).

[107] In 1800 the area's two magistrates, Horton and Pickford, came from the 'mercantile gentry'. The next were direct from the local employers: Rev. John Holme in 1819 (whose wife had interests in local factories – *Manchester Guardian* 7 January 1832, Factory Act case) and James Lees in 1825 (coalowner and son-in-law of Joseph Jones Senior). In 1827 and 1831 two more clergymen were appointed: Revs. James Hordern and T. S. Mills. In 1839 three employers: Jonathan Mellor (cotton), Andrew Schofield (timber), Elijah Hibbert (iron). By 1850 eight more employers had been added (all coalowners but five with money in cotton as well): Abraham Clegg, J. F. Lees, George Lees, Joseph Jones junior, John Duncuft, James Rowland, William Jones and Nathaniel

Worthington. *Proceedings of the Court of Annual General Session for the Palatinate of Lancashire* (LRO).

108 J. Hammond, *Town Labourer* (1927), pp. 83 ff.

109 Lancashire militia books LC/2 & 3, 6 January 1795 to 22 March 1795: return of men liable to serve (LRO). The Oldham militia does not ever seem to have been embodied.

110 Derby, 19 May 1798 (HO 50/42). Derby, 18 September 1803 (HO 50/76). Return of ranks, 10 July 1808 (HO 50/196). It was used in riots in October 1799 and February 1800 (E. Butterworth, *Oldham*, p. 144). During riots in May 1808 it was attacked and stoned (*ibid.*, p. 158). The volunteers appear for the last time in the heavily armoured 'jubilee procession' of 1810 (G. Shaw, *Local Notes*, vol. I, p. 222).

111 Lees to Hopwood, 3 September 1803 (enclosed in Derby, 5 September 1803, HO 50/76).

112 Chippendale gives a vivid description in a letter to his brother Joseph Chippendale, a barrister of Fig Tree Court, Temple (enclosed in Joseph Chippendale to Becket, 25 April 1812 HO 42/122).

113 J. Fortescue, *The County Lieutenancies and the Army 1803-14* (1909), pp. 244-9. Sidmouth gives his reasons for thinking non-propertied volunteers dangerous in a letter to Fletcher, 19 October 1819 (HO 41/5).

114 Sidmouth to Derby, 7 March 1815 (HO 51/89). Hay to Sidmouth, 10 May 1817 (HO 50/360). Taylor to Sidmouth, 29 July 1817 (HO 50/360).

115 Fletcher to Sidmouth, 5 June 1820 (HO 40/13 f 499).

116 Hay to Pelham, 24 May 1801 (HO 42/62). E. Butterworth, *Oldham*, p. 158. Sidmouth to postmaster general, 26 December 1812 (HO 79/2).

117 Chippendale to Byng, 12 November 1820 (HO 40/15 f 295). Bouverie to Peel, 21 July 1834 (HO 40/32 ff 214-225).

118 Bouverie to Peel, 21 July 1834 (HO 40/32).

119 *Leeds Mercury*, 29 April 1820. Norris to Hobhouse, 1 May 1820 (HO 40/13). Lyon to Sidmouth, 6 May 1820 (HO 40/13).

120 Barlow to Hobhouse, 8 June 1821 (HO 40/16 ff 863-70).

121 Eckersley to Duncuft, 12 July 1826 (Giles Shaw ms. XCII, MPL).

122 Phillips to Holme, 15 July 1834 (HO 41/12 f 108).

123 James Barker junior to Graham, 29 June 1843 (HO 45/350).

124 General Arbuthnot, 12 December 1842 (HO 45/268).

125 The pressures came from both genuine business representatives (like Hume, Ricardo and Maberley in the 27 June 1821 'economy and retrenchment' debate, Hansard, V c 1345) and less single-minded working-class spokesmen: see, for instance, the reply to Fielden's petition against barracks in 1834 in E. Stanley to Fielden, 27 July 1834 (HO 41/12 f 113).

126 Lyon to Sidmouth, 6 May 1820 (HO 13/161).

127 The *Manchester Guardian* (9 October 1826) predictably delivered a strong censure.

128 *Manchester Advertiser,* 22 December 1838. *Proceedings of annual general session.*

129 Addington to Chippendale, 28 November 1816 (HO 79/3). 'XY' to Byng, 3 August 1818 (HO 42/179). 'XY' to Byng, 30 April 1820 (HO 40/3).

130 'XY' to Byng, 12 July 1819 (HO 42/189).

131 Chippendale to Hobhouse, 15 November 1819 (HO 42/198).

132 Hobhouse to Harrison, 5 November 1821 (HO 41/6).

133 William Lomas to constables of Oldham, 29 April 1826 (Giles Shaw mss XCII MPL).

134 'Arms Distribution', 30 April 1826 (*ibid.,* XCII).

135 *Manchester Guardian,* 6 May 1826.

136 First report county constabulary, p. 82 (PP 1839 XIX).

137 Sutton to Oldham magistrates, 31 August and 3 September 1842 (HO 41/17). Letters from Rev. T. S. Mills in HO 45/350. General Arbuthnot in HO 45/268 for military intelligence.

138 Sutton to Oldham magistrates, 31 August and 3 September 1842 (HO 41/17).

139 See note 107.

140 *Manchester Advertiser,* 17 July 1847. Magistrates to home secretary, 15 August 1848 (HO 45/241a). Magistrates to home secretary, 29 November and 2 and 3 December 1852 (HO 45/408c).

141 *The Volunteer Movement in Oldham 1859-1939,* OPL.

142 Butterworth diary, June 1832 and E. Butterworth, *Oldham,* p. 200.

143 Hansard, XVI c 365 (7 March 1833).

144 Knight to Fielden, 2 January 1835 (Owen collection, Harvard); Fitton to Fielden, 19 September 1834 (*ibid.*); William Cobbett to Fielden, 24 April 1834 (*ibid.*); John Fielden to Alexander Taylor, 23 November 1845 and 23 February 1846 (OPL); R.B.B. Cobbett to Taylor, 4 November 1846 (OPL).

[145] Hansard, XL c 1103 (13 February 1838). SC combinations of workmen first report (PP 1837-8 VIII).

[146] Hansard, XVI c 731 (18 March 1833).

[147] Hansard XXXVI c 1012 (24 February 1837).

[148] Hansard, XLIX c 117 (10 July 1839), c 694 (23 July 1839), c 738 (24 July 1839).

[149] Hansard, LXV c 1299 (4 March 1841).

[150] Hansard, LXV c 1351.

[151] Hansard, LXXIII c 534 (4 March 1844).

[152] Hansard (31 July 1837).

[153] Hansard, LXXIII c 534 (31 July 1839).

[154] *Political Register,* 16 August 1834.

[155] Hansard, LXIV (20 July 1842). For the other side of the coin R.H. Greg to Chadwick on 17 September 1834: 'Our manufacturers might have sunk with the accumulated poison of high wages, drunkenness, insolence and unions which . . . the masters *cannot* break through. The only escape . . . is in abundant labour. . . . ', and goes on to propose a state-backed plan for moving labour across the country (Chadwick papers, box 69, University College, London).

[156] Hansard, XXXVI c 1012 (24 February 1837).

[157] Hansard, XXXIX c 948 (11 December 1837).

[158] Hansard, XL c 1362 (20 February 1838).

[159] Fielden, Hansard LVII (March 1841 throughout).

[160] Hansard, LXIV (27 July 1842).

[161] Hansard, LXIV (22 July 1842).

Chapter 4: Economics of Class Consciousness

[1] *Northern Star,* 18 March 1838

[2] This is a reclassification of the 1851 published census using Mitchell's adaptation of the 1911 census categories (B. Mitchell, *Abstract of British Historical Statistics,* pp. 59-60). The figures for Great Britain are taken from Mitchell, but the following modifications have been made to them, and to the classification generally. *Combined categories:* public administration has been combined in one category with armed forces, agriculture with fishing, transport with gas and water, building with wood, bricks with chemicals, skins, paper. *Working children:* Mitchell places specifically occupied children *under ten years old* among the unoccupied (about forty thousand in 1851). Here they are classi-

fied as occupied. *Working wives:* Mitchell counts all women classified as wives of shoemakers, innkeepers, farmers etc. as unoccupied. This procedure has been followed here except for shoemakers' wives. The 1851 census tabulated as 'shoemakers' wives' all wives whether they just helped their husbands or performed a specific paid job for·an outside employer. By the 1911 classification the former should be classed as unoccupied and the latter as occupied – and the exclusion of married female labour leaves a big gap in the shoe labour force. A random sample of the 1851 Northampon census schedules (540 out of 5,400) indicates that nine-hundred out of the 1,760 shoemakers' wives had outside paid employment. Accordingly, this number has been added to the Northampton total for 'clothing'. National figures are more difficult. Presumably, as cobbling bulked larger in proportion to mass production in the country as a whole, the national proportion of occupied wives was smaller. The proportion used here (20 per cent of wives occupied) has been estimated from the national proportion of (and demand for) *un*married female shoe labour to male labour. If the Northampton figure of 30 per cent was accompanied by a 50 per cent proportion of working shoemakers' wives, then the national figure of 12 per cent should indicate roughly 20 per cent of wives working. On this basis, eighteen thousand more workers have been added to the national total for 'clothing'.

³ All figures are for parliamentary borough areas and are derived from random samples of the census schedules. In Northampton a one-in-twenty sample was taken (a total of 271 *households*), in Shields a one-in-fifteen (a total of 433) and in Oldham a one-in-thirty sample in 1841 (377 total), one-in-thirty-five in 1851 (387), and one-in-fifty in 1861 (434). The following categories were used. *Magnate:* large business or rentier (defined at £25,000 personalty or over). *Professional:* lawyers, qualified surgeons and physicians, Anglican clergymen, officers in armed forces, annuitants with two or more resident servants. *Tradesmen:* shopkeepers with resident domestic servants (and in Shields including shipowners with servants). *Clerical:* book-keepers, warehousemen, parish officers, unqualified surgeons, preachers. *Small master:* small employers (including shipowners) without servants. *Craft:* building, metal and furniture crafts, pilots and master mariners, overseers and foremen. *Semi-skilled:* the general mass of occupations involving some skill but without any effective union control over labour intake: cotton spinners, piecers, hand and power weavers, carders, coal miners and waggoners, hatters, shoemakers, tailors, sailors, silk weavers, strikers, bolt-screwers, borers and planers. *Labourers:* navvies, carters, porters, willowers,

breakers, building and metal labourers, charwomen and washer-women.

4 From the published census; areas are constant throughout. In Oldham the parliamentary borough corresponded to the pre-1832 chapelry (including the townships of Oldham, Chadderton, Crompton and Royton, but not Lees). In Shields the parliamentary borough corresponded before 1832 to South Shields and Westoe townships. The percentage figures for decennial growth given below have been appropriately weighted where the intercensal period differs from exactly ten years.

	England and Wales	Northampton	Oldham	Shields
1801-11	14 per cent	19 per cent	35 per cent	49 per cent
1811-21	18	28	29	9
1821-31	16	42	32	27
1831-41	14	35	22	9
1841-51	13	29	21	26
1851-61	12	24	31	24

5 Source: random sample of census schedules (as figure 5).

6 Source: published census. The second row of figures for each year indicates how far an industry's local labour force exceeds what one would expect (given the industry's national labour force) in a town of that size. It is calculated by dividing the industry's *local* ratio of labour force to total population by the *national*. Such a method avoids the bias that results from the more usual method of calculating a location quotient (using total area labour force, not population). In mid-nineteenth-century conditions this method would give misleadingly low figures for male-employing industries in towns with exceptionally large female labour forces (like engineering in Oldham). For Oldham and Shields it is not possible to give comparative figures for 1841 as the census of that year gives an occupational breakdown for only a portion of the parliamentary borough areas. *Shoe industry:* the 1851 and 1861 figures have been adjusted to include working shoemakers' wives (see note 2 of this chapter). The 1841 census figure allegedly includes all working wives (Preface to occupation tables, p. 6, PP 1844 XXVII). Mitchell (*ibid.*, p. 59) doubts this, and the *Guide to Official Sources 2: Census Reports of Great Britain* (HMSO, 1951) claims that in 1841 the occupation of wives 'were not required to be stated'. *Cotton:* includes handloom weaving, fustian cutting, calico printing and warehousing.

7 These figures are estimates. That of five hundred men in factories is based on the Crompton census count of 190,000 mule spindles for Oldham and Lees which (using Daniels, *Econ. Journ.*, 1930,

estimate of 240 spindles per mule in 1811 and assuming two mules per spinner) gives a total of just over four hundred men in spinning and allows another hundred for other grades. Men generally composed about 25 per cent of the total spinning labour force. The estimate for weavers assumes that the 50 per cent proportion of weavers among adult males – which held steady through the eighteenth century and stood at 53 per cent in 1780 (Wadsworth, p. 316) – is unlikely to have declined in the interim. Wood (*JRSS*, 1910) calculates a one-to-two ratio between factory and domestic cotton labour forces for 1811.

[8] In 1841 there were forty-three power-weaving firms; in 1832 only ten. The early firms were Collinge and Lancashire (1818), Milne, Travis and Milne (1820), Brierley; Cussons, Bradley and Wilde; and Radcliffe (all 1825), Clegg; Werneth Lees; Wallshaw (Jones); and Greenbank Lees (all before 1832). E. Butterworth, *Oldham* p. 175. SC manufactures, commerce and shipping, Q 10, 943 (PP 1833 VI). E. Baines, *History of Lancashire* (1825). *Manchester and Salford Directory 1832*. A one-in-thirty sample of Oldham's census schedules for 1841 suggests a total of no more than three hundred adult male handloom weavers then.

[9] Source: Factory inspectors' reports, half year ending 31 December 1841, Horner, appendix 1, pp. 33-64 (PP 1842 XXII). For each sector of the industry (coarse spinning, fine spinning, combined weaving and spinning, waste spinning and doubling) Horner lists firms working full-time, short-time, below complement and stopped by the full complement of hands employed. The material tabulated is for Oldham chapelry. Two hundred and fifteen firms are listed as employing (at full complement) 19,548 hands. *Cross-checks:* Butterworth counted 188 firms employing 20,673 hands in late 1846 (*Manchester Guardian*, 20 January 1847 and *Oldham*, p. 118, where the larger firms are given by name). By 1846 some of the smaller concerns seem to have gone out of business (or been missed by Butterworth) and some firms employing two or three hundred hands in 1841 to have moved to the four-hundred range. The patchy employment data in the 1851 census schedules show half a dozen of the small firms to have pushed up over one hundred hands. The 1851 published census gives 20,605 persons as employed in all branches of the cotton industry within the parliamentary borough. *Slaters' 1851 Directory* lists 198 firms.

[10] Sources: for lists of firms, *Slater's 1851 Manchester Directory* and 'Register of Pits and Owners (Oldham)', Mines inspectors reports (PP 1854 XIX). For employment, incomplete returns can be found for 1841 in Joseph Fletcher, 'Report on the Collieries in the Neighbourhood of Oldham', appendix to first report, RC employment of children (mines), part II, p. 819 (PP 1842 XVII); for 1851 there

are also returns in the census schedules. The material for 1841, though patchy and to a degree skewed by depression (there are reasons why failing demand did not mean an all round fall in employment), are complete enough to limit guesswork to the allocation of a relatively small number of workers (five hundred out of sixteen hundred) among well-authenticated claimants. 'Mountain mines' refer to small hillside workings: in 1841 the six mines in this category probably employed less than one hundred workers between them. The 'combine mines' refer to the three colliery companies (Jones, Evans and Lees & Booth) which for most of the period seem to have operated common marketing arrangements. The 'company mines' were those operating independently – almost all directly linked to the local cotton or engineering firms they supplied: Samuel Lees, William Wrigley, James Clegg (Paulden Wood), James Collinge, Charles Taylor, Milne, Travis & Milne, Milne, Taylor (Burnedge), Ainsworth & Lees. The principal estimate is that of three hundred miners for the combine firm Evans, Barker ; in 1846 its output was given as a hundred thousand tons as against a hundred and fifty thousand for Joseph Jones & Co. employing 509 workers in 1841 (Giles Shaw, *Local Notes*, p. 80). Further information on these estimates and the sources used can be found in J. Foster, PhD diss., 1967.

11 Sources: 1851 census schedules supplemented by E. Butterworth, *Oldham*, p. 185, and *Slater's 1851 Directory*. 'Textile machine makers' refer to the three firms mass-producing for bulk orders: Hibbert & Platt (1,309 hands), Lees & Barnes (523), Seville & Woolstenhulme (277). 'Craft firms' include specialists (bolt and gas meter manufacturers) as well the old-style firms that had assembled tailor-made machines on the spot. None of the small subcontract firms employed more than twenty-four workers. In this case estimates were only involved in the allocation of two hundred workers out of two and a half thousand.

12 B. Mitchell, *Historical statistics*, p. 179, and P. Deane, *British Economic growth*, p. 262.

13 As in figure 3, money wages have been weighted by Rousseaux's index of vegetable products. Money wages (for handmule spinners on coarse counts) went as follows:

1810–26	292p	1832	336p	1838	256p	1844	216p
1827	276	1833	312	1840–1	228	1845–6	228
1828	348	1834–8	288	1842–3	204	1847	204

1810-26 from E. Baines, *Cotton Manufacture*. Oldham succeeded in holding off the Manchester reduction till the end of 1826 (Eckersley to Hobhouse, 19 September 1826, HO 40/21 f 523). *1832, 1836 and 1841* are given as a series by Butterworth in

Manchester Times, 2 October 1841. *1833* Oldham spinners' average from 1833 Factory Inquiry Commission (PP 1834 XIX p. 131). *1839* from Butterworth diary, 21 April 1839. *1847* from E. Butterworth, *Oldham,* p. 103. Details of rises and reductions from intervening years come from *Voice of the People,* 30 July 1831, Butterworth diary, 17 October 1833, *Manchester Guardian,* 17 May 1834, *Manchester Advertiser,* 8 April 1837, 26 February, 3 September 1842, 12 and 19 November 1844, and 23 August 1845. No deduction has been made for the pay of piecers (this varied between seventy and a hundred pence a week: Wood, *Cotton Wages,* pp. 22-3, 44-5). Wages of automatic spinning mule operators come from Wood, *ibid.,* p. 22, and are for Manchester district coarse count operators.

14 Source: mill books of the Wallshaw Mill Co. (LRO DDRe 13). Wallshaw mill was a spinning and weaving combine belonging to the Jones family. In 1847 it was owned by Joseph Jones Jnr and employed four hundred (E. Butterworth, *Oldham,* p. 118). The current partnership between Jones and his two managers was dated 1844 but the family had been spinning at Wallshaw, under various names, since at least 1804 (DDRe 13/1 1 & 2). *Profit income* is taken directly from the 1844-51 profit and loss account (DDRe 13/15). To give a rough indication of the balance between the two types of income, *wages* have been interpolated. These are derived mainly from Wood's factory operative average for Oldham and assume a forty-nine week year except for 1847 and 1848 where the wage bill has been cut by one-quarter and one-eighth respectively to allow for two-thirds time working (which lasted in Oldham for most of 1847 and part of 1848: *Manchester Guardian,* 28 April 1847, *Manchester Advertiser,* 26 June 1847 and Factory inspectors reports, Howell, October 1847, PP 1847-8 XXVI). Where necessary Wood's average was supplemented by other local wage material cited in the previous note. The average weekly wage adopted was, year by year, 132 pence, 137, 137, 132, 132, 132, 132 and 134. *The rate of profit* has been calculated from the 1844 stock-taking (DDRe 13/12). The partners put in £8,400 cash. Stock and machinery were valued at £22,342 (for accounting purposes room and power were rented from the Jones's property business).

15 Speaking in 1841 John Doherty claimed that between 1829 and 1841 the number of spinners in Manchester fell from two thousand to five hundred (Butterworth diary, 3 November 1841). Early in 1844 General Arbuthnot became so concerned about the political effects of this process that he instituted a survey which showed that the replacement of men had gone furthest in Ashton and Staleybridge: 'At certain places the adult male population has been thrown out of work to a much greater extent than had been sup-

posed by the improvement of machinery . . . and the employment of women (Arbuthnot to Graham, 8 February 1844, HO 45/650).

16 For power weavers Butterworth (*Manchester Times,* 2 October 1841) gives the following weekly earnings: *1832* eighteen shillings; *1836* fifteen; *1841* twelve. The same trend is apparent in the figures Horner includes in his report for 1842 (PP 1842 XXII). Supporting material can also be found in Butterworth's diary, 21 April 1839, and Stanway's Abstract, Factory Inquiry Commission supplementary report (PP 1834 XIX). For coal Butterworth (*Manchester Times,* 2 October 1841) gives: *1832* twenty shillings; *1836* nineteen; *1841* seventeen. By *1844* (*Manchester Advertiser,* 21 December 1844) earnings in Oldham were down to fifteen shillings a week.

17 Estimate from wages and profit on capital. Figures for local communities can never mean very much. But it is interesting that P. Deane (*British Economic Growth,* p. 247) gives the rent and profit share in national income as 51 per cent for the 1860s. The quotation is from John Knight in *Voice of the People,* 8 January 1831.

18 *Morning Chronicle,* 12 November 1849.

19 The 1851 census makes shoemaking the largest single industrial occupation. The first machines (reaching Northampton in 1857) were sewing machines for closing uppers. Sole riveting came in the early 1860s and sole sewing a few years later. All the machinery originated in the United States: John Strang, 'Sewing Machines', *JRSS,* 1858. John Ball, 'Strike of Northamptonshire Boot and Shoe Makers 1857-9', *Proceedings Society for the Promotion of Social Science,* 1860. H. Lord, 'Fourth Report of the Child Employment Commission', p. 123 (PP 1865 XX).

20 The overseas markets seem to have been mainly the East and West Indies and Spanish America. Evidence of Thomas Bell, John Walter, Joseph Hall, William Collier and William Hickson to 1812 SC on leather duties (PP 1812-3 IV).

21 John O'Neill, 'An Irish Shoemaker in London', *St Crispin,* 19 June 1869. J. Devlin, *Contract Reform* (London, 1856). For an attempt by the Northampton shoemasters to strengthen their bargaining position against the London contractors see 'Articles of Agreement Between Shoemakers of Northampton to Establish a Depot in London', dated 21 June 1815 in NRO (YZ 1600).

22 Estimated from the number of shoemaker burgesses voting in the elections of 1796 and 1818 (*Poll Books,* NPL); following V. Hatley, 'St Giles' Shoe School', *Journ. British Boot and Shoe Institution,* September 1961.

23 Webb Collection EA XXV f 395 & 401 (LSE). *Northern Star,* 26 March 1842. Abortive attempts at wider unionization were made in

1834 and the early 1850s (in the latter case much of the initiative seems to have come from the tramps). *Poor Man's Guardian,* 4 January 1834. *Pioneer,* 11 January and 15 March 1834. 'Boot and Shoemakers of Northampton', *Morning Chronicle,* 23 January 1851, and *Northampton Mercury* 18 December 1852.

24 R. Church, 'Gotch and Sons', *Journ. British Boot and Shoe Institution,* October 1957. Master shoemaker, 'My Life and Recollections', *Boot and Shoemaker,* 9 August 1879 (the anonymous author emigrated to Northampton after involvement in the Cato Street conspiracy).

25 By the 1840s several Northampton firms – Bortons, Edens, Grooms, Marshalls, Parkers – were operating on a fairly large scale and there was considerable concentration. Of the two thousand Northampton shoe workers covered by the thirty-nine returns of employment made to the 1851 census 80 per cent were employed by twelve firms employing over a hundred. On foreign competition, 'Memoirs of a Working Man', *Meliora,* ed. Ingestre (London, 1852), and Church, *ibid.*

26 Census for 1831, 1841 and 1851. The census *samples* for 1841 and 1851 show the proportion of workers employed as binders and closers rising from 30 to 38 per cent of the total work force.

27 Hatley, *op. cit.* In 1838 the operative cordwainers issued a protest against child labour: *Appeal* of the operative cordwainers (NPL).

28 1851 census sample.

29 F. Eden, *State of the Poor* (London, 1928), p. 262. Later wages made up some of the ground lost during the wartime inflation but dropped sharply in 1815-6. John Brown, *Sixty Years Gleanings* (Cambridge, 1858). Webb Collection EA XXV f 372.

30 *Poor Man's Guardian,* 8 February 1834. *Meliora,* 'Statement of a Working Man', pp. 226-8. *Boot and Shoemaker,* p. 411, 9 August 1879. Smith, Sixth Report of Medical Officer to PC, p. 229 (PP 1864 XXVIII).

31 There are two useful histories. William Brockie, *History of the Town, Trade and Port of Shields* (South Shields, 1851) and George Hodgson, *Borough of South Shields* (Newcastle, 1903). Contemporary descriptions can be found in F. Eden, *State of the Poor* (1928 ed.), p. 128, and the reply to the 1842 health of towns RC questionnaire (a copy is enclosed at the back of South Shields Improvement Act Letter Book 1829-48, Town Clerk's Office, South Shields).

32 Broadsheet issued by Robert Anderson JP (leader of the Shields shippers) during the 1852 parliamentary election: folder 'parliamentary election 1852' f 88 (SSPL). Anderson put the number of men and boys employed at four and a half thousand (against the

two and a half thousand seamen recorded as present in Shields on the night of the 1851 census). This corresponds to the figure one would get by multiplying the census figure by the ratio of seamen's wives whose husbands were stated to be away that night (thirty-eight out of eighty-one in a one-in-twenty sample).

33 *Wards North of England Directory 1851* lists public houses and their owners. On prostitution there is the 1850 report of the 'society for the protection of young females', *North and South Shields Gazette,* 24 May 1850. The Shields shipowners were also owners of public house property at the London end of the coal trade and, claims Mayhew, had a large hand in east end prostitution: H. Mayhew, *Life and Labour of the London Poor* vol. III, p. 235. In May 1832 the South Shields shipowners held a protest meeting against a clean-up promoted by the London Coalwhippers Equitable Office: *Newcastle Journal,* 19 May 1832.

34 B. Mitchell, *Historical Statistics,* p. 113 shows an increase of over 50 per cent between 1830 and 1845. P. Sweezy, *Monopoly and Competition in the English Coal Trade* (Harvard, 1938).

35 T. E. Harrison, *Trans Institute Civil Engineers,* 1838. N. Elliott, 'Tyneside', Durham PhD 1955, p. 211. South Shields itself had only two short waggonways. Most of the longer ones ended slightly higher up the river at Jarrow or over the other side at North Shields (1830 SC coal trade, map).

36 Sunderland gained a through route to Newcastle, bypassing South Shields and also one to Durham. Shields, on the other hand, gained a direct Durham route (Durham Junction railway) and also the only route into the coalfields on the other side of Durham (the Stanhope and Tyne railway opened in September 1834: *Newcastle Journal,* 13 September 1834). George Grote (Newcastle branch manager of the Bank of England) gives an interesting account of the economics of this line in his daily report to the London office for 30 November 1840 (out-letter book 1, Newcastle branch, Bank of England record office).

37 Hudson was singled out as the main enemy. James Mather, *Ships and Railways* (London, 1846). 'Parliamentary election 1847', folder, bills 26, 105 & 119 (SSPL). By the mid-1850s over one-third of London coal was brought in by rail and by the mid-1860s more than half (Mitchell, *op. cit.,* p. 113).

38 Mitchell, *op. cit.,* p. 217.

39 Brockie, *History,* p. 122, for the energetic steps taken in 1815 to bring wages down. Series of postwar freight rates for the Shields coal trade can be found in the evidence of Robert Anderson to 1833 SC manufactures, commerce and shipping, Q7, 381 (PP 1833)

VI), to 1844 SC British shipping Q 1,925 (PP 1844 VIII) and 1847 SC Navigation Acts, Q 6,966 (PP 1847 X).

[40] Evidence of G. F. Young to 1844 SC British shipping, Q 84 (PP 1844 VIII).

[41] Evidence of Thomas Young, Thomas Forrest, Robert Anderson and R. B. Roxby to 1833 SC manufactures, commerce, shipping, especially QQ 7,810 & 8,958 (PP 1833 VI).

[42] G. F. Young (Q 53 ff), Joseph Somes (Q 371) and J. Straker (Q 3,050) describe the easy credit conditions that made this shipping boom possible, in evidence to 1844 SC British shipping. For an account from a labour viewpoint see *Northern Liberator*, 16 December 1839.

[43] Evidence of Cuthbert Young to 1833 SC manufactures, commerce, shipping, Q 7,882.

[44] Analysis of shipping registered in the port of Shields whose owners lived in South Shields in December 1850: *Ward's North of England Directory 1851*. Twenty-five of the thirty-one shipowners with more than one ship had other business interests – as did thirty-eight out of forty-two of a one-in-two sample of shipowners with only one ship.

[45] Christopher Wood, owner of six ships in the coal trade, also owned a brewery and a string of thirty pubs when he died in 1836 (A82 & A85, Matthew Wood collection, Newcastle Central Library).

[46] If anything, these figures are on the high side. They come from the evidence of Robert Anderson (deputed by South Shields united underwriters) to the 1833 SC manufactures, commerce, shipping. Anderson obtained them from the books of a vessel employed in the coal trade from 1819 to 1832. They are based on the *average* amount paid out annually to able seamen and therefore take into account the reduced number of voyages made by ships in bad years but *not* the probably even greater unemployment suffered by individual seamen. They exclude the value of provisions (estimated at eleven pence a week). The series is:

1819	£39.50	1824	£43.00	1829	£35.75
1820	36.25	1825	58.00	1830	35.75
1821	35.00	1826	48.00	1831	36.50
1822	38.25	1827	40.50	1832	31.00
1823	38.40	1828	35.00		

Other material which makes it possible to take the series up to the early 1850s can be found in the evidence of Anderson to the 1844 SC British shipping (Q 1,925), and the 1847 SC Navigation Acts (Q 6,966) and in the returns relating to the seamen's wages (PP 1867 LXIV). Money wages reached their lowest point in 1850.

47 *Northern Star,* 13 August 1842. *Newcastle Journal,* 23 February 1839 provides information on the stability of the fifty-four pence a day wage.

48 John Doherty speaking to Oldham workers (Butterworth diary, 3 November 1841).

49 Factory inspectors reports, 31 October 1850 and 30 April 1851 (PP 1851 XXIII). Registration of accidents, especially non-fatal ones, was defective: Horner, report, 31 October 1855, p. 6 (PP 1856 XVIII).

50 For instance, Dr Hawkins' report in Factory Inquiry Commission supplementary report, D 3 Lancashire p. 230 (PP 1834 XIX).

51 Source: General supplement to the registrar general's twenty-fifth annual report (PP 1865 XIII). Rates are calculated by dividing the numbers dying of each disease in each town by the mean population for the decade as computed by the registrar general. A slight bias is involved in using the arithmetic mean but with all three populations increasing at the same rate it is (for internal comparisons at least) of no importance. The three disease groups used comprised between one-quarter and one-third of all deaths and had close ties with the environment. *Typhus* is transmitted by the louse in conditions of famine and war. *Lung diseases* include Phthisis (tuberculosis) and all 'diseases of the lung': inadequate contemporary diagnosis makes finer distinctions unsafe. McKeown and Record (*Population Studies,* XVI, 1962) link tuberculosis with malnutrition. It is not unlikely that overcrowding at home and overwork played a bigger part than they allow. *Scrofula* includes tabes mesenterica. As milder bovine forms of tuberculosis contracted through infected milk, they impart a certain resistance to those who recover. Widespread scrofula could reduce tuberculosis. It is therefore useful as a control for the incidence of lung disease. But it is also important in its own right. McKeown and Record make a higher scrofula rate result from 'any considerable increase in milk consumption'. With milk (and especially inferior skimmed milk) very much a poverty food – the poorest families tended to consume an absolutely greater quantity of milk than their better-off neighbours (see budgets cited in the appendix on poverty) – scrofula is an important index of poor diet. The high Northampton rate would seem to bear out Dr Smith's comment on the large quantity of bad milk drunk by Northampton shoemaker families in his report in the Sixth Report of medical officer to PC (PP 1864 XXVII).

52 Sources: age and sex breakdowns from 1851 published census; births and deaths from the annual reports of the registrar general. All figures refer to registration districts (not municipal boundaries)

and are calculated on three-year averages centred on 1851. *Infant mortality:* calculated from total deaths for the three years 1850, 1851, 1852 against all births for 1850 and 1851 plus three-tenths of the 1849 births and seven-tenths of the 1852 births. *Mortality rate for 1-4 age group:* for registration districts the census only gives numbers for the 0-4 age group. The size of the 1-4 age group in March 1851 had been calculated by subtracting from the total 0-4 age group three-quarters of the 1850 births plus one-quarter of the 1851 births divided by the infant survival rate. *Life expectation:* The annual reports give only a decennial breakdown of deaths after the fourteenth year and the life tables have had to follow. Except for ages over 64 deaths are fairly evenly distributed over a ten-year age period and the figures for England and Wales have here been calculated from the same groupings.

[53] *Boot and Shoemaker,* 9 August 1879.

[54] 'Statement of a Working Man', *Meliora, pp. 226-8.*

[55] H. Lord, Fourth Report of the Child Employment Commission (PP 1865 XX).

[56] J. Devlin, *Contract Reform,* p. 5.

[57] Evidence of John Anderson and Henry Woodroffe to SC shipwrecks (PP 1836 XVII). Samuel Plimsoll, *Our Seamen* (London, 1873). *Annual Reports,* Board of Trade.

[58] Evidence of Woodroffe (QQ 288-295 & 646) to SC shipwrecks. It assumes the correctness of Buddle's estimate of fifteen thousand seamen engaged in the Tyne coal trade (1830 SC coal trade).

[59] *The Life Boat,* 1 November 1870. 1870 Board of Trade annual report.

[60] Evidence of Woodroffe (Q 295) and Anderson (Q 1,789 & 1,859) to SC shipwrecks.

[61] Evidence of Woodroffe (Q 323) to SC shipwrecks.

[62] Appendix 1 gives details of the procedure adopted.

[63] The figures for Northampton and Warrington in 1913 come from A. Bowley, *Livelihood and Poverty* (1915). The methods used in their compilation were largely the same as those used in the poverty estimates for the mid-century. For other details appendix 1.

[64] Sample of 1851 census schedules. Same procedure as described in note 3.

[65] There are, for instance, the arguments of N. Smelser (*Social Change in the Industrial Revolution*) that the upsurge in popular discontent during the 1830s and 1840s is to be explained by the the disruption of conjugal roles – and the threat to male dominance – caused by technicological advances in the cotton industry (espe-

cially the mechnization of weaving). Even if one accepts Smelser's initial assumption that conditions were getting steadily better in this period and *therefore* any discontent has to be explained irrationally, it would seem very difficult to sustain the explanation he puts forward. Neither in Lancashire nor outside does the area of 'unrest' correspond to that of mill communities and one can point to plenty of other areas (like Northampton with its dramatic increase in female working in the 1830s and 1840s) where expansion in non-male working did not bring a corresponding growth in mass militancy. It is also worth noting that as far as Oldham is concerned only an insignificant number of families appeared in the 1851 census sample to show the characteristics which Smelser postulates.

66 After the failure of the 1826-7 weavers' strike any consistent area organization seems to have disintegrated, though there was still action against individual employers, such as that recorded in the Butterworth diary for 7 March 1833.

67 Table 5 for occupational composition of the radical leadership.

68 Articles and Rules of the Friendly Society of Cotton Spinners, Within the Township of Oldham' for 1796 (Webb TU collection XXXVI/2 ff 76-89, LSE).

69 Rowbottom, 22 May 1811 and 5 June 1815, 'XY' to Byng, 3 August 1818 (HO 42/179).

70 James Travis and Joseph Newton: Chippendale to Sidmouth, 4 January 1817 (HO 40/3) and Chippendale to Fletcher, 9 July 1818 (HO 42/178).

71 Norris to home secretary, 13 August 1818 (HO 42/179) and again 29 August 1818 (HO 42/179) where John Haigh of Oldham is listed among the arrested members of the Manchester spinners committee.

72 Fletcher to Sidmouth, 11 July 1818 (HO 42/178).

73 Doherty outlines the development of united action among the spinners at the beginning of his pamphlet *To the Operative Spinners of Manchester and Salford* (Manchester, June 1834, MPL P 2192/2). Also *Report of the Proceedings of a Delegate Meeting of the Operative Spinners* (Manchester, 1829, MPL P 2410).

74 Butterworth diary, 4 September and 12 October 1830.

75 *Ibid.,* November 1833.

76 *Ibid.,* October 1832, 4 March 1833 and 14 April 1834. *Manchester Guardian,* 11 October 1834. The *Manchester Guardian* also prints (7 June 1834) a full version of the Oldham spinners' rule book captured by the police earlier that year.

[77] 'XY' to Byng, 3 August 1818 (HO 42/179). Chippendale, 27 July 1818 (HO 42/179). Norris, 13 August 1818 (HO 42/179).

[78] *Voice of the People*. June-July 1831. Butterworth, 27 February 1841.

[79] pp. 118–20 below.

[80] In the 1770s the minister of College Street Baptist chapel declared: 'if I were General Washington . . . I would call on every man to enter a solemn covenant that we would never sheathe our swords while there was an English soldier in arms remaining in America' (College Street Baptist Church Accounts, f 16 MS NPL). And in 1775-6 there was a split in the Independent congregation of Castle-hill that seems to have similarities (at least in terms of the conflict between wealthy subscribers and manual worker congregation) to the Socinian breakaways noted in Lancashire: T. Gascoigne, *History of Castlehill Church* (Northampton, 1892).

[81] Master shoemaker, 'My Life', *Boot and Shoemaker,* 9 August 1879.

[82] R. Gammage, who spent much of the 1830s in Northampton, gives the most readily accessible description of Northampton Chartism in his *History of the Chartist Movement* (Newcastle, 1894).

[83] The main periods of union activity, 1834, 1848, 1852 and 1857-9, all seem to have ended in defeat. From T. Smith's letter to *Poor Man's Guardian* (4 January 1834) it appears that even most of the craft workers, like the builders, had been unorganized till then.

[84] John Harrison in letter to *Pioneer,* 15 March 1834.

[85] *Morning Chronicle,* 23 January 1851. Even two decades later the situation does not seem to have changed. The National Union of Boot and Shoe Operatives' monthly report for October 1879 describes Northampton as 'a harbour for every kind of scabbery in existence, and no matter how good a man may be when he comes, he soon gets contaminated and gets as bad as the others' (quoted by A. Fox, *History of the National Union of Boot and Shoe Operatives,* p. 78).

[86] 1845 Balance Sheet of the Cordwainers General Mutual Assistance Association (Webb MS EA XXV f 61).

[87] J. Freeman, *History of the Town of Northampton* (Northampton, 1841), p. 85.

[88] Master shoemaker, 'My Life', *Boot and Shoemaker,* 9 August 1879.

[89] G. Cole, *Attempts at General Union* (1953), p. 68 refers to *Northampton and Leamington Free Press,* 10 May and 7 and 14 June 1834 (I have not been able to trace this publication).

90 1818: *A collection of handbills published during the contest by the friends of Sir Edward Kerrison, Captain Maberley and William Hanbury* (Northampton, 1818); 1830: *Northampton Mercury*, 11 September 1830; 1842 (municipal) *Northampton Herald*, 26 November 1842.

91 72 per cent is an estimate based on the census schedule sample.

92 In 1842 the members of the Ladies Boot and Shoemakers Trade Union passed a resolution that 'we, the Ladies shoemakers, seeing the necessity of our labour being protected as well as the produce of it, and seeing the inefficiency of the trades unions to accomplish this object so long as labour is not represented in the House of Commons which cannot be until the People's Charter is made the law of the land; we do therefore agree to join the National Charter Association' (*Northern Star*, 26 March 1842). But nine years later a member of the society was complaining that it would be impossible for a master to reduce wages 'if this society were well supported' *Morning Chronicle*, 23 January 1851).

93 *Northampton Borough Election 1841* (Poll book NPL). *Northampton Mercury*, 17 July 1841 for McDouall's explanation of his defeat.

94 *Northampton Herald*, 29 October 1842 describes the agreement worked out between the Whigs and the Chartists. The candidate, Peter Derby, was a master hatter, a member of the Northampton Total Abstinence Society (Annual Report for 1845, NPL 198/68) and executor to William Tebbutt, brother of Thomas Tebbutt, the boot and shoe manufacturer and leading radical Baptist.

95 *Northampton Mercury*, 31 July 1847 for Epps' election campaign. The Chartist candidates in 1849 and 1850 were Joseph Gurney (a draper who later became one of Bradlaugh's principal supporters), James Pebardy (publican), Pickering Phipps (a Congregationalist coal merchant who was the main local proponent of Miall's Liberation Movement), Gray Hester (a Quaker grocer who was also a keen supporter of the Liberation Movement), George Bass (a Congregationalist watchmaker), John Bates (a working man who reappears – as do Phipps, Gurney and Bass – as a Reform League supporter in 1866-8). In 1848 Nonconformist Liberation Movement supporters (Hester, Latchmore, the Perrys, J. T. Brown, Rev. Thomas Phillips) seem to have more or less taken over the local Chartist organization (*Northampton Mercury*, 1, 8 and 15 April 1848) and even the main working men representatives (West and Pebardy) repudiated the hard-line statements of Northampton's one intransigent militant, Ashton (*Northern Star*, 6 May 1848).

96 James Robertson to General Convention, 1 May 1839, BM Add MS 34, 245A, II, f 372.

[97] This was still the case two decades later. To continue quoting from the October 1879 report of NUBSO: 'All kinds of scab agents do well . . . and the majority are very fond of unionism for the agricultural workers and will go and star it for Messrs Arch, Heywood and their men in the villages . . . but only just mention combination for rivetters and finishers and they will howl at you as if you were some inferior animal'.

[98] The attempts to prevent the introduction of sewing machines (which it was feared would accentuate the already serious unemployment situation) generated a degree of mobilization in both town and country areas quite new to the shoe industry. It also marked the *industrial* emergence of a larger labour critique of economic development (*Northampton Mercury*, 28 August 1858, 26 February and 28 May 1859). But politically the only beneficiaries seem to have been the Nonconformist radicals. 1857-8 saw the setting up of a new Radical Association (run at full anticlerical pitch by Gurney, Pickering Perry and J. T. Brown) able in 1858 to force the Whigs into an electoral pact and secure Gurney a seat on the council (*Northampton Mercury*, 6 November 1858).

[99] Thomas Matthews in a letter to *Poor Man's Guardian*, 4 January 1834.

[100] Particularly interesting on this is J. Fewster, 'The Keelmen of Tyneside', *Durham University Journal*, XIX, 1957-8, and P. Hair, 'The Binding of the Pitmen in the North-East 1800-09', *Durham University Journal*, LVIII, December 1965.

[101] *Copy of the resolutions, rules and orders of the Sailor's Fund, South Shields for mutual relief* (South Shields, 1798), BM 8275 bb. 2. *Copy of the articles of association of the shipwrights association* (South Shields, 1795), SSPL Lp. 334.7/4. Bulmer to home secretary, 18, 19 and 22 February 1793 (HO 42/24) for details of industrial conflict.

[102] C. Wawn in evidence to 1825 SC trade unions, p. 114 (PP 1825 V).

[103] Bulmer to home secretary, 18, 19 and 22 February (as above).

[104] Bulmer to home secretary, 19 March 1793 (HO 42/24).

[105] Mackenzie to Nepean, 4 and 23 May 1803 (ADM 1/2141).

[106] Brockie, *History of Shields*, p. 122.

[107] H. Heath to Sidmouth, 21 September 1820 (HO 52/1).

[108] D. Rowe, 'Strikes of Tyneside Keelmen in 1809 and 1819', *International Review of Social History*, XIII, 1968, and 'The Decline of Tyneside Keelmen', *Northern History*, IV, 1969.

[109] N. McCord, 'The Murder of Nicholas Fairles', *South Shields Archaeological and Historical Society Papers*, 1959.

110 *Newcastle Journal,* 7 July 1832.

111 *Newcastle Chronicle,* 13 July 1844.

112 This was Lowery's reaction to the Tolpuddle prosecution: 'Neither did his tongue utter what his arm was not prepared to defend and executive; and if they did dare to pass a law to put down trades unions he for one would be prepared to resist it to the death' (*Newcastle Journal,* 19 April 1834). Lowery, a journeyman tailor, seems to have moved back and forth between North and South Shields in the 1830s. When appearing at the Burdon Main inquest in 1832 as the 'pitmen's professional adviser', he was described as 'of South Shields' (*Newcastle Journal,* 14 July 1832), at the Tolpuddle protest (as above) he is described as 'of Shields', and at the Blackfell miners' meeting of 1836 as 'of North Shields' (*Newcastle Chronicle,* 24 September 1836). South Shields' petty bourgeois radicals found their base, as in Northampton, among the small employers, especially the smaller ship-owners and shopkeepers. In the 1832 election they backed Hume's protege Gowan (Gowan correspondence, SSPL) and later E. T. Wawn. Their main spokesman was James Mather (see below, p. 122).

113 *Northern Liberator,* 28 October 1837 for founding of the WMA. Extracts from the rules and minute book of the Political Union are in Brockie, *History,* pp 190–1. Early references to its activity are in *Northern Liberator,* 1, 15 and 29 December 1838.

114 For a full list of references 'Labour in South Shields 1800-50: an interim bibliography', *North East Group for the Study of Labour History Bulletin,* 5, 1970.

115 HO 40/42 ff 370, 375, 391, 411, 473. HO 41/14 ff 436, 437, 473.

116 *Newcastle Journal,* 2 February and 17 August 1839.

117 *Northern Liberator,* 15 December 1838 and 26 January 1839.

118 *Northern Liberator,* 10 March and 13 April 1838. *Newcastle Chronicle,* 11 May and 13 July 1844. For Charlton's wider activity in the Miners' Association, R. Challinor, *The Miners' Association* (1968), pp. 19, 66, 116, 128.

119 Descriptions of the Spinners' Factory Act activity between 1815 and 1830 can be found in the evidence of John Lawton to SC Factory Acts 1840, Q 8475 (PP 1840 X), Thomas Worsley to RC Factories, D 1 (PP 1833 XX) and John Doherty to SC Trade Unions, Q 3460 (PP 1837-8 VIII).

120 Already in 1819 the agitation seems to have had wider political implications. The home secretary was replying to the Manchester borough reeve that 'Lord Sidmouth is well aware that you are not singular in your opinion that the renewal of the discussion in

Parliament of the question respecting the cotton mills is likely to revive the turbulent spirit of last year . . . ': Hobhouse to Norris, 24 February 1819 (HO 41/4).

121 *Voice of the People*, 9 April 1831.

122 *Bulletin of the Society for the Study of Labour History*, Spring 1969, pp. 4-5 gives a short outline of this argument and the evidence for it.

123 *United Trades Co-operative Journal*, 26 June 1830 and 14 August 1831, describes Doherty's activity in this field. In 1830, when the Oldham bench refused to convict on a factory offence, the spinners successfully took the case to King's Bench: *Manchester Guardian*, 28 May 1831, *Voice of the People*, 28 May 1831, *Poor Man's Advocate* 3 March 1832, Butterworth diary, 3 May 1832.

124 *Herald of the Rights of Industry*, 1 April 1834.

125 G. Cole, *General Union*, provides a brief history. The principal texts are the society's paper, *Herald of the Rights of Industry*, Cobbett's *Register* and the *Manchester Advertiser* (edited by Condy, a close friend of Fielden and a member of the society's committee). There is also an important letter from Fielden to Owen for 8 February 1834 in the Owen collection, Holyoake House, Manchester (letter 674).

126 *Herald of the Rights of Industry*, February 1834.

127 Cobbett's *Register*, 14 December 1833.

128 *Herald of the Rights of Industry*, 5 April 1834.

129 Bouverie to Phillipps, 17 April 1834 (HO 40/32 f 136).

130 The secret service letter book (HO 79/4) contains a letter for 6 March 1834 from Melbourne to Foster, the Manchester stipendary, asking him to get evidence against the Regeneration Society under 39 Geo II c 79 s 2. On the other hand, it is also possible that the raid was an attempt by local employers to force the government's hand in an increasingly difficult situation. In March 1835 a presentation of silver plate was made to the magistrate who authorized the raid by the Oldham Cotton Masters Association (Butterworth, 6 April 1835). The inscription (according to notes in the front of the first minute book of the Oldham Master Cotton Spinners Association) read 'as a token of respect for his general conduct as a magistrate and particularly during the excitement of the month of April 1834'.

131 Butterworth diary, 14 April 1834, gives a detailed description. The local Regeneration Society committee, in session at the time of the raid, unsuccessfully attempted to go bail for the arrested men.

132 Bouverie to Phillipps, 16 April 1834 (HO 40/32 f 128) enclosing the magistrate's report.

133 Butterworth diary, 17 April 1834.

134 Placard enclosed in Foster to home secretary, 17 April 1834 (HO 40/32).

135 Butterworth diary, 18 April 1834 and *Manchester Guardian,* 26 April 1834.

136 Butterwor h, 18 April 1834.

137 Kennedy to Home Office, 18 April 1834 (HO 40/32 f 351) enclosing Mills to Dornan and Dornan to Kennedy.

138 Butterworth diary, 20 April 1834.

139 William Cobbett to Fielden, 24 April 1834 (from the collection of the late Dr David Owen of Harvard).

140 Butterworth diary, 22 to 24 April 1834.

141 The accounts of the strike in Oldham come mainly from the very full day-by-day descriptions in the Butterworth diary. Correspondence between the Home Office and the Oldham magistrates comes in HO 41/16 f 410, 424, 425, 428, 438, 468, and HO 41/17 f 16-80 & 101, and with the local military in HO 45/268. For the wider political situation in Lancashire the private papers of the home secretary, Graham (microfilm, Cambridge University Library), are invaluable.

142 Butterworth diary, 16 April 1841.

143 *Ibid.,* 9 February 1841.

144 *Ibid.,* 3 November 1841 for Doherty's meeting and 26 November 1841 for account of distress.

145 *Ibid.,* 11 June 1842.

146 B. Brierley, *Home Memories* (Manchester, 1887), pp. 23-4.

147 Butterworth diary, 12 June 1842.

148 *Ibid.,* 5 July 1842. McDouall 'boasted largely of the reported progress of the Charter yet feared that labour would not be properly protected until the trades' unions were revived'.

149 *Ibid.,* 14 August 1842 reports Richard Cooper, an Owenite Socialist and leading figure among the Oldham radicals, speaking on 'the nature of capital and labour' and Swan of Ashton and Clarke and Bailey of Manchester on the 'evils of class legislation and the political degradation of the masses'.

150 Yardley, a shoemaker, was arrested for sedition before the end of the strike (*Manchester Advertiser,* 27 August 1842). 'Rioters' were tried by Special Commission (PL 26/147). But the main concern of

the authorities was to pull in the leaders and arrests of these went on spasmodically for the following four months (*Manchester Advertiser* and Butterworth diary for details).

151 DDR e 9 (LRO) lists purchases of coal rights by the Jones family in the later eighteenth century and DDX 614/19 between 1819 and 1824. In 1810 Barker, Evans paid £12,000 on a forty-year lease for thirty acres belonging to Abraham Crompton (LRO DDX 530/53). There is no firm information on profit levels but we know that Joseph Jones Jnr received for the five years 1830-4 a total income of £10,000 (as dividend on a two-seventh share) from just one of his three main mining ventures (DDX 614/19).

152 The three main partnerships were Werneth colliery (mainly owned by the Werneth Lees and the Jones's – 1794 partnership deed DDR e 6/2), Greenacres (mainly Clarksfield Lees and Booths – 1803 deed DDR e 6/3) and the Evans, Barker group to the north (formed sometime before 1810). Further south on the Ashton border the Fairbottom colliery was principally owned by the Jones's and Clarksfield Lees (DDR e 6/7 and DDX 614/19). There seems to have been close cooperation in marketing and in 1841 Jones (Fletcher, Report, appendix IX to first report of the commissioners (mines), part II, p. 819, PP 1842 XVII) speaks of the proprietors meeting to discuss output (there are also some scraps on this for the late 1850s in DDR e 8/9). In 1879 most of the Oldham mines were consolidated into the Chamber Colliery Co Ltd (Companies House 11821).

153 Garforth, evidence (Fletcher, Report).

154 Mitchell, *Historical Statistics*, p. 482.

155 The Manchester-Leeds branch line reached Werneth (at the foot of the long climb to Oldham) in 1842 but was not extended to the town centre till 1848.

156 For wages see note 16 above. Of the 1,015 workers in the collieries who made returns to Fletcher in 1841, 408 were under fifteen and 144 under thirteen. According to the 1851 census there were 588 workers out of 2,048 aged under twenty. Also Fletcher, 'Register of Accidents at Chamber Colliery', *JRSS*, 1842.

157 Wild, evidence to Fletcher, Report.

158 Warrener and Walkden to Fletcher.

159 R. Challinor, *Miners' Association*.

160 In 1843 the influential Tory *Durham Advertiser* (3 February 1843) came out in favour of much more stringent government enforcement of safety precautions (including costly items like ventilation shafts).

161 *Manchester Advertiser*, 1 March 1845.

162 Butterworth diary, 27 February 1841. Speakers were Robert Warwick (imprisoned for sedition in 1842) and John Greaves (delegate to the 1839 convention).

163 Mills to home secretary, 19 December 1843 (HO 45/350). For the rest of the winter detailed weekly reports were sent to the Home Office on the output of Oldham pits (Mills, 30 December to 26 January 1844, HO 45/350). *Manchester Times*, 29 and 31 July, 1 and 16 August, 1 September and 2, 13 and 26 December gives main reports on MAGB activity in Oldham.

164 For reports of mass meetings at which these ideas were put forward see *Manchester Advertiser*, 31 August 1844, 1 March 1845, 31 May 1845.

165 Place collection BM Add 27803 ff 22, 53, 77, 79, 92, 109, 102, 103, 106, 110, 114 and 188 for correspondence with Woodroffe and ff 82 and 119 for correspondence with Rippon. Both backed Place in his dispute with Gast. There is also a letter from Woodroffe to Place (1 August 1832) in the Gowan correspondence (SSPL). Woodroffe gives an account of his career in SC Merchant Seamen's Fund, Q 353-466 (PP 1840 XIII).

166 On links with Trinity House SC Merchant Seamen's Fund, Q 385 and *Newcastle Journal*, 14 February 1835 and 18 August 1838. The Loyal Standard Association *Quarterly Meeting*, 23 September 1837 (SSPL Bills folder 'Shipping and Seamen') describes how Robert Anderson and Robert Ingham became trustees.

167 Empressment – Bill dated 11 November 1833 and signed Henry Woodroffe (Miscellaneous Bills folder 3, SSPL). Registration – *Newcastle Journal*, 24 May 1834, 6 June 1835 and Q 370, SC Merchant Seamen's Fund. Shipwrecks – dialogue between G. Young and Woodroffe, Q 288-646, SC Shipwrecks (PP 1836 XVII).

168 *North and South Shields Gazette* 24 and 31 January, 7 and 14 February 1851. SSPL Miscellaneous Bills folder 3. There were, of course, still very violent strikes despite the political collaboration, as that in 1844 (*Newcastle Chronicle*, 13 January and 24 February 1844).

169 *North and South Shields Gazette*, 15 December 1873 and *Shields Chronicle*, 16 December 1873 give brief obituaries.

170 SSPL Gowan correspondence. SSPL Bills Folder 'Parliamentary Elections 1832-41'. Mather also took a leading part in founding the South Shields Chamber of Commerce, originally (in 1839) intended to put pressure on the government for a more aggressive foreign policy (*Northern Liberator*, 6 December 1839).

171 SSPL Bills Folder 'Parliamentary Election 1852' (Mather's non-electors committee is listed on f 109). Mather withdrew from the election for personal reasons.

172 James Mather, *Ships and Railways* (London, 1846).

173 *To the Seamen of Great Britain,* 11 January 1849 (SSPL Miscellaneous Bills folder 3). On 24 February 1849 a meeting of seamen and shipwrights resolved 'to take necessary measures to resist by every means in their power the repeal of the navigation laws and the admission of cheap foreign ships and ill-fed foreign seamen to do the work of British seamen and British shipwrights'. The report was signed by John Harper, secretary of South Shields shipwrights society, and John Jobling, secretary of the Loyal Standard Association.

174 *Newcastle Chronicle,* 31 March 1848.

175 B. Porshnev, *Social Psychology and History* (Moscow, 1970).

Chapter 5: Class Struggle and Social Structure

1 Marx and Engels, *Holy Family* (Moscow, 1956), p. 53.

2 A full description of these sources and the methods used is given in appendix 2.

3 The 'central cluster' represents (statistically) those families within one standard deviation of the mean income for the group. Craft occupations are defined as metal crafts, building crafts, printers, furniture and coachmakers and (in Shields) shipbuilders. Labourer families include paupers and washerwomen. The samples are the same as those used in the poverty survey described in appendix 1. The results turn out to be quite contrary to the preliminary assumption made in Foster, 'Class Dimension', *Studies in Urban History* (ed. H. Dyos, 1968) that – as today – the existence of work for women and children would tend to reduce the effect of male differentials. In fact, it was the skilled workers (presumably with more influence in the factories) who secured the lion's share of this work for their own families. This itself is eloquent testimony to the pressures which even the 'better-off' families were then exposed to.

4 Using the significance test described in appendix 2, the figures for Oldham in 1841 are significant at 20 per cent ($X^2 = 1.87$) against those for Oldham in 1851 and at 5 per cent ($X^2 = 3.82$) against those for Shields in 1851. In Northampton (1851) the sample of 5,110 households included 1,097 neighbouring relations involving craft workers and 1,066 involving labourer families. Of these 119 were *between* the two categories as against a 'random expectation' of 114. Oldham (1841): total 2,748; craft 553; labourers 490;

cross 54 against 50 expectation. Oldham (1851): total 5,889 ; craft 1,474 ; labourer 1,546 ; cross 171 against 194 expectation. Shields (1851): total 2,069 ; 701 craft ; 707 labourer ; cross 96 against 119 expectation.

5 In Northampton there were 159 craft/labourer marriages against 206 expectation (3,146 total marriages), Oldham 81 against 101 5,550 total) and in Shields 53 against 76 (3,180 total).

6 The same hierarchies are repeated (with one or two minor variations) if one follows through the mutual interrelations of the component occupations.

7 RC state of towns, second report part 2, appendix p. 185 (PP 1845 XVIII).

8 The 1851 figures are taken from the religious census returns PRO HO 129/168 (Northampton) 475 (Oldham) and 550 (South Shields). For Oldham the returns relating to churches outside the parliamentary borough (in Tonge and Middleton) have been taken out. The figures are for congregations on 30 March 1851 and do not include Sunday school children. Following E. Hennock ('Birmingham Dissent', Cambridge PhD, 1956, p. 265) 'real' attendance has been abstracted from the usual two or three Sunday services by taking the total attendance at the largest and half that at the next largest. The Oldham figures for 1829 come from the return made to the clerk of the peace by constables of 'the total number of places of worship not of the Church of England . . . and the total number of each sect' within each township (LRO QDV 9/267, 301 and 309) and for the Church of England the 1821 visitation report (Chester RO EDV 7/6) of 'usual attendance'.

9 Census schedules. The figures are for households, not *families* or *houses*. One could find more than one family in a household and more than one household in a house.

10 *Morning Chronicle,* 23 January 1851.

11 *Good Words,* 1 November 1869, p. 758.

12 Taken from the same survey of marriage certificates used in appendix 2. Up to 1838 all marriages (apart from special dispensations for Quakers) had *by law* to be performed in Anglican churches. Afterwards they could be conducted in the Registry Office or any other duly licensed place of worship (Anglican or not). But it was still far easier to be married in the traditional way and in Oldham the district registrar's office was anyway associated with the introduction of the new poor law (of whose machinery it was an integral part).

13 The sources are described in the notes to table 8 (at the end of the chapter). 'Main working-class leaders are defined as those whose

names are *recorded* as being active three or more times in different years or who were arrested for sedition. 'Other craft' includes cloggers and basket makers (both occupations highly organized). Factory skilled are dressers, carders and twisters, and semi-skilled weavers.

[14] Butterworth diary, 8 November and 30 December 1831. The radicals were Mills, Swire, Augustus Taylor, Wilde and Knight — who was secretary; the tradesmen Holladay and Halliwell.

[15] *Ibid.,* 14 June and 16 August 1830.

[16] *Ibid.,* 13 October 1831.

[17] William Spier, *A List of Voters in the Borough of Oldham* (Manchester Looney, n.d.).

[18] Butterworth diary, 20 December 1836.

[19] This 'compromise' move (a committee to 'confer with the employers') must be distinguished from the local Chartist attempt to keep their members in line till the national executive had met (Butterworth diary, 12 August 1842).

[20] These are figures abstracted from table 8(b). They include all shopkeepers and publicans (though not beerhousekeepers, coffee shops or cookshops) for whom there is *any* reference of radical political activity.

[21] 1841 census schedule and will (LRO proved June 1853). B. Grime, *Memory Sketches 1832-52* (Oldham, 1887), pp. 59, 212 and 269.

[22] Butterworth diary, 2 January 1840, for some particularly outspoken statements by Taylor.

[23] Police commission minute book 1843-9 (Oldham Town Clerk's Office), 4 January 1843. *Manchester Guardian,* 8 July 1847.

[24] Fielden to Taylor, 23 November 1845 (OPL).

[25] Fielden to Taylor, 23 February 1846 (OPL).

[26] *Northern Star,* 7 July 1838.

[27] p. 223 below for details of this.

[28] Butterworth diary, 31 April and 20 December 1834. E. Butterworth, *Oldham* p. 207. *Manchester Advertiser,* 27 June 1835, 4 and 18 July and 29 August 1835.

[29] *Northern Star,* 7 July 1838. Butterworth diary, 10 September 1838. John Holladay (1798–1852) was originally a millwright who set up a small cotton factory in 1835 in partnership with a Rochdale tea dealer. By 1846 he employed 136 persons. In 1828 he became a trustee of Queen Street Congregational Church.

[30] Abstracted from table 8(G). Includes all those active in the political

campaigns of 1832, 1842 and 1848 which involved confrontation with the authorities. 'Schoolmaster' includes one 'Socialist lecturer' (Richard Cooper) and a 'dissenting minister'. 'Shop-pub' includes John Haigh who only became a shopkeeper after being victimized as a cotton spinner.

31 Chippendale to Fletcher, 25 December 1807 (HO 42/91).

32 Chippendale to Ryder, 22 May 1812 (HO 42/123).

33 Fletcher to Sidmouth, 29 March 1818 (HO 42/175).

34 *Cobbett's Register,* 29 December 1832.

35 In 1801 'John and William Knight' of Stonebreaks, Saddleworth still had £1,500 of stock insured (Royal Exchange fire register 7253/42). The collapse of the firm seems to have come some time after 1812 (probably as a result of Knight's repeated imprisonment). Obituary by William Fitton in *Northern Star,* 22 September 1838. Some biographical information is also included in Cole's edition of Cobbett, *Rural Rides* (1930), vol. III, p. 998.

36 *The Trial of the Thirty-Eight Men from Manchester at Lancaster on 27 August 1812* (Manchester, 1812, MPL 942.730731 P70). Already in 1812 Knight was writing 'labour (the poor man's only property) ought to be held as sacred as any other'.

37 The *Register* ran from 4 January to 1 March 1817. It was printed by Wardle. For Knight as editor of the *Spectator,* Norris to Home Office, 18 November 1818 (HO 42/182).

38 1817 index (HO 40/5 (7)).

39 W. Bennett, *History of Burnley* (Burnley, 1948) for Knight in Burnley.

40 In 1834 he was put on trial for forging a workman's reference and was described by the *Manchester Guardian* as the union's secretary (*Manchester Guardian,* 11 October 1834). Knight denied this in the *Manchester Advertiser,* 10 December 1834.

41 Fitton's obituary in *Northern Star,* 22 September 1838.

42 Knight's introduction to the 1812 *Trial.*

43 *Northern Star,* 7 July 1838.

44 B. Grime, *Memory Sketches,* p. 81.

45 Chippendale to Fletcher, 20 April 1818 (HO 42/176).

46 'XY' to Fletcher, 10 January 1819 (HO 42/183).

47 Chippendale to Sidmouth, 6 July 1819 (HO 42/189).

48 Chippendale to Sidmouth, 10 February 1817 (HO 40/10).

49 Chippendale to Fletcher, 4 September 1816 (HO 42/153).

L

50 Fletcher to home secretary, 20 October 1818 (HO 42/181), reporting AB.

51 Graham to Lyndhurst, 21 August 1842 (Graham papers, microfilm spool, 32 Cambridge University Library).

52 Chippendale to Byng, 8 August 1819 (HO 42/191). Byng to Sidmouth, 10 August 1819 (HO 42/191).

53 Warre to Home Office, 10 August 1842 (HO 45/268).

54 Arbuthnot to Home Office, 17 September 1842 (HO 45/268).

55 Depositions *Regina* v. *Benson* QJD 1/215, *R.* v. *McCabe* QJD 1/214 (LRO). Magistrates of Oldham to Home Office, 31 May 1848 (HO 45/2410A).

56 Fletcher to Hobhouse, 25 April 1818 (HO 42/176).

57 *Manchester Chronicle,* 23 September 1817.

58 'XY' to Byng, 3 August 1818, Chippendale to Fletcher, 4 August 1818, Fletcher to Sidmouth, 5 August 1818 and Norris to Sidmouth, 13 August 1818 (all HO 42/179) give a running commentary on the struggles between 'moderates' and 'extremists' among the weavers and colliers.

59 Chippendale to Fletcher, 25 July 1818 (HO 42/178). Hobhouse to Fletcher, 30 July 1818 (HO 79/3). Fletcher to Hobhouse, 5 August 1818 (HO 42/179).

60 Butterworth diary, May 1832, 9 September 1833, October 1833.

61 Hansard, XCIX c 933-944 (20 June 1848).

62 *Manchester Advertiser,* 25 September 1834.

63 Butterworth diary, 17 April 1834.

64 *Leeds Mercury,* 17 May 1834 and *Manchester Guardian,* 17 May 1834.

65 Ratcliffe to Melbourne, 15 May 1834 (HO 40/32).

66 Bouverie to Phillipps, 11 August 1834 (HO 40/43 f 234).

67 *Manchester Advertiser,* 1 November 1834.

68 *Manchester Advertiser,* 19 and 26 April 1834. King's Bench intervened to grant bail and no Bill was found at the summer assizes. *Manchester Advertiser,* 24 May 1834 and *Manchester Guardian,* 23 August 1834.

69 *Manchester Advertiser,* 25 June 1834.

70 Butterworth diary 22 June 1834.

71 Stanley to Fielden 27 July 1834 (HO 41/12 f 113).

72 Bouverie to Phillipps 17 April 1834 (HO 40/32 f 136).

73 Phillipps to Bouverie, 9 July 1834 (HO 41/12 f 97).

[74] Phillipps to magistrates of Oldham, 10 July 1834 (HO 41/12 f 98) and Phillipps to Bouverie, 21 July 1834 (HO 41/13 f 102).

[75] Bouverie to Phillipps, 21 July 1834 (HO 40/32 ff 214-225).

[76] Phillipps to Holme, 15 August 1834 (HO 41/12 f 20) and Phillipps to Bouverie, 26 July 1834 (HO 41/12 f 102).

[77] The main sources are the Home Office papers (discussed in note 106 to chapter 3), Treasury solicitor and privy council papers, Rowbottom and Butterworth diaries, *Manchester Observer, Manchester Guardian, Voice of the People, Manchester Advertiser, Northern Star, Manchester Times.* The *total* number of people recorded as involved in radical activity of one kind or other – and not just the 'main leaders' – runs to 105.

[78] The table includes all those active in working-class politics for whom either occupation is known or more than one involvement recorded. This covers 137 out of a total 243 names recorded. The sources, in addition to those already listed, include the PRO Palatinate of Lancashire papers PL 26/147 and the LRO Quarter Sessions depositions (1848) QJD 1/214 & 5. 'Corruption/class power 1832' is an attempt to distinguish between the different types of rhetoric used in the parliamentary reform campaign of 1830-2: that of those advocating reform of a corrupt establishment and those demanding labour's representation. 'Regeneration' refers to the National Regeneration Society 1833-4. '1842 strike/compromise' distinguishes *all* those ultimately backing the political strike from those actively engaged in finding an *industrial* compromise solution with the employers ('strike' therefore, includes *both* groups of Chartists). 'Arrest' includes those arrested for riot as well as conspiracy and sedition. '1847 Holladay/Cobbett' distinguishes those backing James Holladay's abortive candidature against Morgan Cobbett, the origin of the main split in the working-class caucus. 'Anti-police': those involved in the campaign against the county police. 'Strike support': those taking part in support actions on behalf of spinners, miners, and other sections involved in industrial action. 'Irish protests': those taking part in protests against British government actions there (principally in 1834 and 1848).

Chapter 6: Crisis of the Bourgeoisie

[1] Marx and Engels, *Selected Works* (London, 1968), pp. 118-9.

[2] Horner in factory inspectors' reports, 31 December 1842 (PP 1843 XXVII) and Engels in *Marx and Engels on Britain*, p. 75.

[3] Count from 1851 census schedules.

[4] Houses assessed to window tax PP 1852-3 LVII (244).

[5] The methods used are described in appendix 2.

6 *Morning Chronicle,* 12 November 1849.

7 *An Appeal to the Christians of Oldham* (Oldham, 1852, Hirst) p. 16.

8 R. S. Andrew, *Oldham, a Satirical poem* (Oldham, 1846, Thompson).

9 A list of members is given in the note on methods at the end of the chapter.

10 *Grand and Novel Attraction* (30 August 1852, broadsheet, OPL).

11 *Appeal to the Christians of Oldham* p. 1.

12 A Bridges and G. Lee, *Centenary History of Queen Street Congregational Church* (Oldham, 1921), p. 37.

13 A Tait, *History of the Oldham Lyceum* (Oldham, 1897), pp. 11 and 19.

14 *Manchester Advertiser,* 4 and 11 September 1847, and *Manchester Guardian,* 20 November 1852.

15 *Manchester Guardian,* 13 February 1847 for a list of partners.

16 BT 41/888/5286 (8 July 1845) for list of promoters.

17 Table 12.

18 *Manchester Guardian,* 18 January 1851 for list of officers.

19 *Manchester Guardian,* 2 November 1850 for attack on hawkers and 28 January 1852 for gas and railway charges.

20 Summerscales to Home Office, 30 July 1838 (HO 43/55). Ninety cases were tried before the second county court for small debts to be held in Oldham (Manchester Guardian, 12 May 1847).

21 *To the Irish and Catholic Residents* (Oldham, 25 November 1852, Hirst, OPL).

22 Butterworth diary, 19 June 1834.

23 *Ibid.,* 12 and 17 April 1843.

24 *Manchester Guardian,* 10 March 1847.

25 Butterworth diary, 25 January 1842 and 25 January 1843 for lists of subscribers.

26 *Industry of the People* (22 July 1847, signed James Holladay, OPL).

27 Factory Act offences (Oldham) 1839-40 (PP 1840 XXXVIII, 171).

28 G. Shaw, *Oldham Annals,* vol. III p. 47.

29 Butterworth diary, 7 January 1839.

30 *Manchester Guardian,* 17 February 1847. The Provident Loan Society was founded in 1837 and in 1847 had a capital of several thousand pounds.

31 Hansard, XCIX c 933-944, 20 June 1848.

32 R. Garnett, *The Life of Fox* (London, 1910), p. 290.

33 *Manchester Guardian,* 17 June 1848.

34 *Morning Chronicle,* 12 November 1849.

35 Hansard, LXXXIX c 492, 26 January 1847.

36 S. Andrew, *Fifty Years Cotton Trade* (Manchester, 1887), p. 2.

37 Butterworth diary, 26 October and 1 November 1838.

38 For instance, the Coopers, Cromptons, Milnes, Travises and Holdens in Shaw, and the Greaves, Lees and Hagues at Greenacres.

39 1851 sample of census schedules for general population (based on 106 households). Only two of the nineteen big employers were born outside Oldham.

40 R. Davies, born in Derbyshire 1818, minister in Oldham from 1843. G. Waddington, educated at Airdale College, minister in Oldham from 1850. W. Walker (1802-57), born Edinburgh, educated Brazenose, Oxford, married daughter of John Hague, large cotton manufacturer of Greenacres. Docker Grundy (1807-1901) born Liverpool merchant background, educated Brazenose. Oxford, Daniel Brammal, born Sheffield 1791.

41 R. Davies, 'Congregationalism in Oldham', *Oldham Express,* 28 July 1883.

42 S. Andrew, *History of Hey* (Oldham, 1905), p. 92 – a note by Grundy's son.

43 Sample estimate (3 + 12) against (0 + 1).

44 Sample estimate. There seems to be no correlation with Anglican or Dissent church attendance as such: of the eleven Nonconformist over-£25,000 employers eight had two or more servants; of fifty-four Anglican twenty-five had two or more servants.

45 The table refers to *families* not households (e.g. the three Radcliffe households count as one family) and to *domestic* servants only. 'Rural': Royton, Crompton, Lees, Hey, Greenacres and Waterhead. It includes all those leaving over £25,000 personalty, or for whom there is evidence of equivalent wealth.

46 S. Andrew, *Hey,* p. 93.

47 R. Andrew, *Oldham.*

48 Clauses instituting sons as tenants in common can be found in the the wills of John Cooper of Royton (died 1847), James Milne of High Crompton (died 1847), Elijah Hibbert (died 1846), Henry Platt (died 1842), Samuel Hague of Vineyard mill (died 1842). Tenancy in common permitted any tenant to sell out at will. The

Andrews of County End seem to have secured their property by the more stringent device of joint tenancy (note under John Andrew in Higson, 'Pedigrees', OPL). For the pre-1926 interpretation of joint and common tenancy Charles Sweet, *Challis's Law of Real Property* (1911), pp. 364-74.

49 *Manchester Guardian*, 11 October 1834 for case against spinner using a forged quittance paper.

50 *Royton Vindicator*, 20 November 1852.

51 Butterworth diary, 3 May 1832.

52 There were thirty convictions among twenty-five out-township big employers against twelve among twenty-four town employers. PP 1836 XLV (77). PP 1837 L (97). PP 1837-8 XLV (120). PP 1839 XLII. Factory inspectors reports, December 1838 (PP 1839 XIX) and from then on in the half yearly factory inspectors reports.

53 *Royton Vindicator*, 20 November 1852.

54 1851 census schedules.

55 H. Bateson, *History*, p. 135.

56 The number of households with two or more resident servants declined from ninety-three in 1841 to forty-five in 1861 (and most of these were by then those of large tradesmen and professional families). Most moved to Cheshire, North Wales, Shropshire, Worcestershire and a few to London and the home counties. The new addresses of twenty-five families are listed in Foster, 'Oldham', PhD, pp. 221-2.

57 42 Geo III c 34.

58 Chippendale to Hobhouse, 3 October 1819 (HO 42/196) mentions a fellow Volunteer officer, Barker, in London to attend the beaver sales.

59 Lists in HO 50/76 (1803) and HO 50/196 (1808).

60 'XY' to Fletcher, 18 March 1819 (HO 42/185). Chippendale to Sidmouth, 7 July 1819 (HO 42/189). Chippendale to Sidmouth, 26 July 1819 (HO 42/190).

61 *Manchester Advertiser*, 12 January 1839.

62 *Ibid.*, 29 July 1837.

63 Butterworth diary, 30 June 1834.

64 R. Andrew, *Oldham*.

65 1832 Poll book.

66 Butterworth diary, 17 December 1840.

67 *Ibid.*, 9 March 1840, 16 April 1841, 25 January 1842, 25 January 1843.

68 Marriage certificates for St. Mary's (Superintendant Registrar's Office, Oldham). *Oldham Chronicle*, 19 February 1870 for bill of fare at the Oldham Assembly (the last to be held).

69 1835 Poll book.

70 Butterworth diary, April 1836.

71 A few years before his death in 1855 Joseph Jones Jnr had moved to his estate at Severn Stoke, Worcester (*Oldham Chronicle*, 3 September 1855), his brother William moved to Stapley House, Nantwich (*Oldham Chronicle*, 28 August 1878) and his son Joseph Jones III to Abberley Hall, Worcester (probate 1880).

72 5 Geo IV c 76.

73 6 Geo IV c 171.

74 Minute book, Oldham branch British and Foreign Bible Society 1813-5 (OPL).

75 E. Butterworth, *Account of the Public Charities of Oldham* (Oldham 1856, Hirst).

76 Barlow to Hobhouse, 8 June 1821 (HO 40/16 f 863).

77 Note 107 to chapter 3.

78 Hansard, XLIX c 1253-4, 5 August 1839.

79 On 31 August 1842 Graham was writing to Earl Powis (lord lieutenant of Shropshire) that 'they [the present disturbances] are inherent in the state of society at which we have arrived and which is highly artificial. It will be seen that a manufacturing people is not as happy as a rural population, and this is the foretaste of becoming "the workshop of the world"' (Graham papers, microfilm, Cambridge University Library).

80 M. Blaug, *Ricardian Economics* (Yale, 1958), pp. 240-2.

81 This is particularly clear in the evidence to the 1841 SC on exportation of machinery (PP 1841 first series VII). Thomas Ashton (who had given evidence against raising the ban on the 1825 committee) now felt that there 'is more machinery . . . then we can employ' (Q 290) and Holland Hoole (vice-president of the Manchester Chamber of Commerce) reported that the Chamber itself had been able to come to no conclusion on the issue – attributing it 'to the present very depressed condition of our manufacturing industry; the master manufacturers are almost desponding as regards the state of our trade . . . ' (Q 2991). There was no serious opposition (as there had been in 1825).

82 Estimates from wages and profits on capital.

83 Barker to Graham, 29 June 1843 (HO 45/350).

[84] R. Broome, *Address to the Inhabitants of Oldham* (Oldham, 1848, Hirst OPL), pp. 16-18.

[85] 1850 report of Oldham Lyceum quoted in Tait, *Lyceum*, p. 25.

[86] R. Johnson, 'Educational Policy and Social Control in Early Victorian England', *Past and Present*, November 1970 provides a detailed analysis of the relationship.

[87] J. Kay-Shuttleworth, *Moral and Physical Condition of the Working Classes* (first ed. London, 1832), p. 50.

[88] Shuttleworth, *Training of Pauper Children* (London, 1839), p. 2.

[89] Quoted by Fielden, *Curse of the Factory System* (London, 1837), p. 52. For Rickards and the Oldham millowners Butterworth diary, 1 March 1934.

[90] Broome, *op. cit.*, p. 18.

[91] *Report of the Proceedings at the First Anniversary Meeting of the Oldham Ragged School*, 21 November 1860 (Oldham, 1861, OPL).

[92] J. Kay-Shuttleworth, *The School in its Relation to the State, Church and Congregation* (London, 1847), p. 14.

[93] Speech at Oldham branch National Association for Protection of Labour, quoted in *United Trades Cooperative Journal*, 3 July 1830, pp. 146-9.

[94] N. Holland, 'Psychological depths in "Dover Beach" ', *Victorian Studies*, supplement IX 1965, provides a stimulating analysis of Victorian social etiquette.

[95] R. Andrew, *Oldham*.

[96] B. Grime, *Memory Sketches*, p. 271.

[97] *Ibid.*, p. 246.

[98] G. Perry Gore, *St. Mary's* (Oldham, 1912).

[99] Andrew, *Oldham*.

[100] T. Whitworth, *The Tories Riddled* ('at the English Press, Antwerp', 1853, OPL). Whitworth reported for the Manchester papers and wrote a *Memoir* of Butterworth (also in OPL).

[101] Andrew, *Oldham*.

[102] Butterworth diary, 10 February 1834.

Chapter 7: Liberalization

[1] Lenin, *Selected Works* (London, 1969), pp. 174-5.

[2] J. S. Mill, *Principles of Political Economy* (Toronto, 1965 ed.), vol. II, p. 758, vol. IV, p. 751, vol. II, p. 755.

³ The following figures are based on the occupations of all men over twenty taken from the census schedules of 1841 (1/30 sample of households), 1851 (1/35) and 1861 (1/50). The earnings figures were taken from Chadwick (*JRSS*, 1860) and are for 1839, 1849 and 1859. Those for 1839 have been corrected by those given in the Butterworth diary for 21 April 1839. The mean and median *real* wages figures are calculated on a price index taken as 1839 = 110, 1849 = 100 and 1858 = 106. This combines Chadwick's Manchester retail price list for 1839 to 1849 with P. Deane's (unpublished) consumer price index for 1849-59. This index gives the *smallest* price increase between 1849 and 1859. Phelps Brown's cost of living index and the Jevons-Sauerback wholesale price index both make the increase considerably larger.

Earnings of men over twenty

	1839–41 per cent	1849–51 per cent	1859–61 per cent
— 8s	4	2	0
—12s	14	17	3
—16s	13	17	30
—20s	17	20	19
—24s	15	21	17
—28s	20	5	20
—32s	14	12	9
—36s	2	6	2
—36s	—	1	—
	100	100	100
sample	393	396	470
mean money wage 20.2s		18.9s	21.3s
median money wage 20.5s		18.7s	19.3s
mean real wage 18.5s		18.9s	19.9s
median real wage 18.7s		18.7s	18.0s

⁴ *Manchester Advertiser*, 30 October 1847.

⁵ The *Manchester Advertiser* reports for 15 and 22 April 1848 suggest a high level of revolutionary sentiments among unemployed spinners and the Irish. In the *Northern Star* for 8 April 1848 Samuel Kydd (Oldham delegate to the National Convention) reported that 'in Oldham there was a general feeling of discontent so long and continuous had been the misery that the people began to feel reckless. They entertained the idea that constant starvation was worse than death'. On the other hand, the attempt at a general strike on 31 May 1848 gained only partial support (magistrates to Home Office, 31 May 1848 HO 45/2410A) and only seventy actively responded to McDouall's call – made covertly at a meeting on 12 August – for National Guards to enroll for the action on the

night of 14-15 August (magistrates to Home Office, 15 August 1848 HO 45/2410A).

6 The severity of the 1846-7 depression is examined in the appendix on poverty.

7 Note 65 below.

8 Area reports enclosed in Gomm to Home Office, 2 May 1852 (HO 45/268).

9 *Manchester Examiner*, 24 January 1846 and again 16 January 1847.

10 *Manchester Advertiser*, 14 and 28 March 1846.

11 *Ibid.*, 5 and 19 June 1847.

12 *Manchester Guardian*, 3 July 1847.

13 *Manchester Advertiser*, 19 June 1847 and 10 July 1847.

14 *Ibid.*, 10 and 17 July and 7 August 1847.

15 *Oldham Monthly Remembrancer and Workingman's Friend* (Oldham, 31 August 1847, OPL).

16 *Manchester Advertiser*, 12 and 26 February 1848 and *Manchester Guardian*, 23 February 1848 and 8 March 1848. Jonathan Mellor Jnr was son of Jonathan Mellor, the magistrate, and like the Worthington brothers came from an Anglican family which had been active in promoting Methodism fifty years before.

17 *Manchester Guardian*, 5 August 1848 and 19 August 1848.

18 Richard Cooper and Kinder Smith were among the attesting witnesses to the anti-incorporation (PC 1/852) beside the Tory lawyers Tweedale and Summerscales.

19 The radicals were Daniel Newton, John Schofield, John Earnshaw and George Leach. Alexander Taylor was narrowly defeated but elected Alderman by the joint radical-Tory majority on the council (*Manchester Guardian*, 4 August 1849). A joint radical-Tory dinner to celebrate the election victory was held in September (*ibid.*, 29 September 1849).

20 The main source for the post-1854 period is the *Oldham Chronicle*. The Liberal-radicals were William Halliwell, John Grimshaw, James Greaves, Len Haslop, Richard Haslam, Sam Yardley, Thomas Wilde, A. F. Taylor, John Swire, James Schofield, John Nield, J. Quarmby, William Knott, James Holladay, Ambrose Hirst. The Tory-radicals Richard Cooper, John Earnshaw, Richard Fletcher, John Haigh, John Halliwell, Francis Lord, James Mills, John Schofield, Kinder Smith, Alexander Taylor and William Thompson.

21 The Reform Association (founded in May 1850) provided a continuing focus for the Liberal-radicals throughout the 1850s and

1860s, and the annual 'Cobbett' dinners seem to have performed a similar function for the Tory-radicals.

22 B. Grime, *Memory Sketches 1932-52* (Oldham, 1887, OPL), p. 271.

23 Hansard, XCIX c 933-944, 20 June 1848.

24 Figures 18 and 21.

25 Figure 20.

26 The sources (and method of calculation) used are described in the notes to figure 20.

27 *Religious Statistics of Eight Towns of South Lancashire* (1880, OPL).

28 From marriage certificates for 1846 to 1857. The total number of fathers were: old Dissent 364, Methodists 84 (many others married in Anglican churches), *all* marriages (11,100).

29 Butterworth gave figures for 1825, 1831, 1838 and 1846 in the *Manchester Guardian*, 23 January 1847.

30 Evidence of W. F. Walker to James Fletcher, 'Report on the Collieries in the Neighbourhood of Oldham', appendix to the first report of the commissioners (mines), part II, p. 819 (PP 1842 XVII).

31 1851 religious census (PRO HO 129/475). As the same children were involved all day, the largest attendance figure has been taken (whether morning, afternoon or evening) and the others disregarded.

32 Rowbottom diary, 22 October 1794.

33 William Bates, *Handy Book of Oldham* (Oldham, 1877, OPL), p. ix.

34 Average lodge memberships are calculated from Bates.

35 Butterworth diary, 17 April 1843.

36 Non-registration was of course more the rule than the exception but Oldham stands out among other Lancashire towns for its complete lack of *any* registration (LRO QDS 1/1 & 4).

37 *Manchester Guardian*, 7 October 1848. For the Neilds' links with Oldham Conservatism, Butterworth diary, 1835-6 *passim* and *Manchester Guardian*, 11 October 1848.

38 *Manchester Guardian*, 13 October 1849.

39 Frederick L. Pick, *The Lodge of Friendship Number 277* (Hinchliffe, Manchester, 1934, OPL).

40 Rowbottom diary, 12 July 1803.

41 For instance Butterworth diary, 12 June 1834 and *Oldham Chronicle*, 15 July 1854.

[42] Butterworth diary, 6 January 1837 and *Manchester Advertiser,* 12 January 1838.

[43] Advertisements in support of the Crimean War in *Oldham Chronicle,* 20 September and 9 December 1854 and 6 January 1855.

[44] *Oldham Chronicle,* 7 April 1855 for anti-Catholic lecture attended by Duncuft and the Revs Walsh and Ireland, and 3 February 1855 and 1 May 1858 for activities of Oldham Protestant Association.

[45] A. Tait, *Oldham Lyceum* (Oldham, 1897), pp. 12-18 for lists of officers and an occupational breakdown of membership for 1840-3.

[46] The Crompton Atheneum (*Manchester Guardian,* 6 March 1850) and the Lees People's Institute (*ibid.,* 29 March 1854) both had employer backing. Northmoor Workingmen's Mechanics' Institute was Methodist supported (F. Kelly, *Northmoor Methodist Church,* Oldham, 1955) and Glodwick Mutual Improvement Society Unitarian (J. Taylor, *Unitarian Chapel,* Oldham, 1913).

[47] *Oldham Chronicle,* 30 September 1854.

[48] *Manchester Guardian,* 7 February 1852.

[49] Among the Methodists John Riley was active in this field in 1838 (Giles Shaw *Oldham Annals,* vol. III, p. 477) and the same year the Baptist coalowner Jesse Ainsworth is reported by Butterworth (diary, 23 May 1838) as an advocate of teetotalism.

[50] *Oldham Chronicle,* 27 January 1855.

[51] Annual celebration, *Oldham Chronicle,* 12 January 1861 and AGM, *Oldham Chronicle,* 26 January 1861.

[52] Rowbottom diary, 27 August 1808 reports legal action being taken against the committee of the Union Provision Warehouse.

[53] G. Hoylake, *History of Cooperation* (London, 1906), p. 295.

[54] *Oldham Chronicle,* 13 November 1858.

[55] P. Redfern, *The Story of CWS 1863-1913* (Manchester, 1913), pp. 19-21, and R. Tyson, 'The Sun Mill Company Limited 1858-1959', MA thesis Manchester 1962.

[56] The 1890 elite sample was constructed along the same lines as that for 1850. Of the eighty-seven employers and professional men for whom there is information fifteen came from manual worker backgrounds. Of the seventy-one office-holders (including members of the school board) another fifteen had similar backgrounds. The yield of information was much poorer than the 1850 sample.

[57] W. Fairbairn, *Mills and Millwork,* preface, describes the skills of the millwright.

[58] Twenty-five machine-makers are listed for Oldham in Edward Baines, *History of Lancashire* (1825).

59 J. Jefferys, *Story of the Engineers* (1947), p. 12, G. Daniels, 'The Organisation of a Turnout of Bolton Machine-Makers in 1831', *Econ. Journ. Hist. Suppl.*, 1930. The Oldham branch of the iron moulders was founded in 1809 (*Manchester Advertiser*, 22 July 1843). A hundred mechanics attended the annual dinners of the Mechanics Friendly Society (*Manchester Advertiser*, 3 January 1835) and of the Journeymen Steam-engine Makers (*Manchester Times*, 24 July 1841).

60 Edward Baines, *History of Lancashire* (1825), vol. I, p. 499 and vol. II, p. 450. Hibbert was son-in-law of Abraham Hilton (cotton spinner and manufacturer. *Commercial Directory 1814* (Manchester, 1815), p. 183). He was also a brother-in-law of Joshua Radcliffe (of Samuel Radcliffe and Sons): probate of Elijah Hibbert, 10 October 1846 LRO. Henry Platt (1793-1842) who joined Hibbert in 1824 was the son of a Dob Cross (Saddleworth) machine-maker insured for £400 in 1791 (Royal Exchange 7253/72 p. 96 Guildhall). Clapham's apocryphal account of the firm (*Economic History*, vol. I, p. 477) seems to be based on a confusion of the Oldham firm of Hibbert & Platt with the Manchester firm of Mather & Platt.

61 Figure 9c.

62 Evidence of William Jenkinson (Q 1274) to SC Exportation of machinery (PP 1841 first series VII).

63 J. Jefferys, *Engineers*, pp. 25-6.

64 Two Oldham members of the Journeymen Steam-engine Makers were expelled in 1842 for acting as piecemasters (W. McLaine, 'The Engineers' Union', PhD London, 1939, p. 192). The progress of dilution had gone sufficiently far by 1845 for the Oldham and Bury branches to ask the Steam-engine Makers delegate conference to abolish apprenticeship altogether: 'By adopting this plan many good men might be united with us' (*Minutes of the Delegate Meeting of the Journeymen Steam-engine Makers . . . , 12 May 1845,* Manchester, 1845, p. 33).

65 A random sample of census schedules (1842 1/30; 1851 1/35; 1861 1/50) gives the following results:

	1841 per cent	1851 per cent	1861 per cent
skilled	71	66	41
apprentice	16	13	16
semi-skilled	3	8	23
labourer	2	14	20
total sample	*29*	*65*	*127*

The published census gives the following proportions of engineering workers under twenty (the 1841 figure is for Oldham township; those for 1851 and 1861 for the parliamentary borough):

	1841	1851	1861
machine-making	16 per cent	22 per cent	27 per cent
iron manufacturing	10	21	24

[66] *The Operative* (BM), vol. I, p. 316 (17 May 1851).

[67] *Ibid.,* 17 May, 24 May, 31 May, 16 August, 27 December 1851.

[68] *Ibid.,* 31 May 1851.

[69] The employers' declaration is printed in *The Times,* 20 December 1851.

[70] Quoted in full by Jefferys, *The Engineers,* p. 40. Accounts of the lock-out can be found in Jefferys (who seems to overemphasize the the overtime aspect), T. Hughes, 'Lockout of Engineers', *Transaction of the National Association for the Promotion of Social Science,* 1860, and K. Burgess, 'Technological Change and the 1852 Lock-Out in the British Engineering Industry', *(Int. Rev. Soc. Hist.,* 1969.

[71] Hansard, CCXXXII c 865, 23 February 1866.

[72] Estimates from figures given above in note 65.

[73] Palmer, evidence in H. W. Lord, 'Metal Manufactures of Lancashire', RC employment of children 1862, third report p. 186 (PP 1864 XXII).

[74] *Ibid.*

[75] W. Marcroft, *Inner Circle of Family Life* (Manchester, 1886), p. 22 and W. Marcroft, *Ups and Downs: life in a machine making works* (n.d.), p. 12. This was also the system finally accepted by the ASE in 1861 (J. Jefferys, 'The Skilled Engineer in 1861', *Econ. Hist. Rev.,* XVII 1947).

[76] Tait, *Lyceum* and *Oldham Chronicle,* 15 August 1868.

[77] *Oldham Chronicle,* 30 September and 21 October 1854.

[78] *Ibid.,* 28 December 1861.

[79] Copies of Platt's balance sheet for 1853, 1854 and 1867 can be found in MPL MS M13/5/4. In 1868 Platts was floated as a public company with £1 million (PRO company file 3838 R163 Box 1380). Nine years later the main unit of the Oldham coal industry, the Chamber Colliery, became a public company with only £230,000 capital (Company House file 11821).

[80] Estimates from records now in the jobbing department of Platt Brothers' Hartford Works, Oldham. These are card indices prepared at the beginning of this century listing individual machinery

orders by year for each customer (the original order books seem to have been lost). Separate indices cover orders going back to the 1840s for roving machines; ring, throstle and doubling spindlage; and mule spindlage. The A to G portion of the mule index has been lost and only the G to J section was sampled. The other indices were sampled in full. The percentage of *foreign* orders was as follows:

	roving (per cent of machines)	rings and throstles (per cent of spindles)	mules (per cent of spindles)
1845–9	82	95	95
1850–4	34	16	82
1855–9	48	17	85
1860–4	59	62	56
1865–9	59	45	60

[81] J. Jewkes, in 'The Localisation of the Cotton Industry', *Economic History*, 1930, describes this process as the 'rather violent change in the location and organization of the industry between 1840 and 1900'.

[82] Powerloom wages were uniformly lower in the north: G. Wood, *History of Wages* (London, 1910), pp. 36-7 for Manchester district and p. 71 for the north. The censuses for 1851 and 1861 show a lower number of immigrant women in all the southern textile towns.

[83] *Manchester Advertiser*, 18 November 1843; 2, 9 and 23 December 1843; 27 January 1844; 10 February 1844; 2 and 6 March 1844. For 23 August 1845 the *Manchester Advertiser* notes 'scarcely a day passes without short-lived turnouts, chiefly on the part of the piecers and cardroom hands for purpose of obtaining an increase of wages'. In September 1845 the Oldham masters threatened a lock-out of any workers who supported striking weavers at the Jones' Wallshaw mill (*Manchester Advertiser*, 6 September and 8 November 1845 and 27 June 1846). E. Hopwood, *Amalgamated Weavers' Association* (Manchester, 1969), p. 42, notes the exceptional strength and prosperity of the Oldham Weavers' Association (founded in 1859 or before) during its early days; *Manchester Guardian*, 22 April and 13 May 1850 for reports of industrial action.

[84] Articles of agreement signed 5 November 1856 (DDRe 14/12 LRO).

[85] In the 1866-75 Levy Book of the Oldham Master Spinners Association (in the association office, Yorkshire Street, Oldham) the two firms were bracketed under the same ownership on entry in 1866.

[86] *Slater's Directory of Manchester and Salford 1851* and *Slater's Directory of Cheshire and Lancashire 1869*.

[87] Based on a comparison of the 1841 figures (PP 1842 XXII) with 1851 census employment returns.

[88] Oldham Master Spinners Levy Book 1866-75 and Minute Book 1866-73 (entries for 26 September, 10 October and 28 November 1866).

[89] Both R. Smith ('Lancashire Cotton Industry 1873-1896', PhD Birmingham, 1954, pp. 190-4) and D. Farnie ('Cotton Industry 1856-96', MA Manchester 1953, pp. 260-8) stress the absence of share purchases in the new limited companies from any large investors (either from the traditional Oldham families or outside the area). On the other hand, Smith's analysis of the early share registers also destroys the myth that they were owned by the 'working-class'. While some investment came from supervisors and managers (and much more from local shopkeepers, accountants, builders, etc.) almost nothing was subscribed by the great bulk of semi-skilled workers (Smith, p. 194). This is confirmed by S. Andrew (secretary to the Oldham Masters Spinners) in his evidence to the RC depression of trade and industry (PP 1886 XXI Q 4335).

[90] S. Andrew, *Fifty Years in the Cotton Trade* (Manchester, 1887), p. 2: 'I very much doubt if any profit has accrued to cotton spinners between 1876 and 1887'. Smith finds the average annual dividend of eight Oldham limited companies (generally with somewhat newer machinery than the non-limiteds) between 1873 and 1896 to be: two companies 3 per cent; three 4 per cent; one 6 per cent; two 10 per cent (Smith, pp. 165-81).

[91] M. Blaug, 'Productivity of Capital in the Lancashire Cotton Industry', *Econ. Hist. Rev.*, 1960-1.

[92] Horner (Factory inspectors report, 31 December 1841, PP 1842 XXII, app. 6) describes the successful use of women on automatic mules in a Manchester factory – cutting the wage bill by half between 1838 and 1841.

[93] F. Merttens ('Hours and Cost of Labour in the Cotton Industry', *Transactions of the Manchester Statistical Soc.* 1893/4) gives comparative figures on manning for a wide range of countries in the 1890s. Further material on the labour-intensive nature of the English industry can be found in G. von Schulze-Gaevernitz, *Cotton Trade in England and on the Continent* (London, 1895), pp. 95-6.

[94] Printed reports of the 'Association of Operative Cotton Spinners, Twiners and Self-acting Minders of UK' (bound in the blue scrapbook 'Circulars and Bills 1840-70', Oldham Spinners' Office, 24 Barker Street, Oldham) for 6 July, 3 August, 28 December 1845 and 25 January 1846).

95 Balance sheet, 30 September to 21 December 1845 (same place).

96 *Manchester Examiner*, 1 August 1846.

97 *Manchester Advertiser*, 16 October 1847.

98 *Ibid.*, 30 October 1847.

99 *Ibid.*, 18 March 1848. Eight acres were leased. On 1 April 1848 John Mills wrote to Fielden asking for a loan to help the union rent land (Owen collection, Harvard).

100 The early officers of the reorganized Oldham district can be found in the *Fourth Annual Report*, 1868 (bound in the 1840-70 scrapbook) and its auditors in the union's Account Book 1869-80. There seems some doubt about the Webb's claim (on the authority of Thomas Ashton) that the union was founded in 1843. The slogan 'founded in 1843' does not appear on the notepaper till the late 1870s. Information on the formation of the trades council can be found in the circulars and reports bound into the spinners' 'scrapbook' and in the *Oldham Chronicle*, 27 July 1867. The trades council secretary, Johnathan Corbett, was also secretary of the Liberal Reform Association, and its president, Charles Yardley, was auditor to the spinners as well as the trades council (J. Corbett to E. Stanley, 25 September 1872 and following letters, Rylands Library MS 1095).

101 Ashton's obituary, *Oldham Chronicle*, 20 September 1919.

102 J. Ward, *Factory Movement*, pp. 372-88.

103 *Manchester Guardian*, 3 May 1848.

104 *Ibid.*, 18 and 29 June and 9 July 1853. Two court cases involving pickets (reported 18 June and 9 July) make it clear that the strike was over short time and took place in defiance of the spinners. These had 'concurred' (according to Eli Lees on 18 June) in the running of the mills after six p.m. The Chartist meeting held in support of short time was described as having 'a great proportion' of its audience made up of 'young lads'.

105 Hansard, CIX c 924, 14 March 1850.

106 *Oldham Chronicle*, 28 March 1855.

107 S. Broome to E. Stanley, 23 September 1871 (Rylands Library MS 1095 f 39).

108 *Oldham Chronicle*, 2 August and 13 October 1856, 18 September, 16 October, 27 November and 18 December 1858. J. Smethurst, *Strikes and Strike Breakers in the Worsley Coalfield* (Eccles History Society, 1967) provides the most detailed study of Lancashire mining unions in the 1850s and 1860s so far available.

109 The argument on checkweighmen is developed at length by R.

Challinor in 'Alexander MacDonald and the Miners', *Our History*, 48, winter 1967-8. R. Page Arnot notes the adverse effect of the sliding scale when introduced in the 1870s in *The Miners* (London, 1949), p. 59.

110 Those involved in 1841-4 were James Greaves, Robert Whitworth and John Hallsworth (*Manchester Times*, 11 March 1841, *Manchester Advertiser*, 4 May 1844, *Oldham Chronicle*, 27 November 1858 and 19 March 1859). The members of the Reform Association on the sympathy committee were its secretary John Grimshaw and James Bailey. James Greaves was also a member of the association, and Greaves, Bailey and Grimshaw all spoke at a dinner in honour of Fox in March 1858 (*Oldham Chronicle*, 16 January, 6 March and 27 November 1858).

111 *Oldham Standard*, 18 May 1867.

112 S. Broome to Stanley, 25 September 1872 (as above) and John Mills to Stanley, 25 September 1872 (Rylands MS 1095 f 41).

113 *Oldham Chronicle*, 16 March 1861.

114 The two Tory ex-workingmen were both town councillors and both grocers: Thomas Hawkins (1826-1900 – obituary *Oldham Chronicle*, 13 June 1900) and William Horrabin (1826-1905 – obituary *Oldham Chronicle*, 16 May 1905).

115 Table 20. Politically the shopkeepers (at least those selling food and clothing) were more Liberal than Tory by the 1860s (table 4).

116 R. Roberts, *The Classic Slum* (Manchester, 1971) vividly describes the gradation of credit-worthiness imposed by Salford shopkeepers before the First World War.

117 John Platt took a leading part in its formation in April 1853 (*Manchester Guardian*, 6 April 1853).

118 *Oldham Chronicle*, 14 October 1854.

119 *Ibid.*, 17 February 1855.

120 Two of the most outspoken proponents of total war were George Seville and William Woolstenhulme, partners in Seville and Woolstenhulme, Oldham's third largest engineering firm. Later in 1855 the firm's financial difficulties forced it to abandon machine-making altogether and switch to millwrighting (J. Brierley, *Oldham 1849-99*, p. 35).

121 *Oldham Chronicle*, 23 March 1855.

122 *Ibid.*, 17 February 1855.

123 *Ibid.*

124 *Ibid.*, 3 March 1855.

125 *Ibid.*

126 *Ibid.*, 15 and 22 September 1855. There is a slight possibility that this John Schofield was the temperance leader (*Oldham Chronicle*, 27 January 1855) and not the Cobbett councillor. However, the tone of the speech makes it far more likely to have been the latter.

127 *Ibid.*, 8 June 1861.

128 *Ibid.* One of the chapels attacked was in Shaw Street to the north of the town centre and the other at Banktop half a mile to the south.

129 The census figures (2,743 in 1851 and 5,830 for 1861) are only for those born in Ireland. Allowing for children born in England, the number of Irish could not have been much below eight thousand by 1861.

130 At least certain sections of the Oldham Irish had always played an active part in the Chartist movement. The trial of Thomas Emmett had been the main item at a Chartist defence fund concert in December 1840 (*Northern Star*, 12 December 1840) and in February 1842 Butterworth describes the Chartists who put down an anti-corn law meeting as 'mainly Irish'. In August 1842 a Chartist meeting was reported as 'crowded to overflowing with both English and Irish' (*Star*, 6 August 1842). At least five of those arrested in Oldham between August and September 1842 were Irish. In 1847-8 the Oldham Irish played a still more prominent role and their most active leader, Edward McCabe, had been one of the leaders of the tailors' strike in 1844.

131 *Oldham Chronicle*, 3 February 1855.

132 *Ibid.*, 30 March, 20 and 27 April 1861.

133 St Peter's parish in the town centre probably contained the biggest Irish concentration. Six hundred of a thousand households visited in 1855 were described as Catholic (*Oldham Chronicle*, 3 February 1855).

134 *Ibid.*, 15 June 1861.

135 The Irish seem to have taken a considerable part in both the tailors' and shoemakers' strike activity in the mid-1840s. Edward McCabe, the tailors' strike leader in 1844 (*Manchester Advertiser*, 23 November 1844) was active also in the ten-hours movement (*ibid.*, 16 March 1844) and against Irish coercion (*ibid.*, 27 and 31 May 1848).

136 Weekly reports can be found in the *Oldham Chronicle* from 1854 on (e.g. 8 March 1855). Such societies undoubtedly existed in the 1840s also but it seems clear that they increased their scope markedly in the 1850s.

137 *Oldham Chronicle*, 25 May 1861.

138 *Ibid.,* 22 July 1861.

139 *Ibid.,* 16 July 1861.

140 When the train bringing the released English rioters back from Manchester quarter sessions passed Platts, the workers turned out to demonstrate support (*ibid.,* 22 July 1861). The assault case brought against Michael Ford (*ibid.,* 8 June 1861) also indicates that the main force of English opposition came from younger semi- and unskilled workers.

141 *Ibid.,* 22 July 1861. Roberts blamed the riots on Irish provocation.

142 *Ibid.,* 12 January 1861.

143 *Ibid.,* 26 January 1861.

144 On the clash over gas prices: letter signed 'B' in the *Oldham Chronicle,* 16 February 1861 and J. Brierley, *Oldham 1849-99,* p. 42 (on George Hamilton). On the resignation issue: *Oldham Chronicle,* 26 January 1861.

145 Letter from Rev. R. M. Davies, *Oldham Chronicle,* 9 April 1861.

146 *Ibid.,* 9 February 1861.

147 *Ibid.,* 2 February 1861. The mechanics institute leaders who supported Platt were John Pollitt of Hollinwood Mechanics Institute (who was a member of the five-man deputation that requested Platt not to resign), Councillor Milnes of the Werneth Mechanics Institute (also on the deputation) and Joseph Baxter of Hollinwood Mechanics Institute. The deputation also included William Lees, who could have been William Lees the cooperator. The following week Councillor Taylor of the Glodwick Mechanics spoke in favour of Platt at the Liberal Registration Association dinner.

148 *Ibid.,* 2 February 1861. The troublemakers were E. C. Cropper and Joseph Scholes (Cropper had long been the mainstay of the Oldham Chartist Association – *ibid.,* 13 November 1858). For their attack on the businessmen cooperators, *ibid.,* 8 June 1861.

149 For attacks on Bright and Gladstone, *ibid.,* 23 February and 23 March 1861. For Reform Association, *ibid.,* 16 January 1858 and 9 March 1861. The Chartist Association gave its backing in 1858 – *ibid.,* 13 November 1858.

150 *Ibid.,* 9 and 23 February 1861.

151 *Ibid.,* 23 February 1861.

152 *Ibid.,* 15 August 1868.

Appendix 1: Poverty

1 B. Rowntree, *Poverty: a study of town life* (London, 1902) and A. Bowley, *Livelihood and Poverty* (London, 1915).

2 Rowntree, *op. cit.*, pp. 90ff.

3 D. Chadwick, 'Rates of Wages', *JRSS*, 1860.

4 W. Nield, 'Manchester and Duckinfield', *JRSS*, 1841. H. Ashworth, 'Bolton', *JRSS*, 1842. J. Grieve (shipwright) in evidence to Q 8038, SC Navigation laws (PP 1847 X). Chadwick, *JRSS*, 1860. Dr E. Smith in fifth (1862) and sixth (1863) reports of medical officer to privy council (PP 1863 XXVIII and 1864 XXIV). The preference patterns of those on or near the subsistence lines are very similar to the actual budgets quoted by Bowley and Rowntree. The mid-century standards of poor relief, though lower than those at the end of the century, were not all that lower. The 1833 Oldham overseers gave 2s 6d relief for each family member (evidence J. Milne, SC commerce, manufactures, shipping, PP 1833 VI) which in current prices and including rent and fuel but not clothing was about 80 per cent of the Rowntree minimum for a two parent two child family.

5 As *temporary* unemployment is not included in the survey, no family in poverty could reasonably defer the purchase of clothing materials.

6 A. Imlah, *Pax Britannica*, index of export priecs of cotton piece goods.

7 Bowley uses a slightly different weighting.

8 Assessment of rateable value made Spring 1851 (PP 1852 XLV (2)) ; rateable value in Oldham corresponded closely to gross rental value and schedule A property tax estimate of rackrent (PP 1860 LV (322)).

9 Same source for Northampton rateable values. The returns for South Shields are incomplete (covering only 2,059 of a total 3,439 houses in the borough).

10 Chadwick (*JRSS*, 1860) allows 1s 6d weekly for fuel in 1849. Grieve (shipwright 1847) puts the annual average weekly coal bill as 1s.

11 In 1850 agricultural labouring wages in Northamptonshire and Lancashire were 12s and 15s respectively (Bowley, *JRSS*, 1898). Roughly the same relationship still seems to hold for 1877 when fuller information is available for building wages in both Northampton and Manchester (PP 1887 LXXXIX p. 641).

12 Comparable earnings are available for Manchester and Newcastle in 1850 (PP 1887 LXXXIX p. 348) which cover a fairly wide range of occupations. There is also information on the wages of glass workers (*North and South Shields Gazette*, 16 December 1853) and masons (*Newcastle Chronicle*, 26 March 1847) for Shields itself.

13 'Returns Relating to Seamen's Wages' (PP 1867 LXIV).

14 E. Welbourne, *Miners' Unions* (Cambridge, 1923), p. 79, and T. Burt, *Autobiography* (1924), p. 112.

[15] Comparison of market prices quoted by local papers fail to show any consistent difference.

[16] Two hundred and sixty-eight such families were found in Northampton, 324 in Oldham and 342 in Shields (a 1/10 sampling fraction was used in Northampton, 1/35 in Oldham and 1/15 in Shields). Many of those families excluded from the survey as non-wage-earning (especially the small farmers and shopkeepers) were scarcely better off and usually had wives and children out working.

[17] Little is known of lodging practices. Bowley (*op. cit.*, p. 76) is not very explicit about the 1913 customs. To assess the significance for family income one would want to know the proportion paying for board and lodging and those for lodging alone. The *mean* lodger payment given by H. Oates ('Deansgate', *Trans Manchester Statistical Society*, 1865) confuses the two practices and is probably not very representative.

[18] There were no more than a dozen of these in each town.

[19] Rowntree, *op. cit.*, p. 117.

[20] Horner, factory inspectors report, March 1847 (PP 1847 XV) and Howell, factory inspectors report October 1847 (PP 1847–8 XXVI).

Appendix 2: Marriage and Neighbouring

[1] Somewhat similar use of marriage material has been made by C. Tilly, *The Vendee* (London, 1964), and T. Geiger, 'Soziale umschich-tungen in einer daenischer mittelstadt', *Acta Jutlandica*, 1951.

[2] I would like to thank the registrar general and the superintendent registrars of Bury, Northampton, Oldham and South Shields for permission to use these certificates.

[3] J. Berent, 'Social Mobility and Marriage' in D. Glass (ed.), *Social Mobility in Britain* (London, 1954), p. 327.

Bibliography

The concrete analysis of English social development has hardly begun, and it is not possible to provide anything like a comprehensive bibliography. The works listed below are those which have been found particularly useful in the present study or which open up parallel themes.

Approach

Marx, *Economic and Philosophic Manuscripts of 1844* (London 1970) pp. 107-16. Marx and Engels, *The German Ideology* (Moscow 1968) pp. 31-7. Marx, *Pre-capitalist Economic Formations*, ed. E. Hobsbawm (London 1964). I. Meszaros, *Marx's Theory of Alienation* (London 1971). B. Porshnev, *Social Psychology and History* (Moscow 1970). L. Seve, *Marxisme et Theorie de la Personnalité* (Paris 1968). Y. Vasilchuk, 'The Productive Forces Dialectic', *Social Sciences* (USSR Academy of Sciences) 3, 1972.

Methods

H. Dyos (ed.), *The Study of Urban History* (London 1968). R. Pahl (ed.) *Readings in Urban Sociology* (London 1969). B. Robson, *Urban Analysis* (Cambridge 1969). S. Thernstrom (ed.), *Nineteenth Century Cities* (Yale 1969). E. Wrigley (ed.), *Historical Demography* (London 1966). E. Wrigley (ed.), *Nineteenth Century Society* (Cambridge 1972). The *Bulletin* of the Society for the Study of Labour History, the *Urban History Newsletter* and the *Working Papers in Contemporary Cultural Studies* are the best places of reference for future development.

Studies

M. Anderson, *Family Structure in Nineteenth Century Lancashire* (Cambridge 1971). D. Jones, *Before Rebecca: popular protests in*

Wales (London 1973). G. Stedman Jones, *Outcast London* (Oxford 1972). P. Hollis, *Pauper Press* (London 1971). E. Hobsbawm *Labouring Men* (London 1964) and *Captain Swing* (London 1969). B. Harrison, *Drink and the Victorians* (London 1971). R. Roberts, *The Classic Slum: Salford* (Manchester 1971). D. Thompson, *The Early Chartists* (London 1971). E. Thompson, *The Making of the English Working Class* (London 1963), 'The Moral Economy of the English Crowd', *Past and Present* (February 1971) and 'Le Charivari Anglais', *Annales* (March 1972). R. Tressell, *Ragged-trousered Philanthropists* (London 1955).

Index

Elcho, Lord, 236
electoral system, Oldham, 52–6
employees, and wealth, 202
employer-dominated household, 24–5
employers, proportion of
  bourgeoisie, 163
employment, 76, 79; cotton industry,
  294; engineering industry, 229;
  Northampton, 74–6, 85–7;
  South Shields, 76, 88
empressment, 121
engineering industry, 204, 224–9;
  see also machine-making;
  machinery exports
engineers (industrialists), 182, 194,
  199
England, pattern of industrialization,
  13–22
exclusive dealing, 53, 55, 59

Factory Acts, 110, 111, 171, 181,
  233
factory inspection, 210, 233
Fairles, Nicholas, magistrate, 105
false consciousness, 4–6, 254
family labour, 199, 200, 201
family structures, 94, 97, 99, 253
farmer, marriage patterns, 267,
  268, 269
female labour, 96, 230, 231, 259,
  292, 293; see also labour dilution
feudal system, 23; antagonistic to
  industrialization, 14–17
Fielden, John, 53, 54, 69, 70, 71,
  110, 115, 135, 138, 153, 175, 186
Fitton, Richard, 169, 198
Fitton, Robert, 169, 198
Fitton, William, 69, 131, 133, 142,
  151, 155
Fletcher, Colonel, 37, 50, 65, 101,
  138, 183
Fletcher, Richard, 155, 176
flour, price control, 37
food and clothing, minimum
  subsistence level, 255–6
food prices, 52
food riots, 30–1, 103
foreign policy, 247; see also
  Crimean War
Fox, W. J., 55, 147, 167, 170, 172–3,
  207, 209, 210, 221, 233, 249
franchise, 52–3, 251
free trade, 121, 232
freemasonry, 30, 217, 218–20
freight trade, South Shields, 90
French revolution, reaction to, 34, 35
friendly societies, 101, 105, 216–18;
  state control, 30
friendship groupings, 195–6;
  servants, 179
Friends of Freedom, 38, 281
fuel costs, 256

furniture craft workers, marriage
  patterns, 267

Gardeners, friendly society, 217
Gas and Water Act of 1825, 185
glassworks, 88, 128
Gledhill, James, millowner, 9;
  family, 182
Glodwick Mutual Improvement
  Society Unitarian, 326
Great Vend, 89
Greenacres, 180; congregation,
  178; cooperative society, 222
Grimshaw, Mortimer, 180, 181
groups, changes of identity, 213
Grundy, minister, 178, 179
guerrilla tactics, 143–4

Hague family, 179, 196
Haigh, John, 62, 131, 137, 145,
  152, 156
Halliwell, John, 152, 156, 176
Halliwell, William, 136, 156
handloom weavers, 78–80; wages,
  36, 43–6; work force, 294
Hardman, Thomas, 57, 156
Haslam, Richard, 156, 207
Haslop, Len, 137, 156, 207
hatters, marriage patterns, 268
hatting industry, unemployment, 259
hatting manufacturers, 181–2,
  183, 199; private wealth, 165
Health of Towns Bill, 208
Herald of the Rights of Industry, 111
Hibbert family, 182, 184, 198
Hibbert and Platt, 225, 295; role
  in engineering lock-out, 226–7
Hirst, John, 169, 172, 198, 248
Holladay, James, 136, 153, 157, 170,
  171, 172, 174, 207
Holme, William, Rev., magistrate,
  150, 160, 182
Horton, merchant, 23, 37, 38
household composition, 97, 257–8
household employment group see
  Puritan households
housing, 97, 163; as measure of
  social distance, 126

ideological development, and mass
  action, 140–9
incomes, bourgeois families, 188;
  working-class families, 188; see
  also wage levels, wealth
incorporation, radical-Tory alliance
  against, 208–9; and religion, 201
indices of association, 263, 267–9;
  see also marriage patterns
industrial coercion, 103
industrial revolution, Oldham,
  8–13; political aspects, 34–41